In this unusual study, Emanuele Senici explores the connection between landscape and gender in Italian opera through the emblematic figure of the Alpine virgin. In the nineteenth century, operas portraying an emphatically virginal heroine, a woman defined by her virginity, were often set in the mountains, most frequently the Alps. The clarity of the sky, the whiteness of the snow and the purity of the air were associated with the 'innocence' of the female protagonist. Senici discusses a number of works particularly relevant to the origins, transformations and meanings of this conventional association including Bellini's *La sonnambula* (1831), Donizetti's *Linda di Chamounix* (1842), Verdi's *Luisa Miller* (1849), and Puccini's *La fanciulla del West* (1910). This convention presents an unusual point of view – a theme rather than a composer, a librettist, a singer or a genre – from which to observe Italian opera 'at work' over a century.

EMANUELE SENICI is University Lecturer in Music at the University of Oxford, where he is a Fellow of St Hugh's College. In 2002 he was awarded the Jerome Roche Prize of the Royal Musical Association. He is author of *'La clemenza di Tito' di Mozart: i primi trent'anni (1791–1821)* (1997), editor of *The Cambridge Companion to Rossini* (2004) and co-editor of the *Cambridge Opera Journal*.

CAMBRIDGE STUDIES IN OPERA

Series editor: Arthur Groos, *Cornell University*

Volumes for *Cambridge Studies in Opera* explore the cultural, political and social influences of the genre. As a cultural art form, opera is not produced in a vacuum. Rather, it is influenced, whether directly or in more subtle ways, by its social and political environment. In turn, opera leaves its mark on society and contributes to shaping the cultural climate. Studies to be included in the series will look at these various relationships including the politics and economics of opera, the operatic representation of women or the singers who portrayed them, the history of opera as theatre, and the evolution of the opera house.

Published titles

Opera Buffa in Mozart's Vienna
Edited by Mary Hunter and James Webster

Johann Strauss and Vienna: Operetta and the Politics of Popular Culture
Camille Crittenden

German Opera: From the Beginnings to Wagner
John Warrack

Opera and Drama in Eighteenth-Century London: The King's Theatre, Garrick and the Business of Performance
Ian Woodfield

Opera, Liberalism, and Antisemitism in Nineteenth-Century France: The Politics of Halévy's *La Juive*
Diana R. Hallman

Aesthetics of Opera in the Ancien Régime, 1647–1785
Downing A. Thomas

Three Modes of Perception in Mozart: The Philosophical, Pastoral, and Comic in *Così fan tutte*
Edmund J. Goehring

Landscape and Gender in Italian Opera

The Alpine Virgin from Bellini to Puccini

Emanuele Senici

CAMBRIDGE
UNIVERSITY PRESS

CAMBRIDGE UNIVERSITY PRESS
Cambridge, New York, Melbourne, Madrid, Cape Town, Singapore,
São Paulo

CAMBRIDGE UNIVERSITY PRESS
The Edinburgh Building, Cambridge, CB2 2RU, UK

Published in the United States of America by Cambridge University Press,
New York

www.cambridge.org
Information on this title: www.cambridge.org/9780521834377

First published 2005

Printed in the United Kingdom at the University Press, Cambridge

A catalogue record for this book is available from the British Library

Library of Congress Cataloguing in Publication data

ISBN-13 978-0-521-83437- 7 hardback
ISBN-10 0-521-83437   - 6 hardback
ISBN-13 978-0-521   - paperback
ISBN-10 0-521-   - paperback

CONTENTS

List of illustrations | vii
Acknowledgements | ix

1   Virgins, mountains, opera | 1

2   'At the foot of the Alps': the landscape of *La sonnambula* | 21

3   *Linda di Chamounix* and the ideology of chastity | 93

4   The politics of genre in *Luisa Miller* | 143

5   Deflowering the Alps: from *I promessi sposi* to *La Wally* and *Fedora* | 181

6   *La fanciulla del West*: a new landscape for a new virgin | 228

Notes | 263
Bibliography | 327
Index | 349

ILLUSTRATIONS

Fig. 2.1. Alessandro Sanquirico, stage design for Act 1, scene 1 of Bellini's *La sonnambula* (Milan, Teatro Carcano, 1831) | 45

Fig. 2.2. Alessandro Sanquirico, stage design for Act 2, scene 1 of Bellini's *La sonnambula* (Milan, Teatro Carcano, 1831) | 46

Fig. 2.3. Alessandro Sanquirico, stage design for Act 2, scene 2 of Bellini's *La sonnambula* (Milan, Teatro Carcano, 1831) | 47

Fig. 2.4. Alessandro Sanquirico, stage design for Act 1, scene 2 of Bellini's *La sonnambula* (Milan, Teatro Carcano, 1831) | 48

Fig. 2.5. Costume for Teresa in Bellini's *La sonnambula* (Milan, Teatro Carcano, 1831). (Milan: Ricordi, 1831) | 49

Fig. 2.6. Costume for Elvino in Bellini's *La sonnambula* (Milan, Teatro Carcano, 1831). (Milan: Ricordi, 1831) | 50

Fig. 2.7. Filippo Peroni, costume for Rodolfo in Bellini's *La sonnambula* (Milan, Teatro alla Scala, 1855). (Museo Teatrale alla Scala, Milan) | 75

Fig. 2.8. Filippo Peroni, costume for Elvino in Bellini's *La sonnambula* (Milan, Teatro alla Scala, 1855). (Museo Teatrale alla Scala, Milan) | 76

Fig. 2.9. Filippo Peroni, costume for Lisa in Bellini's *La sonnambula* (Milan, Teatro alla Scala, 1855). (Museo Teatrale alla Scala, Milan) | 77

Fig. 2.10. Filippo Peroni, costume for Amina in Act 1 of Bellini's *La sonnambula* (Milan, Teatro alla Scala, 1855). (Museo Teatrale alla Scala, Milan) | 78

Fig. 2.11. Filippo Peroni, costume for Amina in Act 2 of Bellini's *La sonnambula* (Milan, Teatro alla Scala, 1855). (Museo Teatrale alla Scala, Milan) | 79

Fig. 5.1. Adolf Hohenstein, stage design for Act 1 of Catalani's *La Wally* (Milan, Teatro alla Scala, 1892). (Archivio Storico Ricordi, Milan) | 223

Fig. 5.2. Adolf Hohenstein, stage design for Act 2 of Catalani's *La Wally* (Milan, Teatro alla Scala, 1892). (Archivio Storico Ricordi, Milan) | 224

Fig. 5.3. Adolf Hohenstein, stage design for Act 3 of Catalani's *La Wally* (Milan, Teatro alla Scala, 1892). (Archivio Storico Ricordi, Milan) | 225

Fig. 5.4. Adolf Hohenstein, stage design for Act 4 of Catalani's *La Wally* (Milan, Teatro alla Scala, 1892). (Archivio Storico Ricordi, Milan) | 226

ACKNOWLEDGEMENTS

I would like to acknowledge the Faculty of Music, Christ Church and
St Hugh's College, Oxford, and the Arts and Humanities Research
Board of England for institutional and financial support during the
writing of this book. I am thankful to the staff at the Music Faculty
Library (especially John Wagstaff), the Bodleian Library and the
Taylorian Library of the University of Oxford, and the Biblioteca
del Conservatorio 'Giuseppe Verdi', the Museo Teatrale alla Scala
and the Archivio Storico Ricordi (especially Maria Pia Ferraris),
Milan, for their gracious help. I am also grateful to David Bretherton
for setting the music examples, Enrique Sacau-Ferreira for compiling
the index, and Lucy Carolan for copy-editing the text, all expertly
and expeditiously, and especially to Victoria Cooper of Cambridge
University Press for shepherding the book from proposal to production and offering friendly support and skilful editorship all along. An
earlier version of chapter 4 was published in *19th-Century Music* 22
(1998–9): I acknowledge the University of California Press for
granting authorisation to reproduce that material here, and James
Hepokoski, co-editor of the journal, for greatly improving the article.
In 1997 a much earlier version of parts of chapter 3 was submitted for
publication in the proceedings of the conference *Donizetti e il teatro
musicale europeo* (Venice, Teatro La Fenice, May 1997), forthcoming
from the Fondazione Donizetti, Bergamo.

David Rosen, my adviser at Cornell, who supervised the dissertation from which this book originated with an unparalleled combination of challenging engagement and contagious enthusiasm,
continued to dispense precious advice and invaluable encouragement, as did Arthur Groos, who smoothly metamorphed from
dissertation reader into series editor; I am very grateful to them
both, *per tutto*. My warmest thanks to all those who commented on

early drafts, answered queries, provided unpublished or otherwise unavailable materials, and offered suggestions and encouragement: Suzanne Aspden, Davide Daolmi, Gabriele Dotto, Michelle Duncan, Linda Fairtile, Peter Franklin, Andy Fry, Maria Fusaro, Michele Girardi, Karen Henson, Gundula Kreuzer, François Lévy, Anna Linton, Sarah McKibben, Roger Moseley, Cormac Newark, Pierluigi Petrobelli, Pierpaolo Polzonetti, Alessandro Roccatagliati, Emilio Sala, Laura Tunbridge, Benjamin Walton. Alessandra Campana, Suzie Clark, Mary Ann Smart and Anya Suschitzky have been especially close to this book, and to me, and are especially deserving of my profound and affectionate gratitude. The most deeply heartfelt thankyou is for Roger Parker, who has done more than anybody else, with infinite patience and endless good humour. Finally, a very special *grazie* to Vincenzo Borghetti who, among many other things, keeps reminding me of the importance of the Apennines in the cultural geography of Italy.

This book is dedicated to my godchildren Giulia Gitti, Elizabeth Yearsley, Florian Solinas Newark and Giovanni de Jaegher, with love.

Oxford, July 2004

The English county of Devon and the French province of Brittany are not renowned for their mountains, and for a perfectly good reason: there are none in either place. Except, that is, on the operatic stage. The stage direction at the beginning of Carlo Pepoli's libretto for Bellini's *I Puritani* (1835), set near Plymouth, calls for 'very picturesque mountains in the background, forming a beautiful and majestic sight: the rising sun gradually illuminates them'.[1] Strictly speaking, the stage directions in Michel Carré's and Jules Barbier's libretto for Meyerbeer's *Le Pardon de Ploërmel* (1859), set in Brittany, never mention mountains – although Dinorah, the heroine, does so in her *romance* 'Le vieux sorcier de la montagne'. But the rocky, picturesque site of Act 1 and the ravine over which a bridge is suspended in Act 3 point to a mountain setting, forcefully evoked by Meyerbeer's recurring echo effects, most explicitly at the beginning of Act 3. The original Parisian audience of *I Puritani* (premièred at the Théâtre-Italien) would not have objected to a mountainous Devonshire, since no one would have had an idea of what the region looked like. Mountains in Brittany could potentially be harder to accept for the audience at the Opéra-Comique, the theatre where *Le Pardon de Ploërmel* was premièred (hence, perhaps, the absence of the word 'mountains' in the libretto's stage directions), and yet the authors were evidently not deterred by geographical correctness.

Why the need to invent mountains where in reality there are none? In short, because the female protagonists of *I Puritani* and *Le Pardon de Ploërmel*, Elvira and Dinorah, are virgins. To be sure, the nineteenth-century lyric stage was densely populated by virgins who live happily in flat or modestly undulated lands, from Rosina in Rossini's *Il barbiere di Siviglia* (Seville) to Amelia in Verdi's *Simon Boccanegra* (Genoa), from Fenella in Auber's *La Muette de Portici*

(Naples) to Charlotte in Massenet's *Werther* (a German town), from Marzelline in Beethoven's *Fidelio* (a castle near Seville) to Eva in Wagner's *Die Meistersinger von Nürnberg* (Nuremberg). These characters' virginity is not one of their defining traits, however, nor does it constitute a central theme of the operas to which they belong – it is not the object of elaborate choral praise, for example. In the cases of Bellini's Elvira and Meyerbeer's Dinorah, though, bodily purity and what the nineteenth century considered its emotional and psychological manifestations, such as innocence and modesty, are emphatically thematised. In nineteenth-century opera the portrayal of an emphatically virginal heroine is often associated with a mountain setting, most frequently the Alps, where the clarity of the sky, the whiteness of the snow, the purity of the air function as symbols for the innocence of the female protagonist. The ideal playground for two virgins with a capital V, then, is the mountains, and amidst mountains they were duly placed, notwithstanding geographical reality.

This conventional association between a vividly depicted mountain landscape and emphatically virginal female characters is present in all the main national traditions of nineteenth-century opera. Beside *I Puritani*, an Italian serious opera, and *Le Pardon de Ploërmel*, a French *opéra comique*, Wagner's *Ring* immediately comes to mind, with its fiercely (rather than modestly) virginal Valkyries roaming freely 'on the summit of a rocky mountain' ('auf dem Gipfel eines Felsenberges') at the beginning of Act 3 of *Die Walküre*. When, at the end of *Siegfried*, Brünnhilde gives herself to Siegfried with wild laughter (after having initially pleaded with him not to touch her virginal body), her act appears all the more portentous for taking place in the same location. When Henry Meilhac, Ludovic Halévy and Bizet decided that *Carmen* needed a character to embody an ideally pure femininity against which Carmen's dangerous seductiveness would emerge more prominently, they invented Micaëla, a seventeen-year-old orphan girl who has followed Don José's mother to a village not far from Seville. Like José and his mother, she comes from the mountains of Navarre and wears the region's typical costume: blue skirt and hair in braids falling on her shoulders – 'it reminds me of home' ('ça me rappelle le pays'), José comments.[2] And it is amidst the mountains of Act 3 that she will accomplish her good deed, convincing José to leave Carmen and go back to his dying mother. As H. Marshall Leicester has suggested, Micaëla's symbolic investment in the mountainous landscape as an emblem of her virtuous self-sacrifice is underlined by director Francesco Rosi in his film version of *Carmen* (1984) with visual references to the sequence in Robert Wise's film *The Sound of Music* (1965) when Maria bursts into song in the middle of a spectacular mountain landscape ('The hills are alive').[3] Singing mountain virgins will survive well into the twentieth century, then, on stage and on screen.

It was in Italian opera, however, that the convention of setting an opera with an emphatically virginal heroine in the mountains emerged with particular frequency from the 1820s until the beginning of the twentieth century. In this book I discuss a number of works particularly relevant to the origins, transformations and meanings of such a convention: Bellini's *La sonnambula* (1831), Donizetti's *Linda di Chamounix* (1842), Verdi's *Luisa Miller* (1849), various operas based on Alessandro Manzoni's novel *I promessi sposi* (*The Betrothed*, 1827, rev. 1840), a few titles from the 1880s and 1890s, most prominent among them Catalani's *La Wally* (1892), and, finally, Puccini's *La fanciulla del West* (1910). Although the chapters are arranged roughly according to dates of first performance, mine is not an attempt to narrate the birth, life and death of a convention. For one thing, such a narrative would require considering many more operas than are treated here. Rather, the convention functions as an unusual point of view – a theme rather than a composer, a librettist, a singer or a genre – from which to observe Italian opera 'at work' over a century.

In chapter 2 I place Bellini's *La sonnambula* in the Alpine landscape, real and imagined, of early-nineteenth-century Europe. The discourse about the Alps was shaped, on the one hand, on Rousseau's influential conceptualisation of them as a present-day Arcadia (especially in *La Nouvelle Héloïse*), and, on the other, on their recent discovery as a tourist site. The cultural construction of the Alps as a modern Arcadia built on the much older topos of the sentimentalised countryside. This topos had had a significant influence on Paisiello's *La Nina ossia La pazza per amore* (1789), one of the foremost examples of late-eighteenth-century sentimental opera and a strong inter-textual presence in *La sonnambula*. What interests me are the differences between the two operas, especially the reasons why Bellini and his librettist Felice Romani chose an Alpine setting for a subject that would previously have been set in the countryside – the action of the pantomimic ballet which is the main source of the opera takes place in the Camargue region of southern France. Analysis of the textual, visual and musical topoi employed to create a mountain setting leads to a discussion of the relationship between *La sonnambula* and previous Alpine operas, from Cherubini's *Elisa ou Le Voyage aux glaciers du Mont St. Bernard* (1794) to Rossini's *Guillaume Tell* (1829). The refusal on the part of Bellini, Romani and Alessandro Sanquirico, the stage designer for the opera's première, to take full advantage of the devices traditionally used to create an Alpine ambience opens up space for an interpretation of the relationship between the two main characters, Amina and Elvino, as less idyllic and idealised than critics have suggested. This interpretation is finally tested against the reception of the opera, focusing both on the evolution of stage designs and on the numerous cuts and transpositions to which the roles of Elvino and especially Amina have been subjected over the decades.

Virginity is the most important 'quality' of these heroines, nowhere more explicitly than in Donizetti's *Linda di Chamounix*. In chapter 3 I approach this work through discourses about virginity and female sexuality in nineteenth-century Europe. These discourses are exemplified by both contemporary psychiatry and canonical psychoanalytic investigations such as Freud's, which mark the point of arrival of a century-long preoccupation with the preservation of female purity. I then turn to Lacan's conceptualisation of voice as a love object, especially as expanded and developed by post-Lacanian critics such as Kaja Silverman, Julia Kristeva and Michel Poizat, in order to foreground the mechanisms of power and desire at work in the opera, observed in particular through the lens of its handling of recurring themes. Throughout the chapter I emphasise the differences between the workings of these mechanisms in the opera and in its source, a French play entitled *La Grâce de Dieu*, focusing especially on the fundamental ways in which music contributes to their articulation and, ultimately, meaning.

My point of departure for chapter 4 is the hypothesis that the transfer of location in Verdi's *Luisa Miller* from the *Residenzstadt* of Schiller's play *Kabale und Liebe* to librettist Salvadore Cammarano's Tyrolean village, usually considered an attempt to draw Schiller's political sting for the censors' sake, can be interpreted as a way of placing *Luisa* in the context of Alpine operas such as *La sonnambula* and *Linda*. The dramaturgy and worldview of these two works are much indebted to those of their sources, which belong to the sphere of French *mélodrame* widely intended. I investigate the ways in which *mélodrame*'s peculiar reliance on visual devices and its concern with familial as well as social issues are translated into a different theatrical genre and socio-cultural milieu, while preserving both their innovative dramaturgy and their conservative social and political stance. I then interpret *Luisa Miller*'s trajectory from Alpine idyll to full-blown tragedy as a kind of fusion of genres different from the oft-invoked Shakespearean or Hugolean mixture of comic and tragic. This interpretation suggests a reconsideration of the traditional account of Verdi's middle period: supported by the early reception of the opera, I argue for *Luisa Miller*'s role in Verdi's multi-faceted exploration of dramaturgies and styles between the mid 1840s and the late 1850s. This opera's play with genres had wider resonances, however, ideological and political as well as dramaturgical. The final section of the chapter explores the political reception of *Luisa Miller* in the wake of the 1848 revolutions and their violent repression, which cast a long shadow on the Italian cultural and political climate of the 1850s.

Chapter 5 examines the evolution of the association between mountains and virginity in Italian opera of the second half of the century. The works range from adaptations of Manzoni's *I promessi sposi* to mid-century operas by Pedrotti and Mercadante, and from Puccini's early *Le Villi* and *Edgar* to Catalani's *La Wally* and

Giordano's *Fedora*. The perception and construction of the Alps was affected, on the one hand, by an emerging aesthetic of literary and musical realism, and, on the other, by the direct experience of this landscape on the part of audiences made possible by the continuous increase of tourism. Both factors were potentially at odds with the traditional operatic representation of Alpine landscape. Librettists and composers responded to these evolving contexts in widely different ways. Their responses led to new ways of representing not only landscape, however, but also the characters' interaction with reality, especially in its sonic manifestations, *La Wally* proving the most interesting and complex work in this respect. Its text as well as the scenes painted by Adolf Hohenstein for its first production reveal startling similarities to poems by Giosuè Carducci and paintings by Giovanni Segantini from the same period. The common goal of these diverse artistic products was re-consecrating a landscape whose idealisation was under serious threat. The third act of *Fedora*, on the other hand, stages the failure of such an attempt in terms of the failure on the part of Alpine landscape to redeem a character who does not belong in it.

The loss of symbolic potential of the old convention is observed in the final chapter from the vantage point of Puccini's radical gesture of replacing the Alps with the Californian Sierra Nevada in *La fanciulla del West*. Puccini's gesture is placed in the larger context of the culture of modernity, which brought about a shift in the construction and perception not only of landscape, but also of femininity and masculinity. I return to the gender-sensitive perspective of chapter 3, therefore, discussing how the fin-de-siècle concern with new conceptions of femininity influenced the depiction of the protagonist Minnie, of her relationship with the almost exclusively male community in which she lives, and of her link with the 'virgin' landscape surrounding her. In turn-of-the-century Italy the discourse on femininity overlapped significantly with that on the United States of America, locating there its newest and most modern manifestations. I explore the Italian image of the United States, and especially California, through two figures particularly influential on the formation of this image, Buffalo Bill and Bret Harte. The land-scape of the Californian Sierra Nevada was the ideal setting not only for a new kind of virgin, but also for a new construction of sonic space and of ways of hearing it on Puccini's part. I suggest that *Fanciulla*'s modernity is located more profitably in these dramaturgical and representational strategies, rather than in its up-to-date harmonic, melodic and timbral language – where past and present commentators have usually placed it. I conclude with a reflection on the role of landscape as an instrument of cultural force.

It should be clear from the preceding summary that the immediate scholarly context of this book is the exploration of the many kinds of conventions fundamental to the production and consumption of opera in general, and nineteenth-century Italian opera in particular. This exploration has in the past concentrated mostly on formal and structural matters, at least for nineteenth-century Italian opera. I focus on a different kind of convention, one whose investigation involves a broader spectrum of issues; in this sense the book belongs to a larger scholarly context. Recent years have witnessed an impressive broadening of the scope of opera studies, with writers from disciplines such as literary criticism, cultural history, philosophy and feminist/gender/queer studies contributing new and important perspectives. These writers exhibit an ongoing concern with the cultural, social, ideological and political meanings of opera, whose cultural work they investigate in broadly interdisciplinary terms. Following their lead, my approach, interdisciplinary in argument and method, places the operas under scrutiny in a series of inter-related contexts, in turn musical, literary, theatrical, visual, social and ideological. At the same time, I insist on the particular qualities of opera as a theatrical and musical genre, and on the crucial import-ance of the kinds of musical dramaturgy peculiar to nineteenth-century Italian opera. Close readings of librettos and scores thus constitute a fundamental aspect of my work.

The connection between landscape and gender offers an unusual and stimulating point of view from which to consider a number of related issues central to the interpretation not only of single works and the conventions they display, but also of opera in general. Each chapter thus broadens out from a consideration of musical and dramatic detail to an exploration of theoretical and historiographical issues. The chapter on *La sonnambula* suggests ways in which human geography might be incorporated into readings of single works as well as operatic traditions and genres. The discussion of the sexual and vocal relationships linking the main characters of *Linda di Chamounix* invites exploration of ways in which psychoanalytic theories can be imported into and adapted to operatic criticism. A politicised reading of generic subversion in *Luisa Miller* becomes the starting point for a reconsideration of the complex relationships it establishes among opera, history and politics. And the discussion of fin-de-siècle works and of *La fanciulla del West* leads to an investigation of the ways in which the conventions explored in the previous chapters extend into the late nineteenth and early twentieth centuries and adapt to a new operatic, cultural and ideological context.

A further context to which this book belongs is, then, the theoretical exploration of the nature of opera as a genre and its methodological and historiographical implications. Indeed, studying the evolution of the particular convention at the centre of this book offers a valuable perspective on the nature of change and evolution in opera as a genre. Especially in the last two hundred years, the increasing presence on the lyric stage of 'old' works has meant a progressively longer survival of themes and conventions, ones that each generation has absorbed and modified in different ways. An investigation of these ever-changing processes affords a vantage point from which to decode the ever-changing relationship between opera and culture.

NINETEENTH-CENTURY VIRGINITY AND THE DE-EROTICISATION OF CULTURE

In chapters 2 and 3 I discuss in some detail the nineteenth-century discourses on mountains and on female virginity respectively, suggesting why they were often linked in various cultural and artistic manifestations, and specifically in Italian opera. Here I want to reflect on the particular historical locatedness of this connection. To put it bluntly, both mountains and virginity became what they were for nineteenth-century culture only in the nineteenth century. It was only then that, after centuries of progressive emergence, mountain landscape eventually reached a truly prominent position in European imagination, acquiring the panoply of meanings that it still displays to this day. And it was only in the nineteenth century that the preoccupation with female virginity, notably its preservation, became an obsession, affecting all sorts of cultural and artistic manifestations.

To be sure, mountains are promoted as a space linked to female virginity as early as in the Book of Judges: Jephthah's daughter retires to the mountains to lament her fate of dying a childless virgin before being sacrificed by her father.

> Then she said to her father: 'Let me have this favour. Spare me for two months, that I may go off down the mountains to mourn my virginity with my companions'. 'Go', he replied, and sent her away for two months. So she departed with her companions and mourned her virginity on the mountains. [. . .] It then became a custom in Israel for Israelite women to go yearly to mourn the daughter of Jephthah the Gileadite for four days of the year.[4]

In Pseudo-Philo's *Antiquitates biblicae*, which contains an early elaboration of the story, the daughter directly invokes the mountains as witnesses to her grief, and calls for the trees to bend their boughs in sorrow and the wild beasts to trample upon her virginity.[5]

Giacomo Carissimi's oratorio *Jephte* (1649), whose text is based on Pseudo-Philo's dramatisation as well as the Bible, concludes with the daughter's lament, answered by Echo (two sopranos):

FILIA
Plorate, colles; dolete, montes, et in afflictione cordis mei ululate.

ECHO
Ululate.

FILIA

Ecce moriar virgo, et non potero morte mea meis filiis consolari.
   Ingemiscite silvae, fontes et flumina; in interitu virginis lachrimate.

ECHO

Lachrimate.

FILIA

[. . .] Exhorrescite, rupes; obstupescite, colles, valles et cavernae, in
   sonitu horribili resonate.

ECHO

Resonate.

FILIA

Plorate, filii Israel, plorate virginitatem meam.[6]

DAUGHTER: Bewail, hills; grieve, mountains, and howl for the sorrow of
   my heart.
ECHO: Howl.
DAUGHTER: Now I will die a virgin, and at the time of my death I will
   not be consoled by my children. Groan, forests, springs and rivers;
   shed tears over the death of a virgin.
ECHO: Shed tears.
DAUGHTER: Tremble, rocks; be astonished, hills, valleys and caves:
   resonate with terrible sounds.
ECHO: Resonate.
DAUGHTER: Lament, children of Israel, lament my virginity.

The daughter repeatedly implores the landscape to produce sound,
to vibrate in sympathy with her voice and the profound emotions
which compel this voice to pour forth. Echo obeys this request, but
in so doing it amplifies the sound to which it responds: while one
soprano repeats the last few bars of the daughter's melody exactly,
the other harmonises a third above or below (Ex. 1.1). The daughter
asks hills to bewail, mountains to howl, valleys and caves to resonate:
a two-voiced echo gives the illusion that they have come alive, that
they are literally responding to the daughter's call. Landscape has a
musical and emotional voice, it can be heard, even if it cannot be

Ex. 1.1. Carissimi, *Jephte*: Echo responds to the daughter's lament.

seen, not only because *Jephte* is an oratorio and not an opera, but also because there is no attempt to describe ambience, to define a specific location. All that counts is the emotional dimension, and its musical manifestation.

The story of Jephthah's daughter is perhaps the earliest instance in Western culture of the connection between female virginity and mountains. I have lingered on this story and its musical realisation in Carissimi's *Jephte* because they help highlight, mostly by contrast, the meanings of this connection in nineteenth-century Italian opera. In this biblical story virginity is something to be deplored – both in its current meaning and in its etymological sense of 'lamented' – as a provisional, incomplete state: dying without having left it behind marks a woman's life as unfulfilled, a life to be doubly mourned. The virginity of Jephthah's daughter does not make her innocent and pure, nor does it bring her closer to God; quite the opposite. The ideological construction of virginity, specifically female virginity, as an ideal state belongs to Christianity; according to historian Elisja Schulte van Kessel, 'no category of women has ever been held in such high esteem as early Christian virgins: they were the very model of perfect Christian women'.[7] This virginal ideal was of course interpreted and inflected in widely different ways at different times; Catholic Counter-Reformation, for example, reaffirmed it in the face of the Protestant promotion of matrimony.[8] But it was only from the second half of the eighteenth century that female virginity, and specifically its preservation before a marriage fully sanctioned and approved by the woman's family, became a central preoccupation of society and a defining aspect, perhaps *the* defining aspect, of the discourse on female sexuality. In very broad terms, this was a reaction to profound socio-cultural changes that put virginity at risk, such as an increased exposure of women to the company of men in the new living situations created by industrialisation and urbanisation, and a consequent liberalisation of courtship rituals.

Nineteenth-century European culture, from literature to the visual arts, from spoken theatre to opera, did more than simply promote the virginal ideal, and at the same time much less. What happened, especially in Catholic countries, was a pervasive and at the same time superficial de-eroticisation of culture; it was then that the *anciens régimes*, and especially their aristocracies, began to be imagined as morally and, in particular, sexually corrupt, with libertines, *cicisbei* and castratos as their privileged representatives. Theatre was no longer regarded 'as a brothel or even as a comprehensive mirror of nature, but as a school for civilised virtues and sexual decorum', promoting the ingénue and redeemed fallen woman as its defining female characters.[9] But both the ingénue and the redeemed fallen woman are defined precisely by their sexual history (or lack thereof) and their imagined sexual future, and therefore in terms of their eros. As an example, let us consider for a moment the portrayal of the ingénue in the French theatrical genre of *mélodrame* – a genre which will play a significant role in chapter 4.

Anne Ubersfeld has explicitly posited a de-eroticisation, or, in her word, 'castration' of this genre:

> The hero acts on an impulse of pure virtue, without other hope of reward beside the satisfaction of having punished the villain and reunited the families. This de-sexualisation or, better, castration of the hero is one of the characteristics of the popular schema. [. . .] The girl, kidnapped, sometimes tortured, never deflowered, arrives at the last scene *virgo intacta* – another proof of this castration of bourgeois theatre of which *mélodrame* is almost a caricature.[10]

However, the apostrophe to love that opens the chapter entitled 'Innocence persecuted' of the *Traité du mélodrame* – devoted to love as an absolutely essential ingredient for the success of a work – contains a revelatory ironic aside:

> Cruel one! What did this young and innocent girl do to you, that you should pierce her heart, when you know well that she cannot love without being unhappy? Why did you bring this handsome young man under her window – whom, admittedly, you show her from afar? But where cannot a fifteen-year-old virgin's eye see?[11]

If *mélodrame* is a caricature of bourgeois theatre, as Ubersfeld suggests, it might be that the deformation of caricature unveils themes that would otherwise remain hidden. The caricature of the *Traité du mélodrame* seems to suggest that sex lies just below the surface: when it comes to spotting men, a fifteen-year-old virgin sees very far indeed.

In the case of an always already morally problematic genre such as opera, and especially what was considered its most morally problematic national tradition, the Italian one, the ambiguities of this pervasive yet superficial de-eroticisation emerge with particular eloquence. Opera historians are familiar, for example, with the fraught nineteenth-century reception of Mozart's *Così fan tutte* on account of the 'immorality' of Da Ponte's libretto. Less familiar, but no less indicative, is the sharp decline in the critical fortunes of Metastasio, whose texts went from being hailed as the purest, most perfect dramatic poetry in Italian to being reviled as the morally suspect and aesthetically weak manifestations of an emasculated poetaster. During the nineteenth century *Così fan tutte* gave way to *La traviata*, *L'italiana in Algeri* and its sexually and therefore psychologically aware and active heroine gave way to *Rigoletto* and its sexually and therefore psychologically unaware and inactive female protagonist (at least initially). This de-eroticisation may even be implicated in the decline of *opera buffa*, a genre to some extent intrinsically erotic, or at least explicit in its representation of sexuality. In nineteenth-century Italian opera women constantly fall in love, but never have sex, or, better, never have it on stage, or talk about it, or ostensibly ever think about it – they are 'unknowing', as the English language has it. In this sense, virgin girls may at first appear as the genre's perfect character type. And yet, they are defined by their very sexual history, and precisely its absence, thus revealing the nineteenth-century obsession with both female sexuality and its concealment, with both the promotion of female virginity and the taboo of its representation, with its exaltation as the ideal state – presumably to be desired for ever – and at the same time its temporality. Never before had the discourse on female virginity been given such prominence, in all its ambiguities and contradictions.[12]

THE MORALITY OF NINETEENTH-CENTURY MOUNTAINS

Similar considerations can be advanced about the nineteenth-century discourse on mountains, but with one significant difference. While the preoccupation with virginity had been a constituent part of the Western discourse on female sexuality since early Christianity, mountains had for the most part remained hidden within the countryside. The idea of mountains was of course present, but the landscape of mountains as something separate and different from the countryside, and, even more, the experience of altitude as a fundamental dimension in the human perception of nature, only emerged with modernity. In Carissimi's *Jephte* mountains are a name and a sound effect, but not an image, let alone an experience. While mountains had appeared, mostly as 'fantastical' shapes, in European paintings from at least the sixteenth century, they did not become a 'real' landscape, with its own set of symbolic meanings and functions, until the eighteenth, taking pride of place in the Western imagination, literary and musical as well as visual, only in the nineteenth.[13]

Not only did mountains remain hidden within the idea of the countryside until the modern era; once they came to the fore, they also took over some of the meanings that the countryside had had in Western culture since antiquity. The opposition between city and country as embodying fundamentally opposed ways of life goes back at least to Latin literature (Virgil, Horace, Juvenal among others), and the Greek myth of pastoral Arcadia constitutes one of the most powerful tropes of Western culture.[14] When, between the eighteenth and nineteenth centuries, the countryside lost at least some of its associations with peace, innocence and virtue, these characteristics were given to mountains instead, especially the Alps, which, thanks to their location at the geographical heart of Western Europe, have been the mountains *par excellence* of the modern European imagination. In John Ruskin's evocative words, 'the best image which the world can give of Paradise is in the slope of the meadows, orchards, and corn-fields on the sides of a great Alp, with its purple rocks and eternal snows above'.[15] In a widely read book first published in 1871, John Tyndall, an English scientist and mountaineer, was more morally explicit: 'There is assuredly morality in the oxygen of the mountains, as there is immorality in the miasma of a marsh. [. . .] We are recognising more and more the influence of physical elements in the conduct of life, for when the blood flows in a purer current, the heart is capable of higher glow. Spirit and matter are intertwined'.[16]

This construction of mountains, and especially the Alps, as a paradise on earth belongs to what, in Schillerian terms, can be called the 'sentimentality' of modernity. As is well known, Schiller's *On Naïve and Sentimental Poetry* formulates a distinction fundamental to nineteenth- and twentieth-century aesthetic discourse: 'The poet either is nature or he will seek it. The former constitutes the "naïve", the latter the "sentimental"'.[17] These two categories are aligned along the ancient–modern distinction, so that the divided, self-reflective consciousness of the 'sentimental' poet is the consciousness of modernity. The reintegration of individual personality and the regeneration of society, eminently modern issues, are, in Schiller's view, the true goals of artistic creation. Nineteenth-century mountains can be understood as a product of this 'sentimental' search for reintegration and regeneration, but with a stronger nostalgia for a lost Eden than in Schiller's conceptualisation. The nostalgia for a pre-lapsarian innocence that is a characteristic of the arcadian trope connotates these mountains as the modern, 'sentimental' version of classical Arcadia.

The differences between nineteenth-century mountains and previous incarnations of Arcadia emerge not so much in aesthetic and moral terms as in visual and ideological ones. The gradual emergence of mountains in early modern European culture corresponded to the gradual construction of a complex discourse around the idea of landscape, a discourse with countless ramifications in many areas of human activity. In a classic account of this process,

Denis E. Cosgrove has defined the landscape idea as 'a way of seeing – a way in which some Europeans have represented to themselves and to others the world about them and their relationships with it, and through which they have commented on social relations'. According to Cosgrove, landscape is an ideological concept: 'It represents a way in which certain classes of people have signified themselves and their world through their imagined relationship with nature, and through which they have underlined and communicated their own social role and that of others with respect to external nature'.[18] To some significant extent, then, the formation of the idea of mountain landscape can be seen as a prime example of this larger construction of a way of seeing nature as a form of self-fashioning. Ruskin forcefully summed this up when he declared that 'mountains are the beginning and end of all natural scenery'.[19]

The consequences of this way of seeing on the idea of mountains, as well as on the mountains themselves, in the nineteenth century are immense, and this is certainly not the place to explore them – they will be discussed briefly in chapters 2 and 5. What particularly interests me here is that, as recent studies have argued, gendering the object of vision is a fundamental component of landscape construction, and, more in general, of modern attitudes towards nature. Landscape has often been metaphorically associated with the body, and this body has mostly been female – in many ways a consequence of the almost exclusively male gender of the subject of vision.[20] This is even more the case when we restrict the focus from landscape to mountains.[21] If in the nineteenth century mountains are peaceful, innocent and pure, and at the same time they are female, what better place to imagine innocent and pure women? Since both mountains and virginal women are imagined as ultimate embodiments of nature, mountain virgins are the ultimate embodiment of nature.

Only virginal mountains can compete with them for this title. A significant theme in the nineteenth-century discourse on mountains is their celebration as virginal sites, to be either revered from a distance or conquered by climbing, or spoilt by hordes of tourists trampling all over them. Already in 1834 Swiss writer and artist Rodolphe Töpffer compared the touristic exploitation of the Alps to the corruption of a virgin forced to become a prostitute.[22] The Jungfrau, one of the highest Swiss peaks, takes of course pride of place in this discourse – well before Freud's famous case of the young man masturbating while looking at the mountain from his hotel room. In Victor de Laprade's 1849 poem 'L'Alpe vierge (à la Jungfrau)' the poet imagines the mountain as a woman's body enveloped in veils, with a white forehead and blue-veined breasts blushing at the first morning light.[23] What is celebrated as the source of purity is the immense height of the mountain, 'higher than all the clouds' ('plus haut que tous nuages'), which makes the summit inaccessible to human passions: 'O serene region where the infinite sits, your peak remains inaccessible to passions' ('O région sereine où siége l'infini, / Ta cime aux passions demeure inaccessible').[24] There is only one higher place, Heaven, and only one purer woman, the Virgin Mary. But reaching these dizzying heights means losing sight of the body.

One crucial consequence of leaving the body behind is that one moves out of earshot. And while this move is at least potentially possible in the case of literature, and indeed indifferent in the case of visual culture, it is constitutionally impossible in the case of music, and specifically opera. In Carissimi's *Jephte* the only manifestation of the mountain landscape is indeed aural, through the voice of echo: Jephthah's daughter acknowledges that the aural is the only dimension allowed to landscape at this historical juncture and in this medium by asking the mountains and hills to make themselves heard more than seen: 'bewail', 'howl', 'resonate'. That echo's voice is female – insofar as we can link soprano voices to femininity in the castrato-populated seventeenth century – is of course due to its responding to a woman's voice, and perhaps also to the gender of the nymph Echo in classical mythology and of the word 'eco' in the Italian language. But perhaps this feminine voice can also be heard in the context of the incipient gendering of landscape in early modern European culture. In any case, if landscape has a voice in *Jephte*, it is only as an echo of a woman's voice, as an emotional response to her

outpouring of emotions. In other words, nature's true, primal voice
is the voice of a woman. Especially in the case of 'feminine' mountains, nature is female. But, also, women are nature, especially if they
are still in their 'natural' state of virginity. The voice of virgins is
therefore the purest voice of nature.[25]

This set of beliefs means that, at least in Italian opera, nature does
not have a voice of its own. Nor does it need one, as long as there are
women or, better, virgins on stage to sing on nature's behalf. By the
early nineteenth century other musical genres and national traditions
of opera were beginning to grant landscape a voice of its own, from
Beethoven's Pastoral Symphony (notwithstanding the composer's
defensive pronouncements) to Berlioz's Fantastic Symphony, from
Weber's *Der Freischütz* to Rossini's *Guillaume Tell*.[26] In Italian opera,
however, landscape was still primarily a site of human geography,
and its voice was the voice of the human beings, especially the female
ones, who lived in it. When nature makes itself heard, its sounds are
filtered through the emotional states of the characters on stage –
once more, especially female characters – becoming almost an echo
of their emotions.[27] When, hearing the wailing wind (wordless
choral singing in the wings) and the clap of thunder announcing
the storm in Act 3 of *Rigoletto*, Gilda utters with a shiver 'what night
of horror!' ('qual notte d'orrore!'), she is not really describing the
weather, but rather the affective storm within – *pace* her original
creator Victor Hugo's pronouncements on ambience as a 'silent
character' in the well-known preface to *Cromwell* (discussed in
chapter 4 below). Looking out to sea just before dawn at the
beginning of Act 1 of *Simon Boccanegra*, Amelia briefly describes what
she sees (as the orchestra has attempted to do in the prelude), but
then immediately goes on to ask: 'But what do the stars and the
sea tell this wretched orphan?' ('Ma gli astri e la marina che dicono
alla mente dell'orfana meschina?'); she knows full well that landscape's voice can be heard only through her interiority, her 'mente'.
Only in the closing years of the century will landscape begin to make
itself heard, but it will do so in an indirect manner, mostly through
the new ways in which characters hear space. In a sense, the history

of the Alpine virgin in nineteenth-century Italian opera is the story of the progressive emergence of landscape's voice, and of learning how to hear it.

The operas discussed in the following chapters have been chosen because they constitute important moments in this process. But they also serve other, less culturally specific purposes. Observing Italian opera at work through the lenses of the Alpine virgin convention brings to the fore with particular forcefulness the fundamental heterogeneity of opera's constituent dimensions, given the often widely differing textual, visual and musical strategies adopted to represent landscape and gender in nineteenth- and early-twentieth-century Italy. The tensions resulting from the encounter of these different representational strategies can be understood only if they are placed within networks of broad cultural relevance. In turn, this contextualising effort can go some way towards safeguarding against the tendency, endemic to opera studies, to smooth over those differences, to make the textual, the musical and the visual always move in lock-step. The operatic landscape that emerges from the following chapters is anything but smooth, resembling rather the rocky, rugged sites depicted in the operas themselves. But it is in such sites that voices resonate most hauntingly. It is the hills that are alive.

It is hard to take Bellini's *La sonnambula* seriously nowadays. Our culture seems to think its idealised depiction of feminine virtue and its sudden shifts in tone from the tear-jerkingly sentimental to the salaciously comic too distant from present-day sensibilities to grant the work canonical status. A recent production by Marco Arturo Marelli, shared by the Vienna State Opera and London's Covent Garden in the 2001–02 season, may be taken as a telling example of this diffidence. Marelli set the opera in the 1920s in a hotel-cum-sanatorium not dissimilar to the one in Thomas Mann's *The Magic Mountain* – an attempt to find a setting hermetically sealed from external reality, a greenhouse-like isolation. This isolation may translate the 'unreal' actions and emotions put on stage by Bellini and his librettist Felice Romani in 1831 for an early-twenty-first-century audience (supposedly equipped with a good knowledge of twentieth-century European literature). But in the end this 'unreality' is emphasised rather than justified.

When Amina wakes up from her second sleepwalking towards the end of Act 2, the curtain comes down: it goes up again a few moments later to find her wearing a long red velvet dress instead of the white sleeping gown of the previous scene; she sings the cabaletta 'Ah! non giunge' standing on a table, an operatic diva giving a concert in front of the hotel guests now turned adoring fans. Amina even gestures to the conductor to signal that the orchestra can strike up the cabaletta tune. This last scene seems intended as a send-up of the opera, which – the director tells us – we cannot take seriously: after all it is just an opera; worse, a bel canto opera, whose notoriously sole purpose is to present the *prima donna* with as many occasions as possible to display her wonderful voice, amazing coloratura, ear-splitting high notes.

The production's ambivalence reflects fairly accurately present-day attitudes towards the opera on the part of both audiences and critics: reviewers of the Covent Garden run of the production in March 2002 betrayed evident discomfort, seldom failing to point out the outdatedness of the story and the characters' lack of emotional credibility. This ambivalence seems reflected in the relatively small number of productions of *La sonnambula* in theatres around the world in recent years. At Covent Garden the last revival before 2002 had been in the 1981–2 season.

It may be surprising, then, that this modest presence in the repertory is a relatively recent phenomenon. *La sonnambula* was one of the most successful Italian operas through the entire nineteenth century, substantially contributing to the creation of the very concept of an operatic repertory.[1] At La Scala, for example, it was first performed in 1834 and by the end of the century had been heard in thirteen seasons (the longest interval, fifteen years, was between 1882 and 1897). Between 1900 and 1962 it was revived in ten seasons (the longest interval fourteen years, 1910–24), then disappearing until 1986. The most recent production was in 2001. But until the mid twentieth century Milanese opera-goers would have had many other opportunities to see it in lesser theatres, starting of course with the Teatro Carcano, where it was premièred. London first saw *La sonnambula* in the same year of its première, 1831, and innumerable other times in the nineteenth century: between 1847, the year when Covent Garden became the Royal Italian Opera, and 1890, it featured in no fewer than thirty-one seasons. In the twentieth century, however, it was revived only in 1909–11 (for Luisa Tetrazzini) and 1960 (for Joan Sutherland). Before 1981 (when Ileana Cotrubas and Luciana Serra sang Amina) it reappeared twice, in 1965 (again with Sutherland) and 1971 (with Renata Scotto).

During its first century, then, *La sonnambula* was taken seriously. Any regular opera-goer in Milan or London (or in Vienna, Paris, Naples, Madrid, Berlin, St Petersburg, New York, Buenos Aires, and countless minor centres) could see it on stage repeatedly at more or less regular intervals in the course of his or her lifetime.

Each time, a negotiation took place between the culture of the time and the work in performance, and for about a century this negotiation had a successful outcome, reaffirming the continuing value of *La sonnambula* for each cultural context from which it was judged worthy of repetition.

In this chapter I propose to take *La sonnambula* seriously: first as a historical object; secondly (and relatedly) as an aesthetic one. My aim is to explore some of the possible meanings it may have had for the nineteenth century, and therefore at least implicitly to try to understand the reasons for its unqualified and continuous success. While initially the focus will be on the context in which the opera first appeared, in the second part of the chapter reception will play an increasingly important role. The main point of view will remain, however, the participation of *La sonnambula* in an ongoing discourse about landscape, especially in its Alpine incarnation.

FORGETTING ONESELF ON THE ALPS

'The action takes place in Provence, on the island of Camargue, near Arles'. Thus reads Eugène Scribe's and Jean-Pierre Aumer's *La Somnambule, ou l'Arrivée d'un nouveau seigneur*, the source of *La sonnambula*.[2] By contrast, the corresponding indication in Romani's libretto is 'the action takes place in a Swiss village' ('la scena è in un villaggio della Svizzera').[3] Why this change of locale? The only way to answer this question is to investigate the different and often contradictory meanings assigned to Alpine landscape in European culture between the eighteenth and nineteenth centuries, including of course operatic culture. Before the eighteenth century the Alps were at the margins of European culture: a wild, inhospitable land, their only function to isolate, or protect – according to geographical or historical perspective – Italy from northern countries. Aesthetically they were dismissed as freaks of nature, deformities of the earth, bubonic protuberances, their few inhabitants considered beastly savages, hardly worthy of belonging to the human consortium.[4] Opera kept them and their landscape at bay, invoking them only occasionally as markers of savagery and wildness. In Giovanni Faustini and Francesco Cavalli's *Ormindo*, premièred in Venice in 1644, Hariadeno, King of Morocco, declares that he belongs to the human race and is able to feel pity by repeatedly reminding the other characters that 'after all I am human, and was not born amidst Alpine cliffs' ('io son humano al fine, e non trassi il natal da balze alpine').

During the eighteenth century, however, the Alpine landscape shifted towards the centre of visual and literary imagination. When Europe took notice of the Alps, it constructed them in two different if related ways. The first appeared in a few canonical aesthetic texts from the second half of the century: Edmund Burke's *Philosophical Inquiry into the Origin of Our Ideas of the Sublime and Beautiful* (1757), Immanuel Kant's *Critique of Judgement* (1790), and Friedrich Schiller's 'On the Sublime' (published in 1801 but written in the 1790s).[5] This view of the Alps centres around the concept of the sublime, variously described as a feeling of delighted horror, terrible joy or speechless stupor that invades the human soul before a spectacle of grandiose dimensions, immeasurable heights, irregular and fantastic shapes. Burke's experience of the sublime – provoked, among other things, by the sight of an Alpine landscape – represents the defeat of the human subject's rational faculties, overpowered by emotional intuition. For Kant, on the contrary, it is the transcendental subject – as opposed to Burke's empirical subject – that experiences what he calls the 'dynamic sublime' as a reaction to the contradiction between pleasure and pain provoked by certain aesthetic perceptions, such as the sight of high mountains. In the light of what follows, it is important to stress how both Burke and Kant posit the separation between reason and feeling as an innate quality, a given, of the human subject.[6]

But the Alps were also variously described as idyllic, pure, virtuous, innocent, natural. The texts most instrumental in promoting this view were Albrecht von Haller's poem *Die Alpen* (1732), extremely popular throughout the century, and Jean-Jacques Rousseau's *La Nouvelle Héloïse* (1761), whose immense influence on European culture lasted well into the nineteenth century. In his philosophical anthropology, developed in works such as the *Discourse on the Origins of Inequality* and *The Social Contract*, Rousseau rejected Burke's and Kant's notion of the human subject as naturally divided between reason and sensibility: he considered this split subjectivity a degradation, the regrettable outcome of civilisation and society. Instead, his genealogy of the human species posited an *état de nature*, an amoral or pre-moral state, in which the subject is ruled solely by conscience, the 'voice of the soul', and passions, the 'voice of the body'. Rationality, the voice of civilisation and society, silences conscience and passions, thus causing the human subject to lose contact with its inner, 'natural' self.

One of the most explicit expositions of this mythological genealogy is found in 'The Profession of Faith of a Vicar from Savoy', a section of Rousseau's *Emile*.[7] It is the specific locale of Savoy – that is, of a quintessentially Alpine region – that interests me here. In Rousseau's thought the Alps represent the site of a primeval – but not primitive – society, where for a moment the illusion of a return to an original state of innocence could be entertained. As opposed to the Burkean and Kantian sublime Alps, which do not admit human habitation and require a solitary, educated viewer, the Rousseauvian Alps are a site of human geography, where a 'natural' communion between humanity and nature could be believed possible. Here is a modern Arcadia, and it is closer to home than Europe used to think.[8]

Rousseau develops this aesthetics of nature, inseparable from his moral anthropology, in *La Nouvelle Héloïse*. Saint-Preux, the male protagonist of this epistolary novel, writes to Julie, the female one:

> I could have spent the whole time in contemplating these magnificent landscapes, if I had not found still greater pleasure in the conversation of the inhabitants. In my observations you will find a slight sketch of their manner, their simplicity, their equality of soul, and of that peacefulness of mind, which renders them happy by an exemption from pain, rather than by the enjoyment of pleasure.[9]

Later in the same letter Saint-Preux performs a fusion of ambience and human nature, referring to 'the pleasing awfulness of nature, the invariable serenity of the air, the grateful simplicity of the people, their constant and natural prudence, the unaffected modesty and innocence of the sex'.[10] Fundamental to the *montagnards'* innocence is a lack of self-consciousness: they are innocent precisely because they do not know they are.

This pre-lapsarian state was what innumerable travellers longed for when they set out in Rousseau's footsteps for their Alpine *grand tour*, in search of the same loss of self-perception that Saint-Preux experiences when contemplating Alpine scenery:

> It seems as if, being lifted above all human society, we had left every low terrestrial sentiment behind; and that as we approach the ethereal regions, the soul imbibes something of their eternal purity. [. . .] There is a kind of supernatural beauty in these mountainous prospects which charms both the senses and the mind into a forgetfulness of one's self and of every thing in the world.[11]

As Jean Starobinski has noted, Rousseau depicts here the landscape of another, larger, magical world. This otherworldly quality becomes less an innate characteristic of the Alpine landscape than a mythical figure of happiness, 'a metamorphosis that the soul, in its exaltation, is able to project into the world around it'.[12] But this metamorphosis is an illusion. The natural space of the Alpine idyll remains a myth, valid only because of its unattainability: the modern cultivated subject can only reach its threshold, observe it, and describe it. The subtitle of Rousseau's novel significantly reads 'Letters of two lovers living in a small town at the foot of the Alps' ('Lettres de deux amants habitants d'une petite ville au pied des Alpes'). 'At the foot' is the closest we can come.

This unattainability of the Alpine space, and therefore of the *état de nature* it harboured, seems to have escaped Rousseau's followers, but can be observed in the schism between the spectacle of humanity that the Alps presented and what visitors expected and wanted to see. If Shelley could not avoid noticing 'the degradation of the human species – who in these regions are half deformed or idiotic, and most of whom are deprived of any thing that can excite interest or admiration',[13] Byron, travelling with him, was absorbed by Rousseau's magic when they reached the little town of Clarens, where *La Nouvelle Héloise* is set:

> I made a voyage round the Lake of Geneva; and, as far as my own observations have led me in a not uninterested nor inattentive survey of all the scenes most celebrated by Rousseau in his 'Héloise', I can safely say, that in this there is no exaggeration. It would be difficult to see Clarens [. . .] without being forcibly struck with its peculiar adaption to the persons and events with which it has been peopled. But this is not all; the feeling with which all around Clarens, and the opposite rocks of Meillerie is invested, is of a still higher and more comprehensive order than the mere sympathy with individual passion; it is a sense of the existence of love in its most extended and sublime capacity, and of our own participation of its good and of its glory; it is the great principle of the universe, which is there more condensed, but not less manifested; and of which, though knowing ourselves a part, we lose our individuality, and mingle in the beauty of the whole.[14]

In a travellers' guide published in 1838, Clarens is described as 'a poor, dirty village, far less attractive than many of its neighbours, and it probably owes its celebrity to a well-sounding name, which fitted it for the pages of a romance'.[15] Shelley, while aware of this contradiction, was willing to go so far as to praise Rousseau for being 'a mind so powerfully bright as to cast a shade of falsehood on the records that are called reality'.[16] And yet reality remained, stubbornly refusing to stand in the shadow of Rousseau's 'Romantic' imagination, itself casting a shadow on late-eighteenth- and early-nineteenth-century images of Alpine purity, innocence and naturalness.

In the French context this contradiction emerged in a particularly acute way. The tension between the sublime and the idyllic, as well as, within the idyllic, between idealisation and reality, stems from the fact that the French Romantics, while deeply influenced by Rousseau's aesthetics of nature, more or less consciously rejected his mythical genealogy of the human species. It was not the happy human life in perfect harmony with nature that was glorified, but rather landscape itself and its influence on the disenchanted soul. The sublime Alps reflected the tormented state of the solitary viewer, as in Senancour's *Oberman* (1804), while the idyllic landscape soothed his private and incurable sorrows – 'his' since this viewer was almost always male. Rousseau's arcadian myth was re-told with a tone of Romantic nostalgia.[17]

Chateaubriand's Rousseauvian description of the people of Switzerland (and of Scythia) as 'happy and savage' ('heureux et sauvage') in the *Essai sur les révolutions* (1797) was dismissively glossed by the author himself in the 1826 edition of this text as 'the excess of a soul taking pleasure in the view of nature'.[18] Whereas in *La Nouvelle Héloïse* Rousseau had evoked the Alpine landscape through the image of the lifting of a veil that makes objects seem closer, the lyrical description of an Alpine spring dawn that opens the fourth 'epoch' of Lamartine's *Jocelyn* (1836) proliferates with metaphors of distance and accumulates a plethora of minute descriptive details, in search of an effect of indefinite *rêverie* laden with nostalgic overtones. Reviewing the poem for the *Revue des deux mondes*, Saint-Beuve sided with reality: 'People used to life in the mountains [. . .] find the landscape of high valleys severe, sober and precise, different from how our poet has created it in his magnificently luxuriant idyll'. He concluded that one could feel 'really irritated by this blond and blue sweetness and this indefinite optimism'.[19]

This tension between nostalgic idealisation and objective observation marks not only the philosophical and literary discourse on the Alps in the early nineteenth century, but also the operatic one. On the lyric stage, however, the ideological construction of the Alpine idyll was influenced more substantially than in philosophy and literature by late-eighteenth-century notions of sentimentality. This influence emerges most clearly in the case of two operas that contributed indirectly but nonetheless significantly to the Alpine discourse to which *La sonnambula* centrally belongs: Paisiello's *Nina* and Rossini's *La gazza ladra*.

NINA AND NINETTA IN THE COUNTRY

Giovanni Paisiello's *Nina o sia La pazza per amore* (1789) was by far the most popular and influential sentimental opera in the early nineteenth century, especially the two-act version prepared by the composer for an early revival at the Teatro dei Fiorentini, Naples, in 1790. Among famous nineteenth-century Ninas was Giuditta Pasta, who premièred the role at the Théâtre-Italien in 1823 and repeated it in the summer of 1829 at the Teatro Carcano, Milan, the same theatre where she would be the first Amina in *La sonnambula*, and where the work was presented as a *dramma semiserio*.[20]

Nina is set in the countryside, whose inhabitants' simplicity and virtue are exalted in opposition to the wicked city, where Nina's cruel father resides. Only in this blessed environment can the heroine find people who, thanks to their innocent goodness, sympathise with her state.[21] Nina is only the last in a long list of virtuous gardeners and shepherdesses who populate late-eighteenth-century sentimental operas, or comic ones with sentimental traits, from Goldoni and Piccinni's Cecchina in *La buona figliola* (1760), another very popular work, to an anonymous librettist's and Mozart's Sandrina in *La finta giardiniera* (1775). But the geographical location of *Nina* is in several ways more precise than these operas' generic gardens.

Nina was premièred at the so-called 'Belvedere di San Leucio', a hunting lodge near the royal palace at Caserta, the summer residence of the King of Naples, on the occasion of the King's visit to the 'popolazione di San Leucio'. This 'popolazione' was a silk manufacturing plant with attached village for the workers set up by the government in an attempt to create an ideal community built on principles of equality and at the same time boundless submission to the King. According to the rules regulating the 'popolazione', for example, marriages should be free from considerations of wealth or class, the choice of partner made by the bride and bridegroom, without parental interference.[22] The resonances between the unusual location of *Nina*'s première and the opera's story of the ruinous effects of a father's opposition to his daughter's marriage to a man of lower social standing cannot be coincidental. The royal attempt to put into practice Rousseauvian ideals in Campania's countryside is echoed in the idealisation of the villagers in Paisiello's opera. The power of this association was not lost on a group of Turinese spectators, who, after attending a performance of the opera in 1794, wrote to Paisiello himself, confessing that he had awakened in them 'the desire for the simple pleasures of innocent nature'.[23]

These spectators were perfectly justified in writing to Paisiello rather than the librettist, since the evocation of an idealised country-side rests significantly on compositional choices. Scene 8 of the first, one-act version of the opera features a shepherd who plays a tune on the *zampogna*, a bagpipe-like instrument characteristic of the Southern Apennines and well known to Italian urban audiences, thanks to the centuries-old tradition, still alive today, of shepherds playing it in the streets during the Christmas season. With its obligatory drone on the dominant and a 'simple', almost entirely stepwise melody, but above all with the evocatory power of timbre, this 'sonata di zampogna' situates the opera approximately south and east of Rome; more likely still, within *c.* 100–50 miles from Naples – in short, a perfect tune for the 'popolazione di San Leucio', at least in the imagination of spectators normally residing in Naples, such as the royal guests of the première or the Neapolitan opera-goers of subsequent revivals.

In the second version of the opera Paisiello turned this tune into the ritornello of a song performed by the shepherd accompanying himself on the *zampogna*:

> Già il sol si cala dietro alla montagna,
> E il prato al suo partir si fa men bello.
> Colla zampogna sua per la campagna
> Gli armenti suoi raccoglie il pastorello:
> Seco la villanella si accompagna
> Col già pasciuto suo bianco torello;
> E per la via de' loro amanti cori
> Spiegan col canto gl'innocenti ardori.

Al nascer poi della novella aurora
Nel primo aspetto suo ritorna il prato:
Sussurra l'aura tra le fronde allora,
Mormora il ruscelletto allor più grato.
Canta la villanella e seco allora
Ripiglia il pastorello il canto usato.
Gareggiano in amore, e fanno intanto
Un sol concerto il rio, l'auretta e il canto.

The sun is already setting behind the mountain, and at its parting the
meadow becomes less beautiful. With his bagpipe the shepherd boy
gathers his herds in the country; the country girl keeps him company
with her well-fed white bullock, and on their way they set free the
innocent ardours of their loving hearts with their singing. At the new
dawn the meadow returns to its former aspect: the breeze whispers
among the leaves, and the brooklet murmurs even more pleasantly. The
country girl sings, and with her the shepherd boy resumes his usual
song. They vie with each other in love, and meanwhile the brook, the
breeze and the song make one harmonious concert.

This text, presumably by Giambattista Lorenzi, who assisted Paisiello
in preparing the second version, is divided into two stanzas of
endecasillabi rhyming ABABABCC, that is, what scholars of Italian
poetry would call two *ottave toscane*. This structure and the folksy
theme point towards the *strambotto* or *rispetto*, forms of Italian poetry
that since the fifteenth century have been at the border between
popular song and its artful, literary imitations, and have coalesced
into regional traditions with different names but with similar
themes and vocabulary.[24] Paisiello's *canzone*, with its 12/8 metre,
the prevalence of the crotchet-plus-quaver rhythmic pattern in the
vocal melody, the alternation between voice and instrumental inter-
ludes – imitating the effect of a performance by one player/singer,
still the standard practice for *zampognari* – and the piquant harmonic
effect of the uninterrupted dominant pedal, is intensely redolent of
'southern Italian popular music' as imagined by urban audiences,
thus reinforcing the geographical identification of the opera's setting
(Ex. 2.1).[25]

Ex. 2.1. Paisiello, *Nina o sia La pazza per amore*: Shepherd's song.

The southern pastoral utopia of *Nina* acted for decades as perhaps the most powerful operatic model of the sentimentalisation of landscape, thanks to its continued success in the first third of the nineteenth century. *La sonnambula*'s indebtedness to Paisiello's opera was evident to early commentators, and has been a recurring theme

Ex. 2.1. (*cont.*)

of Bellini criticism ever since.[26] Critics from Michele Scherillo to Friedrich Lippmann have mentioned similarities between the two works, for example the prominent symbolic role played by objects that have become tokens of Nina's and Amina's lost love, the ring and the flowers. And it has been rightly pointed out that Nina's madness and Amina's sleepwalking would have been conceived in the early nineteenth century as similar states of altered consciousness, before the modern distinction between a 'pathological' condition like madness and a 'physiological' one like sleepwalking.

Bellini's few published letters dating from the months before the première of the opera do not mention *Nina*, but a few years later several references to Paisiello's work are found in the correspondence about *I Puritani*. As Pierluigi Petrobelli has shown, *Nina* constitutes a crucial model for Bellini's last opera. Most relevant in this context, a letter to Francesco Florimo of 4 October 1834 couples *Nina* with *La sonnambula* as representative examples of the same genre: 'If the libretto does not contain profound emotions, it is nonetheless full of theatrical effects in its atmosphere, and I can say that basically the genre is that of *La sonnambula* or Paisiello's *Nina*, plus some robust military touches and something severely Puritan'.[27] Bellini's word, 'colorito', which Roger Parker, Petrobelli's translator, renders as 'atmosphere', may well have meant something that also implies elements both of genre and of local colour.[28] In short, Bellini also had in mind the similar pastoral ambiences of *La sonnambula* and *Nina*, both repeatedly called 'idylls' by nineteenth- and twentieth-century critics. If, from both a compositional and a reception point of view, it was evident that *Nina* and *La sonnambula* belonged to the same genre, as was this genre's requirement of a pastoral, idyllic ambience, why then did Romani and Bellini decide to set their opera in Switzerland rather than in southern France, like *La Somnambule*, or southern Italy, like *Nina*? Why was the pastoral countryside no longer a preferred solution?

The countryside was kept alive in nineteenth-century opera not only by *Nina*, but by new *opere semiserie*, first and foremost Giovanni Gherardini and Rossini's *La gazza ladra* (1817). This work takes place 'in a large village not very far from Paris', which we may suppose to be Palaiseau thanks to the libretto's source, T. Baudouin d'Aubigny and Louis-Charles Caigniez's *mélodrame historique La Pie voleuse ou la Servante de Palaiseau*. Whereas in works like *Nina* the countryside was constructed in opposition to the city, and could therefore assume the moral weight bestowed on it by the ideology of the pastoral, it seems important that the action of *La Pie voleuse/La gazza ladra* takes place in a village 'not very far from Paris'. This closeness to the city forecloses any idealisation of the locale as a site of pastoral utopia. *La Pie voleuse* and *La gazza ladra* are set in the countryside in order to allow mixing social classes and contemporary characters, something not permitted in an urban environment outside the boundaries of the comic genre. Even if the village people show sympathy for the unjustly accused protagonist Ninetta, the rural ambience is never strongly thematised, nor is an explicit connection established between Ninetta's innocence and the landscape of which she is part.

Stendhal was struck in the *introduzione* 'by a note of rustic energy, by a strong flavour of the countryside, above all by a complete lack of urban sophistication – features that imbue this *introduzione* with a colouring, an atmosphere that is a world removed from that, say, of the *Barber*'.[29] Maybe; but Rossini seems to have resisted other opportunities to imbue the rest of the opera with 'a strong flavour of the countryside'. Gherardini had asked for a 'pastoral symphony' ('sinfonia campestre') to be heard 'from behind the hill' to announce the arrival of Giannetto; but Rossini wrote a very fast orchestral passage that sounds no different from any other transitional kinetic section, and does not evoke the countryside at all.[30] The only moment when Rossini injects some rustic flavour is in the two brief dance tunes that separate the stanzas of Pippo's drinking song 'Tocchiamo, beviamo', especially the first, with its brisk 6/8 and concertante clarinet. These hints of *couleur locale*, however, do not mark the sound world of *La gazza ladra* in any significant way. Nowhere do we find anything like Paisiello's 'sonata di zampogna' and shepherd's song.

The countryside did not disappear from early-nineteenth-century Italian opera, then: what became more and more a remnant of a bygone age, appropriate for old classics like *Nina* but no longer suited to new works, was its sentimental and pastoral idealisation. This loss of symbolic potential was due to a complex web of reasons, related to both social movements and literary trends. In a sense, by the early nineteenth century the countryside had become too close to the city. Many in the audience, recently moved from the provinces to cities, knew the country too well to be impressed by the idealisation that had worked for eighteenth-century audiences.

To return to *La gazza ladra* for a moment, Stendhal explicitly connected it with Milan – a city he knew a great deal about – in the chapter of the *Life of Rossini* devoted to this opera:

Fourteen years under the rule of an inspired despot [i.e., Napoleon] had made Milan, a city once renowned for nothing but over-eating, into the intellectual capital of Italy; and in 1817 it could still number among its citizens some four or five hundred individuals – the remnants of that army of administrators which Napoleon had recruited from every corner of Italy, from Bologna to Novara and from La Pontebba to Ancona, to hold high office in his Kingdom of Italy – who stood head and shoulders above the general run of their contemporaries.[31]

This evolution in the provenance of urban élites, which constituted a substantial portion of the opera-going public, was true of Restoration Paris, where *La Pie voleuse* was first performed in 1815, as well as of Restoration Milan, which saw the première of *La gazza ladra*.[32] A recently urbanised audience may have resisted the utopic idealisation of the countryside, of which it had direct experience. To recall the terms of the tension between opposing views of the Alps mentioned above, this audience may have been reluctant to forget 'reality' altogether and, like Saint-Beuve reading Lamartine, may have felt 'irritated by this blond and blue sweetness and this indefinite optimism'.

Alessandro Manzoni's *I promessi sposi* (*The Betrothed*), first published in 1827 and soon to become the most famous novel of Italian literature, embeds some of the tensions inherent to representations of the countryside and the Alps at this time. Its famous first paragraph signals the triumphal entrance of the Alpine pastoral landscape into Italian 'high' culture:

> Quel ramo del lago di Como, che volge a mezzogiorno, tra due catene non interrotte di monti, tutto a seni e a golfi, a seconda dello sporgere e del rientrare di quelli, vien, quasi a un tratto, a restringersi, e a prender corso e figura di fiume, tra un promontorio a destra, e un'ampia costiera dall'altra parte. [. . .] Il luogo stesso da dove contemplate que' vari spettacoli, vi fa spettacolo da ogni parte: il monte di cui passeggiate le falde, vi svolge, al di sopra, d'intorno, le sue cime e le balze, distinte, rilevate, mutabili quasi a ogni passo, aprendosi e contornandosi in gioghi ciò che v'era sembrato prima un sol giogo, e comparendo in vetta ciò che poco innanzi vi si rappresentava sulla costa: e l'ameno, il domestico di quelle falde tempera gradevolmente il selvaggio, e orna vie più il magnifico dell'altre vedute.

One arm of Lake Como turns off to the south between two unbroken chains of mountains, which cut it up into a series of bays and inlets as the hills advance into the water and retreat again, until it quite suddenly grows much narrower and takes on the appearance and the motion of a river between a headland on one side and a wide stretch of shore on the other. [. . .] And the place from which you look out at those varied scenes itself offers the most beautiful sights on every hand. The mountain on whose lower slopes you walk unfolds its precipices and peaks around and above you, high, clear and changing in form with every step you take. What seemed a single ridge opens out and takes the form of a complex of ridges; a feature which you saw but now as part of the hillside now appears on the skyline as a separate peak. The gentle domestic beauty of the slopes pleasantly moderates the wildness of the landscape, and brings out the magnificence of its other parts.[33]

This description is notable not only for its explicit attempt to re-concile the sublime and the idyllic ('the gentle domestic beauty of the slopes pleasantly moderates the wildness of the landscape'), but also for its theatricality, its emphasis on the point of view of the spectator. The effect is one of concreteness, of specific locatedness, far removed from, for example, Lamartine's Alpine dawn, even allowing for the generic differences between poetry and novel.

This sense of concrete locatedness can be connected with the symbolic role played in the novel by the Alpine landscape, which functions as a backdrop to the action, but is evoked only at a few moments of heightened lyricism, as in the female protagonist Lucia's internal monologue which closes chapter eight: 'Farewell, you moun-tains which raise straight out of the water and up to the sky; you jagged, uneven peaks, which we who have grown up with you know so well, and carry impressed in our minds like the faces of our own family' ('Addio, monti sorgenti dall'acque ed elevati al cielo; cime inuguali, note a chi è cresciuto tra voi, e impresse nella sua mente, non meno che lo sia l'aspetto de' suoi più familiari').[34] The human landscape of *I promessi sposi*, however, is not exclusively Alpine: it shares features of both the countryside and the Alps, ambiguously poised as it is between realism and idealisation. Manzoni's fastidious emphasis on the specific location of the nameless village where most of the novel's action takes place – near Lecco, on the lower slopes of mount Resegone – may indeed be related to the symbolic values of these different kinds of landscape: we are neither in a realistic flat countryside nor high in the idealised Alps, but rather somewhere in between, a site that shares characteristics of both locales without belonging unambiguously to either. We are again 'at the foot', as in *La Nouvelle Héloise*, but for entirely different reasons.

Manzoni's novel, which was first published only a few years before the composition of *La sonnambula*, illuminates the complex web of meanings that both countryside and mountains could have for Italian culture at this time. Bellini could no longer make use of the topos of the pastoral countryside on which the human geography of Paisiello's *Nina* relied so significantly. Where to go, then, was the problem that he and Romani faced. The decision was made by early January 1831, when Bellini announced to a friend that he had started composing 'la *Sonnambula* ossia *I due fidanzati svizzeri*'.[35] The subtitle, later dropped, clearly locates the opera in Switzerland. Why Switzerland? Why the Alps? While the larger cultural and literary trends outlined above surely influenced Romani and Bellini, a more immediate context is that of previous operas set in the Alps.

THE DESCENT FROM THE ST BERNARD (ON THE ITALIAN SIDE)

The first opera commonly thought to have brought the Alps onto the operatic stage is Sedaine and Grétry's *opéra-comique Guillaume Tell* (1791). The work that made the Alpine landscape a central concern, however, was Jacques-Antoine de Révéroni Saint-Cyr and Luigi Cherubini's *Eliza ou Le Voyage aux glaciers du Mont St Bernard*, premièred at the Théâtre Feydeau, Paris, in 1794. As Michael Fend has pointed out, the displacement of the characters to the Alps, that is, to a natural environment very distant from the ordinary and perceived as hostile, is exploited as a powerful source of psychological and musical estrangement.[36] Florindo, the male protagonist, a painter originally from the city (Genoa), arrives at the St Bernard pass after his projected marriage to Eliza has been prohibited by her father (echoes of *Nina*). When a letter tells him that Eliza has left Genoa with his rival, he concludes she has betrayed him and, overwhelmed by the horrible landscape that surrounds him, decides to commit suicide.[37] Later in the opera, when Florindo is about to jump into a precipice, an avalanche sweeps him away; he is eventually saved and marries the faithful Eliza. Alpine landscape is portrayed in a way that resonates with the philosophical and aesthetic discourse of the sublime, including the presence of a solitary urban viewer, the painter Florindo, and is musically realised by Cherubini in a style that strives to convey sublime feelings by a massive and unprecedented use of full orchestral forces, an obsessive repetition of motives, and, above all, a broken, emphatic melodic style that steers wide of the flowing continuity normally associated with 'beautiful' Italianate melody.[38] Clearly, these were not Alps that could serve Bellini's needs in *La sonnambula*.

By 1831, in any case, the most imposing example of the operatic Alps was Rossini's *Guillaume Tell*. While generically and dramatically far removed from the world of *La sonnambula*, *Guillaume Tell* embraces the two musical sides of the aesthetic reception of the Alps, the sublime and the idyllic, starting right from the overture with its juxtaposition of the storm on the lake and the pastoral calmness that follows.[39] As Benjamin Walton has recently argued, Rossini's approach to the representation of the Swiss landscape, and especially his use of the by then well-known *ranz des vaches*, consists in saturating the work with local colour to such a degree that, for example, any musical antagonism between the Swiss peasants and the Austrian hunters is drowned out by this 'Swiss soundtrack'.[40] *Guillaume Tell* represents the culmination of a French operatic tradition spanning the last decade of the eighteenth century and the first three of the nineteenth which had developed a substantial musical vocabulary of the Alps. In fact, as Walton suggests, by the late 1820s the French construction of Switzerland as a site of sublime simplicity and beautiful freedom had become a commonplace and was beginning to lose its power of signification, in opera not less than in other art forms – so much so that Rossini and Pierre-Luc-Charles Cicéri, the stage designer for the première of *Guillaume Tell*, had considerable trouble trying to restore this power through sheer accumulation of aural and visual signifiers.

The situation in Italian opera, however, was rather different. The distance between the French and Italian traditions can be best assessed through a brief look at Giovanni Simone Mayr's frequently revived setting of Gaetano Rossi's *dramma sentimentale per musica* in one act entitled *Elisa, ossia Il monte S. Bernardo* (Venice, 1804), an adaptation of Saint-Cyr's French libretto for Cherubini. The overture comprises a 6/8 slow introduction constructed on melodic cells in the woodwind answered by French horns and then trumpets, conveying a sense of spaciousness and suggesting echo effects, and an Allegro which opens with a rustic drone in the strings supporting a melody by oboes, flutes and clarinets.[41] The beginning of the *introduzione*, which according to the libretto 'represents the rising of the sun', is an instrumental piece with flute, oboe and bassoon solos answering each other in echo.[42] A more impressive use of the echo effect is found in Florindo's *sortita*, however, in which the last words of the first four lines of text are repeated by two voices in the wings, designated 'eco primo' and 'eco secondo' in the score. Finally, Mayr concocts suitably rustic music for the Savoyards' chorus that interrupts from the wings Florindo's *rêverie*. The stage direction in the libretto reads: 'Merry music is heard from afar, accompanied by hurdy-gurdies, triangles, and tambourines, and different voices coming nearer from within sing the following chorus'.[43] While the second violins, violas and basses stay on an A–E pedal, the first violins, muted and divisi, play a 'simple', highly repetitive melody in octaves (Ex. 2.2).

If Cherubini's *Eliza* was hardly an example of Alpine idyll, Mayr's *Elisa* might have offered Bellini a model for a more 'Italian', serene musical representation of a pastoral Alpine ambience. Being 'Italian' and serene, however, could mean losing geographical specificity. The sublime musical vocabulary of *Eliza* leaves no doubt that we are very

Ex. 2.2. Mayr, *Elisa*: Savoyards' music.

high up indeed, while *Tell*'s massive doses of *ranz des vaches* keep reminding the audience that these are the Swiss Alps. In comparison, the musical location of Mayr's *Elisa* is less clearly defined.

This potential lack of geographical specificity emerges more sharply once we turn to a more immediate context for *La sonnambula*, which also owes much to transalpine culture: a number of Italian operas from the 1820s based on one of the most successful French *mélodrames* of the time, Victor Ducange's *Thérèse ou l'Orpheline de Genève*, premièred at the Parisian Théâtre de l'Ambigu-Comique in 1820. The story tells of a young orphan girl, Thérèse, who hides *incognita* in a village near Lausanne after being wrongly accused of murdering her benefactress in Geneva. The son of a local noble-woman wants to marry her, but the villain Valther reveals her identity and she is rejected by her fiancé. Eventually, after the villain has assassinated the noblewoman in her sleep, thinking she is Thérèse, he is forced to confess his wrongdoings by means of a theatrical performance in which he is made to believe that he sees the phantom of the dead Thérèse (played by Thérèse herself). The heroine's innocence is revealed, she marries her beloved, and they live happily ever after.[44]

This *pièce*, translated into Italian and reprinted more than once, provided the outline for a number of ballet scenarios.[45] What is more, it was turned into a libretto, *Amina ovvero L'innocenza persegui-tata*, by Felice Romani, set to music by Giuseppe Rastrelli and premièred at La Scala in 1824. The same libretto was used by Antonio d'Antoni for an opera of the same title written for Trieste the following year, and it formed the basis of Carlo Valentini's *Amina ovvero L'orfanella da Ginevra*, with alterations by Andrea Leone Tottola, premièred at the Teatro Nuovo, Naples, in 1825. Jacopo Ferretti prepared yet another modified version for Luigi Ricci's *L'orfanella di Ginevra*, which scored a considerable success at the Teatro Valle, Rome, in 1829 and was heard in several Italian cities in the following decade.[46]

It is difficult to evaluate the musical impact of the Alps in these works, given the problems in locating their musical sources – if indeed they still survive. In the librettos the Alps do not figure prominently, or constitute a theme, even if evidence from reception points towards some concern over their relevance.[47] Apart from various rustic traits, mostly found in choral interventions, the only 'Alpine' music in Ricci's opera, for example, seems to be the prominent echo effect – woodwinds responding to the strings – in the instrumental accompaniment to the Act 1 chorus 'Alle nozze' (Allegro, 3/8, F major).[48] It is unlikely that this group of works enriched the musical vocabulary for the operatic Alps in any significant way beyond what Bellini could find in Cherubini, Mayr and especially Rossini. Rather, the works based on Ducange's *mélodrame* are important because they introduce the Swiss countryside – for early-nineteenth-century culture the idea of an Alpine locale – into Italian opera as a privileged setting for the representation of virtue and innocence.[49]

According to Pauline Lacoste-Veysseyre, the French stage of the 1820s witnessed the revival of a number of old, pre-Restoration texts made appealing to the audience thanks to new Alpine clothing, as well as the appearance of new works with similar settings, which transported spectators into a world different from the everyday, thus offering playwrights an easy way of renovating stock dramatic situations.[50] The progressive post-Restoration domestication of the countryside, its loss of signifying power, promoted an ascent from the traditional pastoral landscape to the new Alpine one. The fluctuating presence of the word 'Geneva', with all the Rousseauvian images it evoked, in the titles of the operas based on Ducange's

Thérèse ou l'Orpheline de Genève makes for a telling case in point. 'Geneva' was eliminated from the title of Romani's libretto: the soprano Teresa Belloc, contracted to sing the title role, was no longer in her prime in 1824, and Romani was specifically requested 'not to talk about the orphan's beauty and youth', 'to make the orphan less young', and 'to get rid of the word 'orphan' in the title, to make the opera more acceptable';[51] and with "orphan", 'Geneva' also had to go. But Tottola and Ferretti restored it to the title, and in all four librettos it is clearly stated that the action takes place in Switzerland. In 1816 Gaetano Rossi could still locate his *Malvina*, a pastoral *melodramma di sentimento* set to music by Nicola Vaccaj, in 'Abbruzzi', the eastern portion of the central Italian Apennines – an ambience apt for *Nina*. But by the late 1820s the site of a pastoral sentimental action which thematised female innocence and virtue had become the Alps.

ROMANI'S AND SANQUIRICO'S LANDSCAPES

La sonnambula builds on the experience of the Thérèse/Amina operas based on Ducange's *mélodrame* in at least one obvious way, since it is itself a Thérèse/Amina opera: the heroine of Scribe and Aumer's ballet scenario is also named Thérèse. Romani clearly remembered his libretto of 1824 when preparing in haste a new text for Bellini in December 1830, following the last-minute decision not to set Victor Hugo's *Hernani*. A brief comparison between the two texts is revealing: in both cases the action takes place in a Swiss village; in the first scenes the chorus of peasants is heard approaching from afar making 'rustic music' ('musica villereccia') (*Amina*, 1, 6) or 'pastoral sounds' ('suoni pastorali') (*La sonnambula*, 1, 1), and then appears onstage carrying 'rustic instruments' ('stromenti campestri') and 'garlands of flowers' ('ghirlande e festoni di fiori') (*Amina*, 1, 7), or 'rustic instruments and baskets of flowers' ('stromenti villerecci e canestri di fiori') (*La sonnambula*, 1, 2). Moreover, the alternation of outdoor and indoor settings follows a similar pattern, at least for the first three scenes: an initial outdoor scene (the castle park in

Amina, the village square in La sonnambula) is followed by an indoor one (a hall in the castle in Amina, a room in Lisa's inn in La sonnambula), which in turn leads to an open-air setting different from the first (the farm court in Amina, the shadowy valley in La sonnambula).

In *La sonnambula*, however, Romani goes further in defining the Alpine setting. Whereas the initial stage direction of *Amina* does not call for hills or mountains, *La sonnambula* requires 'walk-on hills' ('colline praticabili').[52] And at the beginning of scene 2 the peasants are seen walking down the hillsides and finally reaching stage level. The sung text offers a few further clues: the first line of the chorus in Act 1, scene 2, 'In Elvezia non v'ha rosa'; Lisa's remark that the Count would not arrive at the castle, three miles from the village, before nightfall, 'since the road is very steep' ('tanto alpestre è la via') (1, 6); and, at the beginning of Act 2, set in 'a shadowy valley between the village and the castle' ('ombrosa valletta tra il villaggio e il castello'), the chorus's description of the same route as 'still long, steep, stony' ('lunga ancora, scoscesa, sassosa') – note the alliteration of the *s* sound, considered disrupting, unmusical, hard on the ear in Italian poetic phonology since Dante's 'questa selva selvaggia, ed aspra, e forte' at the beginning of *Inferno*, and presumably employed here to evoke the difficulty of climbing the steep path. The libretto of *La sonnambula*, then, builds on the relatively recent tradition in Italian opera of works set in the Alps, thematising more substantially the mountain landscape. But this remains the landscape of a sentimental idyll. Whereas the sublime Alps of *Eliza* and *Tell* must be an over-bearing, disruptive, almost violent presence, the idyllic Alps of *La sonnambula* and its immediate predecessors gently envelop and protect the people who live at their feet.

A similar gesture of gentle protection could be read into the stage designs prepared by Alessandro Sanquirico for the première of *La sonnambula*, which have survived in coloured engravings. There is no doubt that Sanquirico's four scenes make a significant effort to situate *La sonnambula* in the Alps. The first (Fig. 2.1) and the third (Fig. 2.2) do so by virtue of the high mountain in the background,

Fig. 2.1. Alessandro Sanquirico, stage design for Act 1, scene 1 of Bellini's *La sonnambula* (Milan, Teatro Carcano, 1831).

which, with its steep slopes, would be understood as Alpine by an Italian audience. Perhaps even clearer are the pine trees on the sides in the foreground: on the southern watershed of the Alps, pine trees are common only at a relatively high altitude.

Nonetheless, I would argue that Sanquirico's designs betray some sort of ambivalence towards a fully-fledged Alpine ambience. In Figures 2.1 and 2.2 the effect of the pine trees is counterbalanced by vegetation more characteristic of lower sites, bushes and trees such as oak, chestnut and beech – in fact, in Act 2 scene 2 Amina remembers the times when she and Elvino used to sit 'under the shadow of beech trees' ('di questi faggi all'ombra'). The design for the last scene lacks any iconographical marker of the Alps (Fig. 2.3), and the room in Lisa's inn looks more like the picture gallery of an upper-class residence, complete with mural ornaments and a divan *à l'Empire* (Fig. 2.4). Nor do the costumes (prepared

Fig. 2.2. Alessandro Sanquirico, stage design for Act 2, scene 1 of Bellini's *La sonnambula* (Milan, Teatro Carcano, 1831).

under Sanquirico's supervision if not drawn directly by him) go beyond a generally rural prettiness (Figs. 2.5 and 2.6).[53]

Why this ambivalence? Sanquirico, unlike Romani and Bellini, had virtually no context at his disposal in which to situate his work: he was operating in a kind of iconographical void. Italy did not participate significantly in the iconographical construction of the Alps until the central decades of the nineteenth century, despite the geographical location of a substantial portion of them in regions that considered themselves Italian. Early-nineteenth-century Alpine iconography was the work of the likes of Alexander and John Robert Cozens, Jacques-Louis David, Jean-Antoine Linck, Gabriel Lory and William Turner. The iconography of the hesitant Italian reception of *Guillaume Tell* (or, better, *Guglielmo Tell*, and, in censored versions, *Vallace* and *Rodolfo di Sterlinga*), which has been thoroughly documented by Elizabeth Bartlet and Mercedes Viale Ferrero, might help clarify the situation at the time of *La sonnambula*.

Fig. 2.3. Alessandro Sanquirico, stage design for Act 2, scene 2 of Bellini's *La sonnambula* (Milan, Teatro Carcano, 1831).

From Bartlet's and Viale Ferrero's studies it clearly emerges how difficult it was for Italian audiences to come to terms with the powerfully innovative gesture of setting an heroic, tragic subject in a rustic ambience that did not correspond to the classical topos of the arcadian pastoral.[54] Stage designers found two ways out of this potential impasse: history and sublimity. *Guglielmo Tell*, *Vallace* and *Rodolfo di Sterlinga* are set in the middle ages, and the opportunity to emphasise their historical location was not wasted on stage and costume designers immersed in a visual culture for which 'historical truth' was both a major concern and the yardstick by which their work was customarily judged. By the 1830s, moreover, the sublime Alps were not unknown to northern Italians, exposed as they were to the prints, engravings and later lithographs coming from the North, especially from France. One iconographical topos seems especially relevant: to cite the title of its most famous exemplar, by David, 'Napoleon crossing the St Bernard' in 1796, an event whose

Fig. 2.4. Alessandro Sanquirico, stage design for Act 1, scene 2 of Bellini's *La sonnambula* (Milan, Teatro Carcano, 1831).

importance could hardly be overestimated in post-Restoration Italy. Horrific cliffs, blinding glaciers and scary storms were the stuff Italian stage designers latched onto – and it certainly helped that both *Vallace* and *Rodolfo di Sterlinga* were set not in Switzerland, but in remote Scotland. But the idyllic, pastoral Alps posed new challenges, ones that Sanquirico was forced to confront head-on.[55]

The room in the inn was the only setting for which Sanquirico could rely on an established iconographical tradition. The reviewer of the *Gazzetta privilegiata di Milano* (Milan's daily newspaper), however, did not fail to notice the designer's exuberance:

> At first the scene of act one that, according to the libretto, represents a room in an inn, seemed ill-conceived because of those pictures on the walls, that make it look like the gallery of an ancient castle rather than a room in a poor village inn; but we have been informed that all those portraits were of the ancestors of the innkeeper, who perhaps had previously been the squire of the village, or something like that.[56]

Fig. 2.5. Costume for Teresa in Bellini's *La sonnambula* (Milan, Teatro Carcano, 1831).

Fig. 2.6. Costume for Elvino in Bellini's *La sonnambula* (Milan, Teatro Carcano, 1831).

Sanquirico, surely the most distinguished Italian stage designer of the first half of the century, was famous for his historical and geographical precision. The precise location of the action was usually evoked through the reproduction on stage of historic buildings that immediately identified the urban space in which an opera was set. But *La sonnambula* offered no such option, and it must have been a relief for Sanquirico to be able to turn to at least one established iconographical topos, that of the 'sala', the hall of the mansion or castle, even if, as the Milanese reviewer noted, it went against the letter of the libretto. Put another way, both Romani and Bellini could rely on a set of established literary and musical topoi to represent the idyllic Alps on the operatic stage, but Sanquirico and, perhaps more important, the audience had no visual background on which to build their interpretation. The result of this potential impasse was a substantial recurrence to the old topos of the *locus amoenus*, the arcadian 'luogo delizioso' that had been in the repertory of designers for the operatic stage since the seventeenth century.

The geographical resonances of this recourse to the *locus amoenus* were perhaps unexpected but certainly of consequence. As we shall see, Bellini's stay on the shores of Lake Como during the summer of 1830 has inspired countless commentators to link the composer's direct experience of the Italian lower Alps to his representation of a pastoral Alpine ambience in *La sonnambula*, which was first performed the following winter. The Italian, southern Alps, especially at their most 'Mediterranean' around the lakes of Lombardy, where pines and palms grow side by side, constituted the perfect incarnation of the *locus amoenus*, the perfect fusion of Switzerland and Sicily, Bellini's birthplace. As a consequence, Lombardy has sometimes been suggested as the proper setting of *La sonnambula*.[57] It will come as no surprise, then, that Sanquirico's designs resemble the engravings contained in a volume called *Viaggio pittorico nei monti di Brianza* (*A pictorial journey through the mountains of Brianza*), a collection of views of the region between Milan and the Alps, published in Milan in 1823. The *locus amoenus* of *La sonnambula* ended up looking perilously like the vacation spot of the Milanese upper classes. But this went against the cultural construction of the Alps as an 'other', distant, idealised site. It could be said of Sanquirico's work what I have suggested about Manzoni's treatment of landscape in *I promessi sposi*, then: these four scenes share features of both the countryside and the Alps, without belonging unambiguously to either. We are, once again, 'at the foot'.[58]

BELLINI'S LANDSCAPE

Two kinds of evidence, one based on the genesis of the work and the other on its reception, offer a useful point of departure for interpreting Bellini's representation of landscape in *La sonnambula*. Manuscript sketches by Romani for the libretto bear annotations in Bellini's hand: in Act 1, scene 6, immediately before Teresa's 'ma il sol tramonta: è d'uopo prepararsi a partir', Bellini added 'the call for the flock is heard' ('si fa sentire il chiamo del gregge').[59] In the printed libretto for the première Romani changed this annotation to the more literary 'the sound of the bagpipes is heard, leading the flock back to the fold' ('odesi il suono delle cornamuse che riconducono gli armenti all'ovile'), thus specifying the instrument, or at least the timbre, heard at this point. I would suggest that the immediate reason for Bellini's addition was the need to bolster Teresa's remark about the sunset with an aural signifier: the visual effect requested at this point would have been difficult to realise with the limited technical resources of the small Teatro Carcano.

This staging indication assumes a larger, intertextual function, however, one of which Bellini may have been aware: the appearance of the shepherd in Paisiello's *Nina* is thus explained by Susanna, Nina's governess: 'Night is falling, and the villagers are gathering together on their way home' ('Siam sulla sera, e i villani si raccolgono verso casa'). And Romani's 'cornamusa' is another, more literary word for Carpani's or Lorenzi's 'zampogna'.[60] Both Romani and Bellini, however, knew full well that bagpipe-like instruments are characteristic not of the Alps, but of the central and southern Apennines. If Romani's choice of words can be justified by the

Ex. 2.3. Bellini, *La sonnambula*, Act 1: Horn calls.

weight of a literary tradition that identified 'cornamusa' as the typical arcadian instrument, Bellini knew that he could not follow in Paisiello's footsteps and compose a *strambotto*-type song accompanied by a bagpipe with a dominant pedal. What is more, while in France the operatic stage resonated with more modern, more Alpine sounds, the Italian tradition was less resolute in its aural evocation of an Alpine landscape, less interested in giving this landscape an individual voice. In the end, Bellini made only a passing reference to such a voice: all we find in the score is a simple horn call whose last two chords are echoed (Ex. 2.3).

The reception evidence centres around the definition of *La sonnambula* as a pastoral idyll, an insistently recurring theme in nineteenth-century Bellini criticism, with frequent mention of names such as Theocritus, Virgil and Giovanni Meli.[61] This has traditionally been interpreted as a southern, Mediterranean, Sicilian pastoral, in a move linking biography and art made possible by the rather feeble voice accorded to the opera's landscape.[62] Occasional references to the Alpine ambience are domesticated by the immediate naming of Bellini's 'Greek' origins, as in Florimo's 'with *La sonnambula* Bellini became the Theocritus, the Gessner of music', or in Romani's 'it could be said that Bellini went to Switzerland to be inspired by the sweet tunes of the Muse Gessner, and to fuse them with the beautiful rhythms of Greek melody',[63] in which the reference to the Swiss Salomon Gessner's famous *Idyllen* (1762) is part of the traditional reception of this poet as the 'German Theocritus'.[64]

But biography plays a more specific role in the individuation of *La sonnambula*'s musical geography. As mentioned above, many have suggested a connection between Bellini's holiday on the shores of Lake Como in the summer of 1830 and his representation of a pastoral Alpine ambience in *La sonnambula*. Branca and Scherillo, for example, point to Bellini's summer memories as a reservoir of musical and visual suggestions during the composition of *La sonnambula*.[65] The conclusion has been that, at least for Bellini, the opera's 'real' setting is the Lombard *Prealpi* rather than Switzerland.

This conclusion, as well as all the lyrical enthusing about Sicily and Theocritus and orange trees, has been made possible by the mediated, non-referential quality of *La sonnambula*'s musical landscape, which tends to downplay the definition of ambience. Critics have labelled the *introduzione* 'conventional', claiming that it is external to the intimate substance of the work. The initial 'thoughtless *tarantella*' and the choral song 'In Elvezia non v'ha rosa' have been especially criticised.[66] Some have even attempted to demonstrate the 'generic' quality of Bellini's music by substituting military texts for the words of the two choruses.[67] No matter how questionable these interpretations are – the initial tune is not a *tarantella*, and the tempo and harmonic conduct of the choruses make them impossible as military songs – they nonetheless point to the equivocations to which the opera's musical landscape is open. No *ranz des vaches* and no prominent echo effects avoids situating *La sonnambula* in a precise location immediately identifiable as the Alps. While this lack of geographical specificity was characteristic of the Italian operatic tradition, Bellini seems especially reluctant to give the audience musical clues sufficient to allow them to determine where the action takes place. Instead of climbing the mountain tops, he preferred to stop mid-way at some picturesque but familiar pastoral spot and view them from afar. This point of view, the result of a combination of aesthetic context and compositional choice, has a significant impact on the interpretation of the opera's emotional and psychological landscape.

THE MUSICAL DRAMATISATION OF CONFLICT

I have already mentioned the split between the spectacle of humanity presented to early-nineteenth-century travellers in the Alps and what, having read their Rousseau, they expected to see. A somewhat similar split characterises interpretations of the Alpine people in *La sonnambula*. On the one hand, critics such as Luigi Baldacci and Guido Paduano have taken the chorus seriously, stressing, albeit with differing emphases, its problematic position: having begun as Amina's 'dear companions' ('care compagne') and 'tender friends' ('teneri amici'), they are all too ready to switch sides and congratulate Elvino on his new bride, Lisa; and they end up rejoicing at Amina's triumph. These people's obtuse, pre-Enlightenment readiness to believe in supernatural phenomena such as phantoms goes hand in hand with their absolute faith in authority – they believe Amina is still pure just because the Count says so. This makes them the ideal subjects of Restoration Europe: not only are they willing to submit to a superior authority, but they even desire it, eagerly anticipating the arrival of the new Count – 'everybody wishes him here' ('ciascun lo brama') – after Teresa has sung the praise of the old one, 'the good lord!' ('il buon Signore!').[68]

On the other hand, Francesco Degrada has contrasted Romani's 'smile of benevolent superiority' and 'touch of parody' with the composer's choice of expressive tone for the entire opera, including the choral contribution, which he calls 'religious'.[69] It seems significant that in Scribe and Aumer's *La Somnambule* the villagers express their distress at Edmond's decision to marry Gertrude (Lisa) instead of Thérèse (Amina), while in the opera they congratulate Elvino on his sensible choice. If the portrayal of the chorus was meant to be comic, this would have been the moment to make fun of its readiness to go with the proverbial flow; but it is impossible to take Romani's text other than seriously. The result uncannily resonates with Shelley's observations about the inhabitants of the Swiss Alps. If not 'half deformed or idiotic', our villagers are surely obtuse, servile, narrow-minded and self-righteous. What, then, of the idyllic portrayal of the *montagnards* that had blinded Rousseau's readers to the realities of the Alpine communities they visited?

I want to connect the less than sharply defined Alpine landscape of *La sonnambula* and the ambiguous, if not entirely negative, representation of the village community. From a post-Rousseauvian perspective, emphasis on an unambiguously Alpine ambience would seem to imply an idealised representation of an Alpine community. Perhaps, then, *La sonnambula*'s relative lack of geographical specificity can be connected with the 'realistic' portrayal of the villagers. Stopping at a lower, relatively more familiar spot – in Italy sometimes called 'mezza montagna' – rather than climb the mountain top opens up space for a reading of the opera as a representation of society from a 'realistic', that is to say, middle-class, point of view. This interpretative space becomes available only in the context of the nineteenth-century construction of Alpine landscape. In other words, setting *La sonnambula* in the countryside would not question any idealised representation, since the countryside and its inhabitants were no longer idealised. In order to come down, one needed to go up first, or at least to begin the ascent.

In this light, it is revealing that Romani's scene originally planned for Act 2, in which the Count and Amina find out they are father and daughter, was eventually discarded.[70] The immediate reason behind this decision might have been an attempt to avoid problems with the censor, since the discovery that Amina is the Count's daughter would have coloured the latter's desire for the sleepwalking heroine in Act 1 with the threat of incest.[71] A larger consequence, however, is to distance *La sonnambula* from its source and dramaturgical context, that of French *mélodrame*, by rejecting one of the recurring elements of this theatrical tradition, the recognition scene, and thus ultimately questioning *mélodrame*'s idealised morality and conservative social view.[72]

The Count is problematised in more than one sense: his loss of paternal status inflects his treatment of his subjects with paternalism. His interest in Amina in the first scene, intertextually related to Don Giovanni's arrival at Zerlina's and Masetto's wedding and his immediate lust for the bride, betrays the libertine, whose Giovanni-like concentration on quantity rather than quality explicitly emerges in his monologue in Act 1, scene 8: Amina is 'very pretty' ('assai leggiadra'), but he likes the 'dear innkeeper' ('cara ostessa') as well. Moreover, his idea of authority is absolute and not especially enlightened: he calls Elvino a 'wretch' ('sciagurato') for daring to question his word, again echoing Don Giovanni's conceit 'the honesty of noblemen is written in their eyes' ('la nobiltà ha dipinta negli occhi l'onestà') in his line 'a person of my standing cannot lie' ('un par mio non può mentir').[73]

Romani's portrayal of Elvino is equally problematic. On a dramatic level, his decision to marry Lisa instead of Amina is especially troubling – a gesture perhaps psychologically justifiable if dictated by desperation, but not justified as such in the opera.[74] On a linguistic level, his possessive and egoistic idea of marriage is revealed in constant use of self-referential adjectives and pronouns, in opposition to Amina's preoccupation with her fiancé's feelings.[75] This textual characterisation needs to be verified against its musical counterpart, however, and this cannot be done separately from a consideration of Bellini's characterisation of Amina.

In Amina's *cavatina* 'Come per me sereno' the heroine, ecstatic about her forthcoming wedding, sings of the perfect harmony between idyllic nature and her feelings.

> Come per me sereno
>   Oggi rinacque il dì!
>   Come il terren fiorì
>   Più bello e ameno!
> Mai di più lieto aspetto
>   Natura non brillò:
>   Amor la colorò
>   Del mio diletto.

How serenely is this day beginning for me! How beautifully and pleasantly the earth is blooming! Nature has never glowed more happily: love has coloured it with my joy.

The music clearly depicts this edenic correspondence between nature and emotion, especially in formal and melodic terms. The slow movement flows in a regular succession of four-bar phrases which belongs to the sphere of the so-called lyric form, and can be summarised as an a_4 a'_4 b_4 a''_4 a'''_4 structure. Particularly important for its overall effect is the feeling of both varied repetition and introduction of new material that the last eight bars of the melody convey: even if a'' and a''' contain the structural pitches of a and a', they differ significantly in their harmonic motion (a difference concealed by their labels).[76] While it is risky to establish a direct link between form and affect in the fast-evolving context of Italian opera of this time, the lyric form of 'Come per me sereno' stands out if we compare it with the entrance arias of Bellini's immediately preceding heroines: Imogene's 'Lo sognai, ferito, esangue' (*Il pirata*, 1827) is notoriously idiosyncratic, but Alaide's and Giulietta's *romanze* (in *La straniera*, 1829, and *I Capuleti e i Montecchi*, 1830, respectively) are hardly models of simplicity and predictability, especially the former. While these troubled characters present themselves in 'troubled' forms, Amina's serenity shines through her equally proportioned phrases.[77] Another factor contributing to this feeling of effortless flow is the even distribution and integration of melismas in the melody.

What is more, Amina is in secure control of all her registers, including the top one, in which special emphasis is placed on the high A flat: she reaches it in the very first phrase of her melody, returning to it in both the subsequent phrases (bb. 7 and 12). What enables her to rise to it so easily is made clear in the next phrase (bb. 14–17), where she reaches it on 'amor' – the only word repeated more than twice in the whole movement – and not by a wide leap, but for the first time through G. After this G the reprise of bars 7–9 starting with the high A flat acquires a more secure, radiant flavour, enhanced by a rhythmic integration of the two halves of this phrase. Amina's achievement is crowned in the last phrase (bb. 18–21), in which she eventually reaches the high A flat through a scale, prompted again by 'amor'. At this point she has equipped herself for the climactic rise to scale degree $\hat{5}$, B flat, gloriously achieved in the cadenza (after being briefly anticipated in the preceding bar), and yet again on 'amor' (Ex. 2.4). Given the emphasis on A flat in the slow movement, it should come as no surprise that the cabaletta 'Sovra il sen la man mi posa', in which Amina rejoices in glorious coloratura, is in the key of A flat. At this early stage Amina still entertains the illusion of being in joyful communion with the natural landscape surrounding her and her friends; she still inhabits the Rousseauvian myth unproblematically.

At first it may seem as if Elvino inhabits this myth as well: his musical language in the *cavatina* 'Prendi, l'anel ti dono' echoes Amina's in its fluently ornate ease. A sceptical ear, however, could detect hints of trouble in the relationship between the two protagonists. At the partial reprise of the initial melody of the slow movement, Amina keeps at the respecful distance of a sixth above Elvino, harmonising what is clearly *his* melody. More troubling is her interjection 'Ah! vorrei trovar parole', in which she expresses her inarticulateness, her inability to express her love.

Ah! vorrei trovar parole
  A spiegar com'io t'adoro!
  Ma la voce, o mio tesoro,
  Non risponde al mio pensier.

Ah! I would like to find words to explain how much I adore you! But my voice, my beloved, does not answer to my thoughts.

Her musical voice literally does not 'answer' her thoughts. Her sentence, an a a' eight-bar period in F minor, features a prominent Neapolitan harmony followed by a diminished seventh in the third bar of the a section, and a descending chromatic bass sustaining a series of seventh chords in a', over which Bellini places a hesitant, repetitive vocal line. She had no problem expressing her love before Elvino's entrance, but his presence seems to cause her to lose her voice – a loss she is musically well aware of, and one that troubles her deeply (Ex. 2.5). Elvino seems impatient with his fiancée's inarticulateness: he cuts her off, and the A flat major of his answer

Ex. 2.4. Bellini, *La sonnambula*, Act 1: Amina's *cavatina*, slow movement.

Ex. 2.4. (*cont.*)

bears little sign of having been affected by the preceding F minor.[78]
Again he is preoccupied with himself, with *his* perception of Amina's
feelings – note the relationship between the personal pronouns, with
'me', 'io', 'mia' prominently placed before 'tuoi' and 'tua'.

> Tutto, ah! tutto in questo istante
> > Parla a me del foco ond'ardi:
> > Io lo leggo ne' tuoi sguardi,
> > Nel tuo riso lusinghier!

Ex. 2.5. Bellini, *La sonnambula*, Act 1: Elvino's *cavatina*, Amina's interjection 'Ah! vorrei trovar parole'.

L'alma mia nel tuo sembiante
    Vede appien la tua scolpita,
    E a lei vola, è in lei rapita,
    Di dolcezza e di piacer![79]

Everything in this moment speaks to me of the fire with which you
burn: I can read it in your glance, in your lovely smile! My soul clearly

sees yours depicted in your countenance, it flies to it, it is enraptured by it with sweetness and pleasure!

The Act I duet between soprano and tenor is rather short, a single slow movement followed by a brief, fast codetta. The intervening arrival of the Count and his obvious attentions towards Amina have aroused Elvino's jealousy, but the musical relationship between the two does not seem significantly affected by this potential source of trouble. On the one hand, Elvino still proposes the melody that Amina later repeats, and in the *a due* he sings an ornamented version of the melody at the original pitch level, while Amina simply accompanies him a sixth above. On the other hand, as Mary Ann Smart has noted, her exposition of the melody is not a slavish repetition of Elvino's first statement, but rather a subtly adapted version of it. She makes this melody her own, just as she skilfully turns his language on its head, declaring her love for all the natural objects of which he is jealous.[80]

ELVINO
Son geloso del zefiro errante
Che ti scherza col crine, col velo;
Fin del sol che ti mira dal cielo,
Fin del rivo che specchio ti fa.

AMINA
Son, mio bene, del zefiro amante,
Perché ad esso il tuo nome confido;
Amo il sol, perché teco il divido,
Amo il rio, perché l'onda ti dà.[81]

ELVINO: I am jealous of the wandering breeze that plays with your hair and your veil; of the sun that looks at you from the sky, of the stream that reflects you.
AMINA: My beloved, I love the breeze because I confide your name to it; I love the sun because I share it with you; I love the stream because it gives you its waves.

Reminiscences of both Elvino's *cavatina* and the duet haunt Amina's first sleepwalking scene – formally cast as a loose single-movement duet with the Count. It is significant that this happens in a sleepwalking scene: according to nineteenth-century psychology, we have access here to Amina's 'true', 'authentic' feelings, we can enter her inner self. Moreover, sleepwalking is itself a manifestation of psychological trouble, of a problematic relationship between conscious and unconscious that Amina has not (yet) sorted out. What does her sleepwalking tell us about her position in this Alpine community, of which Elvino, 'rich land-owner' ('ricco possidente'), is the paradigmatic manifestation?[82] Without anticipating the psycho-analytically orientated arguments of the next chapter, here I would simply suggest that, while Amina fully partakes of the Rousseauvian Alpine arcadia of her village when awake, her sleepwalking may cast doubts on the extent of her integration into the community, as well as on the nature of her relationship with Elvino. The cata-strophe that follows – when she is discovered in the Count's room, accused of improper behaviour, and rejected by Elvino – might in a sense have been anticipated by the spectacle of the sleepwalking Amina accompanied by disconnected fragments of the music of her previous encounters with Elvino.

While Elvino has his share of musical distress in his Act 2 aria, this distress is dealt with in ways significantly different from Amina's. His slow movement begins with a French horn solo intro-ducing the melody that he takes up for an a a′ period, in which he expresses his desperation over Amina's supposed betrayal. But again he is self-centred, not even referring to the cause of his despair:

> Tutto è sciolto. Oh dì funesto!
>   Più per me non v'ha conforto.
>   Il mio cor per sempre è morto
>   Alla gioia ed all'amor.[83]

> All is undone. What a terrible day! There is no comfort left to me.
> My heart is dead forever both to joy and to love.

At this point Bellini inserts a dialogue between Amina and Elvino not present in Romani, one that breaks down the lyric form into a *parlante* section (I shall discuss this dialogue below). After sending

Amina away Elvino remembers that he has not completed his slow movement. But seeing Amina and talking to her seems to have changed his feelings too much to allow him to return to his initial melody: he starts a new lyric form on the second stanza of his text, and this time brings it to completion. His cabaletta 'Ah! perché non posso odiarti', notwithstanding the text, confirms his regained control over musical form and process. After all, we should not be surprised to discover in the next scene that he has made the seemingly absurd decision to marry Lisa: fully conscious of his pre-eminent position in the village and of the prerogatives of his sex, Elvino knows that distress must be overcome by action, and he acts. Musically, he brings to completion his interrupted major-mode slow movement, and, dramatically, decides to marry Lisa.

Amina's final *rondò*, 'Ah! non credea mirarti', has always been considered the emotional and musical climax of the opera. In the *scena* the sleepwalking Amina is still vividly preoccupied with Elvino's feelings, something that has characterised her utterances since the beginning of the opera: her last wish is for Elvino's happiness with his new companion. The slow movement of the aria soon became not only the most famous piece of the opera, but an *exemplum* of Bellini's style, the paradigmatic example of what Verdi called his 'melodie lunghe lunghe lunghe'.[84] The text of this movement spells out the breaking of the perfect union between individual and nature portrayed in the first scenes of the opera, as Smart has suggested. The withered flower that Amina holds might be revived by Amina's tears, but these tears are caused by the dying of Elvino's love, which, unlike the flower, will not return.[85]

Ah! non credea mirarti
  Sì presto estinto, o fiore.
  Passasti al par d'amore,
  Che un giorno sol durò. (*piange sui fiori*)
Potria novel vigore
  Il pianto mio donarti. . .
  Ma ravvivar l'amore
  Il pianto mio non può.[86]

I had not thought I would see you, dear flower, perished so soon.
You died like love, which only lasted for a day. (*She cries on the flowers.*)
My weeping could restore your strength, but my weeping cannot
revive love.

Carl Dahlhaus has analysed this piece in an attempt to describe
the musical means by which Bellini achieves a sense of endlessness,
of 'sensuous and spiritual intoxication'.[87] In the initial A minor
section, the centrifugal effect caused by the metrical irregularity
and the avoidance of melodic repetition is subtly counterbalanced
by the cohesive role of harmony, which keeps hinting at a cadence
but does not actually feature a structurally relevant – that is, caden-
tial – dominant seventh chord in root position until its tenth bar.
Moreover, as Smart has observed, after the initial two bars the
melody itself is constantly interrupted by rests, broken down into
short gasps.[88] We could interpret this section as the climax of
Amina's musical confusion, the point to which Elvino's dramatic
and musical behaviour has driven her. Dahlhaus rightly points to the
exceptional status of this piece within Bellini's output: in no other
opera do we find a comparable attempt to eschew the usual patterns
of Italian operatic melody at such a detailed level and with such a
result.[89] I would suggest that 'Ah! non credea mirarti' finds its *raison
d'être* in the musical tale of the relationship between Amina and
Elvino that Bellini has narrated in the preceding scenes.

What, then, is the end of this tale? A happy one, of course, with
the coloratura triumph of Amina's final cabaletta 'Ah! non giunge
uman pensiero'. Several commentators, however, have argued that
the reconciliation between the two lovers takes place during the
sleepwalking scene, within the slow movement, at the point when
Elvino intervenes in Amina's melody with his anguished cry 'I
cannot stand such sorrow' ('io più non reggo a tanto duolo'etta).
Inserting the line that Romani had placed after the end of the *versi
lirici* within them, Bellini anticipates musically what will happen
dramatically immediately after, when Elvino puts the ring back on
Amina's finger: at this point in the slow movement Elvino comes to

a full realisation of his musical relationship with Amina, and, for the first time, shares her music on equal terms, literally in consonance with her most inner self as expressed in her dream.[90] A closer look, however, might offer a slightly different picture.

First, Elvino does not sing 'how unhappy I made her', but 'I cannot stand such sorrow', again focusing on his own feelings, his reaction to the spectacle of Amina's despair. On the musical level, Lippmann has rightly pointed out that Elvino's intervention brings the melody to its climax.[91] One of the most effective features of this movement is its relatively low vocal range: Amina occupies the fifth A–E, reached in the first bar from the lower E, with a rise to F in bars 7 and 12 (in the latter case as a neighbour note to E). Leaving aside for a moment the different octaves in which soprano and tenor operate, Elvino's intervention occupies the upper fourth E–A, with emphasis on the highest note. But Elvino's move does not encourage Amina to explore the upper fourth herself; instead she twice completes his downward stepwise motion, taking it up where he left off, on E, and concludes with the skip E–A, thus emphasising her 'location' there. She seems to hear his music, since she is able to complete his line, but she cannot, or does not want to, join him up there. Some may want to read this division of the melodic space into two separate areas as promising a harmonious division of duties in Elvino and Amina's future household. In the light both of their past interactions and of the relative location of these areas, however – to put it bluntly, with Elvino on top – I am more inclined to interpret it as the latest chapter of the by now well-known story of Elvino's self-centredness and wish for control – a wish that Amina here seems to understand and respect. In the cadenza Amina eventually reaches her high A (which of course has a rather different feeling from Elvino's As at bars 16 and 19–20, given the different tonal/modal context). But what could be a momentous event, given her previous low-lying melodic conduct, fails to impress. This A is merely an upper neighbour note to the G, and, what is more, is immediately inflected by an A flat that suggests C minor (bb. 38–9).[92] The conquest of the top is hardly a victory. The contrast with the *cavatina*, in which she had made ample use of her top register, could not be stronger (Ex. 2.6).

I am not simplistically suggesting that Elvino and Amina are still in conflict. Their musical relationship, however, seems more ambiguous and less unmediatedly positive than the idyllic consonance promoted by critics. In this context 'Ah! non credea mirarti' might be interpreted as another instance of the rather contradictory 'realism' that infiltrates the portrayal of *La sonnambula*'s Alpine community. This interpretation is supported by the text of the final cabaletta, in which Amina voices her need to be reassured that she can believe in her happiness – a reassurance for which, tellingly, she turns to her lover: 'I can hardly trust my senses; reassure me, my beloved' ('A' miei sensi io credo appena; tu mi affida, o mio tesor'). She is now aware that she cannot trust her ability to decipher reality; what used to be buried in her unconscious has now painfully emerged to the rational surface. The myth of her prelapsarian oneness with nature has crumbled, and she knows that the earth is not a natural Eden. Heaven has to be worked for, even in the Alps, as she declares in the second stanza:

> Ah! mi abbraccia, e sempre insieme,
> > Sempre uniti in una speme,
> > Della terra in cui viviamo
> > Ci formiamo – un ciel d'amor.

> Embrace me, and, always together, always joined in one hope, let us make a heaven of the earth where we live.

What are we to make, then, of Bellini's triumphal, coloratura-laden setting of these words? Smart has observed how throughout the opera Amina's florid singing corresponds to the moments of outwardly unproblematical happiness and oneness with self, others and nature, while a more syllabic style is reserved for her exploration of the dark side of this illusory myth: the two sleepwalking scenes and her encounter with Elvino at the beginning of Act 2.[93] Why revert to coloratura at the end? The convention of ending an opera with a virtuoso piece for the *prima donna* could be sensibly

Ex. 2.6. Bellini, *La sonnambula*, Act 2: Amina's *rondò*, slow movement.

Ex. 2.6. (*cont.*)

Ex. 2.6. (*cont.*)

invoked here, and there is no doubt that this convention played an important role in Bellini's compositional decision. While being careful not to smooth over this divergence between words and music, to prove at all costs that they work together, I nonetheless want to call attention to some significant and unusual features of this melody.

Romani writes eight *ottonari trocaici* (the normal form, with accents of varying intensity on the first, third, fifth and seventh syllables) characterised by the constant presence of the *sinalefe* in the fourth syllable. According to standard practice, the *sinalefe* (the fusion of the vowel ending a word and the one beginning the next word) is observed by composers, who will set the two syllables to one note, and expect singers to elide the first vowel sound and pronounce only the second: in the first verse of Amina's cabaletta, therefore, the syllable 'ge u' of 'giunge uman' should be set to a single note, and be sung 'g'u'; in the second, 'to ond' of 'contento ond'io' will become 't'ond'.

Bellini boldly disregards this centuries-old practice for the first three *ottonari* of each stanza, setting them as if they were a *quadrisillabo* followed by a *quinario*: 'Ah! non giunge / Uman pensiero / Al contento / Ond'io son piena', and so on. He then proceeds to place a rest in the middle of each final word of these newly obtained verses, extending this treatment to the word ending with the *sinalefe* (here properly executed) in the final verse of each stanza, 'affida' and 'formiamo'. What is more, the a, a′ and a″ sections of the lyric form begin with an almost literal repetition of the initial melodic unit, corresponding to the *quadrisillabo* and *quinario* forming lines 1, 3 and 7 (Ex. 2.7). The result is a kind of effortful breathlessness, as if Amina lacked the necessary strength to sing even four or five syllables without an intake of breath. Moreover, she seems to have trouble finding her way out of that F–B flat–D arpeggio that weighs her down to earth. Making a heaven out of the earth on which she and Elvino live could prove more difficult than it may seem at first, notwithstanding the coloratura that follows these initial sixteen bars. The divergences between this cabaletta and Amina's

Ex. 2.7. Bellini, *La sonnambula*, Act 2: Amina's *rondò*, cabaletta.

first one, 'Sovra il sen la man mi posa', measure the emotional and psychological distance that she has travelled in the course of the opera, in the process leaving behind the innocence that the Alpine landscape seemed at first to reflect so unproblematically.

IDYLLIC COSTUMING

The emphasis on idyll in the critical reception of *La sonnambula* would seem to deny any awareness of the opera's 'realistic' side. Some aspects of its performance history, however, might raise suspicions about the pervasiveness of this lack of awareness. I will now turn to these aspects, examining first iconographical and then musical evidence in order to investigate some of the meanings that the opera's portrayal of Alpine landscape, of the character of Amina, and of her relationship with Elvino acquired in the course of the performance history of *La sonnambula*.

An important feature of an Alpine ambience is the atemporality of the costumes, which under normal circumstances are the single most powerful historicising device in the staging of opera. For the ethnographic perception of nineteenth-century theatrical audiences, Alpine costumes meant simply 'the Alps', their semantic baggage did not include time. 'Eighteenth-century Alpine costumes', therefore, was a contradiction in terms: at the time of the opera's première the action of *La sonnambula* was perceived as contemporary, as testified by the costumes prepared then.[94] The same is true for most of the nineteenth century, as pictures of Maria Malibran, Jenny Lind and Adelina Patti as Amina, dating from the 1830s, 1847, the 1860s and 1890, confirm.[95] But the Alps and their inhabitants could not, should not be too close. And so, for example, at La Scala in 1855 Filippo Peroni conceived costumes that resolutely locate the opera in the seventeenth century (Figs. 2.7–2.11). Better, these costumes relocate the *male* characters of *La sonnambula* in the seventeenth century, but keep the women, especially Amina, in a less definite temporal frame, one that does not exclude the nineteenth century.

Reviewing a performance of the opera at the Paris Opéra in 1868, the critic J. De Filippi wrote:

> Agnesi, always perfect, as the great singer that he is, has well rendered the role of the Count. But why that black jacket, that present-day hat, that red ribbon, all things that make a jarring juxtaposition with the tone of the work and the costumes of the other characters? Why not wear

Fig. 2.7. Filippo Peroni, costume for Rodolfo in Bellini's *La sonnambula* (Milan, Teatro alla Scala, 1855).

Fig. 2.8. Filippo Peroni, costume for Elvino in Bellini's *La sonnambula* (Milan, Teatro alla Scala, 1855).

Fig. 2.9. Filippo Peroni, costume for Lisa in Bellini's *La sonnambula* (Milan, Teatro alla Scala, 1855).

Fig. 2.10. Filippo Peroni, costume for Amina in Act 1 of Bellini's *La sonnambula* (Milan, Teatro alla Scala, 1855).

Fig. 2.11. Filippo Peroni, costume for Amina in Act 2 of Bellini's *La sonnambula* (Milan, Teatro alla Scala, 1855).

military attire in the style of Louis XV, since he is the *master* of the castle? Singing is an artificial language that does not go well with everyday costumes. It needs a decor, if not artificial, at least ancient enough to allow the imagination of the public to yield to the musical illusion.[96]

A contemporary setting left space for a process of identification between stage and audience that someone at La Scala in 1855 tried to prevent, choosing to move the action two centuries back. One of the consequences of this move is to prevent any possible 'realistic', bourgeois reading – precisely the possibility, I would argue, that made a French critic writing in 1868 uncomfortable when presented with a Count Rodolfo who looked like any Parisian banker sitting in the audience. At the same time, keeping Amina's costumes in a temporal frame that does not exclude the present seems to suggest that the feminine virtues she incarnates are timeless – and timelessly seductive.[97]

AMINA'S MUSICAL BIOGRAPHY

Another aspect of the reception of *La sonnambula* that provides interesting glosses on the opera's representation of femininity and the relationship between the two protagonists is its textual and performance tradition. Alessandro Roccatagliati and Luca Zoppelli, editors of the forthcoming critical edition of *La sonnambula*, have calculated that in about two thirds of the librettos published by the 1850s the Act 1 duet between Elvino and Amina was cut.[98] The reasons for this standard cut were undoubtedly diverse and mostly practical, but one of its consequences was to rob Amina of the one instance where she makes a melody first proposed by Elvino her own through subtle adaptation and skilful subversion. A consideration of the musical sources paints a similar if perhaps more articulate picture.[99]

From 1831 to the present, when Amina sings solo, she sings almost always in the original keys, as a significant sampling of sources, especially printed vocal scores and recordings, proves. There is only one noteworthy exception, the Italian–English vocal score 'adapted by Henry R. Bishop' and published in London in *c.* 1833 (in fact a collection of separate pieces bound together and issued as a whole at a later stage). The frontispiece of each piece that includes Amina proclaims 'as sung by Madame Malibran at the Theatres Royal Drury Lane and Covent Garden'. We know that Maria Malibran sang *La sonnambula* at Drury Lane in May 1833 and at Covent Garden the following month. Bellini saw her at Drury Lane and reported his favourable impressions to Florimo in a letter very likely to be a forgery, and in more sober terms to Alessandro Lamperi.[100] If Malibran performed the opera as presented in Bishop's arrangement, she sang 'Ah! non credea mirarti' in F instead of A, and 'Ah! non giunge' in F instead of B flat. But there is more: at the end of 'Ah! non credea mirarti' a footnote signals that 'in the original of Bellini, the *cavatina* [*sic*] ends here; the remainder is added that it may conclude in the key in which it commenced'. This 'remainder' consists in the literal repetition of the first part of the movement, up to immediately before the modulation to C, followed by a cadenza identical to that concluding the original piece (except for the key, F instead of A).[101]

Are we to think that Bellini heard the opera at Drury Lane performed thus and did not raise any objection? Malibran sang Amina for the first time at the Teatro del Fondo, Naples, in February 1833. A manuscript score now in the library of the Naples Conservatory, clearly of local provenance, announces on the frontispiece that the opera was 'written in Milan, performed at the Real Teatro del Fondo in 1833', and presents it in a version very close to the autograph, and in any case in the original keys.[102] It is perhaps risky to establish a direct connection between this score and the performances at the Fondo with Malibran, but it seems difficult to imagine that the singer agreed to learn the opera anew in such an altered version for London. In any case, apart from this important and complex exception, Amina's arias were transposed only in a few publications aimed more or less explicitly at amateurs, such as a few separate numbers issued by minor English publishers or a Viennese vocal score 'adjusted for the range of every voice' by none other than Anton Diabelli.[103]

The problems for Amina come with Elvino. The vocal profile of Giovanni Battista Rubini, the first Elvino, is well known, and included a strong penchant for lyrical phrases in extremely high tessituras, shaped by the tenor with a languid abandonment which sent audiences, and especially women, into ecstatic shivers. Bellini took full advantage of these abilities, making the part of Elvino murderously high. But Rubini was unique, and even he did not last long, as a letter by Bellini to Florimo following the revival of *La sonnambula* at the Théâtre-Italien with Giulia Grisi and Rubini in October 1834 confirms:

> Rubini was thought sublime for both his singing (I assure you, my dear, that each note touched the heart's deepest recesses) and the intensity and fire with which he acted throughout the opera. However, in order to allow him to master his part fully, I lowered his *cavatina* from B flat to A and the slow movement and the stretta of the finale also by a semitone, since now Rubini's voice produces its effect a semitone lower than the tessitura of six years ago; he could not have delivered the part with more emphasis and made a stronger impact than last night.[104]

Rubini had evidently lost a little of his legendary ease in the top register, and Bellini was more than ready to lower the most exposed passages. There are doubts about the authenticity of this letter, as is the case for all the letters to Florimo whose autograph has disappeared. In the autograph score, however, a note added at a later stage, probably by Bellini, asks for the *cavatina* to be performed a semitone lower.[105] What is surprising is that Bellini lowered only the *cavatina*, 'Prendi, l'anel ti dono', and the slow movement and the stretta of the finale, and apparently not the duet 'Son geloso del zefiro errante' and the Act 2 aria 'Tutto è sciolto. . . Pasci il guardo. . . Ah! perché non posso odiarti', whose tessituras are no less exposed than the pieces mentioned in the letter. In any case, Bellini must have known perfectly well that vocal scores for sale in 1834 had already gone further, that is to say, lower. Both the 1831 Ricordi score and the one published by Ricordi's Parisian partner, Launer, in 1834 print the *cavatina* in A flat, the Act 1 duet in F instead of G, and the Act 2 aria in B flat–D flat instead of B–D.[106] The consequences of this progressive sinking of Elvino's part on Amina are important and interesting.

Amina must count among the most intrusive *pertichini* in nineteenth-century Italian opera. Her numerous and extended interventions in what Bellini unequivocally calls 'cavatina d'Elvino' must be at the root of the reception of this piece as a duet, starting as early as the first Ricordi vocal score and continuing uninterrupted to the present day.[107] As we have seen, it is here that the pattern of the musical encounters between soprano and tenor is set: Elvino has the melody and Amina accompanies him a sixth above. The consequence should be obvious: if Elvino sinks, Amina must sink with him, faithful even down to the abysses of the Es and Ds and Cs of her lower octave. The printed tradition of *La sonnambula* is unequivocal on this point: Amina always keeps a sixth above Elvino, in the *cavatina*, in the duet, in the Act 1 finale. It is Elvino's Act 2 aria, however, that presents Amina's sad fate in all its cruelty.

Bellini wrote the slow movement, 'Tutto è sciolto. . . Pasci il guardo', in B minor–D major, and the cabaletta, 'Ah! perché non posso odiarti', in D major. The first Ricordi vocal score lowered the whole number by a semitone, while Ricordi's 'new edition' of 1858 went down another semitone, to A–C, for the cantabile, but printed the cabaletta in B flat, no less than a major third lower than the original key.[108] All modern vocal scores follow this edition. Bishop's arrangement issued by Boosey had already gone to G–B flat for the cantabile and B flat for the cabaletta, however, at least preserving Bellini's tonal plan. The manuscript tradition presents a more fragmented picture, from the original keys of the Neapolitan copy discussed above or another one now at the Rome Conservatory,[109] to the F–A of another Roman copy and of one prepared in Italy but now at the Bibliothèque Nationale, Paris.[110]

An eloquent testimony of the absurd situation that the nineteenth century had to face is found in an Italian manuscript copy now at the British Library that was clearly used repeatedly for performances, since it is full of performing annotations in Italian, German and especially French. At the beginning of Act 2, at the line 'Gli obbliò il crudele! Ei m'abbandona', two sheets inserted at a later stage declare that they contain 'Scena ed Aria Elvino Trasportata in Re b', but other hands wrote '1/2 ton bas' and '1/2 tono sotto'. At 'Vedi, o madre, è afflitto e mesto', that is, at the beginning of the instrumental ritornello of the cantabile, the type of paper changes but the key remains B flat. Variously deleted and re-written notes by different hands, however, ask for the piece to be performed 'en La mineur', 'in g moll', 'en La b mineur', 'in La b minore', 'un tono sotto', 'mezzo tono sotto', ending with the desperate cry 'plus bas'.[III]

During the cantabile Amina continues her dialogue with Elvino. If the piece is in G or F instead of B, the soprano finds herself forced to descend to the D and C of her lower octave instead of the original F sharp. The dialogue between Amina and Elvino included in this cantabile is of fundamental importance in the narrative and affective economy of the opera, and its text was significantly modified by Bellini. The extent of Bellini's changes is evident from a comparison between Romani's original text, which appeared in the first printed libretto, and the version in the autograph score.

Romani

ELVINO
Tutto è sciolto. Oh dì funesto!
Più per me non v'ha conforto.
Il mio cor per sempre è morto
Alla gioia ed all'amor.

AMINA
Vedi, o madre. . . è afflitto e mesto. . .
Forse, ah! forse ei m'ama ancor.
(*Amina si avvicina. Egli si scuote, la vede e amaramente le dice:*)

ELVINO
Pasci il guardo, e appaga l'alma
Dell'eccesso dei miei mali:
Il più triste de' mortali
Sono, o cruda, e il son per te.

AMINA

M'odi, Elvino. . . Elvin ti calma. . .
Colpa alcuna in me non è.

ELVINO: All is undone. What a terrible day! There is no comfort
left to me. My heart is dead forever both to joy and to love.

AMINA: You see, mother. . . he is sad and upset. . . perhaps he loves
me still.

(*Amina draws closer. He sees her and says to her bitterly:*)

ELVINO: Feed your glance, fill your soul with the excess of my sorrows:
I am the saddest of men, cruel one, because of you.

AMINA: Hear me, Elvino. . . Elvino, calm yourself. . . I am without
blame.

Bellini

AMINA

Vedi, o madre. . . è afflitto e mesto. . .
Forse, ah! forse ei m'ama ancor.

ELVINO

Tutto è sciolto.
Più per me non v'ha conforto.
Il mio cor per sempre è morto
Alla gioia ed all'amor.

AMINA

M'odi, Elvino. . .

ELVINO

Tu!. . . e tant'osi?

AMINA

Deh!. . . ti calma. . .

ELVINO

Va. . . spergiura.

AMINA

Credi. . .
Colpa alcuna in me non è.

ELVINO

Tu m'hai tolto ogni conforto.

Va. . . Va . . . ingrata!

AMINA

Sono innocente, io tel giuro:

Colpa alcuna in me non è.

ELVINO

Pasci il guardo, e appaga l'alma

Dell'eccesso dei miei mali:

Il più triste de' mortali

Sono, o cruda, e il son per te.

AMINA: You see, mother. . . he is sad and upset. . . perhaps he loves me still.

ELVINO: All is undone. There is no comfort left to me. My heart is dead forever both to joy and to love.

AMINA: Hear me, Elvino. . .

ELVINO: You!. . . and you dare this much?

AMINA: Ah, calm yourself.

ELVINO: Go away. . . faithless one.

AMINA: Believe me. . . I am without blame.

ELVINO: You have robbed me of all comfort. Go. . . go. . . ungrateful one!

AMINA: I am innocent, I swear it: I am without blame.

ELVINO: Feed your glance, fill your soul with the excess of my sorrows: I am the saddest of men, cruel one, because of you.

Bellini's changes are significant because they alter Elvino's character, emphasising his selfish concentration on his own feelings and his disregard for his fiancée. As I have suggested, at least until the last scene Elvino does not want to listen to Amina, or cannot. But if Boosey's 1833 score were the only source of the opera, and Elvino's Act 2 cantabile were in G–B flat instead of B–D, could he behave otherwise? And what of the F–A of some manuscript copies? No wonder Elvino does not listen to Amina: he cannot hear her, stuck as she is in the nether parts of her tessitura. The result is what Philip Gossett has called Amina's vocal schizophrenia.[112] At this point she has two completely different tessituras, one for the sections where she sings by herself or with other characters, another when she sings with Elvino.

That such a state of affairs could not be sustained was realised already in the nineteenth century. One attempt to solve the *impasse* was to accept the fact that the printed tradition and the performing one were too different for the latter to be reflected in the former. Sixteen years after publishing one of the most heavily altered scores (the Bishop version discussed above), in 1849 Boosey issued the only vocal score of *La sonnambula* I am aware of that sticks to the original keys. The frontispiece proclaims that this score was 'revised from the orchestral score by W. S. Rockstro', while the preface declares that 'Mr Rockstro has done his duty bravely, having had the assistance of poor Bellini's original MS, to which it will be seen he has made considerable reference'.[113] A long and learned introduction follows, by the translator of the text, J. Wrey Mould, who discusses sleepwalking, Bellini's stylistic evolution, the Milan première, and especially the London career of the opera with intelligence and a profusion of detail. This is a volume for the library shelf even more than for the piano, an extraordinary example of philological intentions applied to a repertory that would have to wait for more than a century to be taken seriously from a textual, and therefore aesthetic, point of view. One of the consequences of these intentions is that Amina's tessitura is kept intact.

Another solution to the problem of this half-floating, half-sinking tessitura was found by the widow Launer, who, when re-issuing the score of *La sonnambula* in 1841, only ten years from the première and seven from the first edition of the same publishing house (when *père* Launer was still alive), adopts Boosey's choice: cantabile in G–B flat and cabaletta in B flat. But in this score, as later in the ones of other Parisian publishers such as Schlesinger (1845) and Leduc (1872), there is no trace of Amina: no supplications, no protestations of innocence, no appeals to divine testimony. Rather than the shame of being forced to shout out in her lowest register to be heard by Elvino, who would not have listened to her anyway, Amina chooses a dignified silence. And I like to think that it was Madame Launer who, with feminine sympathy for the outrage inflicted on Amina, took stock of the situation and acted accordingly.[114]

But this is not always Amina's fate. In a copy of the Schlesinger score now at the Bibliothèque Nationale, Paris, for example, the section in parallel motion of the Act 1 duet is cut in pencil and replaced by an elaborate cadenza for Amina alone.[115] Moreover, in the slow movement of the finale, when as usual Amina should be 'below' Elvino, the same hand wrote twice on the soprano's stave 'unison with the tenor'.[116] In a copy of the full score printed by Ricordi at the end of the nineteenth century now housed in the British Library, part of the *a due* of the Act 1 duet has been cut: in the cadenzas, however, only Elvino's line is cut, not Amina – a situation similar to the one in the Parisian copy.[117] On the basis of these clues we could therefore imagine a performing tradition of *La sonnambula* independent from the printed one, a tradition in which Amina rebels against the progressive sinking of her tessitura when she sings with Elvino, singing instead on a level with him and even more than him.

Such a performing tradition would presumably be reflected in the rich and varied recording history of the opera. To find the first complete recording we have to wait until 1952; during the first half of the twentieth century, however, a few predictable pieces were recorded over and over again, especially the slow movement and cabaletta of Amina's *rondò* (more often separate than together), while the *a dues* between Amina and Elvino appear less frequently.[118] A significant sampling of these recordings leads to the perhaps surprising conclusion that in the vast majority of cases the *a dues* follow the printed tradition in both the choice of keys and the relationship between the two voices, with Amina sunk in the lowest reaches of her tessitura. Among other examples, especially eloquent are Amelita Galli-Curci with Tito Schipa in 'Son geloso' (1923), Maria Gentile with Dino Borgioli in the slow movement of the finale (1927), Toti Dal Monte again with Schipa in 'Prendi, l'anel ti dono' (1933), and again Lina Pagliughi with Ferruccio Tagliavini and

Joan Sutherland with Nicola Monti in the complete recordings of 1952 and 1962.[119]

One name stands out for its absence from this list, that of Maria Callas. Her studio recording of the opera with Nicola Monti as Elvino and Antonino Votto conducting the La Scala chorus and orchestra, made in Milan in 1957 under Walter Legge's supervision during a revival of the famous production by Luchino Visconti premièred two years earlier (then with Leonard Bernstein in the pit), quickly became the *Sonnambula par excellence* of the second half of the twentieth century, a true classic of opera recording.[120] It is here that Amina's rebellion is finally documented. If in 'Prendi, l'anel ti dono' Callas accompanies Monti, as in the vocal scores, in the *a due* of the duet 'Son geloso del zefiro errante' (or, better, of what remains of it after the cuts), a new Amina emerges, an Amina who appropriates the melody and relegates Elvino to a tenth below. In the second half of the slow movement of the finale Callas sings in unison with the tenor, with the result that Monti becomes virtually inaudible. Finally, in the following stretta (much cut), the soprano keeps to the vocal scores, but takes back some of what was hers with a final *puntatura* to the high E flat – a *puntatura* possibly common in the theatre, but which in the recording studio was not attempted even by Pagliughi, a soprano whose reputation rested on high notes much more than Callas's.

It is interesting to note how Joan Sutherland followed all Callas's choices in her *Sonnambula* with Renato Cioni, performed in concert form under Nicola Rescigno in New York in 1961,[121] but in the studio recording of the following year, with Richard Bonynge and Monti, the same Elvino as Callas, she scrupulously keeps to the printed version. This is all the more noteworthy if we keep in mind that both tenor and conductor were unlikely to object, for different reasons, if Amina had wanted to sing what she had sung in New York the previous year. The potential dichotomy between printed versus performing tradition, which I have suggested existed in the nineteenth century, could be seen as replicated in the twentieth between studio recordings versus performances in the theatre, some of which have been preserved in live recordings. The moment when this dichotomy breaks down and the performing tradition enters the recording studio came with Callas's recording, which must therefore be considered exceptional also from this point of view.[122]

It could seem paradoxical that the most famous recording of *La sonnambula* is also the least 'authentic', at least from the point of view of the disposition of the voices. But if we consider for a moment Amina's destiny since that 6 May 1831 when Giuditta Pasta appeared on the stage of the Teatro Carcano, Callas's interventions, or at any rate ones that Callas was the first to preserve in a recording, may seem more justifiable. Callas's Amina rebels against the progressive sinking of her role and takes back at least part of her original tessitura. The innocent girl seems to have learnt that the Rousseau-vian myth of the perfect communion between human beings, and especially man and woman, who live in the Alps – a myth of which *La sonnambula* has been seen as one of the most perfect incarnations – is a fiction. This perfect communion can easily turn into man's oppression of woman. The model of feminine identity which gener-ations of commentators have seen incarnated into Amina is a model by and for men, who, if in need, will not hesitate to force a woman to the level of the Es and Ds and Cs of her lower octave.

THE LANDSCAPE OF *LA SONNAMBULA*

These aspects of the reception of *La sonnambula* offer a vantage point from which to ponder the negotiations that took place be-tween the work in performance and its evolving cultural contexts. These negotiations shed interesting light on the changing meanings of the opera's complex representation of an Alpine landscape and the human interactions taking place in this setting. The change of locale from the Camargue of Scribe and Aumer's *La Somnambule* to the Swiss Alps of *La sonnambula* is located at a crucial point in the progressive replacement of the countryside with the Alps as the chosen setting for an idealised and sentimentalised modern Arcadia. Indeed, *La sonnambula* quickly became one of the foremost operatic

representatives of this discourse, as its critical reception amply demonstrates. At the same time, the relative restraint with which the
Alpine landscape is depicted textually, visually and musically encour-
aged its 'Mediterranean' reception, which also responded to bio-
graphical suggestions. Moreover, this restraint can be related to a
less than idealised representation of the human interactions taking
place in this setting. In particular, Amina's prelapsarian oneness
with nature and its inhabitants is gradually replaced by a painful
awareness that the earth is not a natural Eden, not even amidst the
Alps. But this interpretation seems to go against the critical reception
of *La sonnambula*'s geographical and human landscape as the perfect
incarnation of a modern Arcadia.

This potential contradiction can be seen at work in some aspects
of the opera's reception. On the one hand, the attempt to locate the
opera visually at a distance safe enough to preserve its idyllic idealisation points away from the potentially 'realistic' implications for
which Sanquirico, Romani and Bellini leave room, chiming instead
with the general tone of the opera's critical reception. On the other
hand, the transpositions and cuts to which the part of Amina has
been subjected since the opera's première further complicate the
representation of her relationship with Elvino, at first reinforcing an
interpretation of this relationship as becoming progressively more
problematic in the course of the action, but eventually rebelling
against the more oppressive consequences of this emotional and
musical trajectory. The reception of *La sonnambula* plays out some
of the tensions that characterise the opera's verbal, visual and musical texts, then, responding to both these tensions and the different
contexts in which it was performed, and to which it contributed.

Seen from this perspective, Marelli's Vienna and London production discussed at the beginning of this chapter acquires richer meanings, both supporting and questioning the Alpine idyll. The final *coup
de théâtre* might be understood as a refusal to subscribe to a happy
ending – an ending that at first could appear to silence the 'realistic'
aspects of the opera's portrayal of an Alpine landscape. (Whether
turning Amina into a *prima donna* is the subtlest way to do so is open

to discussion.) This production takes the idyll at face value, therefore – thus chiming with a significant strand in the opera's reception – and then proceeds to question it wholesale, as an integral component of the genre and tradition to which *La sonnambula* belongs. But a more attentive reading of the opera shows that the idyll of *La sonnambula* was under threat from the very beginning. Like Manzoni his betrothed from near Lecco, Romani, Sanquirico and Bellini placed their village, and its inhabitants, resolutely 'at the foot'.

In *La sonnambula* everybody seems to know what references to Amina's purity, innocence and candour mean. What is more, the high value that everybody places on her virginity is presented as a matter of course, a belief so essential to the world represented on stage that there is no need to discuss it – an attitude which suggests that this belief is at least as essential to the world off the stage. In other words, the opera presupposes that representation and reality go hand in hand when it comes to the meanings and value of virginity. Writing in 1917, Sigmund Freud summed up the attitude of the preceding century when he observed that 'the high value which her suitor places on a woman's virginity seems to us so firmly rooted, so much a matter of course, that we find ourselves almost at a loss if we have to give reasons for this opinion'.[1] And yet this 'ideology of chastity', to use Luigi Baldacci's expression, is among the most characteristic traits of nineteenth-century society and culture.[2] Alpine virgin operas reflect, and contribute to, this society and this culture, of course, perhaps never more eloquently than in the case of Donizetti's *Linda di Chamounix*, a *melodramma semiserio* by Gaetano Rossi premièred in Vienna on 19 May 1842. This opera's exploration of the ideology of chastity is not only interesting in itself, but it acquires larger meanings when placed in the context of the literary and theatrical tradition from which it stems and of which it constitutes a prominent manifestation. The first direction which I pursue in this chapter is therefore an investigation of *Linda*'s complex genealogy, since the opera's sources not only significantly shaped its narrative and musical construction, but also highlight, often by contrast, its depiction of virginity. This literary and theatrical tradition is itself part of a larger socio-cultural discourse, however, and it is to this larger context that I then turn.

But *Linda di Chamounix* is not simply about virginity, or about virginity in the French Alps; it also focuses prominently on other themes such as seduction, madness and the power of the human voice. This constellation of themes has been addressed most intensely and productively by psychoanalysis, both in its classic Freudian form and in its later Lacanian and post-Lacanian incarnations. In the third part of the chapter I attempt a psychoanalytic reading of *Linda*, or, better, I look at the opera through the lenses of different psychoanalytic and para-psychoanalytic theories, in turn Freudian, Lacanian and post-Lacanian, the latter especially in their feminist inflections.

This privileging of psychoanalytic discourses, while perhaps controversial to some, finds justification in two related considerations. The first is that, as already mentioned, no theory or discourse has occupied itself more assiduously with the workings and meanings of both human sexuality and the human voice than psychoanalysis. Psychoanalysis therefore illuminates with particular intensity texts that take human sexuality and the human voice as their subject matter, *Linda di Chamounix* not last among them.[3] The second is that psychoanalysis was born at the end of the nineteenth century as a comprehensive theory of the human subject out of the observation of human subjects historically located in the nineteenth century, and therefore it displays from its origins an elective affinity with nineteenth-century subjects, real or fictional.

What is more, to quote Baldacci once more, 'Ottocento come noi', the nineteenth century is us. We are children of the nineteenth century, not least in the ways that psychoanalysis has fundamentally shaped and still shapes our conceptions of human subjectivity. Looking at a nineteenth-century artefact such as *Linda di Chamounix* through the lenses of psychoanalysis means therefore considering it from both a past and a present perspective; it means both keeping it at a distance and bringing it near, without obliterating its historical distance, but also without reducing this historical distance to absolute alterity.[4] I will therefore begin with *Linda* but soon leave it, eventually returning to it by way of a long detour: first to the mid-nineteenth-century French popular stage, and then to the psychoanalytic theatre of the unconscious.

THE TRAVELS OF A SONG

> *Linda*, as you know, is *La Grâce de Dieu*, this famous play so successful at the Théâtre de la Gaîté for so long; *La Grâce de Dieu* is *Fanchon la vielleuse*, this comedy so successful at the Théâtre du Vaudeville for so long, and arranged with variations on the theme of a *romance* by Miss Loïsa Puget, so successful for so long in the salons and in a thousand other places. What glorious origins! What an imposing genealogy! What a multiple success of play, of vaudeville, of song, harbingers of the success of an opera![5]

This reviewer of the first Parisian production of *Linda di Chamounix*, in a revised version prepared by Donizetti himself (Théâtre-Italien, 17 November 1842), needed only one paragraph to summarise the opera's sources, since he knew his readers were well aware of them. It will take me somewhat longer to reconstruct *Linda*'s 'imposing genealogy'.

The immediate source is *La Grâce de Dieu*, a *drame* by Adolphe Philippe Dennery (or D'Ennery) and Gustave Lemoine, premièred at the Théâtre de la Gaîté, Paris, on 16 January 1841; Donizetti saw the play in the same production during that year.[6] This play is in turn based on two main sources: *Fanchon la vielleuse*, a *comédie en trois actes, mêlée de vaudevilles* by Jean Nicolas Bouilly and Joseph-Marie Pain, first performed in 1803 and revived at the Théâtre de la Porte-Saint-Antoine in 1837;[7] and 'A la grâce de Dieu', a song by Loïsa Puget published around 1835 and very famous in Paris during the following decade. The text of this song is by Lemoine, Puget's husband, who enlisted Dennery's help when he decided to capitalise on its success and build a plot based on the old but still well-known Fanchon story.

> Tu vas quitter notre montagne,
> Pour t'en aller bien loin, hélas!
> Et moi, ta mère et ta compagne,

Je ne pourrai guider tes pas!
L'enfant que le Ciel vous envoie,
Vous le gardez, gens de Paris;
Nous pauvres mères de Savoie,
Nous le chassons loin du pays!
En lui disant adieu!
A la grâce de Dieu!

Ici commence ton voyage;
Si tu n'allais pas revenir!. . .
Ta pauvre mère est sans courage,
Pour te quitter, pour te bénir!
Travaille bien, fais ta prière,
La prière donne du coeur;
Et quelque fois pense à ta mère,
Cela te portera bonheur!. . .
Va, mon enfant, adieu!
A la grâce de Dieu!

Elle s'en va, douce éxilée,
Gagner son pain sous d'autres cieux;
Longtems, longtems, dans la vallée,
Sa mère la suivit des yeux;
Mais lorsque sa douleur amère
N'eut plus sa fille pour temoin,
Elle pleura, la pauvre mère,
L'enfant qui lui disait de loin:
Ma bonne mère, adieu!
A la grâce de Dieu![8]

You are leaving our mountains to go very far, alas! And I, your mother and companion, cannot guide your steps! People of Paris, watch over the child that Heaven sends you; we, poor mothers of Savoy, send our children away, while bidding them farewell! To God's mercy! Now your journey begins; what if you were not to come back!. . . Your poor mother is unable to leave you or to bless you! Work, and pray: prayer gives courage; and sometimes think of your mother: this thought will bring you happiness!. . . Go, my child, farewell! To God's mercy! She, my sweet exiled one, goes to make some money under other skies: in the valley her mother follows her with her eyes for a long, long time; but when her daughter cannot see her bitter pain any longer, she will cry, poor mother, for the child who told her from afar: farewell, my good mother! To God's mercy!

In the play, Madeleine sings the song's second stanza to her daughter Marie, who is forced to leave Chamonix (the customary spelling of the town name nowadays) for Paris with the village youths – who travel to the city every autumn to support themselves and their families by singing in the streets – in order to escape the lustful attentions of the Commandeur de Boisfleury, a local aristocrat. Marie is in love with the Marquis of Sivry, Boisfleury's nephew, who courts her disguised as the 'colporteur' André, knowing that his mother the Marquise would never allow him to marry a peasant girl. Acts 2, 3 and 4 take place in Paris: Marie ends up living in a luxurious apartment owned by the Marquis, still a virgin and convinced he is going to marry her; but when she discovers that the Marquis is about to get married to a noblewoman imposed on him by his mother and witnesses the wedding cortège from her window, she goes mad. This happens immediately after her father Antoine, who has come to Paris looking for her, 'discovers' her a kept woman and curses her. In the last act we are back in Chamonix: Pierrot, a young Savoyard friend of Marie's, has taken her back to her parents, but she recognises no-one; it is only when Madeleine sings 'A la grâce de Dieu' to her that she regains her sanity. At this moment the Marquis appears: he did not get married after all, and, since the Marquise has been 'called by God', he is now free to marry Marie. They will live happily ever after.

The song is heard not only in the two instances mentioned above, but several other times: it is repeated by the departing Marie at the end of the first act; played offstage, presumably by Pierrot, it saves Marie from being seduced by the Marquis at the end of Act 2; she starts 'mechanically' repeating its refrain after having gone mad;[9] and Pierrot is able to make her walk back to Chamonix only by ceaselessly playing the song on his hurdy-gurdy. The audience witnesses this pantomime twice: at the end of Act 4, in Paris, and in the middle of Act 5, on Pierrot's and Marie's arrival in Chamonix. This recurring song and, more generally, the large number of musical inserts set *La Grâce de Dieu* apart from the *mélodrames* and the *drames mêlés de chant* of the first half of the century.[10] In fact, the play is constructed around the song itself: the plot dramatises the narrative implied by the text of 'A la grâce de Dieu'. Furthermore, it seems that it was precisely this reliance on music that convinced Donizetti that the play could be transformed into a successful opera.[11] Early on, when he still referred to the work that would become *Linda di Chamounix* as 'La Grâce de Dieu', Donizetti called the song simply 'la ballade de l'opéra',[12] thus acknowledging its centrality to the opera's dramaturgy. However, during its migration from play to opera this song underwent a momentous transformation in both content and function. To understand this transformation, a detailed summary of *Linda*'s plot is in order.

Antonio Loustolot (Rossi's spelling of Dennery and Lemoine's Loustalot) and his wife Maddalena, humble farmers, live in the Alpine village of Chamonix with their young daughter Linda. The Prefetto (a thin disguise for the parish priest, but renamed thus for the censors' sake)[13] warns them of the Marchese di Boisfleury's lustful designs on the girl. Linda, however, is in love with Carlo, who presents himself to her as a young painter but is in fact the Visconte di Sirval, nephew of the Marchese. The Prefetto advises Antonio to send the girl to Paris, where each year the young village people go to make a living. Linda sets out with Pierotto, a young hurdy-gurdy player who had earlier made his appearance singing a *ballata*.

At the beginning of Act 2 Linda has been living for three months in an elegant Parisian apartment made available to her by Carlo, who has by now revealed his true identity and position. Linda is reunited with Pierotto, whom she has not seen for a while owing to an illness. The Marchese appears: he recognises Linda despite her luxurious wardrobe and tries to seduce her, but she scornfully rejects him. Carlo also arrives and, although he knows he is about to marry a woman imposed on him by his mother, tries to convince Linda to yield to his ardour. On hearing the music of Pierotto's *ballata* played in the street, Linda finds the strength to resist Carlo and send him away. Finally Antonio arrives in Paris looking for his daughter. At first he does not recognise Linda in such an aristocratic environment, but, moved to remorse, she reveals herself. Pierotto brings the news that Carlo is about to wed a noblewoman. Believing that she has dishonoured herself, Antonio curses Linda. She is overcome by despair and loses her mind.

Act 3 brings the action, and the young Savoyards, back to Chamonix, where their arrival is greeted with joy. Carlo, who had refused to get married at the last minute, has also come back looking for Linda. Pierotto and Linda appear on the hilltop: she follows him only when he plays his *ballata* on the hurdy-gurdy. Linda is delirious and does not recognise anybody, not even Carlo; yet, on hearing him sing the melody of their Act 1 duet cabaletta, she regains her senses. She and Carlo will be married shortly.[14]

In the play Madeleine sings only the second stanza of Puget's song, but Pierotto's *ballata* includes two stanzas, the second sung to the same melody as the first but with a thickened orchestral accompaniment and a *concertante* clarinet part. The text reads as follows:

PIEROTTO
Per sua madre andò una figlia
Miglior sorte a rintracciar.
Colle lagrime alle ciglia
Le dolenti s'abbracciar.
Pensa a me, dicea la madre,
Serba intatto il tuo candore,
Nei cimenti dell'amore
Volgi al Nume il tuo pregar.
Ei non puote a buona figlia
La sua grazie ricusar.

LINDA
Questa tenera canzone
Mi fa mesta palpitar.

PIEROTTO

Quei consigli, ahi! troppo poco
La fanciulla rammentò.
Nel suo cor s'accese un foco,
Che la pace le involò.
La tradita allor ritorna,
Cerca invan di madre un seno
Di rimorsi il cor ripieno
Una tomba ritrovò.
Sulla tomba finché visse
Quella mesta lagrimò.

LINDA E CORO

Sulla tomba finché visse
Quella mesta lagrimò.[15]

PIEROTTO: A daughter went to seek a better fortune for her mother. They embraced with tears in their eyes. Think of me, said the mother, keep your purity intact; in the midst of love's perils, pray to God. He cannot refuse His help to a good daughter.

LINDA: This tender song makes me sad.

PIEROTTO: Alas, the girl soon forgot those words. In her heart, a fire was lit that robbed her of her peace. The betrayed one returns, and looks in vain for her mother's embrace, but instead, her heart heavy with remorse, she finds a tomb. On this tomb the wretched one cried until her death.

LINDA and CHORUS: On this tomb the wretched one cried until her death.

The differences between the title song in *La Grâce de Dieu* and the *ballata* in *Linda di Chamounix* are not insignificant. While 'A la grâce de Dieu' functions in the play as Madeleine's farewell to Marie, in the opera it is Pierotto who sings the *ballata*. What is more, Linda does not regain her sanity on hearing her mother sing the song, but rather on hearing Carlo sing the principal theme of the cabaletta of their Act 1 duet.

The differences in speaking subjects and between the rhetorical and narrative functions of these two texts are striking. Madeleine's is an exhortation to Marie – to work, pray and remember her mother – made at a highly charged moment in the action both emotionally and dramatically: Marie is about to leave for Paris and Madeleine blesses her. In the opera, Pierotto tells a story whose characters are not called Maddalena and Linda – in fact, they remain nameless – at a relatively static moment in the action, and much earlier. Nobody in the Loustolot family is aware of the cause of Boisfleury's display of protective benevolence towards them, and the audience can only guess that the *ballata* will turn out to be significant. In the recitative immediately following Pierotto's exit Linda muses: 'I don't know: that song touches and saddens me. I have a mother too, and maybe. . . and Carlo. . .' ('Non so: quella canzon m'intenerisce e mi rattrista. Ho anch'io una madre, e forse. . . E Carlo. . .'); but the symbolic value of the song's story remains hidden at least until the last scene of the act. Finally, this symbolic function is at best ambiguous, since Pierotto sings of 'a fire that robbed her of her peace', referring to the nameless daughter's loss of her virginity, whereas it is precisely on hearing the song during Carlo's attempted seduction in Act 2 that the memory of her mother and her duty is awakened in Linda, giving her the strength to impose respect for her innocence on the lustful Carlo. Linda's 'peace' is safely preserved for the obligatory happy ending.

To an early-twenty-first-century sensibility these differences between 'A la grâce de Dieu' and 'Per sua madre andò una figlia' seem crucially relevant for an interpretation not only of the heroine's character, but also of the overall meaning of the two works. Yet the reviews of the opera's productions from its première up to the early 1850s, and especially of the first performance of the revised version for Paris, in which Puget's song and *La Grâce de Dieu* feature as strong intertextual presences, leave us empty-handed. The reception of these texts failed to differentiate the perspectives that each of them offers, concentrating instead on what links them, namely, the representation of a virgin girl from Savoy who goes to Paris, comes close to losing her virginity, loses her mind, and eventually gets her sanity back when she goes back to Savoy.

Three crucial themes emerge from the plots of both play and opera: geographical displacement, the preservation of female virginity, and the causes and cures of female madness. The first two had been connected for almost a century; the link between travel from the mountains to the city and threat to a woman's virginity was common in French literature from at least the second half of the eighteenth century, with Savoy a favourite region to represent mountains, and Paris of course the city *par excellence*. The theme of the corrupting city had been explored in all its titillating potential in such works as Louis Sébastien Mercier's *Tableau de Paris* (1781–8) and *Le Nouveau Paris* (1794–1800), and Rétif de la Bretonne's *La Paysanne pervertie, ou Les dangers de la ville* (1784) and *Les Nuits de Paris, ou Le spectateur nocturne* (1788–94). Sidelined during the Empire in favour of the edifying image of the 'capital of the world', this representation of Paris as a horrid monster feeding on human beings, especially the innocent ones coming from the mountains, resurfaced with renewed strength in the literary production of the Restoration and especially the 1830s and 1840s, including numberless *mélodrames*, and is best known to modern readers through Balzac's novels collectively entitled *Scènes de la vie parisienne*.[16] Reviewing the Parisian première of *Linda*, Théophile Gautier reminded his readers that *La Grâce de Dieu* was 'a subject made up of *Marianne*, *La Paysanne pervertie*, *Claudine*, *Fanchon la vielleuse* and *Clary*', and that the *drame* put on stage an old story:

> The eternal story which used to delight our parents and with which our pale generation has still been rocked to sleep: 'I was born from poor parents amidst the mountains of Savoy; now they send me to Paris, since we were a lot of children' etc. O mountains! What have the flatlands done to you for you to overwhelm them with your virtues? O countryside, what have cities done to you? O Savoy, what has France done to you, where you bring nothing but your marmots, and from where you take away so much money? Is it really necessary for Savoyards to come to Paris to become corrupt?[17]

The song cited by Gautier is a *romance* for Fanchon in Act I of *Fanchon la vielleuse*, a piece that clearly encountered an enormous success.[18]

Insisting on the genealogy of *La Grâce de Dieu* and *Linda di Chamounix* and inscribing them in the context of the story of 'virtuous Savoyards in corrupt Paris', as reviewers did at the time, however, means relegating to a secondary role the third crucial theme of these texts, madness, which also differentiates between them, as I have suggested above. *La Grâce de Dieu* and *Linda* do not put on stage 'l'histoire éternelle' of Fanchon's song; they are not just late variations on the old theme. Jacques Joly has discussed Donizetti's opera and its sources from the point of view of their socio-political ideology, showing the gradual replacement of Fanchon's active independence with Linda's passivity – her 'undoing' as Joly puts it, echoing Catherine Clément. He connects this replacement with the evolution of the texts' ideological resonances from a post-revolutionary egalitarian moralism to the ambiguous poetic and religious peace between the classes that surfaces in *La Grâce de Dieu* and comes to the fore in the opera. Joly notices how 'in Marie and in Linda nostalgia, guilt, and passivity lead to madness, which is the sign of the crisis of the individual in the climate of the Restoration'.[19] I would like to expand on Joly's suggestion and place the opera's connection between virginity and madness in the context of their discourses in mid-century France and Italy, the years that saw the conception and success of *La Grâce de Dieu* and *Linda*.[20]

AN IDEOLOGY OF CHASTITY

Virginity and madness are linked in one of the most powerful scenes of Balzac's novel *Splendeurs et misères des courtisanes*, published in 1844, only two years after *Linda*'s première. Lydie Peyrade, the innocent young daughter of the secret police agent Peyrade, alias Father Canquoëlle, has been kidnapped by order of Jacques Collin, alias Vautrin, alias Carlos Herrera, under the threat that, if her father does not comply with Collin's requests, he will not see her again.

Peyrade cannot do what Collin wants, and Collin poisons him. The dying Peyrade gathers the strength to reach home, only to discover that Lydie has been raped and then released. When Corentin, Peyrade's friend, asks her what happened, she answers: 'Oh! it can be mentioned but not narrated. . . I am dishonoured, lost. [. . .] There is no longer peace for me! The only peace I desire is the peace of the tomb'.[21] Once in her bedroom, she falls prey to delirium: 'She sang gracious tunes, together with shouting horrible expressions she had heard! Her beautiful appearance was mottled with purple stains. She mixed memories of her pure life with memories of those ten days of infamy'.[22] Lydie witnesses her father's death but does not realise that he is dead: she continues to ask for his mercy, repeating that it is not her fault, until she is taken to another room and examined by the doctors Desplein and Bianchon. When Corentin inquires about Lydie's state, one of the doctors answers: 'Place that girl in an asylum: if she does not recover her sanity in giving birth – if, in fact, she is pregnant – she will end her days as a mad-melancholic'.[23]

Linda does not lose her virginity, as Lydie does, but the simple idea that her father thinks her a kept woman is sufficient to drive her mad. The figure of the father looms large in both cases: Lydie is so obsessed by fear that Peyrade may think her in some way responsible for her state that she does not notice his death, which has taken place under her very eyes. In the opera, Antonio is the most explicit mouthpiece of the characters' obsession with Linda's virginity. Rossi's text as well as the entire narrative structure of *Linda di Chamounix* revolve around the enormous importance that everybody attributes to the young girl's innocence. Her very name is a literary adjective that means 'clean and pretty'. Act 1 opens with a vision of a pure Alpine dawn that functions as a metaphorical representation of Linda's purity. Even before she appears on stage, her mother Maddalena informs the audience that Linda is sleeping 'the sleep of innocence' ('il sonno dell'innocenza').[24] The idea of purity dominates the libretto's language, with adjectives such as 'puro' (the most frequent, often linked to 'amore'), 'innocente',

'ingenuo', 'candido', 'onesto', and the related nouns, in addition to
'angelo', 'virtù', 'onore', 'giglio', and such opposites as 'seduttore'
(always, of course, 'vile'), 'rossore', 'perverso', 'deturpare', and so on.
However, the 'technical' term that describes Linda's state, 'verginità',
never appears. This is probably a late legacy of the Petrarchan poetic
lexicon, which does not include 'verginità', and uses 'vergine' only in
association with the Virgin Mary. In any case, the result is a censori-
ous silence that surrounds Linda's virginity. It is as if virginity were
of such value that its name cannot be pronounced. In *Linda di
Chamounix* the uttering of virginity's name is taboo.

Linda's purity is described not only as a characteristic of the
heroine, but an attribute of her entire family, an actual possession
of her parents, closely related to their socio-economic situation.
How this relationship is interpreted depends on the subject: in
Antonio's words, 'they think we are without honour because we
are poor!' ('perché siam nati poveri ci credon senza onor!').[25] At first
the immediate cause of Linda's loss of reason might seem to be the
news that Carlo is about to get married; in other words, her madness
could be compared to Lucia's in *Lucia di Lammermoor*, or Elvira's in
I Puritani, or many other abandoned women in Italian opera from
Monteverdi's Arianna onwards. Indeed, many plot summaries in
early reviews interpret it that way.[26] However, a symptomatological
reading of the last scene of Act 2 demonstrates Antonio's crucial
responsibility. Linda's sanity receives its first blow by his words, sung
'con impeto crescente', 'Linda may be poor, but she is honest. My
daughter cannot possibly stay in a viscount's house' ('Linda è povera
ma onesta. La mia figlia d'un visconte non può in casa soggiornar').
Linda cries 'forgive me!' ('deh! perdon!'), but her father replies 'don't
hope for it' ('non lo sperare'). The girl is 'beside herself' ('fuori di sé')
after learning about Carlo's impending wedding, but she is still in
contact with the world. She goes mad only when Antonio shouts
'I curse you' ('ti male. . .'); Pierotto tries to silence him by putting a
hand over his mouth, but it is too late: Linda, 'dumbfounded and
immobile' ('colpita e immobile') according to the libretto, 'immobile,
with her eyes turned towards heaven' ('immobile cogl'occhi volti al

cielo') in the score, has already reached the high B flat that signals her loss of reason.[27] The Act 2 finale only strengthens Antonio's role in the familial structure of the Loustolots, which had already emerged in Act 1. It is he who sings the *romanza* 'Ambo nati in questa valle', a hymn to the native valley and the farm, whose value can be interpreted metonymically as containers of the family. And it is Antonio who defends his daughter's virginity as a family attribute in the duet with the Prefetto. Knowing the value her father places on her purity, it is scarcely surprising that Linda loses her mind when he curses her.

Lydie Peyrade's and Linda Loustolot's madness becomes possible, indeed necessary, within the nineteenth-century construction of the family as the primary site for sexuality: not only its control, but also, in Michel Foucault's classic analysis, its deployment: 'The deployment of sexuality which first developed on the fringes of familial institutions (in the direction of conscience and pedagogy, for example) gradually became focused on the family. [. . .] In the family, parents and relatives became the chief agents of a deployment of sexuality which drew its outside support from doctors, educators, and, later, psychiatrists'.[28] In Balzac's urban society the outside support comes from the doctors Desplein and Bianchon, but in rural Chamonix Antonio appeals to the Prefetto – the parish priest in thin disguise. The old libertine Boisfleury tries to resist the institutionalisation of the family as focus of the deployment of sexuality, and in so doing reveals his alliance to the *ancien régime*, one that is more ideological than political. Moreover, he implicitly challenges the prohibition of incest: since he is the Marchesa's brother, and the Marchesa is Linda's godmother, 'by the right of blood, I, her Marquis, am also her godfather' ('*de sanguinis jure*, suo marchese, padrin son io pure'). Canon law prohibited marriage between godparents and their godchildren on the principle that, in God's eyes, godparents were 'real' parents, and therefore marriage would have been a kind of incest.[29] If, as Foucault argues, 'in a society [. . .] where the family is the most active site of sexuality, and where it is doubtless the exigencies of the latter which maintain and prolong its existence, incest [. . .] occupies a central place',[30] then Boisfleury's crime is against the laws not only of the Church and, by proxy, of the society, but also of the family.

In the nineteenth century a daughter's virginity was understood as valuable family capital, to be guarded closely by fathers and brothers, who were its primary custodians outside the family itself.[31] The discourse surrounding female purity, however, was rarely explicit, especially when directed towards the virgins themselves. Rather than resorting to coercive measures, in order to postpone the awakening of desire the family attempted to conceal sex from young girls as long as possible; in fact, the very thought of sex was considered a sin. In the words of social historian Yvonne Knibiehler, 'a "pure" girl knew nothing and suspected nothing'.[32] Hence, perhaps, the taboo placed on the naming of virginity itself, not only in *Linda*, but also, for example, in Catholic educational treatises published in Italy up to the end of the nineteenth century.[33]

In Catholic countries like France and Italy, this necessity to postpone the awakening of desire, coupled with the attempt to conceal sex from young girls, took the form of a dramatic spread of the cult of the Virgin Mary. In this sense, I would argue that the most important single 'fact' for understanding the cultural context in which *Linda di Chamounix* and its sources were created and received occurred on 8 December 1854. On that day Pope Pius IX proclaimed the dogma of the Immaculate Conception: alone among God's creatures, Mary the Mother of God had been preserved from original sin. This cornerstone of nineteenth-century Catholic culture marked the culmination of a long process that saw the progressive feminisation of religious practice and the convergence of religious sentimentality and family sentimentalism.[34] The feminine Catholic model became exclusively that of wife and mother, and the young girl had to be trained to fulfil this model, while at the same time being kept unaware of the sexual realities of being a wife and mother.[35] The cult of the Virgin Mary constituted a powerful religious practice that promoted the transcendence of adolescent love in young girls, especially in peasant communities, which saw the spreading of Marian devotion in the month of May. The staging manual compiled by Louis Palianti for the French translation of *Linda* requires 'a little stone fountain with a little statue of the Virgin Mary in a cavity', to which the villagers bow before singing the opening chorus. At the end of the Act 3 pantomime, before beginning the recitative, Pierotto kneels in front of this statue.[36]

In mid-nineteenth-century rural France May, the month of roses, was also the time of the *rosières* ceremony. Young girls of modest means appeared before the mayor, the curate and the schoolteacher with a medical certificate attesting their virginity; if they were recognised as models of virtue, devotion and industry, they were crowned with wreaths of roses, and awarded a monetary prize that would be given them as dowry two months before their marriage. At the opposite end of society, in 1847 Maria Adelaide of Savoy was awarded the 'Rosa d'oro' by Pius IX, a papal honour reserved for the most virtuous Catholic women of regal families.[37] When Boisfleury proclaims Linda 'a pure, candid lily, a smiling April rose' ('un giglio di puro candore, una rosa ridente d'aprile'), the extent of the metaphor goes beyond literary tradition and evokes contemporary social practices.

In light of these social practices and their literary manifestations, it is clear that Linda and Lydie could not escape going mad after losing their virginity (Lydie), or after their families thought they had (Linda). Theirs is a sin not only against religious principles, but also against the laws of family and society. Linda is thought to have betrayed Antonio, Maddalena, the entire village of Chamonix, and more. In Pasquale Contini's *La traviata* (1866), a poem clearly inspired by Verdi's opera, the narrator, assuming the moralistic tones of Germont *père*, tells the story of a young girl whom he had met in a mountain village, and whom he meets again in the city, now a prostitute, eloquently voicing the common judgement when proclaiming:

Come potesti porre in obblio
L'Onor, la Fede, la Patria, e Dio?
Quando, infelice, corri al delitto

Che sul tuo fronte leggesi scritto,
Ma non ti senti coglier da un gelo,
Ma non paventi l'ira del cielo?. . .
De' tuoi più cari, che più non hai,
Non vedi l'ombre, non odi i lai?. . .[38]

How could you forget Honour, Faith, Homeland, and God? When you,
wretched one, hasten to the sin that is written on your forehead, are
you not frozen with guilt? Are you not afraid of Heaven's rage?. . .Do
you not see the shades and hear the cries of your dear departed ones?

I would suggest that it is the echo of such words that drives Linda
and Lydie to madness, the fear of hearing their fathers' condemna-
tion repeated by an entire nation ('la Patria'), and sanctioned by God
himself.

These considerations can be extended to Marie, the heroine of *La
Grâce de Dieu*, steeped in the same socio-cultural context. Like Lydie
and Linda, she would have been described as a 'folle-mélancolique'
and, without Pierrot, would have ended up in a 'maison de santé'.
Parisian madwomen were customarily sent to the Hôpital de la
Salpêtrière or to the asylum at Charenton, on the outskirts of the
city; there the three girls might have become friends and perhaps, in
rare moments of lucidity, told each other their sad stories. Yet, as I
have suggested above, Marie's story is different from Linda's in what
seem to us fundamental ways. The mid-nineteenth-century discourse
on virginity and madness was not equipped to describe or perhaps
even perceive these differences, however, centred as it was on the
moral and social aspects of both female sexuality and female mental
sanity. The differences between Marie's and Linda's stories needed to
wait a few decades to be brought to the fore by psychoanalysis and its
focus on the profound causes of human behaviour and thought.

MOTHERS, FATHERS AND DAUGHTERS

In his 1893 obituary of Jean-Martin Charcot, the French *médecin
aliéniste* who had become the most famous authority on hysteria
and whose work he had observed in Paris a few years earlier, Freud

insinuated that Charcot was concerned with description but paid little or no attention to the aetiology of the disease.[39] The late nineteenth century brought to the fore a new concept, hysteria, and a new concern for the causes of madness. Hysteria was hardly new, actually: earlier in the century a number of French psychiatrists had studied this type of *folie*, but the impact of their work was relatively limited and became part of the cultural horizon only in the 1860s.[40] According to historian Jan Goldstein, in 1841–2 (the years of the premières of *La Grâce de Dieu* and *Linda*) only about 1 per cent of the women admitted to the Salpêtrière were diagnosed as hysterics, while forty years later, in 1882–3, when Charcot was working at the hospital, this figure had risen to about 20 per cent. Jean-Etienne-Dominique Esquirol, the preeminent *aliéniste* between the 1820s and the 1840s, was indifferent to hysteria.[41] When Desplein and Bianchon diagnosed Lydie as a 'folle-mélancolique', they proved themselves doctors of their time.

As Foucault has argued, psychoanalysis was born out of a century-long development of a discourse of sexuality which involved first medicine, then psychiatry and criminal justice, and eventually an articulated system of social control that awoke and later intensified awareness of sex as a constant danger. This development brought about a hystericisation of women's bodies, which were first analysed as being thoroughly saturated with sexuality, then integrated into the sphere of medical practices, and eventually placed in organic communication with the entire social body, first of all the family space.[42] Psychoanalysis 'rediscovered the law of alliance, the involved workings of marriage and kinship, and incest at the heart of this sexuality, as the principle of its formation and the key to its intelligibility'.[43] This observation fits especially well Freud's early work on hysteria, which was born out of his contact with Charcot, and centred around the attempt to develop a theory of the disease's aetiology in the family history of patients.[44]

Reading *Linda* and its sources through the lens of psychoanalysis, especially Freud's early work on hysteria, means adopting the point of view of the most comprehensive and arguably most insightful theory of nineteenth-century subjectivity in terms of sexuality and the family. Moreover, it offers a framework within which the differences between *La Grâce de Dieu* and the opera, so far overlooked, come to the fore, since attention to the origins and workings of power relations in Dennery and Lemoine's Loustalots will highlight Rossi's innovations and Donizetti's musical working of them.[45]

Linda's case presents intriguing similarities with the fourth of Freud's cases in *Studies on Hysteria* (1895), that of Katharina.[46] Most interestingly, both take place in an Alpine setting, Savoy and the Hohe Tauern. Freud, who had travelled to the mountains to forget medicine and neuroses for a while, is approached by Katharina, a girl of about eighteen who serves his meal in a refuge hut and asks his help on account of her 'bad nerves'. The doctor declares himself 'interested to find that neuroses could flourish in this way at a height of over 6,000 feet', and starts questioning her.[47] Katharina's story – her father's attempt to have intercourse with her, and her later discovery of him and her cousin Franziska engaged in sexual activity – confirms Freud's finding that 'in girls anxiety was a consequence of the horror by which a virginal mind is overcome when it is faced for the first time with the world of sexuality', and leads to the diagnosis, 'hysterical attacks the content of which is anxiety'.[48] The girl's anxiety attacks and hallucinations are hysterical because they are a reproduction of the anxiety that had first appeared in connection with a sexual trauma; even if Katharina had not decoded her father's approach as sexual at the time, Freud comments that 'a mere suspicion of sexual relations calls up the affect of anxiety in virgin individuals'.[49]

Freud observes in passing that he owed Katharina 'a debt of gratitude for having made it so much easier for me to talk to her than to the prudish ladies of my city practice, who regard whatever is natural as shameful'.[50] This crucial aside points to further similarities between Linda and Katharina. Both girls develop their pathology precisely because, in the simple Alpine innocence that city-dwellers attribute to them, they do not admit – at least initially – into the sexual sphere what audience and analyst alike immediately recognise as seduction attempts, in both cases unsuccessful but nonetheless disastrous for the psychic equilibrium of the two virgins. As Baldacci has noted, Rossi knew well that, in the Act 2 duet, desire is 'intense' ('fervido') for Carlo, but 'unknown' ('incognito') for Linda.[51]

What, then, is Linda's pathology? Freud describes Katharina's case in terms of anxiety hysteria, but for the Savoyard girl the diagnosis is more serious: in the mature Freud's terms, a reaction psychosis with schizophrenic symptoms. Freud's early writings still contemplate the possibility of hysterical psychosis, and it is ultimately in these terms that Linda's madness would have been described. Rossi and Donizetti do not significantly change the symptoms staged in *La Grâce de Dieu*, and therefore both pathology and diagnosis can be extended back to Marie. Freud, however, was centrally concerned with the causes of hysteria and its roots in the family history of the patient; from this point of view, the play presents a scenario significantly different from the opera.

As noted above, Antonio first asserts his power over Linda and his family in the *romanza* 'Ambo nati in questa valle'. In the play, however, it is Madeleine who invests the farm with the metonymical representation of the family: 'Sell this farm, where we got married?... And where my mother died? And where our daughter Marie was born? Is it in God's name possible? What will become of us, Antoine, what will become of us?'[52] Already at the beginning of Act I Madeleine had revealed her active, central contribution in the shaping of Marie's character and the special bond that linked her to her daughter. When Pierrot marvels at the fact that Marie is still asleep while her mother kills herself with work, she answers: 'MADELEINE: Oh, I don't mind fatigue and lack of sleep!... I am strong! PIERROT: Not like Miss Marie! One would never guess she is your daughter!... She looks more like a city girl than a Savoyard!... What is it with her this morning, anyway? MADELEINE: She is sleeping!... She is young... she needs sleep!... But, me, I work!... Besides, this way she can sleep longer and our work doesn't suffer'.[53] In the opera, Maddalena's first words say exactly the opposite:

Linda, mia dolce figlia! Tu nel sonno
Dell'innocenza ancora giaci; a lungo
in assiduo lavoro,
provvida tu per noi vegliasti, e lieti
saranno i sogni tuoi.

Linda, my beloved child! You are still sleeping the sleep of innocence.
You prolonged your dutiful waking hours in assiduous labour for your
parents, and may pleasant dreams lull you to rest.

The most revealing evidence of Madeleine's hold on Marie is, of
course, the song she sings to her daughter before the entire village at
the end of Act 1, the second stanza of 'A la grâce de Dieu':

MARIE
Ma mère, ne voulez-vous pas bénir vostre Marie?

MADELEINE
Oh! oui, oui! chère enfant! la bénédiction que me donna autrefois ma
mère. . . elle m'a toujours préservée du danger!. . . la mienne t'en
préservera, Marie!. . . A défaut de ma voix. . . que bientôt tu n'entendras
plus!. . . emporte dans ton coeur ce chant, que ma mère me donna pour
sauve-garde!. . . Ma fille, me dit-elle. . .
(*Madeleine étend ses mains sur la tête de Marie*)

AIR: *A la Grâce de Dieu (L. Puget)*
Ici, commence ton voyage;
Si tu n'allais pas revenir!
Ta pauvre mère est sans courage,
Pour te quitter!. . . pour te bénir!. . .
(*Ici, Madeleine, affaiblie par la douleur, s'assied; Marie tombe à ses pieds.*
    Madeleine continue le couplet.)
Travaille bien. . . fais ta prière,
La prière donne du cœur.
(*Peu à peu la voix de Madeleine est éteinte par les larmes.*)
Et quelquefois pense à ta mère!. . .
Cela te portera bonheur!. . .
Va, mon enfant. . . adieu!. . .
A la grâce de Dieu!
Adieu!. . .à la. . .

(*Mais ici la voix lui manque et elle s'évanouit.*)

MARIE

Ma mère! ma mère!. . .[54]

MARIE: Mother, won't you bless your Marie?

MADELEINE: Oh! yes! yes, my child! the blessing that my mother used
to give me. . . it has always protected me from peril. . . and mine will
protect you, too, Marie!. . . in lieu of my voice. . . which soon you
will hear no longer!. . . keep this song in your heart, the song my
mother gave me as token of her protection!. . . My daughter – she
told me – . . . (*Madeleine places her hands on Marie's head.*) Now your
journey begins; what if you did not come back!. . . Your poor mother
is unable to leave you or to bless you! (*At this point, Madeleine,
weakened by sadness, sits down; Marie falls at her feet. Madeleine
continues.*) Work. . . pray: prayer gives courage. (*Little by little
Madeleine's voice is choked by tears.*) And sometimes think of your
mother!. . . this thought will bring you happiness!. . . Go, my child. . .
farewell! To God's mercy! Farewell. . . to. . . (*Here her voice fails her
and she faints.*)

MARIE: Mother! Mother!. . .

The song is passed down from mother to daughter as a sort of magic
talisman, but is also the sign of the pre-eminent role played by women
in the family. Antoine Loustalot has much less control over Marie's
personality than Antonio Loustolot has over Linda's. In short, the
Loustalots are a matriarchy, while the Loustolots are a patriarchy.

It is not surprising, then, that Marie loses her mind not when
Antoine curses her, but when she witnesses Arthur's wedding cortège from her window: 'Marie lets out a terrible cry and backs away
from the window horrified; from this moment on, she looks at the
audience with a fixed, disturbed gaze'.[55] Why, then, did Rossi and
Donizetti decide to alter the family interaction of *La Grâce de Dieu*?
The answer is simple: the conventions of Italian opera did not allow
for an 'important' mother if the *prima donna* was somebody else,
especially if the mezzosoprano was already cast as the *musico*, i.e.
Pierotto. The 'serious' baritone, Antonio, however, was not excluded
either by the serious bass or by the *buffo*, in this case the Prefetto and
Boisfleury. The psycho-narrative consequences of this eminently

practical choice are momentous, and emerge especially in the light of Freud's mature work on female sexuality.

The interest in female sexuality that runs through *Studies on Hysteria*, although never absent from the development of psycho-analysis, returns to the centre of Freud's thought in a few essays published in the early 1930s, especially 'Female Sexuality' (1931) and 'Femininity' (1933), which implicitly re-address and re-interpret the set of questions opened up by the early research in hysteria. In the light of these essays' interpretative strategies, the aetiology of Linda's madness can ultimately be located in the permanence of a strong Oedipus complex, which she has not outgrown – not surprisingly, given Antonio's overwhelming presence. Marie's case is altogether different. In 'Female Sexuality' Freud observes that 'we had to reckon with the possibility that a number of women remain arrested in their original attachment to their mother and never achieve a true change-over towards men', first and above all the father.[56] 'This being so, the pre-Oedipus phase in women gains an importance which we have not attributed to it hitherto'.[57] Most important for an interpretation of Marie, 'this phase of attachment to the mother is especially intimately related to the aetiology of hysteria, which is not surprising when we reflect that both the phase and the neurosis are characteristically feminine, and further, that in this dependence on the mother we have the germ of later paranoia in women'.[58] Marie's attachment to her mother is predicated on Madeleine's matriarchal strategies: working hard to let her daughter sleep longer, imparting her blessing and singing her 'A la grâce de Dieu' are symbolic signs of Madeleine's role as guardian of Marie's chastity, a role that Maddalena never performs.

Rossi and Donizetti's dramatic and musical decisions – having Pierotto sing the *ballata*, making Linda go mad only when Antonio curses her – create not only a different type of Alpine virgin from the heroine of *La Grâce de Dieu*, but one constructed and categorised by Freud almost a century later. The uncanny ability of Freudian psychoanalysis to paint full portraits of mid-nineteenth-century dramatic characters proves its relevance for an interpretation of these characters and the artistic artefacts in which they appear, and at the same time confirms the genealogy of psychoanalysis in the nineteenth-century discourse of sexuality.[59] Subjecting *Linda di Chamounix* and its sources to a classic Freudian psychoanalytic interpretation means recognising psychoanalysis as both the product of nineteenth-century culture and a powerful tool with which to perform a sort of 'analysis with original instruments' of this culture – which, as I have already suggested, is also to some significant extent the culture of the present.

THE THERAPEUTIC CABALETTA

The function of psychoanalysis as an interpretative framework for literary, artistic and musical texts is by no means exhausted by a Freudian (or Jungian, or Kleinian) analysis of characters, authors or readers/audiences. As many have argued, psychoanalysis, especially as expounded in the writings of Jacques Lacan, can be employed to read a text in a structural and rhetorical sense. In Peter Brooks's words, 'Lacan [. . .] has taught students of literature to understand the basic operations of the "dream-work", condensation and displacement, as the master tropes of rhetoric, metaphor and metonymy, reconfigured as fundamental psychic manifestations presented to analysis: symptom and desire'. Since human subjects constitute themselves, at least in part, through their fictions, 'the study of human fiction-making and psychic process are convergent activities, and superimposable forms of analysis'. More specifically, if 'sexuality belongs not simply to the physical body, but to the complex of phantasies and symbolisations which largely determine identity', we can read these phantasies and symbolisations in terms of sexuality, and therefore interpret them psychoanalytically.[60] *Linda di Chamounix*, a work saturated with sexual fantasies and symbolisations, seems a promising candidate for such an interpretation, especially since in many ways it does not conform to psychoanalytic theories, and therefore it may resist the kind of reductively symptomatic interpretation all too often encountered in psychoanalytic criticism of art.[61] In order to perform this interpretation, however, a closer consideration of the representation of sexuality and voice in the opera and in texts closely connected with its genesis is necessary.

As I have argued, one of the most significant differences between the song in *La Grâce de Dieu* and Pierotto's *ballata* in the opera centres around the question of the girls' purity: while in 'A la grâce de Dieu' there is no suggestion of seduction, Pierotto explicitly sings of 'a fire that robbed her of her peace', transparently referring to the daughter's loss of virginity. In a letter to Antonio Vasselli dated 24 December 1841, Donizetti summarises the plot he is about to set in the following way:

> Don't look for the plot for Vienna in history books. There are children leaving Savoy for Paris to make some money. Some are good, others bad. Many times this girl almost lets herself be seduced, but each time, she hears her village's song, thinks of her father and mother, and resists. . . But then she no longer resists. . . the seducer wants to marry somebody else. Then she goes mad (humph!); then she goes back to the village with a poor boy who induces her to walk by playing her the song: if he doesn't play, she stops. . . Both almost die of starvation; the seducer arrives. . . he didn't get married. The girl regains her wits, since when she hears. . . a woman regains immediately her wits.[62]

'Then she no longer resists'. At first, then, Rossi and Donizetti had in mind a successful seduction. The story narrated in the *ballata*, however, does not correspond to the final version of the opera's plot.

Moreover, the *ballata* fails therapeutically: although it enables Linda to walk from Paris to Chamonix, it does not succeed in bringing her back to sanity. Its failure is due to a multiplicity of reasons. First, it is not sung by Maddalena, either in Act 1 or Act 3; and even had Maddalena sung it, it would equally have failed, since Maddalena is not the object of Linda's libido, who is instead in a fully-fledged Oedipal phase. If Antonio had sung it, then, Linda would have fallen back into the arms – metaphorical, and perhaps also real – of her father, who, substituting for Boisfleury in his lust for the girl, would have raised the suspicion of incestuous desire.

In order for Linda to leave her family behind – and with the family her virginity, which belongs to the family – it is Carlo who must make his voice heard. However, Carlo does not sing the *ballata* – of course: why would he make her hear the song that stood between them in Act 2? He repeats the theme of the cabaletta of his duet with Linda in Act 1, 'A consolarmi affrettisi tal giorno desiato'.

The sources offer different readings of the text, oscillating between the literal repetition of the Act 1 incipit and the modification of its third-person subjunctive into the second-person imperative 'A consolarmi affrettati'.[63] The latter emphasises the fulfilment of the wish expressed in the Act 1 cabaletta, the fact that the desired day has eventually arrived: Carlo knows that his voice will call Linda back from madness and bring about the happiness they could only dream of earlier. He seems sure that, in Donizetti's words, 'the girl regains her wits, since when she hears. . . [*ché a sentire.* . .] a woman [*la donna*] regains immediately her wits'. In Italian 'sentire' means both to hear and to feel, and 'la donna', although grammatically singular, implies the entire feminine gender, all women. What does Linda actually hear/feel?

In the last scene of the opera Carlo sings the first eight bars of the cabaletta of their Act 1 duet. A simple motivic reduction of this G major melody highlights its characteristic stepwise descent from G to B (scale degrees $\hat{8}$ and $\hat{3}$), with a significant emphasis on D (scale degree $\hat{5}$) (Ex. 3.1). The D minor vocal line of Pierotto's *ballata*, on the contrary, rises from D to B flat (scale degrees $\hat{1}$ and $\hat{6}$), with emphasis on A (scale degree $\hat{5}$) (Ex. 3.2). If we add to these two melodies the Larghetto 'Cari luoghi, ov'io passai', sung by Pierotto in the wings immediately before the *ballata* and inserted by Donizetti in the Paris version, we obtain the same collection of pitches of the *ballata* and a similar upward motion – not to mention the same key (D minor), metre (6/8), tempo (Larghetto) and instrumental colour (an attempt to imitate the sound of a hurdy-gurdy) (Ex. 3.3).

This strong similarity between the first Larghetto and the *ballata*, which extends to the metrical structure of their texts (*ottonari*), could be thought a miscalculation, perhaps dictated by time constraints.

Ex. 3.1. Donizetti, *Linda di Chamounix*, Act 3: Reprise of 'A consolarmi affrettisi'.

While the reason behind the insertion of the Larghetto probably resides in the need to give the *musico* something that could balance the new *cavatina* 'O luce di quest'anima', added for the soprano of the Parisian première, Fanny Tacchinardi-Persiani, there seems to be

Ex. 3.1. *(cont.)*

no compelling reason why the Larghetto should be so similar to the *ballata*.[64] I would draw attention to the Larghetto's text, however, an invocation of the 'dear place, where I spent the first years of my life'. Keeping in mind the genealogy of Pierotto's *ballata* in Madeleine's song in *La Grâce de Dieu* and its function, in both play and opera, of

Ex. 3.2. Donizetti, *Linda di Chamounix*, Act 1: Pierotto's *ballata*.

Ex. 3.2. (*cont.*)

safeguarding the heroine's virginity, I would suggest that Pierotto's voice is the voice of the community, of Chamonix, of the native valley, and therefore, by metonymy, of the family. Singing a melody motivically, modally and gesturally opposed to Pierotto's music, therefore, Carlo sings *against* the community and the family – that is, against the owners and guardians of Linda's virginity. And Linda knows it.

When Carlo proposes the melody to her for the first time, she promptly accepts it, but before repeating it together, they 'look around to see if somebody is coming' ('guardan pria se viene alcuno'), and then they attack it 'pianissimo, as if hiding' ('come di soppiatto').[65] The reassuring promise of a proper wedding contained in the text – 'tuo/a sposo/a diverrò' – seems to counteract this subversive gesture. When, in Act 2, Linda goes mad, her first musical gesture is to sing the incipit of 'A consolarmi affrettisi' – the musical counterpart of the stage direction 'she becomes calmer' ('va serenandosi'). For a moment it seems as if this were to become the cabaletta of the finale, but, in the middle of the second phrase, at the words 'tua sposa', she loses the thread of the melody, and on a rallentando in the orchestra, 'almost crying, mezza voce', lands on a repeated E flat (in a G major context).[66] She tries again, but to no avail, and then starts what turns out to be the real cabaletta, the wonderfully disjointed 'No, non è ver, mentirono', in E flat major.[67] However, the memory of 'A consolarmi affrettisi' haunts her: note the motivic similarities between the melodies – the

Ex. 3.3. Donizetti, *Linda di Chamounix*, Act 1: Pierotto's first Larghetto.

Ex. 3.3. (*cont.*)

second sounds like a fractured, disfigured transformation of the step-wise descent of the first – the doubling in thirds, and the double appoggiatura in the second bar of 'A consolarmi affrettisi' and the third of 'No, non è ver'.[68] Moreover, before the coda of the latter, the voice slips back into an unorthodox, unprepared G major, the key of 'A consolarmi affrettisi', only to return to E flat by way of a deceptive cadence that highlights the prominent melodic tritone E natural–B flat (Ex. 3.4).[69]

At her reappearance in Act 3, Linda sings the entire second phrase of 'A consolarmi affrettisi', 'in faccia al cielo e agl'uomini tua sposa diverrò', thus completing the musical non-sequitur of the previous act, but she does so in the 'wrong' key of F (Ex. 3.5). It is only when Carlo sings it to her in the last scene that the cabaletta theme comes back complete and in its original key of G (Ex. 3.1 above). This utterance not only resolves a long-range musical and emotional tension, but also represents the climax of an almost painfully concentrated pressure that involves the text, the music and the action of the last musical number.

According to the autograph score, the last number of the opera begins with the pantomimic scene of Linda and Pierotto arriving in Chamonix. The long *scena* is saturated with fragments of the *ballata* reworked contrapuntally and contains the aforementioned appear-ance of the cabaletta melody in F major. Linda, who believes she is still in Paris, hears sounds she interprets as part of the festivities for Carlo's wedding and flees to her parents' house. Antonio comes on stage and tells the Prefetto, Carlo, Boisfleury and the chorus that

Ex. 3.4. Donizetti, *Linda di Chamounix*, Act 2: Finale, reprise of 'A consolarmi affrettisi' and first statement of the cabaletta.

Linda 'trembled at the sound of my voice, but remained unmoved by her mother's, whom she loved so much' ('ha tremato alla mia voce, restò immobile a quella di sua madre che amava tanto'). After the *ballata* theme is heard from within, Maddalena comes to report that

Ex. 3.4. *(cont.)*

her daughter 'shook herself and got up at the sound of Pierotto's playing' ('s'è scossa, s'è alzata al suono di Pierotto'). Linda, clearly still mad, appears 'with her eyes turned upwards to the sky, as if talking to her mother' ('con gli occhi rivolti al cielo, come parlando a sua madre'), and proclaims her innocence. Carlo, 'as if inspired'

Ex. 3.4. (*cont.*)

Ex. 3.4. (*cont.*)

('come ispirato'), asserts that 'love will perhaps cure her' ('riserbato all'amore è forse il ridestarlo'), and calls her name, to which she answers 'this voice!' ('qual voce!').

At this point Carlo launches into a cantabile about his voice:

CARLO
È la voce che primiera
Palpitar ti fece il core,
È l'accento dell'amore,
È il sospir di chi t'amò.

Ex. 3.5. Donizetti, *Linda di Chamounix*, Act 3: Fragment of 'A consolarmi affrettisi'.

LINDA
Egual voce un dì nel petto
Mi discese e vi regnò.

CARLO
È il tuo ben che ancor t'adora,
Che da te perdono implora!
Uno sguardo, un tuo sorriso,
E felice tornerò.[70]

CARLO: It is the voice that first made your heart beat, it is the accent of love, it is the sigh of him who loved you.

LINDA: This same voice once entered into my heart and ruled it.

CARLO: It is your beloved who still adores you, who implores your
pardon! Give me one look, one smile, and I will become happy again.

Linda remains motionless, still mad: she understands Carlo's description of his voice, but not that the voice talking about the voice of love
is *his* voice. He is about to leave in desperation, but she stops him:

LINDA
Se tu fossi Carlo mio,
Tu m'avresti il cor beato,
Ripetendo un caro accento,
Che rammenta il più bel dì.

CARLO
Ah! sì, Linda, ti consola!
Carlo a te dicea così:

LINDA
Dillo! dillo![71]

LINDA: If you were my Carlo, you would have made me happy by
repeating the sweet words that recall our happiest days.
CARLO: Ah! yes, Linda, console yourself! This is what Carlo used to say
to you.
LINDA: Say it! Say it!

It is at this moment that Carlo sings 'A consolarmi affrettisi'. Linda
'listens to him with all her attention' ('lo ascolta con tutta l'atten-
zione'); at the words 'tuo sposo' 'she is overcome by emotion and is
about to lose her senses' ('alterata per l'emozione va mancando'):
she shouts a G sharp and faints (Ex. 3.1 above). Pierotto, Carlo,
Antonio, Boisfleury and the Prefetto invoke Heaven's help with an
a cappella prayer, after which Linda regains her senses and recognises,
in the following order, her mother, her father and then Carlo.
Overwhelmed by joy, Linda cannot believe the scene is real, and
asks Carlo for confirmation: he responds with the cabaletta 'Di tue
pene sparve il sogno', and is joined by Linda after twelve bars.
According to the autograph score, 'this cabaletta can also be sung
by Linda the second time', and Linda's vocal line for the first twelve
bars is added in pencil.[72]

An interpretation of this finale should start by acknowledging that this is in fact a long double aria in D major for the tenor, the pillars of which are the slow movement 'È la voce che primiera' and the cabaletta 'Di tue pene sparve il sogno'. The exceptional length of the *scena* and especially the *tempo di mezzo* – which contains the return of 'A consolarmi affrettisi' and the prayer 'Compi, o ciel, la nostra speme' – should not blind us to the fact that it is Carlo who musically 'owns' the opera's last number, and that its central movement thematises his voice as the object of Linda's desire and the only possible treatment for her madness.[73]

Not only the centrality of the voice as manifestation of desire and of hearing as access to the subject's innermost recesses, but also the theorisation of this centrality are by no means a twentieth-century phenomenon, as many recent discussions seem to imply. On the contrary, they have characterised Western discourse on subjectivity for a very long time, as Michel Poizat, Mladen Dolar and Corrado Bologna have argued among others.[74] For example, voice and hearing are often presented in these terms in the writings on virginity by the Fathers of the Church (St Ambrose's *On Virginity* and *On the Education of Virgins* are especially eloquent texts). Most interestingly (and seldom mentioned), they re-surface in late-eighteenth-century French culture, where both the story of the Savoyard girl and modern conceptions of subjectivity find their roots. According to Diderot, for example, 'the power that hearing has on our soul is immense'.[75] In *Les Cent vingt journées de Sodome*, a text centrally occupied with desire, sexuality and virginity, Sade writes:

> True libertines know well that the sensations transmitted by the sense of hearing are the ones that give the utmost pleasure and whose impressions are the strongest. Therefore, our four scoundrels [the four libertine protagonists of the novel], who wanted pleasure to impregnate their hearts as deeply and completely as it could penetrate, had to that end imagined a very strange thing. It consisted in this: after having surrounded themselves with everything that could satisfy the other senses with lubricity, in this situation they wanted to be told in the greatest detail, and in an orderly fashion, all the different possibilities of

debauchery, all its kinds, all its conventions, what in sum is called, in the libertine language, all the passions.[76]

Sade's words resonate uncannily with Lacan's concepts of hearing as the most powerful access to the subject's unspeakable compulsions and voice as a tool of penetration – that is, with the richest and farthest-reaching twentieth-century theorisation of the voice.[77]

In Lacanian terms, Carlo's voice constitutes the *objet a*, the manifestation of Carlo's desire which becomes the 'object' of Linda's desire. Lacan remarks that the invocatory drive is 'the closest to the experience of the unconscious' and that 'in the field of the unconscious the ears are the only orifice that cannot be closed'.[78] Linda's madness allows her to let the voice of her unconscious speak, to recognise the therapeutic potential of Carlo's voice and invoke it: 'If you were my Carlo, you would have made me happy by repeating the sweet accent that recalls our happiest days' – Donizetti adds the interjection 'dillo! dillo!', not present in the libretto and clearly perceptible above the silence of the orchestra. In her madness, or, better, thanks to her madness, she knows that her ears, the only point of entrance open to Carlo, cannot be closed, and asks him to penetrate her unconscious, to suture the original rift between child and mother and give her the illusion of wholeness, to make it possible for her to ignore her division and re-constitute herself as subject. It is first and foremost Linda's voice, then, that moves towards the Other; it is Linda who requires that Carlo make himself heard. Paraphrasing Lacan's theory according to which 'the Law appears to be giving the order, *"Jouis!"*, to which the subject can only reply *"J'ouis"* (I hear), the *jouissance* being no more than understood', it is Linda who cries 'fais moi t'ouir / fais moi jouir': Carlo cannot but respond 'jouis!', to which Linda answers 'j'ouis', experiencing *jouissance* – or, as Lacan would say, understanding it.[79]

In other words, the cabaletta's theme acts as a tool by which Carlo penetrates Linda. In Lacan's theory, therefore, his voice stands for the phallus, the symbol of the original lack, of what the subject lacks in order to attain his or her mythical wholeness and that the Other supposedly owns – the power of the Other to reconstitute the subject as such. The phallus, *not* the penis: Donizetti and Rossi changed their minds in January 1842, the seduction does not take place, Carlo does not penetrate Linda physically. In this respect, Donizetti's original plot summary is inaccurate. But Donizetti's own words support the interpretation of Carlo's voice as the phallus: 'Since when she hears. . . a woman regains immediately her wits'. The rhetorical use of reticence and the double meaning of the verb 'sentire' open up this sentence to *double entendre*. Carlo obviously shares Donizetti's view of the feminine psyche, since he seems to understand immediately Linda's plea and hastens to make himself heard, that is, to perform the act of penetration by singing the cabaletta theme. He responds to Linda's invocation with his own invocation, reciprocating Linda's movement towards him by moving towards her.

Do Linda and Carlo meet? Lacan would answer with a resounding 'no'. And yet this is what *Linda di Chamounix* seems to stage: the eventual encounter of two desiring subjects who have moved towards each other for three long acts. However, this encounter takes place within a frame of reference and according to the terms set by Carlo, at the level of both plot and musical structure. Carlo goes back to Chamonix to look for Linda after he has conquered his mother's resistance and is no longer obliged to marry the aristocratic woman she had imposed on him. And, as I have mentioned, the crucial final scenes of the opera are musically constructed as a double aria for him. Finally, it is to Carlo that Linda turns for confirmation that she is not dreaming, to which he answers with the final instance of his musical control, the cabaletta 'Di tue pene sparve il giorno'.

Until now I have oscillated between general references to Carlo's voice and more specific instances of his utterance of 'A consolarmi affrettisi', but these two objects perform very different functions in the therapeutic scenario. Carlo's voice alone fails to bring Linda back to sanity; it is only when he sings 'the sweet accent that recalls our happiest days' that she is cured. Why is 'A consolarmi affrettisi' Linda's only cure? According to Lacan, 'the *objet a* is something from which the subject, in order to constitute itself, has separated itself off as organ'.[80] As Lacanian exegete Bruce Fink has recently elaborated, the *objet a* can be understood 'as the *remainder* produced when that hypothetical unity breaks down, as a last trace of that unity, as a *reminder* thereof'.[81] The Act 1 duet between Linda and Carlo, in which 'A consolarmi affrettisi' makes its first appearance, represents the primal unity of which the cabaletta theme is both remainder and reminder. This symbolic function is highlighted by the fact that Linda keeps singing it in her madness: to remind herself of that literally prelapsarian unity with Carlo, clinging to it as the remainder of this unity. In Act 1 this unity is no less hypothetical than in Lacan's theory, since it is only an imagined future unity. But when Linda recalls it, she remembers it as if it had actually happened. In the light of this retrospective construction of reality, Carlo's betrayal and Antonio's curse come to signify the phallic split, the rift of the perfect unity of the two lovers. It is therefore only the repetition of 'A consolarmi affrettisi' sung by Carlo, who had sung it first in Act 1, that can suture the phallic split and fill Linda's ears with the *jouissance* of understanding.

'The ear of understanding' is Julia Kristeva's formulation in a feminist gloss on the Lacanian conception of voice that touches upon virginity as well:

> We are entitled only to the ear of the virginal body, the tears, and the breast. With the female sexual organ changed into an innocent shell, holder of sound, there arises a possible tendency to eroticise hearing, voice, or even understanding. By the same token, however, sexuality is brought down to the level of innuendo. [. . .] The virginal maternal is a way [. . .] of dealing with feminine paranoia. [. . .] The Virgin obstructs the desire for murder or devouring by means of a strong oral cathexis (the breast), valorisation of pain (the sob), and incitement to replace the sexed body with the ear of understanding.[82]

With the help of Kristeva I would like to take a Lacanian reading of the final scenes of *Linda di Chamounix* a step further in a feminist direction. Since for both Lacan and Kristeva the original unity is that of mother and child, *La Grâce de Dieu* represents its perfect example, configuring as it does Madeleine's song as its symbol and her voice as the object of Marie's desire. But in the opera Maddalena is mute, and Pierotto's music, rather than the musical embodiment of this original unity, metonymically represents the voice of the Father, and of the Law, against which Carlo already sings in Act I. For Linda the retrospectively constructed union with Carlo must therefore belong to a stage other than what both Lacan and Kristeva name 'the symbolic'. In any case, Rossi and Donizetti eliminate the possibility of imagining Carlo's voice as an echo of the mother's voice, since the mother has no voice, *is* not voice, but only an image, which Linda dutifully recognises once she has regained her senses.

In the light of these observations, a feminist reading of *Linda* according to Kristevan formulations can develop in two directions. On the one hand, since 'the female sexual organ has changed into an innocent shell, holder of sound' (in this case the sound of the tenor's voice), Linda's sexuality 'is brought down to the level of innuendo' – the innuendo of Donizetti's letter – which, moreover, can be staged only within a narrative and musical frame provided and controlled by male desire. On the other hand, as Kaja Silverman has commented discussing the connection between motherhood and muteness running through Kristeva's essay, 'if the mother is mute, she is also irrecoverable; [. . .] once her voice has been silenced, it can no longer help to weave the anaclitic enclosure which figures her union with the child'.[83] Not simply irrecoverable, I would add with an eye to the opera's musical construction, but altogether absent. Linda knows that her mother's voice can no longer help to weave the anaclitic enclosure which figures Maddalena's union with herself, not because that voice has been silenced, but because it was not there in the first place. In the opera Linda hears only two voices, her father's – 'she trembled at the sound of my voice' – and Carlo's, the former symbolised by the *ballata*, the latter by the cabaletta. Their changing musical status in the course of the opera can be interpreted in terms of their evolving symbolic meaning.

The *ballata* is heard in its entirety only once, when Pierotto introduces it in Act 1. Its theme, the eight-bar period that moves from D minor to F major, appears several times in the course of the opera: its head motif infiltrates the instrumental coda to the Act 1 finale; Pierotto plays it under Linda's window at the beginning of Act 2; he does so again (in G minor) during the *tempo di mezzo* of Linda's and Carlo's duet later in the same act; the Act 3 pantomime presents fragments of it;[84] later Pierotto plays it again in the wings, and the orchestra continues it in *parlante* style, completing not only its minor-mode stanza, but also its major-mode refrain. After its first appearance, the *ballata* music is never sung again, only played on Pierotto's hurdy-gurdy or by the orchestra. Moreover, in Act 3 its initial status as stage music is obfuscated: when the orchestra picks it up from Pierotto and completes it, it is unclear whether the characters on stage still hear it, or whether it has descended from the stage into the pit, becoming, in Carolyn Abbate's famous formulation, 'unheard'.[85]

A feminist reading of *Linda* focusing on the presence/absence of the maternal voice cannot leave unremarked that Pierotto is a mezzosoprano *en travesti*; in a post-castrato age, therefore, his voice is not only that of a woman, but is also exclusively associated with women. In fact, Pierotto is one of the last representatives of that peculiar vocal-dramatic category, called *musichetti* in technical jargon, which enjoyed a certain popularity in Italian opera of the 1830s and 1840s: mezzosopranos impersonating adolescent boys who are not full-blown protagonists (like the older *musici*), but, according to Marco Beghelli, 'tend to inhabit the social and geographical ambience of the drama, expressing with their voice its characteristic *couleur locale*', especially in songs, ballads and serenades (among other prominent Donizettian *musichetti* are Smeton in *Anna Bolena* and Gondì in the Parisian version of *Maria di Rohan*).[86] Pierotto is a mezzo just like Maddalena, and it is therefore tempting to consider the possibility that his voice acts as a substitute for the maternal one. At this point, however, it is important to distinguish between Pierotto's voice and his *ballata*. As I have mentioned above, Pierotto never sings the *ballata* a second time, not even a fragment of it: separated from the sound of a voice which could act as maternal, the theme is heard in the mechanical timbre of the hurdy-gurdy, or its orchestral imitations. Once this theme is deprived of the 'warm' timbre of the human voice, what comes more prominently to the fore is its abstract, 'cold' melodic profile, which, as suggested above, is associated with Linda's familial sphere. Such 'cold' music can make Linda walk all the way from Paris back to Chamonix, but not cure her madness.

Pierotto's voice, however, is heard prominently in another number beside the *ballata*: his one-movement duet with Linda at the beginning of Act 2.[87] The most significant musical feature of this duet is undoubtedly the coupling of Linda's and Pierotto's voices in a long passage in parallel thirds, which is repeated in its entirety, since formally the movement is structured like a cabaletta (Ex. 3.6). This pairing of two female voices has a mighty genealogy in a number of Italian operas of the two decades preceding *Linda*, foremost among them Rossini's *Semiramide* and Bellini's *Norma*, specifically the slow movement, 'Giorno d'orror!', of the Semiramide–Arsace duet in Act 2 of *Semiramide*, and the same movement, 'Mira, o Norma', of the Norma–Adalgisa duet in Act 2 of *Norma*. The precedent most directly related to Linda, however, is the duet for Ninetta and Pippo 'E ben, per mia memoria' in Act 2 of another *opera semiseria*, Rossini's *La gazza ladra*, placed in the same position as the Linda–Pierotto number and expressing similar sentiments of compassion, support and love. As Heather Hadlock has noted in her discussion of the Semiramide–Arsace duet, 'the voice of the *musico* becomes [. . .] the feminine voice of a mother – a beloved object of vocal imitation, a "tutelary goddess" with whom the child prays. [. . .] Arsace and Semiramide become not hero and heroine, but rather two *women* in a reciprocally maternal relation to each other'.[88] Much the same could be said of Linda and Pierotto, who are literally praying to God to hasten the day of Linda's wedding, and especially her return to her family and the valley of Chamonix: 'I imagine your parents' joy in embracing you, the entire valley coming

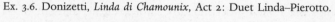

Ex. 3.6. Donizetti, *Linda di Chamounix*, Act 2: Duet Linda–Pierotto.

down to meet you' ('De' genitori immagino la gioia in abbracciarvi, tutta la valle in giubilo fuor esce ad incontrarvi').[89]

In the context of the entire opera, however, this indulgence in reciprocal breast-feeding is constructed as momentary and perhaps even regressive, a moment of delusory fantasy from which Linda is awoken, in a powerful crescendo, first by the lustful attention of the Marchese (duet Linda–Marchese), then by the equally lustful and much more dangerous attention of Carlo (*romanza* Carlo and duet Linda–Carlo), and finally by Antonio's arrival and his curse (Act 2 Finale). In fact, Pierotto's voice virtually disappears from the *musical* action of *Linda di Chamounix* (unlike the theme of his *ballata*); this

Ex. 3.6. (*cont.*)

action is brought to a forceful conclusion by Carlo's voice instead, which becomes the subject of the opera's last musical number. Carolyn Abbate memorably describes the effect of a similar trajectory in Snow White's wishing-well song from Walt Disney's *Snow White*, in which an echo voice, playing Adalgisa to Snow White's Norma (Abbate's formulation), sings with her a third below. Towards the end of the song 'the Prince appears out of nowhere, as if conjured up by the impossible duet. By singing a final *"today"* back to the real Snow White, he ends the vertiginous play of female voices with a firm masculine hand'.[90] A firm masculine voice, rather, and in *Linda* doubly masculine, in fact, keeping in mind not only the female sound of Pierotto's voice, but also the gender ambiguity of a woman playing a boy vis-à-vis the unambiguous masculinity of a man playing an adult male.

In this sense, *Linda* seems characteristically suspended between the past of those lullaby-like parallel thirds and the future of the sexually charged tenor voice, whose appeal will surpass anything that another female voice can offer Italian opera for the rest of the century. On the one hand, Verdi will seldom make two women sing together, let alone arrange them in parallel thirds: the few bars in which Ulrica and Amelia attempt something of the sort in the Act 1 trio of *Un ballo in maschera* are precisely part of a trio with the tenor Riccardo. On the other, it is difficult to imagine the mature Verdi not taking advantage of the situation at the end of Act 2 for a full-blown father–daughter duet – another instance of the distance between his dramaturgy and Donizetti's, who is more interested in the explicit erotisation of the sex-charged tenor voice than in the implicit erotisation of the power-charged baritone one at the centre of Verdi's musical theatre.[91] Similarly, the parallel thirds still appear in *Linda*; but they do so only to be constructed as a remnant of the old familial order, from which Linda frees herself by invoking the intervention of Carlo's voice and, more, of their cabaletta theme, whose symbolic meaning is closely connected with its evolution in the course of the opera.

After its threefold repetition in the Act 1 duet, this theme resurfaces, truncated, during Linda's mad scene, and she sings its second half in Act 3, before Carlo presents it in its entirety at the climax of the last scene. 'A consolarmi affrettisi' never comes back without its text: at first 'unheard', it begins to acquire phenomenal status once Linda starts singing fragments of it in her madness, and it fully becomes stage music when Carlo offers it to her in the last scene. Finally, Linda never sings the *ballata*, only hears it, while she sings the two occurrences of the cabaletta before the last one. In previous dream or mad scenes – in *Lucia di Lammermoor*, *I Puritani* and *La sonnambula*, for example, all influential points of comparison in the authors' and audiences' minds – fragments of 'unheard' music are perceived only by the deranged heroine, and 'phenomenal' music remains so throughout the score. But 'A consolarmi affrettisi' makes a complete journey from one status to the other: in the last scene all the characters on stage hear Carlo sing it. They cannot understand its power, however, since they are not aware of its story and its meaning for Linda – only Pierotto, who has heard her repeating it many times during their return to Chamonix, knows that this music has been haunting Linda, but cannot possibly fathom why.[92] What is most surprising is that Carlo seems to understand perfectly what Linda is referring to when she asks him to repeat the 'caro accento', even though he has never been informed that Linda has been singing it over and over again.

The psychoanalytic implications of this fact are important. Carlo knows that there is a privileged point of entrance into Linda's unconscious, he is aware that he can cure Linda's mind with his voice and reconstitute her split subjectivity – that is, he knows he owns the phallus. While this subject position is not contemplated in Lacan's psychoanalytic landscape, Rossi and Donizetti, and with them an entire culture, believed it possible. From a feminist point of view, it is relevant that in *Linda di Chamounix* this subject position is gendered masculine – an observation not necessarily true in the case of *Lucia di Lammermoor*, *I Puritani* or *La sonnambula*. Generally speaking, however, the nineteenth century agreed with *Linda*, and granted to women, specifically to virgins, nothing but the ears of understanding.

A hundred and sixty years after *Linda*'s first appearance we may want to distance ourselves from this resolute construction of woman as the hearing subject *par excellence*. By way of conclusion, however, I would like to linger for a moment on the resulting alignment of Linda with the audience of opera, which occupies the hearing position in the theatre. In this sense, the question I have prominently asked above – 'what does Linda actually hear?' – can be given a different and perhaps unexpected answer. The opposite trajectories of the *ballata* and the cabaletta, and the latter's final triumph as the only successful therapeutic treatment for Linda, can be interpreted as the triumph of what could be called the 'true' music of opera, the very reason of its existence. What would be 'real' music in 'real' life – or in a play – is here staged as temporary, ineffectual and ultimately 'fake'. The victory of 'A consolarmi affrettisi' as the provider of *jouissance* metonymically promotes the genre of opera as the only possible cause of *jouissance*.[93] Echoing Sade I would say that, because of its music, opera gives the utmost pleasure and leaves the strongest impressions. In Lacanian terms (and paraphrasing a set of possible definitions of the gaze and the voice by Fink), opera brings us as close as possible to experiencing our unconscious; it is the phantasmatic partner that ever arouses our desire; it belongs to the real, and therefore resists imaginarisation and symbolisation, and yet is closely related to our most important experiences of pleasure and pain, excitement and disappointment, thrill and horror. Opera resists analytic action, but is related to a *jouissance* that defines our very being.[94] Obliquely and reticently, Donizetti seems to be saying that Linda, the innocent Alpine virgin, is *us*, opera's audience: we, like Linda, are in search of an aural penetration that will (re)constitute us as subjects – we want the phallus. We may or may not like this position, take pleasure in it or not; but if we listen to *Linda di Chamounix* and believe what we hear, we have no choice but to repeat 'Dillo! dillo!' – '*Sing it! Sing it!*' – and to succumb to the aural power that our cry has evoked.

The critical literature on Verdi's *Luisa Miller* (Naples, Teatro San Carlo, 1849) has paid only scant attention to the transfer of location from the *Residenzstadt* of Schiller's play *Kabale und Liebe*, the opera's source, to the Tyrol. David Kimbell has discussed it briefly as an attempt to 'draw Schiller's political sting'.[1] Piero Weiss has commented more extensively on the opera's 'woodsy Tyrolean setting', faulting the librettist Salvadore Cammarano in the following terms: 'Cammarano mercilessly cut down Schiller's drama, not simply to the requirements of a libretto, but to those of a conventional tragedy [. . .] [and] went still further: he transferred the locale from town to country (for the sake of the choruses, as he explained more than once), thus depriving the drama of its almost claustrophobic menace'.[2] For Alessandro Roccatagliati, who has emphasised the political problems posed by Schiller's text and the librettist's drastic refashioning, the change of locale was specifically not a matter of ambience: the invention of what he calls 'a fabulous Tyrol', removed by a hundred and fifty years from Schiller's late eighteenth century, was a pre-emptive move against anticipated censorial interventions.[3]

It seems that the idea of moving the action to the Alps was Cammarano's. Never discussed in the extensive correspondence between composer and poet, the new setting first appeared in the prose draft (*programma* or *progetto*) that Cammarano sent Verdi on 3 May 1849.[4] In a later letter to Verdi (11 June 1849) Cammarano asserted that moving the action to a village had been 'most useful to a subject where, at first sight, finding a role for the chorus seemed not so much difficult as impossible'.[5] Cammarano had of course been able to make room for the chorus in many librettos he had written before *Luisa* without opting for a village. But, even if we grant that the move from a city to a village was useful in practical terms, why a village in the Tyrol rather than in Saxony or the Rhineland? Why the ascent to the Alps? In this chapter I will argue that the opera's location in a Tyrolean village, far from being a trivial detail, lies at the core of *Luisa Miller*'s dramaturgy and meaning. What is more, I will suggest that Verdi and Cammarano, in search of inspiration for the comparative novelty of projecting an Alpine ambience in *Luisa Miller*, embarked on an excursion to the operatic Alps which had profound effects on the final product, influencing not only the dramaturgy of the opera, but also its wider cultural, ideological and even political meanings.

VIRGINAL ENTRANCES

The sound world of *La sonnambula* and *Linda di Chamounix*, not to mention their idyllic ambience and happy endings, seems very far from early Verdi. And yet it is precisely to Bellini's and Donizetti's operas that Verdi and Cammarano turned for the initial number of *Luisa Miller*. Significantly, it is in the *introduzioni* of these works that the Alpine world and the bodily purity of the protagonists are most explicitly connected.

La sonnambula, Act 1, scenes 1–2

> *Piazza d'un Villaggio. Da un lato un'osteria, dall'altro un mulino, in fondo colline praticabili.*
>
> *All'alzarsi del sipario odonsi da lungi suoni pastorali e voci lontane che gridano*: viva Amina. *Sono gli abitanti del villaggio che vengono a festeggiare gli sponsali di lei.* [. . .]
>
> *Durante il colloquio di Lisa e Alessio, i suoni si son fatti più vicini, e più forti le acclamazioni.*
>
> *Scendono dalle colline villani e villanelle, tutti vestiti da festa, con stromenti villerecci e canestri di fiori – Giungono al piano.* [. . .]

ALESSIO E CORO
In Elvezia non v'ha rosa
    Fresca e cara al par d'Amina:
    È una stella mattutina,
    Tutta luce, tutta amor.

Ma pudica, ma ritrosa,
  Quanto è vaga, quanto è bella:
  È innocente tortorella,
  È l'emblema del candor.[6]

A village square. On one side, a tavern, on the other a mill, in the background hills.
  As the curtain rises, pastoral music is heard, and distant voices shouting:
  'Long live Amina'. It is the villagers, coming to celebrate her nuptials. [. . .]
  During the conversation between Lisa and Alessio, the music comes nearer, and
  the acclamations grow louder. Men and women of the village descend from the
  hills, dressed in their Sunday best, with rustic musical instruments and
  baskets of flowers. They reach the level of the stage. [. . .]

ALESSIO AND CHORUS: In Switzerland there is no rose fresher and
  dearer than Amina: she is a morning star, all brightness and all love.
  But modest and reserved as she is charming and beautiful: she is an
  innocent turtle dove, she is the emblem of purity.

Linda di Chamounix, Act 1, scene 1

L'aurora, il sole va poi gradatamente illuminando la scena. Interno d'una
  cascina. A destra verso il fondo la porta d'una stanza. Una rustica sedia
  a bracciuoli, vicina. Una panca, qualche sedia. Il prospetto è aperto, e da
  esso scorgesi un sito pittoresco sulle montagne di Savoja, e parte del
  villaggio. Una chiesa sull'alto.
Si odono gli ultimi tocchi d'una campana. Varie voci da opposte parti, che si
  ascoltano: si vedono poi uomini, donne, fanciulli avviarsi al tempio, poi
  Maddalena, indi Antonio.

CORO
Presti! al tempio! Delle preci
Diè il segnal la sacra squilla!
Già del Sol vivo scintilla
Sulle cime il primo raggio,
Già dal Ciel fausto viaggio
Cominciamo ad implorar.
La speranza, ed il coraggio
Non potranno vacillar.

Terminato il coro apresi la porta della stanza a destra, e vi esce pian piano
  Maddalena, che si ferma sulla soglia, guardando ancor dentro.

MADDALENA
Linda, mia dolce figlia! Tu nel sonno
Dell'innocenza ancora giaci – a lungo
In assiduo lavoro
Provvida per noi vegliasti, e lieti
Saranno i sogni tuoi. (*chiude la stanza*)[7]

*It is dawn; the sun gradually illuminates the stage. The interior of a farmhouse.
On the right, towards the back, the door of another room. In the foreground
a rustic wooden armchair. A bench, some chairs. The back wall opens upon
a picturesque tableau of the Savoy mountains and part of the village. Above,
a church. The last chimes of a bell are heard, and various voices from
different sides, listening to each other: men, women and children are seen
going to church, then Maddalena, eventually Antonio.*

CHORUS: Let us hasten to the temple. The sound of the church bell has
given the signal for prayers. The first rays of the sun are now
sparkling on the mountain tops: let us begin to implore Heaven for a
safe journey. Our hope and courage cannot vacillate.

*After the chorus, the door on the right opens and Maddalena comes out slowly and
softly: she stops on the doorstep and looks back into the room.*

MADDALENA: Linda, my beloved child! You are still sleeping the sleep
of innocence. You prolonged your dutiful waking hours in assiduous
labour for your parents, and may pleasant dreams lull you to rest.
(*She closes the door.*)

In both texts the purity of the air and the clarity of the skies become
emblems of Amina's and Linda's spotless virginity, which goes hand
in hand with their simple religious faith and boundless love for their
parents – Teresa's mill and the interior view of Linda's farmhouse
point to the family as a central element in the construction of both
heroines. Amina's purity is praised at length by the chorus, with
particular emphasis on metaphors of light and whiteness, while
Linda's innocence is indirectly associated with the bright Alpine
dawn evoked by the chorus by Maddalena's description of Linda's
sleep as 'the sleep of innocence'.

Similar observations can be made on a musical level. *La sonnam-bula* begins with an *introduzione* in three parts: a short opening chorus, Lisa's one-movement aria followed by a reprise of the chorus, and a long concluding choral passage. Even before the curtain opens the brief orchestral introduction suggests a rustic setting by virtue of its 6/8 metre,[8] its instrumentation – French horns and solo clarinet – and its echo effects between the on-stage band and the pit orchestra. The two choruses 'Viva Amina' and 'In Elvezia non v'ha rosa' manifest such rustic traits as a vocalisation on a simple 'Ah', melodies with a limited range and repetitive rhythms, and a harmonic language that seldom ventures beyond tonic and dominant triads. The simplest gesture is the renunciation of language altogether, the 'la la la la' that ends the first chorus. The opening of *Linda* is different from that in *La sonnambula*, but the essential rustic feeling is conveyed through the use of the same musical devices. The full-scale overture opens with a pastoral introductory Larghetto in 6/8 played by muted strings. When the curtain rises, a bell calls the village people to Mass; they answer from different sides with a simple melody, pastoral-flavoured by virtue of the repeated grace note on the downbeat 6/4 chord and the extended pedal points. Seeing the mountain settings in the stage decorations, audiences would have associated these generically rustic stylistic features with an Alpine ambience. Innocence is therefore not only a defining emotional and bodily characteristic of the operas' protagonists: it is also a trait of the musical language 'spoken' in these Alpine locations, whose inhabitants know only simple melodies and basic harmonies. At least initially, in Switzerland and in Chamonix *tout se tient*: heart and body sing the same simple song.

Before December 1849, when *Luisa Miller* was premièred, *La sonnambula* had been performed at the Teatro San Carlo in five seasons. *Linda* had proved initially more popular, being staged in four out of the eight seasons following its *prima assoluta*, while other Neapolitan theatres had ensured that the opera was seen there every year between 1843 and 1849.[9] In the 1849 revival at the San Carlo (7 performances, the first on 10 July), Eugenia Tadolini and Felice

Varesi appeared as Linda and Antonio (roles they had created), Teresa Salandri sang Pierotto, Settimio Malvezzi Carlo, and Antonio Selva Il Marchese di Boisfleury. A few months later in the same theatre Salandri was Federica, Malvezzi Rodolfo, and Selva Count Walter in the première of *Luisa*.[10] Cammarano, who was resident poet and stage director at the San Carlo from 1834 until his death in 1852, was responsible for numerous revivals of both operas as well as for the first production of *Luisa*.[11]

Cammarano's stage directions for the first scene of *Luisa Miller* and the text of the opening chorus read as follows:

> *Ameno villaggio: da un lato la modesta casa di Miller, dall'altro rustico tempietto; in lontanza, ed a traverso degli alberi, le cime del castello di Walter.*
>
> *Un'alba limpidissima di primavera è sull'orizzonte: gli abitanti del villaggio si adunano per festeggiare il dì natalizio di Luisa – Laura è fra dessi.*
>
> CORO E LAURA
> Ti desta o Luisa, regina de' cori;
>   I monti già lambe un riso di luce:
>   D'un giorno sì lieto insiem con gli albori
>   Qui dolce amistade a te ne conduce.
>   Leggiadra è quest'alba sorgente in Aprile,
>   Ma come il tuo viso leggiadra non è:
> È pura, soave quest'aura gentile,
>   Pur meno è soave, men pura di te.[12]

> *A picturesque village. On one side Miller's humble dwelling, on the other a little country church. In the distance, through the trees, rise the towers of Count Walter's castle. A crystal-clear spring day is dawning on the horizon; the villagers are gathering to celebrate Luisa's birthday. Laura is among them.*
>
> LAURA, VILLAGERS: Awake, Luisa, queen of our hearts; the smiling sunlight is already brushing the top of the mountains with its lips: together with the dawn of such a joyful day, sweet friendship leads us to you. Fair is this dawn rising in April, but not as fair as your face; this gentle breeze is pure and sweet, yet less sweet, less pure than you.

At the end of the *introduzione* 'the church bell rings' ('odesi la sacra squilla') and everybody enters into the church singing: 'Did you hear? The bells are ringing: let us go, Heaven invites us' ('Udiste? I bronzi squillano: andiam, ne invita il ciel').

The similarities between this text and the opening scenes of *La sonnambula* and *Linda* are striking. As in Bellini's and Donizetti's works, the initial stage direction defines not only a mountain setting, but also the social and moral world of the heroine, with Miller's house joining Teresa's mill and Antonio's farm in symbolising the power of the family in a rural, low-class society. In *Linda* and *Luisa* the church and the crystal-clear Alpine dawn are also emphasised in the sung text, the connection made explicit by the recurring alliteration of 'sacra squilla'. In both operas the first rays of the sun shine on the mountain tops, while hope and courage cannot vacillate for both Savoyards and Tyroleans – their Rousseauvian state of nature now transformed into a Christian state of faith, whose consequence is the natural capacity to feel pity before and above rationality. Similarly, Bellini's and Verdi's heroines are subjected to the same kind of metaphors by the laudatory chorus, with emphasis placed on images of light and whiteness: 'light' and 'candour' in *La sonnambula*, 'smiling sunlight' and 'dawn' ('albori', 'alba') in *Luisa*.[13] Verdi initially imagined that his opera would be called *Amore e raggiro* (*Love and Intrigue*, i.e., *Kabale und Liebe*), but the change of title to *Luisa Miller* shifted the focus from the abstract situation to the heroine herself. From the very first line of the opening chorus Luisa is unmistakably the protagonist: her social, moral and emotional situation constitutes the topic of the *introduzione* – which in this case is literally an introduction. *Luisa Miller* is an opera about Luisa Miller very much as *La sonnambula* is an opera about Amina and *Linda di Chamounix* about Linda.

Inasmuch as moving the action to the Tyrolean Alps seems to have been Cammarano's idea, he must be credited with the idea of connecting the opera with *La sonnambula* and *Linda di Chamounix*, the most representative works of the Alpine virgin tradition, and therefore with transforming *Amore e raggiro* into *Luisa Miller*. Did

Verdi follow his lead? Julian Budden has noted that *Luisa's introdu-zione* represents an idyllic country scene similar to those from *La sonnambula* or *Linda*.[14] The opening gesture, which sounds like a *ranz des vaches*, is given to the clarinet – the solo clarinet also plays a prominent part at the beginning of *La sonnambula*. As in *La sonnam-bula*, the opening chorus is in G major and in 6/8, although Verdi's instrumentation is more complex than Bellini's, especially in the second stanza of the chorus, with its flute and clarinet arpeggios.

As for Donizetti's work, *Linda's sortita* (entrance piece), 'O luce di quest'anima', is not the usual double aria with slow movement and cabaletta – the kind that had been given to Amina – but a peculiar piece constructed like a cabaletta but not preceded by a slow move-ment. The text, a double quatrain of *settenari* rhyming ABBC DEEC, is sung twice to the same music, rhythmically similar to a *tyrolienne* and with prominent use of staccato in the voice.[15] Luisa's *cavatina* 'Lo vidi, e il primo palpito', a double quatrain of *settenari* rhyming ABBC DEEC (exactly as in *Linda*),[16] seems to be a manipu-lation of Donizetti's structure. The second half of the melody, which exhausts the text, avoids tonic closure, cadencing on V in-stead; the transition back to the tonic is accomplished by a vocal cadenza, which, however, cadences not into the expected ritornello, but into a *Linda*-like repetition of the text and the melody, albeit with the substitution of a prominently virtuosic conclusion for the second half. The similarity between the two pieces is strengthened by Luisa's 'canto staccato', which closely resembles Linda's vocal style (Ex. 4.1 and 4.2).[17]

A further relationship can be established between Linda's and Luisa's *sortite* and the cabaletta of Amina's *cavatina*, the Moderato 'Sovra il sen la man mi posa'.[18] 'Canto staccato' seems again a fitting description of this melody's style, again employed by a young Alpine virgin who sings of her happy love. Why did Bellini, Donizetti and Verdi all employ a staccato vocal style for the first arias of these characters? The answer is in their texts, at least in the cases of *La sonnambula* and *Luisa Miller*. Amina and Luisa recognise that they are happily in love by the fact that their hearts palpitate:

AMINA
Sovra il sen la man mi posa,
Palpitar, balzar lo senti:
Egli è il cor che i suoi contenti
Non ha forza a sostener.

Put your hand on my bosom, feel how it palpitates and throbs: it is my heart, that does not have the strength to sustain its happiness.

LUISA
Lo vidi, e il primo palpito
Il cor sentì d'amore:
Mi vide appena, e il core
Balzò del mio fedel.

I saw him, and my heart felt its first palpitation of love; as soon as my faithful lover saw me, his heart started to throb.

The melodies attached to these texts try to embody the palpitations of the characters' hearts by adopting a predominantly staccato articulation. Amina alternates stepwise melodic motion with wide leaps, fittingly reserving the widest one, an octave, on 'balzar' (literally 'to leap') (Ex. 4.3). Luisa is the heroine who employs staccato most consistently, even if her only significant wide leap is, tellingly, on 'balzò'. Linda's heart does not palpitate so much as it sighs and desires. By 1842, however, *La sonnambula* already constituted a powerful example of which kind of vocal style was appropriate for a young Alpine virgin singing happily about her love, and Donizetti did not simply follow this example slavishly; rather he built on it: Linda's 'O luce di quest'anima' is the aria for which the term 'staccato' can be employed most meaningfully.[19] By the time of *Luisa Miller*, Amina's and Linda's entrance arias had coalesced into a dramatic and musical topos that linked innocence, hopes of happiness in love, a bright Alpine morning and 'canto staccato'.[20]

Connecting *Luisa Miller* with *La sonnambula* and *Linda* has shown revealing similarities in the ways these operas' heroines are introduced and initially characterised. If we take into account how the characters are developed later in the opera, however, this comparative

Ex. 4.1. Verdi, *Luisa Miller*, Act 1: Luisa's *cavatina*.

Ex. 4.2. Donizetti, *Linda di Chamounix*, Act 1: Linda's *cavatina*.

Ex. 4.3. Bellini, *La sonnambula*, Act 1: Amina's *cavatina*, cabaletta.

approach points in a different direction: Luisa's fate is famously different from Linda's and Amina's. The alliance between Count Walter, who opposes her reciprocated love for his son Rodolfo, and Wurm, who wants her for himself, proves fatal to both the heroine and her lover, who, believing Luisa unfaithful, poisons her and himself, their agonies just long enough for Luisa to reveal her innocence. It is perhaps only on the level of the characters, and specifically in light of the heroine's fate, that the modelling of the beginning of *Luisa* on *La sonnambula* and *Linda* reveals its dramaturgical function. In other words, one of the reasons for which Cammarano and Verdi established an initial connection between *Luisa* and Bellini's and Donizetti's operas was to break that connection later in the opera: the expectations set up by the Alpine idyll are left unfulfilled, and the plot shifts unexpectedly towards tragedy. *Luisa* is *La sonnambula* or *Linda* run amok. But why does *Luisa* run amok? Why did Verdi and Cammarano want to break the intertextual connection they had established between their opera and *La sonnambula* and *Linda*? In order to answer these questions, the context in which I have initially placed *Luisa* and its intertextual references must be broadened, addressing directly issues of genre, and specifically the generic position of Alpine virgin operas. The question of genre will in turn require discussion of the literary sources of these operas, since they crucially influenced these operas' dramaturgy.

THE MELODRAMATIC MORALITY OF
OPERA SEMISERIA

Alpine virgin operas belong almost exclusively to the nineteenth-century Italian genre of *opera semiseria*. Evidence from the reception history of *La sonnambula* and *Linda di Chamounix* highlights their pastoral setting and sentimental tone as crucial factors in determining the genre of these works.[21] To take one illustrious example, in a letter to Antonio Somma dating from the period of their collaboration on the *Re Lear* project, Verdi wrote: 'I just want to let you know that I would like not a plot that requires elaborate scenic effects, but a sentimental one, a kind of *Sonnambula* or *Linda*, but distancing [ourselves] from that genre, because it is already known'.[22] The composer explained what he meant by 'sentimental' in another letter to Somma: 'I told you that I would have liked to compose a quiet, simple, tender drama: a kind of *Sonnambula* without being an

imitation of *Sonnambula*'.[23] The designation of *La sonnambula* and
Linda as belonging to the sentimental genre, frequent in reviews of
their performances, can be explained by the emphasis they give to
the family and to the emotions harboured within it.[24]

Besides the sentimental, the other characteristic most often mentioned in conjunction with Alpine virgin operas was their pastoral
ambience. Italian reviewers of a literary bent rarely missed an opportunity to refer to the two most famous *exempla* of Italian pastoral
poetry, Tasso's *Aminta* and Guarini's *Il pastor fido*.[25] Closer to home,
the name that appeared most frequently as the pastoral ancestor of
La sonnambula and *Linda* was Paisiello's *Nina*. Early commentators
generally classified these works as belonging to the 'mezzo carattere'
genre, the best example of which was *La gazza ladra*, mentioned time
and again in the reviews as the standard-setter. In the first half of the
century the most common designation for these 'mezzo carattere'
works was 'opera semiseria'. This term did not begin to appear with
consistency until the second decade – previous terms included
'(melo)dramma sentimentale', 'dramma serio-giocoso', and, especially if the work was in one act, 'farsa sentimentale'. *La sonnambula*
was called simply 'melodramma' in the first libretto. Eventually,
however, the adjective 'semiseria' came to overshadow all other
terms and has crystallised in music-historical writings as the generic
designation of *La sonnambula*, *Linda* and the vast majority of Alpine
virgin operas.

Virtually all these operas are based on French dramatic productions of the early nineteenth century known as 'Parisian boulevard
theatre'. This category includes spoken dramas, *mélodrames*, panto-
mimes, vaudevilles and all the works normally associated with
Parisian theatres other than those mainly devoted to operatic genres
(the Opéra, the Opéra-Comique and the Théâtre-Italien) and the two
main stages for spoken plays (the Comédie Française and the
Odéon). In particular, *mélodrame*, which has come to epitomise
French popular theatre of the time, provided the sources for a
large majority of *opere semiserie*. Even when this was not the case,
the original sources – *opéras comiques* or, more rarely, novels – betray

the influence of *mélodrame*'s modes of communication. This genre's dramaturgy thus acted as a filter between an original text and its operatic incarnation. This is especially true in the case of *opéra comique*, from which several *semiserie* are derived. In 1832 Guilbert de Pixérécourt, the most representative author of *mélodrames*, commented on the links between the two French genres: while retrospectively finding in *opéra comique* a precedent for *mélodrame*, he pointed to the latter as a regulating, codifying force, one that coalesced elements already present in *opéras comiques* into genre-defining features.[26] Therefore an investigation of the dramaturgy and ideology of *mélodrame* might help explain their counterparts in *semiseria*.[27]

In his preface to the collected works of Pixérécourt, Charles Nodier wrote:

> It is certain that, in the circumstances in which it came into being, *mélodrame* was a necessity. The people had recently played out in the streets and public squares the grandest drama in history. Everybody had acted in this blood-drenched play, everybody had been a soldier, or a revolutionary, or an outlaw. These solemn spectators, who had smelled gunpowder and blood, needed emotions equal to those of which the return of order had deprived them. [. . .] In stories whose conduct was always new, but whose outcome was always the same, these spectators needed to be reminded of that great lesson to which all philosophical doctrines, based on all religions, come down: even on earth, virtue is always rewarded, crime is always punished. Let no one be fooled: *mélodrame* was no small thing; it was the morality of the revolution![28]

Mélodrame was thus charged with the symbolic redemption of the Revolution and, more specifically, of the execution of the King, the parricide *par excellence*. It could perform this cultural work through its obsessively recurrent plot structure and strictly codified characters: the greedy and hypocritical villain; the virtuous and courageous hero; his comically common-sensical servant or sidekick; the young heroine, victim of the lustful attentions of the villain, frequently abducted but always remaining pure and innocent; and her father, unjustly persecuted but, thanks to the hero, eventually reunited with his daughter and reinstated in his rightful position.[29]

Mélodrame went well beyond the limits of a didactic genre, assuming a foundational, symbolically constitutive role: it was the site where a kind of ideal reconciliation of society could take place, and in which the bourgeoisie constructed itself as the totality of the nation. The presence of the comic servant, representative of the lower classes, assured this totality and at the same time placed these classes in a firmly subordinate role: in a reconciled society evil can only derive from the moral failings of individuals, never from social injustice. The unity of society was mirrored in the unity of discourse, never dialectic or even dialogic, but only exclamatory or assertive: in Anne Ubersfeld's words, 'the word of *mélodrame* answers itself with an echo'.[30]

The most effective and original element of the poetics of *mélodrame*, however, is its reliance on the visual as the crucial device for capturing the audience's attention and emotional participation. The central concept here is that of 'tableau', defined by Diderot, its first theorist, in his *Entretiens sur 'Le Fils naturel'* (1757), as 'a disposition of the characters on stage so natural and true that, if faithfully rendered by a painter on canvas, it would please me'.[31] Clearer, and closer to our concerns, is the description given in the parodic *Traité du mélodrame* (1817):

> At the end of each act, one must make sure to bring all the characters together in a group, and to place each of them in the attitude that corresponds to the situation of their souls. For example: sorrow will place a hand on its forehead; despair will tear out its hair, and joy will kick a leg in the air. This general perspective is called *tableau*. It is clear how agreeable it is for the spectator to comprehend at a glance the moral state of each character.[32]

According to Pierre Frantz, Pixérécourt's extended use of the *tableau* not only at the end of the play and each act, but also within acts, constructs a dramaturgy of the suspensive pause: the *tableau's* codification and ritualisation respond to a lack of theatrical experience in *mélodrame's* popular audience. This dramatic practice hides an inherent paradox: the tableau is made up of gestures, but these gestures are fixed, immobilised.[33] It is precisely to this paradox, however, that the *tableau* owes its theatrical impact, an impact based not on mimetic illusion, but on the power of signification that gestures acquire when they become fixed. In Barthes's memorable words:

> The (pictorial, theatrical, literary) *tableau* is a pure projection, sharp-edged, incorruptible, irreversible, which banishes into nothingness everything around it, which is therefore unnamed, and promotes to the status of essence, to light, to sight, everything it brings into its field; this demiurgic discrimination implies a high level of thought: the tableau is intellectual, it has something (moral, social) to say, but it also says that it knows *how* this must be said; it is at once significative and propaedeutic, impressive and reflexive, moving and conscious of the means of emotion.[34]

The strong emotional response that the *tableau* awakens in the public does not impede the deciphering of the precise social and moral message at the heart of *mélodrame*: on the contrary, it encourages it, making its impact stronger. This unambiguous deciphering becomes possible within the immutable dramatic rules of *mélodrame* and its highly ritualised performance.[35]

It is especially important that the *tableau* was theorised by Diderot and other prominent authors associated with the creation of bourgeois drama, such as Mercier and Beaumarchais. In their intention, bourgeois drama – in French simply called 'drame', or 'genre sérieux' – was to be a third genre that would break the conventions of tragedy and comedy. As Stefano Castelvecchi has argued, the *genre sérieux* acted as stimulus and model for late-eighteenth-century sentimental opera.[36] At the same time, the visual dramaturgy explored in the *genre sérieux* constitutes the direct antecedent to its employment in *mélodrame*.

How, then, does the influence of *mélodrame* differentiate *opera semiseria* from its sentimental predecessor? Castelvecchi has noted the absence of narrative complexity in sentimental opera, a trait shared by much contemporary sentimental literature and theatre, and especially by examples of the *genre sérieux*.[37] Neither sentimental opera nor *drame ever became massively popular genres, however, while hundreds of mélodrames were produced on Parisian stages of the early decades of the new century. If the characters were fixed and the happy outcome was known in advance, how did each mélodrame manage to engage the interest of its audience? On a dramaturgical level, the answer is twofold: first, a complicated plot, full of unexpected turns and coups de théâtre. Second, novelty of setting and a painstaking attention to what at the time was referred to as couleur locale.[38]*

Both *mélodrame* and *opera semiseria* often featured exotic ambiences in the broad sense of the term: ambiences different from the urban environment in which audiences lived. Even if the countryside of the pastoral tradition was still found, as in Caignez's *La Pie voleuse ou La Servante de Palaiseau* and *La gazza ladra*, the search for more unusual, picturesque locales took the characters to 'remote' European countries: places like Ireland (Delamarre's *Adelson et Salvini* and Bellini's *Adelson e Salvini*), Scotland (Ducange's *La Fiancée de Lammermoor* and Carafa's *Le nozze di Lammermoor*), Russia (Pixérécourt's *La Fille de l'exilé ou Huit mois en deux heures* and Donizetti's *Otto mesi in due ore*), or Spain (the island of Majorca in Pixérécourt's *La Citerne* and Donizetti's *Chiara e Serafina*), and beyond (Pixérécourt's *Robinson Crusoe* or Donizetti's *Il furioso all'isola di San Domingo*).[39] The characters of *mélodrame* and *semiseria* went not only further, but also higher, of course: up to the mountains, most often the Alps.

As a consequence of this broadening of the horizon, the *mise en scène* of *mélodrame* acquired an importance unprecedented in previous theatrical genres, even if its theoretical justification dates once again from the second half of the eighteenth century, generally under the rubric of 'costume'.[40] If, on the chronological level, 'costume' is based on a new awareness that owes much to recent developments in the theory and practice of historical writing, it is on the geographical level that the fantasy of the *metteur en scène* is free to 'invent truth', to use Verdi's famous words. The illusion of truth, however, requires specificity and precision, and the beginning of the century saw the publication of several treatises on the technique and art of the *mise en scène*.[41] Pixérécourt himself controlled all aspects of the staging of his *pièces*, going as far as to sketch the stage designs himself.[42]

In his classic study of *mélodrame* and its influence on the nine-teenth-century novel, Peter Brooks argues that pantomime became an essential element of the visual dramaturgy of the *genre sérieux* first, and of *mélodrame* later, thanks to the theorisation of gesture as the language of nature, the instinctual language of primal reactions and emotions.[43] Pierre Frantz has shown, however, that the promin-ence of pantomime in the *genre sérieux* derives also from the necessity of integrating this acting style into the aesthetics of the *tableau*. Diderot theorised and systematised the new performing style of such actors as Garrick and Mlle Clairon, making it an essential factor towards the goal of involving the public emotionally, especially its less literate members.[44] Once again, *mélodrame* radicalises the eighteenth-century heritage.

The influence of the dramaturgy of *mélodrame* on *semiseria* emerges in the latter's extended pantomimic scenes, not normally found in serious or comic operas. To mention one of the most striking examples (besides Linda's arrival at Chamonix already dis-cussed in chapter 3), in Act 2 of Donizetti's *Otto mesi in due ore* the appearance of the protagonist Elisabetta on a mountain and her descent to the bank of the river downstage occupy a separate number in the autograph score, called 'Elisabetta's descent' ('discesa di Elisabetta'). The composer specifies that 'the pantomime must be executed in time with the music' ('la pantomima va espressa a tempo di musica'), and carefully synchronises the movements of the heroine with the succession of contrasting melodic fragments and harmonic nonsequiturs that characterise the orchestral part.[45]

Pantomime, the recurrent use of *tableaux*, and attention to *mise en scène* and *couleur locale* constitute the central factors in what Brooks has called *mélodrame*'s 'aesthetics of muteness', its reliance on means of signification other than verbal language. As theorised by Diderot, this aesthetics owes much to the philosophical reflection on the origin of languages that Rousseau was elaborating at the same time. What is more, Diderot's and Rousseau's aspirations towards a 'natural' form of communication, which became a staple of the dramaturgy of *mélodrame*, was connected to the search for Rousseauvian 'natural' spaces, evident in the geographical setting of many representatives of the genre.

This 'naturalness' stood in opposition to the 'artificiality' not only of the traditional dramatic genres of tragedy and comedy, but also of the discursive and social spaces in which both author and audience found themselves enclosed in everyday life. The visual dramaturgy of *mélodrame* can be seen as 'an effort to recover on the stage something like the mythical primal language, a language of presence, purity, immediacy'.[46] But the same could be said of *mélodrame*'s geographical expansion, an effort to recover on the stage a mythical Eden, where presence, purity and immediacy are still a reality; where the mythical tale of a united society can still be told; where, according to a contemporary critic, 'crime always appears odious and is always punished, where sincerity triumphs, where innocence is protected by an invincible hand – in sum, where the world is shown not as it is, but as it should be'.[47]

The genealogy of *opera semiseria* in French *mélodrame* fundamentally shaped not only its dramaturgical profile and its choice of settings, therefore, but also its social, moral and ideological meanings. *Mélodrame* first, and *opera semiseria* later, may have been dramaturgically innovative genres, but their dramaturgical innovations were placed at the service of an essentially conservative ideology: showing the world 'as it should be' aligned them with other politically charged aesthetic manifestations of the Restoration. Contradictions abound: ideologically conservative genres such as *mélodrame* and *semiseria* owe some of their most significant dramaturgical features to a potentially revolutionary genre such as *drame*; an essentially bourgeois genre such as *mélodrame* promotes a conservative worldview at a time when the bourgeoisie aspired to political reform, or even revolution. The fact remains, however, that, by the late 1840s, thanks to a significant degree to its melodramatic genealogy, *opera semiseria* promoted a conservative ideology, one of social reconciliation and moral idealism.

By that time *La sonnambula* and *Linda di Chamounix* had attained a classic status, coming close to epitomising the whole genre of *semi-seria*. Establishing an intertextual connection between *Luisa Miller* and these works, therefore, meant placing it within the context of *opera semiseria*. What can *Luisa*'s running amok mean, then, if seen in this context?

THE PROSAIC MODERNITY OF *LUISA MILLER*

One consequence of the Alpine setting of *La sonnambula* and *Linda di Chamounix* was a change in the perception of the time of the action. In nineteenth-century Italian opera contemporary settings were reserved for the comic genre; serious opera required an action involving aristocratic or generally high-class characters and taking place in a past sufficiently removed to be the object of distancing historisation. The generic constraints of *opera seria* seem to have been at least partly valid for *semiseria*, but the latter was able to break the rules by removing the action to some 'other' location, most often the Alps. *La sonnambula* and *Linda* were assumed to take place in contemporary times for lack of other evidence.[48]

In his *Studio sulle opere di Giuseppe Verdi* (1859) Abramo Basevi offered an interesting gloss on *semiseria*'s chronological setting: 'Verdi was the only one in Italy to treat seriously the emotions of characters of our modern and *prosaic* society, as in *La traviata*. *La sonnambula*, *Linda* etc. are similar subjects, but not *prosaic*'.[49] *La sonnambula* and *Linda* expressed 'seriamente' – meaning both 'seriously' and 'in the (semi)serious genre' – the emotions of characters who belonged to modern society. But why were they not prosaic? Because, unlike *La traviata*, they took place in the Alps and their heroines were virgins. I want to suggest that *Luisa Miller* is the crucial link between the 'poetic' modernity of *La sonnambula* and *Linda* and its 'prosaic' incarnation in *La traviata*.[50] The context in which *Luisa*'s prosaic modernity emerges most clearly is that of the politics of French theatrical genres.

Several scholars have advanced the hypothesis that, while in Paris in 1847, Verdi must have seen Schiller's drama in a French adaptation by Alexandre Dumas *père*, premièred at the Théâtre Historique on 11 June.[51] While the composer had already mentioned the text as a possible operatic subject in a letter to Cammarano (probably dated 31 August 1846), seeing a French adaptation of it on the stage in Paris created a potential link with Parisian boulevard theatre. *Kabale und Liebe*, published in 1783, was not, of course, a French *mélodrame* – Schiller called it 'bürgerliches Trauerspiel' – but from the point of view of the 1830s and 1840s it could be read as a text that embedded some elements of French *mélodrame* only to turn them upside down, to show how false they rang to the new Romantic sensibility.[52]

Dumas's adaptation, *Intrigue et amour*, was reviewed by Théophile Gautier in revealing terms:

> It may be easier to have our public accept Shakespearean reality, which related to historical and conventional subjects, than the analogous procedure employed by Schiller for modern subjects. The details of bourgeois life, mixed with situations in which the strongest tragic passions explode, often run the risk of provoking a smile. [. . .] The French public [. . .] has never completely accepted the mixture of the pleasant and the serious; it readily enough accepts the foolish *mélodrame*, or a familiar scene coming on the heels of a tragic one; but strident laughter which all at once gets entwined with the shock of exalted passions has something about it that still astonishes [our audiences].[53]

Mutatis mutandis, Cammarano and Verdi probably saw in Schiller's drama what Gautier had seen, and they surely realised that the potential subversion of the rules that governed French theatrical genres could be transferred into the world of Italian opera once a suitable 'initial' generic context in which to place *Luisa Miller* was found. This genre was that of *semiseria*. If, in both *mélodrame* and *semiseria*, 'crime always appeared odious, and was always punished; sincerity triumphed, innocence was protected by an invincible hand', Verdi and Cammarano were prepared to turn these maxims on their head. For in *Luisa Miller* crime is odious but is not punished (not Walter's, at least); sincerity does not triumph; nor is innocence protected by an invincible hand. The world is shown 'as it is', and not 'as it should be'.

In this context the meaning of Basevi's opposition between 'modern' and 'prosaic' to explain the difference between *La sonnambula* and *Linda* on one hand and *La traviata* on the other can be expanded by aligning it with the opposition elaborated by Pixérécourt in his most important statement of poetics, 'Le mélodrame' (1832), between his own *mélodrame classique* and more recent texts grouped under the name of *mélodrame romantique*. Modern critics have singled out *L'Auberge des Adrets* by Benjamin Antier, Amand Lacoste and Alexis Chapponier, premièred in 1823, as the first example of this new type of *mélodrame*, in which the breaking of the unities of action and place observed by Pixérécourt in his works goes hand in hand with a reversal of these works' moral stance. The heroes of *mélodrame romantique* were no longer *les bons*, but *les méchants*: the character of the bandit Robert Macaire in *L'Auberge des Adrets* became instantly famous, and his first interpreter, Frédérick Lemaître, even co-authored a *pièce* entitled *Robert Macaire* (1834). *Mélodrame*, originally the genre of bourgeois conventions, rapidly became the genre of excess and rebellion.

Pixérécourt felt the need to distinguish between *mélodrame classique* and the new genre, not only on dramaturgical grounds, but on moral ones as well, calling the more recent titles 'monstrous': '[From these works] all conscience is banned; they outrage common sense, morals and modesty in every scene; they are essentially licentious works that cannot but inspire horror of society, by showing it constantly to us from a revolting angle'.[54] One of the main figures in the formation of *mélodrame romantique* was Charles Nodier, who in the 1820s adapted for the Parisian popular stage old Gothic novels that had fallen out of fashion during the preceding twenty years – it was precisely against the late-eighteenth-century *drame noir* and the *genre sombre* that *mélodrame classique* had asserted itself.[55] Seen in the context of French theatrical debates of the 1830s, Basevi's

distinction between 'modern' and 'prosaic' implied a moral judgement on 'our modern society', whose 'prosaicness', that is, ethical
decadence, allowed a prostitute to become the heroine of an opera
(*La traviata*), just as it allowed a bandit to become the hero of a
mélodrame (*L'Auberge des Adrets*).[56]

But there is more to this connection. In the 'Dernières réflexions'
published at the end of his *Théâtre choisi*, Pixérécourt abandoned the
term *mélodrame romantique* and referred simply to 'modern dramas',
thus including in his censure both the 'high' genre of *drame romantique*, *à la* Hugo and Dumas *père*, and the 'low' one of *mélodrame
romantique*.[57] Far from being an invention of the old and embittered
Pixérécourt, the confusion between *drame romantique* and *mélodrame
romantique* was widespread, at least for the first few years after *drames*
started to be performed on Parisian stages, both 'serious' (Dumas
père's *Henri III et sa cour* and Hugo's *Hernani* at the Comédie Française, in 1829 and 1830 respectively) and 'popular' (Dumas *père*'s
Antony and Hugo's *Marion De Lorme* at the Théâtre de la Porte-
Saint-Martin, both in 1831). Hugo's conscious attempt to conquer
the entire Parisian theatrical arena came clearly to the fore in his
double enterprise of 1832, *Le Roi s'amuse* at the Comédie Française
and *Lucrèce Borgia* at the Porte-Saint-Martin (the latter performed in
early 1833).[58]

A review of Milanese performances of *Amore e raggiro* in 1834
explicitly connected Schiller's play with 'the satanic school that, as
it seems, was recently born and is growing in France, thanks to the
works of Hugo, Balzac, and their ilk'.[59] The 'modern' genre of
Romantic drama was morally and dramaturgically at war with
mélodrame classique, and Schiller's text could appear to be so as well,
if seen from the point of view of the French theatrical debates of the
early 1830s. Romantic drama, however, owed to *mélodrame* more than
its authors were willing to acknowledge. One of the levels on which
mélodrame – *classique* first and *romantique* later – influenced Romantic
drama was that of *couleur locale*, or, as Hugo named it, 'le caractéristique'. Hugo's pronouncements on this subject in his well-known
preface to *Cromwell* (1827) are worth quoting:

Exactness in the matter of locality is one of the most essential elements
of reality. The speaking or acting characters are not the only ones who
leave a faithful impression of the facts upon the mind of the spectator.
The place where this or that catastrophe occurred is an incorruptible
and convincing witness to the catastrophe; and the absence of this
species of silent character would render incomplete upon the stage
the grandest scenes of history. [. . .] It goes without saying that if the
poet is to make a selection for a work of this kind (and he certainly
should), he should select what is characteristic rather than what is
beautiful. Not that he ought to manufacture local colour, as they say
today – that is to say, add a few discordant touches here and there
to a whole that is utterly false and conventional. If local colour is to
be applied at all, it should not be on the surface of the drama, but at
its very heart, whence it will spread out of itself, naturally and evenly, to
every corner of the drama, as the sap ascends from the root to the
topmost leaf on the tree.[60]

As discussed above, attention to ambience had been a central tenet
of *mélodrame*: it was often the work of nature (a shipwreck, a storm,
an avalanche) that caused the lovers to meet, or the villain to come
back to the site of his misdeeds, or the heroine to be believed dead.
At the same time, a remote, exotic location had been crucial to the
process of idealisation necessary to show the world 'as it should be',
but, in Paris, was not. Romantic drama, of course, wanted to show
the world 'as it is', and therefore, in Hugo's poetics, attention to
ambience no longer served idealisation; rather, it supported a
heightened perception of what he called 'la réalité'. But *le caractéristique* as a 'silent character' (Hugo) migrated from Pixérécourt to
Hugo, from *La Fille de l'éxilé* to *Lucrèce Borgia*, and set them apart
from French classical theatre (not only Racine and Corneille, but
also, and perhaps especially, Voltaire) and its lesser nineteenth-
century offspring, the *tragédies* of such authors as Etienne de Jouy
or Alexandre Soumet.[61]

By now it should be obvious that I intend to link the concern for
ambience in Romantic drama, Cammarano's move of *Luisa* to Tyrol,
and Verdi's efforts to follow him in musical terms. The Italian

operatic genre in which attention to locale consistently occupied a central place was *semiseria*, specifically its Alpine subset, which, in Hugo's terms, afforded the composer the possibility to place *couleur locale* at the core of the work. Thus *Luisa*'s Alpine setting became the *sine qua non* for the authors' subversive dramaturgical and generic gesture, one that resonated with Hugo's and his fellow Romantics' pronouncements and practice. It is not difficult to imagine Pixéré-court objecting to *Luisa Miller* in terms similar to those he employed against 'modern dramas'.

THE MUSICAL MODERNITY OF *LUISA MILLER*

Establishing an intertextual connection between *Luisa Miller* and its two illustrious Bellinian and Donizettian predecessors required no special boldness on Verdi's part: it was simply a matter of incorporating Bellini's and Donizetti's musical depiction of Alpine innocence in his compositional language as it had developed by 1849. Finding a musical equivalent for his and Cammarano's generic subversion, however, was a harder challenge. What could it mean to compose 'modern' music for a 'modern' drama? How to make music sound 'modern'? A character-based approach proves again especially suited to this line of enquiry. I will turn first to Wurm, one of the opera's two villains.

In a letter of May 1849 Verdi asked Cammarano 'to imbue the latter's [Wurm's] entire character with a certain comical quality that will give greater emphasis to his shrewdness and villainy'.[62] This might seem a puzzling request even in the light of Schiller's partly comic treatment of the Chamberlain von Kalb (whose character Cammarano conflated with Schiller's Wurm to shape the Wurm of the opera), since Verdi eventually portrayed only Wurm's dark side.[63] If we keep in mind the connection between *Luisa* and *semiseria*, however, we can hypothesise that, when writing to Cammarano, Verdi had in mind the usual *buffo* of *semiseria*. When Wurm enters after the *introduzione*, with his violent language and sinister tremolos, the innocent world of the Alpine village starts to look dangerously fragile. The following scene between Wurm and Count Walter, with its strongly chromatic harmony, unisons and trills in the low register, dissipates any remaining doubts about the character's real nature: Wurm is no *buffo*. Still, he was conceived in the shadow of the *buffi* of *semiseria*.[64] The generic tension of *Luisa* is revealed, then, not only by the contradiction between its beginning and its development and conclusion, but also by the discourse surrounding Wurm. Wurm also violates the expectations of his traditional character type. He loses all sense of generic propriety and performs, in effect, a personal subversion of genres. In this sense, the character of Wurm can function as a metonymy for the whole opera, whose *semiseria* ancestry sets its tragic, Romantic conclusion in higher relief.

The musical 'modernity' of Wurm emerges only from the point of view of his compositional history; it is only because we know that Verdi conceived him initially as sharing traits with *buffi* that we can interpret as meaningful the composer's eventual decision *not* to attribute to Wurm any comic quality. But Verdi made compositional decisions that can be interpreted as subverting generic expectations, as modern, even without resorting to compositional process. The most interesting instance is probably Luisa's aria at the beginning of Act 2, and particularly its slow movement, 'Tu puniscimi, o Signore', whose text is printed in the first libretto as follows:

> Tu puniscimi, o Signore,
>   Se t'offesi, e paga io sono,
>   Ma de' barbari al furore
>   Non lasciarmi in abbandono.
>   A scampar da fato estremo
>   Innocente genitor
> Chieggon essi. . . – a dirlo io fremo! –
>   Della figlia il disonor!

Punish me, O Lord, if I offended you, and I will be content, but don't leave me, abandoned, to the fury of the cruel ones. To save an innocent from a mortal fate, they ask – I shudder to say it – his daughter's dishonour!

The first unusual feature of this text is its syntactic complexity. The first two lines contain a conditional sentence ('punish me. . . if I offended you') and an independent clause ('I will be content'), while the second couplet consists of a single independent clause that indicates an opposition to the concept expressed in the first one. The second quatrain is occupied by a single unit, constituted by a subordinate phrase in lines 5–6 and the controlling main clause in lines 7–8; but the latter is interrupted by another independent clause that functions as an aside ('I shudder to say it!').

A rhetorical reading of this text reveals a potentially problematic tension. The image that causes Luisa's lyric outburst, her dishonour – that is, the unwilling sacrifice of her virginity to Wurm – is placed in the final line, a conventional feature of aria texts in nineteenth-century Italian opera. Syntactically, however, this image is weak, since Luisa refers to it in the third person as 'his daughter's dishonour' (no doubt to emphasise the connection with the father), and as the object of somebody else's request ('they ask'), without the emphasis produced by the first- and second-person verbs of the first quatrain. The prayer, stated in the imperative form, has already been heard more forcefully in lines 3–4 ('do not abandon me'), and in a much weightier syntactical and rhetorical context.

Verdi set this text as an Andante agitato in A major. This movement contains the components of a traditional lyric form, but they are separated by interpolated sections and expanded so radically as to render the form barely recognisable. The conventional sections are: phrase a (bb. 3–6); a′, an almost entirely new melody which acts harmonically, however, as a consequent to the preceding antecedent (bb. 7 through the beginning of b. 9, which connects to the end of b. 15 and b. 16); b (bb. 17–20); c (bb. 21–4, replacing the music for the repetition of 'della figlia il disonor' with that for 'non lasciarmi in abbandon' at bb. 30–1). If the movement were constituted only by these sections, text repetition would be limited to 'non lasciarmi' in bars 9/15 and, from the last couplet, 'chieggon essi' and 'della figlia il disonor'. We could consider such a setting a sensible, logical response to Cammarano's text (Ex. 4.4).

Verdi found a much more creative solution, however, one that addresses the syntactical and rhetorical tensions of the text head-on. The obsessive repetition of 'non lasciarmi in abbandono' in bars 9–16 – as far as I know the most extended internal text repetition in Verdi's arias – promotes this line to the rhetorical high point of the movement. The melody is fixated on the semitone C sharp–D, supported harmonically by a directionless alternation between V/vi and iv/vi (bb. 10–11) that threatens to move to vi (and therefore alludes to the vi harmony in b. 5) but eventually evades it. The rhetorical opposition contained in the first quatrain is compressed and heightened at bars 13–15 by rearranging the text: 'Se t'offesi mi punisci, ma non lasciarmi'. The deceptive cadence on the downbeat of bar 24, again involving V/vi, recalls bar 10 and introduces a further repetition of line 4 similarly harmonised. The ascent to B and the subsequent coloratura passage resolve the tension created by the isolated high A at bar 21, partly filling the tenth left open previously. Only in bar 31 does the music reach a structural cadence, the coda beginning no sooner than this point. Here Verdi exploits the possibility of truncating 'abbandono' and 'Signore' and ends the movement with two *tronco* rhyming lines, 'abbandon' and 'Signor', thus reinforcing closure and retroactively making the first four lines into a separate stanza, while undercutting Cammarano's *tronco* endings in lines 6 and 8. Normally the last two lines would be repeated, but Verdi must have regarded them as rhetorically and syntactically unfit to provide the climax of the piece, and therefore decided to alter the standard form.[65] As a consequence, Verdi's setting changes the perception of Luisa's state of mind. While in the text she expresses terror and desperation but remains in control of her discourse, the music portrays her as almost beside herself. The shadow of obsession and perhaps even hysteria looms large on *Verdi's* Luisa.

The conventions of the lyric form leave wide scope for manoeuvre: there are many instances in Verdi's early- and middle-period operas of texts that do not fit the quadripartite structure, and of melodies that manipulate the lyric prototype considerably.[66] 'Tu puniscimi, o Signore' constitutes an extreme instance of such

Ex. 4.4. Verdi, *Luisa Miller*, Act 2: Luisa's aria, slow movement.

Ex. 4.4. (*cont.*)

Ex. 4.4. (*cont.*)

Ex. 4.4. (*cont.*)

manipulations, however, even in the flexible context of mid-century lyric form. This is as far as a composer could go if he wanted to keep within the frame of reference of the lyric prototype. In this sense, the subversion from within which Verdi operated on the conventions of a standard formal framework is comparable to the similar treatment that he and Cammarano reserved for the genre of Alpine *semiseria*. *Luisa Miller* is a 'modern drama', a 'prosaic' one, from both a generic and a musical-formal point of view. It is not only *Luisa Miller* that runs amok, then: Luisa Miller does so too. Or, rather, she comes within an inch of doing so, but ultimately does not: she does not walk in her sleep like Amina, and she does not go mad and hallucinate like Linda. She remains in touch with reality, however fragile and stretched to the limit this connection may be. She sees the world 'as it is', rather than as what it had appeared to her in the opera's *introduzione*, and faces the devastating consequences that confronting reality may have on the human subject – and her music.

'ITALIAN TYROL' IN 1849

Why, then, do *Luisa Miller* and Luisa Miller run amok? In short, in order to show the world as it is, in all its modern prosaicness. But why did Verdi and Cammarano want to show the world as it is? Viewing *Luisa Miller* in the context of its early reception might help answer this question. The evidence implicitly supports viewing the opera within the tradition of Alpine *semiseria*, but at the same time furnishes an unexpected twist. The critic Vincenzo Torelli, reviewing the première for the Neapolitan newspaper *L'omnibus*, affirmed that with *Luisa* Verdi moved into his 'second period', and traced the sources of this development in the composer's art:

> The composer, after going to the other side of the Alps, after studying French lightness, German combinations, what could be called the harmonic prose of the spoken melodramas, and the elaborate or *picchettati* accompaniments, wanted to test the rustic genre against the heroic, the countryfolk's innocence against aristocratic arrogance, and eventually a troubled love to which death puts an end, touching the chords, nearly always effective, of pity and terror! [. . .] Were the reminiscences of French and German music really needed? [. . .] Whoever left Italy either died or dried up: thus Rossini, thus Bellini, thus Donizetti.[67]

The connection between *Luisa* and French *mélodrame* and the explicit mention of 'the rustic genre against the heroic', an accurate description of the opera's trajectory from Alpine *semiseria* idyll to full-blown *seria*, seem especially relevant. The link polemically established between Verdi's 'second period' and the international careers of Rossini and Donizetti, which gave birth to *Guillaume Tell* and *Linda*, is equally revealing.

A more familiar Verdian critic, Basevi, also wrote of the composer's 'second manner' in connection with *Luisa*; indeed, according to him, that work was its first true product. Basevi connected Verdi's first period, which he characterised as 'grandiose' and 'passionate', with Rossini's last operas, while in the second period, which showed 'a calmer melodic style, shorter and lighter melodies, more mobile rhythms', Verdi came closer to Donizetti.[68] If we bear *Linda* in mind, Basevi's words make more sense than they have for Verdians so far, who have commented on the influence of *Lucrezia Borgia* on *Rigoletto*, or of *Maria Stuarda* on *Nabucco*, but have not linked *Luisa* to any of Donizetti's works.[69]

Basevi, however, seems to be more interested in other, not strictly musical aspects of Verdi's second manner. He opens his chapter on *Luisa Miller* by reminding the reader that this was Verdi's first opera after the so-called '1848' revolutions, which in Italy lasted well into the following year. In his view, Verdi was profoundly affected by the failure of the revolutions and his 'genio' changed accordingly. Thus was born the 'second manner':

> Verdi took advantage of the strong passions on which the plot is constructed. Since people's hearts were no longer able to feel enthusiasm, they didn't disdain those characters that do not immediately come across as imposing because of the prestige they receive from the ancient time of the action, or from their elevated class, or from the actions caused by them; it is because of these characteristics that the tragedy takes the name of 'bourgeois', what we would call 'domestic'.[70]

In other words, Cammarano and Verdi chose Schiller's 'bourgeois tragedy' as more fitting to the times but gave it some of the characteristics of *semiseria* only to make the generic, moral and ultimately political reversal more powerful.

The politicisation of *Luisa*, however, can go beyond Basevi's connection between the temper of the times and the opera's generic genealogy. In a general sense *La sonnambula*'s Switzerland, *Linda*'s Savoy and *Luisa*'s Tyrol are equally effective as Alpine settings. But in the wake of the 1848 revolutions and the return of the Austrians to domination of northern Italy, Cammarano's choice of the Tyrol could hardly have been coincidental. The Tyrol, the largely German-speaking, Habsburg-dominated Alpine region closest to Italy, was the place where an Italian opera with possible anti-Austrian resonances could be safely located without being too far removed to lose these resonances entirely.[71] Not all of the Tyrol was German-speaking, however: in its southern part, roughly corresponding to what is now the province of Trent, Italian was the native language of the large majority, and its common nineteenth-century geographical designation was in fact 'Italian Tyrol'.

The clarification of the linguistic, cultural and social differences between 'the region improperly called Italian Tyrol' and 'German Tyrol' was the first task that Princess Cristina Trivulzio di Belgioioso set herself in her 'La Guerre dans le Tyrol italien', the fourth of a series of essays published after September 1848 in the Parisian *Revue des deux mondes* and collectively entitled 'L'Italie et la révolution italienne'.[72] Cristina Belgioioso was a long-time friend of Giuseppina Strepponi, by now Verdi's companion, and Verdi had first been in contact with her family during his student years in Milan.[73] A vehement anti-Austrian patriot already in exile, on 6 April 1848 she entered the (temporarily) free Milan (dressed as Joan of Arc) at the head of 160 volunteers she had brought to Lombardy all the way from Naples, welcomed by a cheering crowd. Verdi was in town. When the Austrians returned, the Princess fled to Paris, where Verdi had preceded her, and where both were living when she published her essays in the *Revue des deux mondes* in late 1848 and early 1849.

Whether or not Verdi read Princess Belgioioso's articles or heard her or Giuseppina talk about them, the devastating effect that the arrival of a new ruler, the 'Austrian' Count Walter, had on the life of the idyllic Tyrolean village resonates with many passages of Belgioioso's essay: 'Austria possesses to a superior degree the art of uprooting peoples from their native regions, of wiping out national-ities and creating fictitious ones, with no other reason than caprice, or, even worse, the politics of the sovereign'.[74] 'The Austrians, having become the masters again, declared Trent under military law;

arrests, confiscations, executions multiplied. Towns, villages, and farms were sacked'.[75] 'The valleys of Italian Tyrol have fallen again under Austrian domination. The imperial police operates there with a pitiless rigour. The entire Tyrol, down to the most secluded valleys, has been turned into a huge camp under military law, and in many instances Austrian soldiers have been seen perpetrating acts of violence that recall the saddest scenes of Galicia'.[76] Compare Count Walter's throwing Miller into jail, or the way he came into power through murder, or Wurm's attempt at forcing Luisa to yield to him. The year 1848 influenced *Luisa* even more deeply than Basevi thought.

Moreover, even if the libretto tells us that *Luisa Miller* takes place in the first half of the seventeenth century, the same argument could be made for it as has been advanced for *La sonnambula* and *Linda*: the 'where' superseded the 'when' and therefore gave the action a potentially contemporary flavour. Moving the action to the Alps had two contrasting results: it connected *Luisa* with *semiseria* and French *mélodrame* – their idealised morality and political conservatism – and at the same time made *Luisa* as contemporary as was allowed in serious opera at the time, thus making more transparent the moral pessimism of the plot and its resonances with the post-1848 political restoration. *Luisa Miller* is not only, dramaturgically and from a French point of view, a post-1830 'Romantic' opera, but also, politically and from an Italian perspective, a post-1848 'realistic', 'patriotic' one.

And yet this is a strange kind of 'patriotic realism'. Basevi, commenting on the monothematicism of *Luisa*'s *sinfonia*, informed its readers that 'this kind of overture is unusual for Italy; but examples can be found among the overtures by composers beyond the Alps (*oltremontani*)', and compared it to the overture of *The Magic Flute*.[77] Verdi had ended up sounding 'oltremontano' – French and, even worse, German – and the critic Torelli, as we have seen, did not like what he heard.[78] Seen in this light, Verdi's 'second period' opened poised precariously on a contradiction. When he had appropriated from foreign musical traditions the means to depict ambience with sufficient skill to let it take centre stage, he put this skill to use in *Luisa Miller*. But the opera's patriotic resonances were potentially at odds with these 'foreign' influences. While this contradiction should not be explained away, we might wonder whether it was one of the reasons for the opera's mixed reception during the 1850s and 1860s, and for the fact that Verdi quickly lost interest in promoting its performance. *Luisa* never acquired a stable position within the repertory: *Rigoletto's* immense and immediate success overshadowed it, and the opera fell into almost complete oblivion for the rest of the century and longer. Once Verdi's early works began to be historicised from the point of view of *Rigoletto's* popularity, the at best ambiguous position of *Luisa Miller* in the traditional narrative of the composer's career was assured. It is worth examining this position in some detail, since it has undoubtedly influenced the negative critical assessment of the move to the Tyrol from Schiller's German town.

THE POLITICS OF GENRES IN VERDI'S MIDDLE PERIOD

It has long been a critical commonplace that with *Rigoletto* Verdi created new musical forms and processes. Many have praised the opera, for example, for its frequent rejection of 'la solita forma', the standard formal layout of musical numbers in Ottocento opera. What is more, critics have often linked these musical innovations with equally striking novelties in the dramaturgy of the opera. Among others, Gary Tomlinson has connected them to the influence of Hugo's theatrical ideals, while Piero Weiss has traced the source of these novelties in the composer's reception of Shakespeare and has explored his various attempts to bring comedy into tragedy (following Shakespeare's example) in the operas composed between his first Shakespearean work, *Macbeth* (1847), and *Rigoletto*, which represents the best example of what Weiss calls the 'fusion of genres'.[79]

One consequence of this view of *Rigoletto* is that Verdi's previous operas tend to be regarded, at least in the final analysis, as musically and dramatically undeveloped – as mere stepping-stones on the way to the real thing. But this critical move is not so easily executed, especially in the case of operas that steer clear of any hint of the

Shakespeare–Hugo fusion of genres. In this context *Luisa Miller* is especially problematic. Weiss has praised *Rigoletto* for 'breaking down the barrier that separated the serious and the comic', for 'transcending [. . .] a stubborn literary convention that had reduced far more "normal" characters – Rodolfo and Luisa, for example – to two-dimensional stock figures operating in a shop-worn theatrical tradition'.[80] From a musical point of view, Roger Parker has properly noted that 'it is difficult to see in the formal aspect of *Luisa* an essential stylistic turning-point'.[81] Instead, what is remarkable is its skilful use of conventional musical forms, which makes it, according to Parker, a crucial step not towards *Rigoletto*, but towards *Il trovatore*, traditionally considered not only the most formally conservative of Verdi's middle-period works, but also perhaps the least concerned with the fusion of genres in Weiss's sense. In the cases of both *Luisa Miller* and *Il trovatore*, then, musical conservatism might appear to go hand in hand with dramaturgical traditionalism.

Furthermore, critics have tended to discover and discuss manipulation and transformation of musical structures primarily in operas that tend to be associated with dramaturgical experimentation on Verdi's part, such as *Macbeth*, *Stiffelio* and *Rigoletto*.[82] 'Fusion of genres' – the type of dramaturgical experimentation on which Verdians have concentrated – goes hand in hand with musical innovation, and especially manipulation of forms. Different domains of the operatic work are thus collapsed, and the musical and the dramaturgical become simply different aspects of the same historical trend towards freedom from formal and generic shackles.[83]

After placing *Luisa Miller* in the context of Alpine virgin operas, however, can we still maintain that 'Cammarano mercilessly cut down Schiller's drama to the requirements of a conventional tragedy'? Rodolfo and Luisa might look like 'two-dimensional stock figures operating in a shop-worn theatrical tradition', but only from the point of view of the mixture of comic and tragic in *Rigoletto*. What Cammarano and Verdi did with *Luisa Miller* was to use the 'stubborn' operatic conventions of *opera semiseria* only to break them and reach an equally 'modern', but different, juxtaposition of genres, one that matched the 'realism' and political engagement of Schiller's bourgeois tragedy. Saving what could be saved of Schiller's socio-political critique by transferring its location from a German town to an Alpine village testifies to an acute dramatic consciousness, to an awareness of a wide spectrum of possibilities in dealing with operatic genres in mid-century Italian opera.

Recuperating the sense of novelty and surprise that struck the first commentators of *Luisa* and repositioning it in the context of Alpine *semiseria* might help us to rethink the concept of Verdi's treatment of genres. Playing with genres – Verdi scholars' most frequent trope for dramaturgical innovation – can imply manipulating, mixing, 'using' not only forms, but also ambience and plot types. *Luisa Miller*'s important position among pre-*Rigoletto* operas is assured not, or not only, by its control of conventional musical forms, or by the 'modern' manipulation of them that can be detected in some of its numbers, but by its innovative play with genres in the sense outlined here – by its *ranz des vaches* and echoes and 6/8 metres at the beginning of a *melodramma tragico*. To extend the implications of this aspect, the future opera *Luisa* most resembles is not *Il trovatore*, but rather *La traviata*. Basevi introduced his discussion of the music of the latter opera with the following remarks: '*La traviata* is a kind of composition that, thanks to the nature of the characters, the domestic affects, and the lack of spectacle, comes close to comedy. *Verdi* began a third period, which in more than one sense moves towards the French genre of *opéra comique*'.[84] 'The nature of the characters' was exactly what had made him consider Schiller's *Kabale und Liebe* a 'bourgeois [tragedy], what we would call domestic'. *Luisa* had started Verdi's second period as *La traviata* started the third, and if for the former the play with genres was implied, in this case it was spelled out clearly: 'Comes close to comedy', 'moves towards *opéra comique*'. Not by chance was Basevi reminded of *La sonnambula* and *Linda* when he discussed 'our modern and prosaic society' of *La traviata*: he could have mentioned *Luisa*, which, thanks to its setting, also comes very close to being both 'modern' and 'prosaic'.

Deflowering the Alps: from *I promessi sposi* to *La Wally* and *Fedora*

Luisa Miller's subversion of genres for socio-political critique could only be effective in a theatrical and cultural context in which Alpine virgin operas were still a noticeable presence. It was not only the robust repertorial health of *La sonnambula* and *Linda di Chamounix* that contributed to such a context: new operas centred on the established topos were composed and performed throughout the nineteenth century. It was only natural, however, that the association between mountains and virginity would evolve as the century progressed. This evolution involved not only the different ways in which the theme was treated on the stage, but also its meanings, which could hardly remain fixed in a rapidly changing socio-cultural environment. In the present chapter I explore this evolution through a discussion of a few significant works, from a number of operatic adaptations of Manzoni's *I promessi sposi* to mid-century works by Pedrotti and Mercadante, and from Puccini's early *Le Villi* and *Edgar* to Catalani's *La Wally* and Giordano's *Fedora*. The diverse dramatic and musical strategies of these works testify to the problematic relationship between the traditional representation of landscape (Alpine or otherwise) in Italian opera and an emerging aesthetic of textual and musical realism at least potentially at odds with operatic tradition. The solutions attempted by librettists and composers in the second half of the century lead to new ways of representing not only landscape, however, but also the characters' interaction with reality, especially in its sonic manifestations.

I PROMESSI SPOSI AT THE OPERA: REALITY VERSUS REPRESENTATION

As suggested in chapter 2, Manzoni's *I promessi sposi* not only introduced the Alpine landscape into Italian literary culture, but also did so in a remarkably theatrical way, not least in its famous opening paragraph. Given the apparent unsuitability of such a complicated, chronologically extended and geographically mobile plot for operatic reduction, it is nonetheless surprising that the novel became the source of several operas premièred between the 1830s and the 1860s. It is not difficult to imagine, however, how the immense popularity of the book must have been irresistible for librettists and composers. Less surprising, given that the novel's action constitutes a typical example of an Alpine virgin story, is that all these works are *opere semiserie*. These Manzonian operas offer a vantage point from which to consider some of the changes undergone by the Alpine virgin convention in the central decades of the century.

A few of these works date from the years immediately following the first edition of the novel in 1827, taking us back to a period when the tradition was still less than fully established. Giuseppe Checcherini's *melodramma* for Luigi Bordese, first performed at the Teatro Nuovo, Naples, in 1830, shows a complete disregard for what could be considered key features of the book: its language and sense of ambience. In typical Neapolitan *semiseria* fashion, prominence is given to the *buffo caricato* who expresses himself in local dialect, in this case incongruously impersonating Don Abbondio, the 'mayor' of a village near Lecco. If Lucia's arrival is accompanied by stage music played on 'tambourines, castanets and pipes' ('tamburelli, nacchere e ciufoli'), instruments more typical of Neapolitan than Lombard folklore, it nevertheless follows the iconography strongly associated with her from the novel's first appearance. Here is how another character describes her: 'That garland of roses and lilies, those beautiful long pins that surround your head like rays, how fittingly they adorn the many turns of your black braids' ('Quella ghirlanda di rose, e gigli, quei belli spilloni, che t'irradiano la testa, oh come adornano bene gli spessi giri delle tue nere trecce').[1] Apart from this visual connection to the novel – a gesture towards an ambience with some degree of specificity, and in any case different from the assumed *napoletanità* of this sub-genre – the rest of the opera shows virtually no awareness of the Alpine virgin convention. Evidently, this convention was not yet fully established, at least on the Neapolitan stage – *La sonnambula* would be premièred in Milan one year later.

The incipient classicisation of *I promessi sposi* and its influence on operatic transpositions is already evident in an anonymous libretto set to music by Pietro Bresciani and premièred in Padua in 1833, a work that now seems aware of the Alpine virgin convention, perhaps through the mediation of *La sonnambula*. Characteristic linguistic imports from the novel (for example, in Don Abbondio's entrance aria, his duet with Renzo, and Lucia's final farewell to her village) go hand in hand with an increased attention to locale, as in the rather specific stage direction at the beginning of the opera. While attention to locale is not a prominent feature of another anonymous *I promessi sposi* (set to music by Luigi Gervasi and premièred at the Teatro Valle, Rome, in 1834), the characterisation of Lucia in this work owes much to that of the protagonist in *La sonnambula*.[2] Perhaps an additional connection was provided by the first interpreter of this Lucia, Fanny Tacchinardi-Persiani, who had already established herself as a famous Amina and would be an equally famous Linda, as we have seen.

More than twenty years separate these early operatic appearances of *I promessi sposi* from another group of operas based on the novel: Amilcare Ponchielli's on an anonymous libretto, premièred in Cremona in 1856; Andrea Traventi's on a libretto by Pietro Micheletti and Emanuele Bardare (Rome, Teatro Argentina, 1858); and Errico Petrella's on Antonio Ghislanzoni's text (Lecco, Teatro Sociale, 1869). The work that connects Manzoni's story with the Alpine virgin theme most explicitly is undoubtedly Ponchielli's, whose opening chorus seems a distillation of *La sonnambula*'s and *Linda*'s corresponding numbers: a picturesque valley at dawn, women praising the 'beautiful virgin' Lucia, shouts of 'Evviva Lucia' and 'la la la la', metaphors of light and whiteness, 6/8, G major, echo effects, and so on. A revision by Enrico Praga for the Milanese Teatro Dal Verme (1872) emphasises even more prominently the central role of landscape, as emerges clearly through comparison of the initial stage directions in the two versions:

Cremona, 1856

> Luogo campestre. Veggonsi varie case villereccie tra le quali a destra dello spettatore, quella di Don Abbondio Pievano del villaggio. In distanza il palazzotto di Don Rodrigo.[3]

> A place in the countryside. Several rustic houses, among which, on the right, Don Abbondio's, the village priest. In the distance Don Rodrigo's manor.

Milan, 1872

> Amena valle fiancheggiata da promontorii. Sopra uno dei quali è posta una chiesuola; accanto a questa la casa di D. Abbondio, con porta praticabile; dal lato opposto varie case villereccie, fra le quali quella di Lucia, essa pure con porta praticabile. Nel fondo la scena è chiusa da alte montagne; sovra il fianco di una di esse s'innalza il palazzotto di Don Rodrigo, al quale conduce un difficile e tortuoso sentiero. È l'alba.[4]

> Beautiful valley enclosed within promontories. On one of these promontories a little church; beside it Don Abbondio's house, with functioning door; on the opposite side various rustic houses, among which Lucia's, also with functioning door. In the distance the scene is bounded by high mountains; on the side of one of them Don Rodrigo's palace, reached through a steep and tortuous path. It is dawn.

The classic status attained by *La sonnambula* and *Linda* was never equalled by *Luisa Miller*, whose career was less distinguished. The stage directions for Ponchielli's second version, however, may owe something to *Luisa*; what is certain is the visual and emotional centrality of the evil ruler's castle seen in the distance, dominating the space where the action begins and casting a dark, menacing shadow.

It is instead the echo of *La sonnambula* that is most distinctly heard in the opening sequence of Micheletti and Bardare's 1858 libretto for

Traventi, from the level of the action and succession of scenes (opening chorus praising the bride Lucia's beauty and purity; *cavatina* for Lucia on the joys of this blessed day; Renzo's arrival followed by duet for the two *promessi sposi* about to be wed) down to details of poetic diction, as in the opening chorus of women peasants:

Di sposa il tenero
   Serto di fiori
   Ricevi, o Vergine,
   Dall'Amistà.
Ma delle vivide
   Rose i colori
   Non ponno vincere
   La tua beltà.
La Rosa è il simbolo
   Del casto affetto
   Che in te fra palpiti
   Arse finor;
Sorridi, o Vergine,
   Al tuo diletto,
   Che anch'esso palpita
   D'eguale amor![5]

O Virgin, receive from your friends the tender nuptial bouquet. But the colours of vivid roses cannot surpass your beauty. The rose is the symbol of the chaste affection that has burned with palpitation within you until now; smile, o Virgin, at your beloved, who feels an equally palpitating love!

Writing 'Virgin' with the capital V, as in the original libretto, emphasises the connection between the virgin on earth and the Virgin in Heaven. One of the most famous moments of the novel (not set in this particular libretto) is Lucia's vow to the Virgin Mary to remain a virgin for ever if she is rescued from the dungeon of the Innominato's castle. Putting such emphasis on Lucia's virginity engenders an effect of narrative irony: the girl's friends remind her that her virginity is her most precious possession, so that at a future moment of great danger she will know that this is the most valuable gift that she can make to that ultimate virgin, the mother of God. The popularity of Manzoni's novel was such that it mattered little whether the vow scene was included in the opera or not, since the majority of spectators would have had it very clearly in their minds.[6]

The book's ever-growing fame as the classic novel of Italian literature may be detected behind the desire to compress the entire plot in the librettos for Ponchielli and Petrella, as opposed to earlier poets' willingness to limit their transposition to the initial eight chapters (out of a total of thirty-eight), that is, to the part of the action that takes place in the surroundings of Lecco, before Lucia's journey to Monza and Renzo's to Milan. The novel's status, however, had clearly reached a point at which operatic transposition would be considered almost an act of *lèse majesté*. That it was at least an act in need of justification is confirmed by the brief disclaimer preceding the second version of the text for Ponchielli,[7] and especially by the much longer preface that Ghislanzoni wrote for his libretto. Aware that 'all spectators will bring with them to the theatre an ample knowledge of the novel', the librettist assures the reader that 'sometimes I have copied almost word for word; and, as much as the verse form would allow, I have always tried to imitate that naturalness and simplicity of language of which Manzoni is supreme master'.[8]

The language of Ghislanzoni's libretto is undoubtedly its most explicit acknowledgement of the novel's reputation, specifically in its characteristic choice of words and constructions. There are passages in which the novel is openly invoked as a validating intertextual presence, going well beyond the similarities due to the fact that *I promessi sposi* is the source of the opera. Witness the evident attempt to preserve as much as possible from one of the most famous passages of the novel, Lucia's farewell to her mountains, in the recitative preceding her Act 2 aria:

> Addio montagne sorgenti dall'acque,
> Cime ineguali, note
> A chi crebbe tra voi. . . Addio torrenti,
> Villette biancheggianti in sul pendio,

Come branco di pecore pascenti,
Addio! addio! addio![9]

Farewell, you mountains which raise straight out of the water; you
uneven peaks, which we who have grown up with you know so well. . .
Farewell, you brooks, you little white houses dotting the slope like a herd
of grazing sheep, farewell! Farewell! Farewell!

Compare the novel's 'Farewell, you mountains which raise straight
out of the water and up to the sky; you jagged, uneven peaks,
which we who have grown up with you know so well. [. . .] Farewell,
you streams, [. . .] white houses spread glimmering across the slope,
like flocks of grazing sheep, farewell!'[10] The linguistic influence of
the novel on the libretto goes beyond such moments of explicit
intertextuality, however, extending to the general level of poetic
diction. The significant presence of contemporary colloquial expressions, for example, is quite unusual in Italian librettos up to this
time, differentiating this kind of linguistic realism of novelistic provenance from the traditional colloquialisms common in *opera buffa*
librettos.

One of the results of this aspect is the construction of characters,
such as the two protagonists Renzo and Lucia, who are relatively
unusual for the Italian stage of this time, unusual precisely in their
wide spectrum of discursive strategies. This 'realism' was openly
censured after the Milan première of the opera in 1871. Ghislanzoni
replied with a surprisingly explicit declaration of poetics:

Renzo and Lucia are two *real* peasants, scrupulously reproduced from
reality, two peasants such as can be seen by the hundred around Lecco.
[. . .] If you take the trouble to read the novel, you will be convinced that
their language is exactly equal to that which they speak in my libretto.
Could I, should I have idealised when Manzoni had proven himself so
great, so inimitable a master of *the real*? [. . .] My first and foremost
intention was that of remaining faithful to the original text as much as
possible. In many instances I copied almost literally, sacrificing
versification and the facile bombast of poetic language to the duty of
being true to reality.[11]

One cannot help asking: what kind of reality? The reality of Manzoni's novel? Or the reality of the villages around Lecco, where Ghislanzoni himself came from? Why was the idealisation of the Alpine landscape and its inhabitants subjected to corrosion by the lowering of the level of poetic diction? Why had 'the real' become a goal to be attained, a worthy aspiration? This is a kind of 'realism' different from the ideological and political one invoked in *Luisa Miller*. In the case of operas based on *I promessi sposi*, the connection with the Alpine virgin convention and its baggage of idealisation did not have to be established, as was the case with Cammarano and Verdi, since this connection was guaranteed by the novel's ambience and action. In Ghislanzoni's libretto for Petrella, then, we witness an attempt to distance the text from idealisation, at least on the linguistic front: a clear symptom that the aesthetics of the Alpine virgin convention were evolving.

This attempt at some sort of realism, or at least at mitigating idealisation, emerges with startling clarity in the opening scene. A reticent stage direction is glossed by a footnote referring to the first chapter of Manzoni's novel 'for the precise reproduction of the scene' ('per l'esatta riproduzione della scena'). The famous opening paragraph (discussed in chapter 2 above), with its insistence on a specific and realistically described ambience, becomes what must be the longest (and most poetic) stage direction in the history of Italian opera, at least up to 1869. To the text of the opening chorus is appended another footnote: 'The author has followed the metre and the bizarre structure of two very ancient popular songs from Lombardy, mentioned also by the illustrious historian Cesare Cantù in his *Documenti alla Storia Universale*. In order to furnish this scene with an entirely local colour, Maestro Petrella has striven to reproduce these traditional melodies'.[12] One of the purposes of Ghislanzoni's footnote is surely to justify the irregular metric structure of the men's chorus, with its alternation of *settenari piani* and *ottonari tronchi*. But there are other features which would not normally have right of citizenship in a libretto of the time, most prominently the repetition of entire verses or parts of them:

DONNE
Quell'augellin del bosco
  Vola per la campagna;
Quell'augellin del bosco
  La notte e il dì si lagna;
La notte e il dì si lagna
  Perché non trova amor.

UOMINI
Cantiam, danziam, fanciulle,
  Nell'aprile dell'età;
Cantiam, danziam, fanciulle,
  Presto il verno tornerà.

DONNE
Quell'augellin si arresta
  Sul tuo verone, o bella;
Quell'augellin ti desta,
  Allo spuntar del dì;
Ti reca una novella:
  'L'amante tuo morì'.

UOMINI
Cantiam, danziam; la vita
  Per noi scorra nel piacer;
Cantiam, danziam, la vita
  È un baleno passeggier.[13]

WOMEN: The little bird from the wood flies in the countryside; the little
  bird from the wood laments day and night, laments day and night
  because it does not find love.

MEN: Let us sing and dance, girls, in the springtime of life; let us sing
  and dance, girls, winter will soon return.

WOMEN: That bird lands on your window, o beautiful girl; that bird
  wakes you up at dawn; it brings you news: 'Your lover is dead'.

MEN: Let us sing and dance; life must pass in pleasure for us; let us sing
  and dance; life is a passing flash.

This text is indeed an elaboration of two distinct popular songs from northern Italy, of which several versions exist, a few of them already available in print in 1869.[14] Ghislanzoni, who was originally from Lecco, may have combined evidence from printed sources with direct experiences of these songs. In any case, they count among the earliest instances of direct quotation from the folk repertoire of any provenance in Italian opera.

According to his footnote, Petrella 'reproduced' the melodies traditionally associated with these songs, but this is difficult to verify. Petrella's simple melodic gestures are as 'characteristic' and 'popular' as Bellini's 'la la la la' or 'In Elvezia non v'ha rosa' at the beginning of *La sonnambula*. Even the irregular metre of the men's song, potentially the source of an unusual rhythmic arrangement, is easily neutralised by exploiting the equality in number of syllables between *settenario piano* and *ottonario tronco* (Ex. 5.1). The only folk melody associated with these songs and published relatively close to the date of the opera's première that I have been able to trace is found in Costantino Nigra's *Canti popolari del piemonte* (1888), probably the most exhaustive such publication in nineteenth-century Italy (Ex. 5.2). Even though Petrella's melody and the folk tune are obviously not the same, they share a few significant traits, such as the recurrence of the dotted-quaver-plus-semiquaver rhythm and the long note values at the end of most lines. I am certainly not claiming that Petrella based his melody on this specific tune, especially since the song, attested all over northern Italy and Tuscany, was probably sung to substantially different melodies in different regions.[15] But we have no reason not to believe the claim made in the libretto for Petrella's setting.[16]

Despite sharing some important traits with a nineteenth-century northern Italian folk melody linked to an almost identical text, then, Petrella's music sounds entirely operatic, in no significant way different from Bellini's choruses for the opening scene of *La sonnambula*. In other words, were it not for that footnote in the libretto, it would never have occurred to anyone to track down 'L'uccellin del bosco' in nineteenth-century collections of Italian folk songs. The only

Ex. 5.1. Petrella, *I promessi sposi*, Act 1: Opening chorus.

Ex. 5.2. 'Bel uzelin del bosc', nineteenth-century northern Italian folk song.

possible conclusion is that it was very difficult, if not impossible, for nineteenth-century Italian opera to include music that sounded authentically folk-like, whether borrowed from reality or invented, since the musical idioms of folk song and opera were too similar to permit it; or, in a different formulation, that the stylistic spectrum of nineteenth-century Italian opera included a 'popular', 'folk' idiom close to the idiom of 'authentic' folk music. Hence the long-held belief, mentioned in chapter 2, that in *La sonnambula* Bellini had reproduced the popular songs he had heard on Lake Como during the summer preceding the opera's composition. Composers who wanted to include 'real' folk music in their operas, however, were left stranded: nobody would have noticed. The only way out of this impasse was to footnote the use of folk music explicitly in the libretto.[17] The limited effectiveness of such a gesture is revealed, for example, by the complaint, voiced by the theatrical journal *Il trovatore*, that there was not enough local colour in the opera.[18]

Ghislanzoni and Petrella's *I promessi sposi* was premièred in Lecco, surely for commercial reasons, in order to secure a local success that would – and did – have national resonance. This resulted in an unprecedented attempt to match the ambience depicted on the stage with the one visible from the streets just outside the theatre, in textual and musical as well as visual terms. In order for the connection between stage and reality to be meaningful, ambience had to be depicted with a precision well beyond what was common in Italian opera of the time. Moreover, in Manzoni's *I promessi sposi* ambience was indeed depicted with a high degree of precision, as the aesthetics of the historical novel required; and the descriptive passages were among the most famous pages of the book, especially the opening paragraph and Lucia's 'Addio monti'. This unusual combination of factors opened the door to an aesthetic of textual and musical realism that throws new light not only on the evolution of the topos of the Alpine virgin in opera, but also on the evolving relationship between reality and its operatic representation.

'Realism' was a concept fraught with tensions and contradictions on the Italian stage of this time, however, and not only there. 'L'uccellin del bosco', the source of the opening chorus of Ghislanzoni's *I promessi sposi*, was championed as an example of authentic Italian folk song in Cesare Correnti's 'Della letteratura popolare' of 1856, one of the foundational critical texts of so-called *letteratura rusticale*.[19] 'Rustic literature', which emerged in Italy in the 1840s in the works (mostly short stories) of Giulio Carcano, Caterina Percoto, Ippolito Nievo and other, now forgotten authors, acted as a catalyst for an important theoretical and critical debate on the meanings and scope of realism in Italian literature.[20] Despite repeated pledges of allegiance to 'the true' and 'the real', however, this Italian brand of literary realism, which flourished especially in the 1850s, owed its most substantial debt to the rural idylls of George Sand's *romans rustiques* and their self-confessed intention to remind an urban society badly shaken by the 1848 revolutions that 'pure mores, tender sentiments and primitive equanimity still are, or can be, of this world'.[21] Despite claiming that writing *La Mare au diable*, the first of her *romans rustiques*, had been nothing more than reproducing 'an actual scene that I had under my eyes', Sand was quick to assure her readers that 'art is not a study of actual reality; it's a search for ideal truth'.[22] Among the manifestations of rustic purity, tenderness and equanimity, Sand accorded pride of place to singing: 'The singing of peasants is the purest and best, since it takes its inspiration especially from nature, since its contact with nature is the most direct'.[23] Italian literary realism between the 1840s and the 1860s, which found its inspiration in Sand rather than Balzac, subscribed wholeheartedly to these views.

It is in this context that the realism of Ghislanzoni and Petrella's *I promessi sposi* emerges in all its limitations. On the textual side, being true to Manzoni did not and could not amount to being true to reality, as Ghislanzoni well knew, despite his implicit claim to the contrary. On the musical side, being true to reality – taking inspiration from the 'pure' and 'natural' singing of peasants, as Sand would have it – ultimately meant being true to operatic tradition. The inclusion of reality into operatic representation was far from the simple, smooth operation claimed by that footnote on the first page of the libretto. For the audience of Lecco's Teatro Sociale in 1869, the Alps and their inhabitants as depicted in Ghislanzoni and Petrella's opera were close indeed, but also very, very distant. Operatic convention made sure that this distance would be maintained for the rest of the century.

A SWISS TYPE

That by mid-century the Alpine virgin tradition was a fully established presence in the world of Italian opera is attested not only by *Luisa Miller*'s subversive manipulation and by the considerable influence of this tradition on operatic transpositions of Manzoni's *I promessi sposi*. New operas exploited the conventional pairing of female virginity and the Alps. Full adherence to the topos did not necessarily mean slavish repetition of the characteristics of its classic titles: new representational strategies were adopted in a few works from the second half of the century. After following the fortunes of *I promessi sposi* on the operatic stage into the 1870s, we must go back to the 1850s in order to consider two operas that, although taking the topos for granted, at the same time sought a degree of distance from it, through significantly different strategies.

Luigi Serenelli Honorati's libretto for Carlo Pedrotti's *Fiorina o La fanciulla di Glaris* (Verona, 1851) features the character of Giuliano, a French painter travelling through Switzerland in search of picturesque sights, who ridicules the Alpine virgin convention at every possible turn. Fiorina displays the conventional characteristics of her type to such a high degree, however, that an ironic stance seems fully justified. Not only does she enter at dawn exclaiming: 'Limpid crystal envelops my mountains. . . this is my sky' ('È limpido cristallo quel che avvolge i miei monti. . . egli è il mio cielo'); she proceeds to sing a refrain on the notes of the *ranz des vaches* (heard previously) to the words: 'Oh my country where I was born, I will always love you' ('Oh! mia terra ov'io son nata, sempre, sempre io t'amerò!'). In the next scene the local boy Ermanno, who is in love with Fiorina, exclaims: 'Rise, my beautiful solitary virgin; a dawn of roses adorns your hair' ('Sorgi, mia bella vergine romita, l'alba di rose t'inghirlanda il crin'). Fiorina's second aria, in Act 2, is preceded by a recitative opening with an apostrophe to the local breeze: 'Comfort me, o sweet native breeze, that dances lightly on my brow in the ecstasy of a virginal joy' ('O dolci aure natie, che nell'ebbrezza d'una vergine gioia, mi danzate sopra il ciglio scherzando, confortatemi voi'). Such sentiments would not be out of place for a Metastasian heroine, except that Metastasian heroines never needed to explain that their joy was virginal, since this was obvious to everybody on stage and in the audience. And this is only a selection of the numerous instances where Fiorina is described or describes herself as an astonishing concentration of purity, goodness, love for her native mountains, honesty, beauty, and so on.

Giuliano is not only a painter: he is French and, what is worse, 'a perfumed ruin from the galant century' ('un profumato rudere [*sic*] del secolo galante'), who cannot take all this purity and goodness seriously. For Giuliano, an inveterate tourist (sexual as well as artistic, one suspects), Fiorina is just another piece of local colour: as he starts to draw her, he asks her to let him take back to France 'a Swiss type' ('un tipo elvetico'). When she assures him that her only love is her valley – literally 'these breezes', 'quest'aure', an ever-present metonymy – he reacts in a mocking, incredulous aside: 'È puro sangue!'. This literally means 'her blood is pure', but 'purosangue' also means 'a thoroughbred' – a crude remark that undermines the venerable topos in one bold stroke.[24] But Giuliano remains on the margins of the Swiss village community, who staunchly believe in

Fiorina's physical and emotional innocence, and in her communion with the landscape. And the outcome of the rather intricate action proves them right. What is more, the music seems to reject Giuliano's subversive perspective, fully subscribing to the textual and visual representation of Fiorina and keeping Giuliano within the safe boundaries of his role as 'buffo comico' (his libretto designation), destined by operatic tradition to be proven wrong – an operatically literate audience would know that he is a loser from the moment he starts singing, not least because of his vocal style.

While the music does contribute to the identification of Fiorina as local colour, as 'a Swiss type', it seemingly does so utterly devoid of irony or critical distance. The 'famous' *ranz des vaches* (as the libretto calls it) played by off-stage horns in the first scene is brought back, this time in the orchestra, for the instrumental prelude to Fiorina's entrance, and then actually *sung* by her as a refrain punctuating the following *scena*.[25] The fusion between ambience and character is thus accomplished musically as well as textually: the *ranz des vaches* occupies all possible musical territories, from stage music and stage song to 'unheard' orchestral sound, indicating a complete interiorisation of ambience and, conversely, an exteriorisation of affect into natural sound. Natural and emotional landscapes mirror each other in perfect unison, as they can only do in a perfect Eden called Switzerland populated by perfect women such as Fiorina.

The other opera from mid-century that subscribes to the Alpine virgin topos but inflects it in new ways is Saverio Mercadante's equally successful *Violetta*, on a libretto by Marco D'Arienzo, premièred at the Teatro Nuovo, Naples, in 1853. Here the practices of Marian devotion discussed in chapter 3 are transplanted to the theatre: a full-blown *rosière* ceremony is staged in a Swiss village. This incorporation of social ritual into the fabric of the action not only testifies to ritual's importance for an effective theatrical representation of the society to which it belongs. The injection of realism provided by the staging of a *rosière* ceremony goes hand in hand with a remarkable multiplicity of points of view from which the action is considered, a multiplicity that becomes tangible in the text's mixture of linguistic levels. The comic perspective – comic in the linguistic sense – is no longer restricted to the *buffo*, but can occasionally be taken on by other characters. The most startling example is perhaps the dialogue opening Act 2, in which the three female characters, the protagonist Violetta and the *seconde donne* Rosalba and Fiorina, discuss their duties as farm workers:

ROSALBA (*a Fiorina che è discesa dai colli*)
Al vicin borgo i tori
Mandato hai tu?

FIORINA
          Vi par!

ROSALBA (*a Violetta che segue Fiorina*)
              Nè ti rimuovi
Dal tuo passo di piombo. . .

VIOLETTA
                Ah no, non sento
Meritar tal lamento.

ROSALBA (*alle due*)
            Ai mietitori
Su, su, il pasto allestite. . .

ROSALBA: (*to Fiorina who is coming down from the hills*) Have you sent the bulls to the nearby village?
FIORINA: Of course!
ROSALBA: (*to Violetta who is following Fiorina*) You never abandon your leaden pace. . .
VIOLETTA: Ah no, I do not feel I deserve this reproach.
ROSALBA: (*to both*) Come on, prepare the meal for the harvesters.

It is not so much that Rosalba refers to Fiorina's shepherding duties: shepherdesses had enjoyed full operatic citizenship since the seventeenth century. What is new is, for example, Rosalba's specific reference to prosaic 'bulls' ('tori') instead of the usual, generic and poetic 'herds' ('mandrie' or 'armenti'), to which Fiorina appropriately answers 'of course' ('vi par!'); but the tone implied is 'don't even ask', 'what do you think?'), keeping the linguistic tone as low as the question. There is nothing 'funny' in this scene; this is no *buffo* spitting out his patter – although there is plenty of Leporellian language elsewhere in the opera. This is the comedy of reality, the reality of a modern village ritual and the reality of farming, encroaching on the idyllic idealisation of ambience and characters at the core of the Alpine virgin convention in operas from the first half of the century. This convention is by no means discarded in *Violetta* or in Pedrotti's *Fiorina*, or even radically questioned; rather, it is injected with moderate but nonetheless noticeable doses of irony and realism that begin to alter some of its meanings, at least in their librettos.

Irony and realism certainly do not affect a startling example of the longevity of the Alpine virgin tradition, Ponchielli's *La savojarda*, on a libretto by Francesco Guidi (premièred at the Teatro della Concordia in Cremona in 1861, it was subsequently revised as *Lina* with the textual help of Carlo D'Ormeville and presented at the Teatro Dal Verme, Milan, in 1877). The position of this work well within the confines of the convention is defined by its saturation with elements derived from *La sonnambula*, *Linda* and *Luisa*: a countess returning to the village after many years and remembering her happiness there (*La sonnambula*); the Savoy setting in the first version, an opening chorus of peasants going to church at dawn, and a love duet melody recalled at later crucial moments (*Linda*); the Tyrol setting in the second version, a chorus of villagers singing homage to the heroine outside her house on the morning of her birthday (*Luisa Miller*). The language of the libretto is replete with direct citations and intertextual references to these three operas, but at the same time it displays a remarkable unity of tone and register, allowing for none of the multiple points of view that momentarily temper the idealisation in *Fiorina* and *Violetta*. Even the visual discourse partakes of this intertextual frenzy; the opera's last scene, with a tree trunk functioning as a bridge suspended high above a precipice, unmistakably refers to the corresponding scene in *La sonnambula*, for which by this time a board or a tree trunk suspended above a mill wheel or a torrent had become *de rigueur*. The intention to compile a *précis* of the 'best' moments of these three classics becomes even clearer when we discover that in *La savojarda/Lina* the rustic bridge is neither crossed nor mentioned in the dialogue, its sole function being as intertextual reference to *La sonnambula*.[26]

Ponchielli rose to the intertextual challenge without hesitation, at least in *Lina*.[27] Opening horn calls with their obligatory echo are followed by a long chorus of villagers, arriving on stage and then leaving with carefully prescribed dynamic effects to match their movements; while on stage they give voice to their merriment by repeating 'la la la la la'. After a solo number, and a chorus and a song of hunters, the entrance sequence for the heroine Lina begins. She is first heard singing off-stage a virtuosic piece preceded by an improvised cadenza and generously peppered with short bursts of coloratura; a *tyrolienne* for the chorus follows, in which her beauty and purity are praised at length. At this point a new number begins, her *cavatina* proper, whose slow movement and cabaletta both sound as if they came straight out of Act 1 of *La sonnambula* (both are addressed to her 'compagne' and 'amici'): gentle arpeggiated accompaniment, textbook lyric prototype for both movements, expressive ornamentation, 'canto staccato' for the cabaletta (even if there is no reference to beating hearts in the text), and so on.[28] The respected critic Filippo Filippi, reviewing the first performance of *Lina*, had no doubt that 'the idyllic, rustic, sentimental colour dominates, and Ponchielli, setting to music Lina's chaste affects, has found suavely melodious phrases and Bellinian intonations', but concluded that 'this *Lina*, despite all the efforts to make of it another *Sonnambula* or *Linda*, has come out a mess'.[29] Another critic pointed to the gap between the limited scope of a sentimental idyll and Ponchielli's outsized score as the main reason for the opera's failure.[30]

By the early 1860s, it seems, only a young and inexperienced composer like Ponchielli, living in provincial Cremona, could accept at face value the Alpine virgin convention as presented by works from the first half of the century. This attitude must have seemed even more old-fashioned in 1877, despite the updated musical language of *Lina*. Trying to fashion another *Sonnambula* or *Linda* was no longer worth the effort, despite, or perhaps because of, the continuous presence of these two titles in the repertory. But the conventional coupling of Alpine landscape and female virginity did not disappear from the Italian operatic stage in the last decades of the century. It re-emerged in a number of operas, transformed in ways that acquire meaning when placed in the cultural context of fin-de-siècle Italy.

FIN-DE-SIÈCLE FLOWERS

Like his composition teacher Ponchielli, Giacomo Puccini also exploited variants of the Alpine virgin theme in his first two operatic essays, *Le Villi*, an *opera-ballo* (later re-christened *leggenda drammatica*) on a text by Ferdinando Fontana (Milan, Teatro Dal Verme, 1884, revised several times), and *Edgar*, a *dramma lirico* also by Fontana (Milan, La Scala, 1889, also repeatedly revised). Although neither is set in the Alps, both exhibit connections to a mountain setting, and the characterisation of their female protagonists refers to the traditional representation of virginity in operas from earlier in the century.

Le Villi is set in a clearing in the Black Forest, and the villagers are called 'montanari'. A link to *La sonnambula* is established by the initial stage direction calling for a bridge connecting two rocky sites in the background, as in *La savojarda / Lina* (and, as in Ponchielli's operas, this bridge does not fulfil any specific dramatic function). What is more, the heroine Anna is invested almost obsessively with a blanket of flowery metaphors, as in the following chorus of women mourning her death:

> Come un giglio reciso
> Nel feretro ella giace!
> Raggio di luna è il pallor del suo viso. . .
> O pura virgo, requïesce in pace!. . .[31]

> She lies in her coffin like a cut lily! The pallor of her face is a moon ray. . .
> O pure virgin, rest in peace!

Anna herself sets the metaphor in motion in her entrance aria, in which she gives voice to her desire to be like the flowers she is holding, a bunch of forget-me-nots:

Se come voi piccina
   Io fossi, o vaghi fior,
   Sempre sempre vicina
   Potrei stare al mio amor.
Allor dirgli potrei:
   'Io penso sempre a te!'
   Ripeter gli vorrei:
   'Non ti scordar di me!'
Voi di me più felici,
   Lo seguirete, o fior;
   Per valli e per pendici
   Seguirete il mio amor. . .
Deh, se il nome che avete
   Menzognero non è,
   Al mio amor ripetete:
   'Non ti scordar di me!'[32]

If I were as small as you, dear flowers, I could always stay near to my beloved. I could tell him: 'I always think of you!' I would repeat to him: 'Forget me not!' You flowers, luckier than me, will follow him; you will follow him through valleys and slopes. . . If the name that you carry does not lie, repeat to my beloved: 'Forget me not!'

As has been repeatedly noted, early Puccini heroines make their first appearance in a flowery context, and *Edgar*'s Fidelia is no exception. First she invokes flowers to describe a Spring dawn:

O fior del giorno, salve alba serena!
   Speranza ed esultanza!. . . Inno gentil!
Di celestial profumo è l'aura piena. . .
   O fior dell'anno, salve alba d'april![33]

Hail, serene dawn, flower of the day! Hope and exultation!. . . Gentle hymn! The air is full of a heavenly perfume. . . oh flower of the year, hail, April dawn!

Then she offers her beloved Edgar a branch of almond blossom. Several other heroines of fin-de-siècle Italian opera make their appearance within a flowery frame, among them Elda in Catalani's opera of the same title (1880; a direct model for *Le Villi*) and Suzel in Mascagni's *L'amico Fritz* (1891).[34] Entering the stage surrounded by metaphors steeped in the world of flowers is something that these girls learned from their elder sisters Amina and Linda; and, as for Bellini's and Donizetti's heroines before them, flowers and spring dawns are symbols of the girls' purity and innocence – which each opera's ensuing action will variously place under threat, uphold triumphantly, or unmask as unable to prevent the male protagonist from turning to women of lower virtue.

Edgar is especially interesting in this respect. Puccini's opera is set in a Flemish village in 1302, but its source, a *poème dramatique* by Alfred de Musset called *La Coupe et les lèvres* (1832), takes place in the Tyrol. Given the nature of the play, the extreme brevity of its stage directions is not surprising (Act 1, scene 1: 'A public square. A large fire burning at its centre'); hence the limited presence of landscape in the text. However, de Musset opens with an 'invocation' to the Tyrol, 'simple and naïve region' ('terre simple et naïve'), in which all the recurring themes of mountain discourse are present, from innocence to liberty, from the purity of the air to the clarity of the sky. It is not only the air which is 'virginal', but the Tyrol itself.[35] But Déidamia, de Musset's equivalent of Fidelia, makes her first appearance, simply as 'une jeune fille', in a very short scene half way through Act 1, when she gives Frank (Puccini's Edgar) a bunch of eglantine withered by snow and wind. There is no attempt to integrate her in the mountain landscape (the stage direction simply asks for 'a plain').[36]

Fontana and Puccini may have moved the action to Flanders, but they supply the opera with an *introduzione* worthy of any operatic Tyrol. The composer's skill as orchestrator is especially in evidence, with piccolo, glockenspiel and harp summoned to give sonic substance to the 'pure dawn' ('alba pura') mentioned in the libretto. The distant tolling of the church bell is answered by a chorus of villagers in the wings, followed by Fidelia's opening song, prepared in the orchestra by oboes and clarinets suggesting rustic pipes. After a dialogue with Edgar, Fidelia moves from metaphoric to real flowers in her short aria 'Già il mandorlo vicino', in which she tells him that her first thought on waking that morning was to pick almond blossoms to give him as her 'morning greeting' ('mattinal saluto'). The musical world in which she moves is characterised by a repeated crotchet–quaver rhythm in a 6/8, F major context, the orchestra providing open fifths in the bass to give the whole an unmistakable pastoral flavour, inflected only by unresolved dissonances above the orchestral bass. The scene is rounded off by the chorus reprising her song 'O fior del giorno'.[37] According to Julian Budden, this scene would provide an excellent start to an opera in the tradition of *La sonnambula* and *Linda*, but is dramatically disastrous for the continuation of this particular chain of events, as it fatally undermines the reasons for Edgar's subsequent behaviour.[38] If this is the case, then the power of the Alpine virgin convention is even more clearly in evidence: we may no longer be in the Alps, but the memory of Musset's 'virginal' Tyrol lies just beneath the surface of the Flemish setting, enough to send Fontana and Puccini back to the traditional coupling of virgin landscape with virginal heroine.

Neither *Le Villi* nor *Edgar* is actually set in the Alps, however, and neither follows the traditional outline of a *semiseria* plot – of the operas mentioned thus far, only *La savojarda/Lina* shares with *Le Villi* and *Edgar Luisa Miller*'s tragic ending. In *Le Villi*, for example, the evil city (Mainz) corrupts the hero Roberto, not the heroine Anna. Even more striking is the presence of the supernatural: the ghost of Anna appears to Roberto in the forest together with the Willis, the spirits of girls who died because of love. The decadent, nocturnal atmosphere emerges also in the fact that the villagers sing a prayer (a free paraphrase of the Catholic invocation 'Angelus Domini') not at dawn, as in *Linda*, but at nightfall.

The novelties are not only dramatic, but also symbolic. While Amina, Linda and Luisa are compared only to two 'classic' kinds of flowers, roses and lilies, the fin-de-siècle operatic flower garden has been updated, from Anna's humble, Madonna-blue forget-me-nots to

Fidelia's white, slightly exotic (and for Flanders perhaps unrealistic) almond blossom. Suzel picks violets for Fritz and, like Anna, interprets their language, speaking on their behalf: 'We are the shy and modest daughters of spring' ('Noi siamo figlie timide e pudiche di primavera'). As Fritz remarks, she seems to have privileged access to the language of nature, since later in *L'amico Fritz* she also interprets the song of sparrows, which 'jokingly play among the white hawthorn blossoms' ('agili scherzano dei biancospini tra i fiori candidi').[39]

But the truly momentous botanic discovery of the fin de siècle is that of the edelweiss, the flower that will become one of the most powerful symbols of the Alps for twentieth-century culture (e.g. *The Sound of Music*). The 'flower of the Alps' in the title of Alberto Franchetti's *Fior d'Alpe* (libretto by Leo Di Castelnovo, Milan, La Scala, 1894) is the edelweiss, emphatically drawn on the cover of the vocal score.[40] The libretto proceeds to make all the possible symbolic connections explicit: in Act 3 the protagonist Maria returns, Linda-like, to her native Savoy from the city where she had spent Act 2 (in this case Turin rather than Paris), and upon her arrival her adopted parents offer her two bunches of edelweiss:

> Nel dì sacro alla Vergine,
> Nel dì della tua festa,
> Di tuo candore il simbolo
> Prendi dell'Alpe i fior![41]

> On the day consecrated to the Virgin, your name day, take the flower of the Alps, symbol of your purity!

Apart from its substitution of the edelweiss for the lily or the rose, however, *Fior d'Alpe* is remarkably traditional in its re-packaging of the old classics, especially *Linda* – Verdi thought the subject 'rather naïve', and Boito reported to him that at the first performance 'the audience was divided into three parties: those who were bored and stayed quiet, those who were bored and applauded, those who were bored and hissed'.[42] Di Castelnovo's and Franchetti's naïveté emerged in their wholehearted adherence to the Alpine virgin convention, without any attempt at updating a theme which might still hold the stage in its classic incarnations (although performances of *La sonnambula* and *Linda* became less frequent in the last two decades of the century), but needed to be treated from fresh angles in the cultural climate of fin-de-siècle Italy, as Puccini had already showed. Two years earlier, however, another, more successful opera had already introduced the edelweiss on the Italian lyric stage, presenting not only a new kind of flower, but also a new kind of Alpine virgin.

WALLY HEARS THE LANDSCAPE

The transformations that the Alpine virgin convention had undergone in the second half of the century came together in what proved to be its most popular and influential incarnation after Bellini and Donizetti, Alfredo Catalani's *La Wally* on Luigi Illica's 'riduzione drammatica' of the novel *Die Geyer-Wally* by the German writer Wilhelmine von Hillern, premièred at La Scala in 1892. Far from being just a collection of changes made previously, however, *La Wally* became the most original contribution to the tradition of Alpine virgin operas since Verdi.

The novelty of the work emerges most clearly in the character of Wally, most boldly drawn at her entrance:

> *Ad un tratto una strana creatura irrompe violentemente in mezzo a quella folla, urtando gli uni, ricacciando gli altri. È una bizzarra fanciulla, bizzarramente vestita; ha i lunghi capelli disordinati e sciolti e intrecciati di edelweiss; le braccia forti, completamente ignude; gli occhi larghi e profondi pieni di fuoco; è la Wally! Vedere suo padre a terra presso all'Hagenbach, afferrare costui alle spalle e cacciarlo con forza lontano così da farlo barcollare, è un colpo solo.*
>
> WALLY
> Chi osò levar sul padre mio la mano?
> HAGENBACH (*furioso si volge; ma vedutosi di fronte una fanciulla, resta sorpreso dapprima, poi, quasi vergognoso balbetta*)
> Primo ei m'offese!

(*La Wally ha riconosciuto l'Hagenbach! Una profonda sensazione di dolcezza passa nei suoi sguardi; impallidisce e rimane immobile, muta, sorpresa, gli occhi suoi fissi nel volto di lui*).

[. . .]

HAGENBACH (*guardando bieco la Wally*)

Strana creatura![43]

Suddenly a strange creature bursts violently into the midst of the crowd, bumping into some, pushing others away. She is a bizarre girl bizarrely dressed. She has edelweiss twined in her long untidy hair, strong arms completely bare, huge dark burning eyes: it is Wally! Seeing her father on the ground at Hagenbach's feet, she seizes the latter by the shoulders and pushes him away with such force as to cause him to stagger.

WALLY: Who dared lift a hand against my father?

HAGENBACH (*turning furiously, he is nonplussed at finding himself face to face with a girl; then, almost ashamed, he stammers*): He insulted me first! (*Wally recognises Hagenbach! An expression of profound tenderness covers her face; turning pale, she remains still, mute, surprised, and is unable to take her eyes off him*)

[. . .]

HAGENBACH (*looking askance at Wally*): What a strange creature!

Wally is a 'strange creature', a 'bizarre girl' who leaps onto the stage from nowhere, disrupting the scene with her physical appearance as much as with violent behaviour. Her untidy hair, strong, naked arms and large, deep eyes proclaim her an untamed child of nature, while the edelweiss entwined in her hair makes clear what kind of nature has mothered her: the highest snow-covered peaks, where the flower grows. What is more, she is prey to sudden changes of mood: as soon as she recognises Hagenbach, violence immediately gives way to gentleness; she freezes, transfixed. Were she in an opera from the 1830s, we could be sure that she would go mad at some point during the ensuing action.

Her language seems to contradict this characterisation, since she speaks the literary and poetic Italian traditionally employed in nineteenth-century opera librettos: compare not only the perfect *endecasillabo* 'chi osò levar sul padre mio la mano?', but especially her next utterance, 'proud youth is more inclined to forgiveness than to hate and curse' ('la balda giovinezza più a perdonar che all'odio e al maledir è avvezza'), with its rhetorically skilful use of the abstract 'youth', giving the sentence a proverbial flavour, and with the poetic postponement of the verb to the end of the sentence. This kind of sustained high language has not been heard until Wally's entrance, except in Walter's song 'Un dì, verso il Murzoll, una fanciulla'; and, as Walter himself confesses, the song was composed by Wally. She speaks a more literary language than anybody around her because she is a poet/composer, and she has privileged access to a level of poetic diction unavailable to other inhabitants of the valley. Her language, just like her behaviour, sets her apart from the community to which she nominally belongs.

Musically, Wally's entrance is no less disruptive than her physical appearance and language. Her leap onto the scene is accompanied by a chromatic run worthy of a Valkyrie; her first vocal phrase explores the upper triad of a dominant seventh in last inversion, with the menacing seventh held by the basses. The motive that immediately follows in the orchestra maintains the tension, refusing to cadence properly in A flat; its final semitonal inflection reveals its Tristanesque nature by eventually blossoming, at the moment when Wally recognises Hagenbach, into a chromatic progression that ends on a diminished version of her initial seventh chord (Ex. 5.3). Wally confirms her allegiance to chromaticism and unresolved harmonies in her next phrase, 'la balda giovinezza', supported by a downward sequence of the orchestra ending again on an unresolved dominant seventh in A flat (Ex. 5.4). This degree of chromaticism and lack of resolution has not been heard thus far in the opera, except for a few passages in Hagenbach's narrative of his encounter with a wild bear, which he eventually kills, and here only in the orchestra supporting a declamatory vocal line. Wally is clearly a much wilder animal, and Hagenbach will need more than his knife to deal with her: witness the dissonant context in which a fragment of his hunting motive is heard when he exclaims 'strana creatura', immediately followed by another fragment, this time of the motive heard at his first sighting

Ex. 5.3. Catalani, *La Wally*, Act 1: Wally's entrance.

of Wally (Ex. 5.5). Rather than appearing as a perfectly integrated component of an idyllic mountain community, as Amina, Linda, Luisa, Lucia and their sisters had done, Wally immediately sets herself apart from this community, making it abundantly clear that she speaks a language profoundly different – bodily, verbally and musically.

Wally's behaviour, her language and her music in the rest of the opera enrich her initial characterisation without ever denying its salient traits. To restrict ourselves to her actions, for example, on

Ex. 5.4. Catalani, *La Wally*, Act 1: Wally, 'La balda giovinezza'.

Ex. 5.5. Catalani, *La Wally*, Act 1: Hagenbach, 'Strana creatura'.

the one hand she answers Gellner's declaration of love with a direct refusal, 'emphasising each word' ('spiccando le parole'): 'I don't love you and I will never love you. . . understand?' ('Non t'amo né t'amerò giammai. . . comprendi?'). To her father's injunction to marry Gellner or be thrown out of the family home she responds by leaving her village and moving into a hut high up in the mountains, from which she returns only after her father's death. In Act 2 she takes pleasure in tormenting Gellner 'with savage and ferocious force, as if swearing' ('con impeto selvaggio e feroce, come un'imprecazione'). In Act 3 she does not hesitate to descend into the ravine herself in order to save her beloved Hagenbach who has fallen into it, leaving the onlookers 'almost terrified by her strong act of courage' ('quasi atterriti dal suo forte atto di coraggio'). And at the end of the opera she will throw herself into the precipice to follow Hagenbach, who has been swept away by an avalanche. On the other hand, she can also be shy and emotionally fragile, and is prey to melancholy and sudden mood swings. In Act 2 she confesses that she has never been kissed, and has always dreamt of resting her head on Hagenbach's breast and staying close to him for ever. After saving him in Act 3 she renounces him and gives all her possessions away to Afra, his fiancée, so that they can live happily together while she retreats once more to her hut up on high. Wally's behaviour never ceases to surprise and unsettle her community.

This new kind of character is accompanied not so much by a new kind of landscape – although unusual vistas are open – but rather by a new kind of representation. The critic Giuseppe Depanis wrote in 1893 that 'La Wally brings high mountains into the opera house', adding that 'in La Wally local colour is promptly and spontaneously brought to the foreground' and comparing the opera's ambience to that of Aida and Carmen.[44] While high mountains had of course been in the opera house for decades, La Wally does indeed constantly promote a vivid awareness of the landscape in which the action takes place and by which the characters are influenced. What is more, the precise location of each act (the hamlet of Hochstoff, the village of Sölden, the glaciers by the peaks of the Murzoll and the Similaun) is explicitly designated and minutely described, in an unprecedented effort to reproduce as faithfully as possible a very specific kind of reality. This is not simply the 'Tyrol', or 'Switzerland', or 'Savoy': this is the Oetz valley (located in the present-day Austrian Tyrol, west of Innsbruck), a place whose exotic aura is due precisely to its being both real and at the same time fantastically remote for the opera-going public of fin-de-siècle Italy. Catalani and Adolf Hohenstein, the stage and costume designer for the opera's première at La Scala, made a trip especially to the Oetz valley 'in order to copy the costumes and the landscapes from reality', as Catalani himself said.[45] Before going there, however, they had spent a few days at Hillern's villa in Oberammergau, upper Bavaria.[46] Why go especially to the Oetz valley? Did they think they would find costumes substantially different from those they could see at Oberammergau? Why the need to copy the landscapes 'from reality'? Who would have noticed had they not?

These questions will be explored below. For the moment it is important to note that this realism is also significant for the musical dramaturgy of *La Wally*. We do not know whether Catalani attempted to reproduce folk songs or dances, as Petrella had done for *I promessi sposi*. Given the complexity of the opera's stage music, this seems unlikely. What is certain is the centrality of the musical depiction of ambience to the opera's characterisation. Not only does each act begin with a substantial scene-setting introduction, whether for the orchestra alone (Acts 3 and 4) or with the participation of the chorus (Acts 1 and 2), but each act also explores the interaction between 'characteristic' stage music, be it song or dance, and the characters' musical expression.

Walter's edelweiss song, with its various reappearances, is the most obvious example of this interaction. The connection with *Linda* cannot be missed: Walter, a boy sung by a soprano *en travesti*, accompanies himself on the hurdy-gurdy ('cetra') in a song which foreshadows the fate of the heroine (a girl is so enamoured by the candid, resplendent snow that she climbs the highest peaks to be as near as possible to it, only to be buried by an avalanche; she has been turned into a flower which grows in the snow, the edelweiss). After singing it for the first time, Walter reveals that Wally composed it, to everybody's surprise except Gellner's, who has heard Wally sing it before. From this moment onwards, fragments of the song reappear at various points in different guises, not only as stage vocal music or as 'unheard' orchestral music, but also in the vocal lines of Wally and Hagenbach.

More interesting in this respect, however, is the duet for Wally and Hagenbach in Act 2. They dance a *ländler* throughout the scene, but, as the stage direction indicates, 'one could say that they dance without realising it, and often stop dancing in order to talk to each other, as if the harmony that guides them is not that of the instruments, but comes from their lips' ('si direbbe che danzino senza accorgersene e spesso cessano di danzare per parlarsi, quasi che l'armonia che li conduce non sia già quella degli strumenti, ma quella che esce dalle loro labbra'). Catalani translates this scenic and psychological indication into music by starting off with a 'real' *ländler*, but one that soon turns to a degree of chromaticism beyond any folk idiom.[47] After the opening choral intervention is completed, the musical spotlight focuses on Wally and Hagenbach, who sing to each other in a *parlante melodico* style, their freely declamatory vocal line sustained by the orchestra. What is remarkable is the constant presence of the rhythmic articulation of the *ländler*, no matter how mentally isolated from their surroundings Wally and Hagenbach become. This rhythm survives not only modulations to distant keys (from E flat major to E major, for example), but also metrical changes, from the initial 3/4 to 12/8 at Hagenbach's 'Perché, Wally, sei bella' – Catalani expressly indicates 'continuando lo stesso movimento'.[48] After the climax of the duet, when Wally has yielded to Hagenbach's pressing requests for a kiss, the *ländler* does not stop immediately, but is brought to a proper conclusion by the chorus laughing at Hagenbach's success; only at this moment do the protagonists snap back into the physical reality surrounding them – as opposed to the reality of their emotions.

What begins as a realistic musical depiction of ambience turns into the perception of this ambience by the characters on stage: at times, engrossed as they are in their exchange, all Wally and Hagenbach hear of the *ländler* is a distorted echo of its rhythmic scansion. But this is not a one-way street from a faithful depiction of external reality to its internal interpretation and distortion. Sonic reality keeps moving in and out of focus as the listening point of view shifts from the crowd to the interiority of the two main characters and back to reality. The fact that stage music and 'unheard' music cannot be kept apart can be interpreted as a sonic translation of the impossibility of keeping ambience and interiority separate. Ambience penetrates the characters' inner selves, and, conversely, these selves transform the perception of ambience. While the Act 2 duet brings this representational give-and-take to the surface, I would argue that the principle pervades the opera. Ambience is always heard through the characters' investment in it, and the characters are heard through their participation in a specific sonic ambience. Landscape is not a character in *La Wally*, but a very specific visual and sonic presence of which each character partakes.

The character who seems most vividly aware of this predicament is of course Wally herself: not by chance is she a poet/composer. Alone in the opera, she is constantly aware of the sonic reality in which she is embedded. Most famously, in her Act 1 aria she sings that she will go far away, 'just like the echo of the church bell' ('Ebben?. . . Ne andrò lontana, come va l'eco della pia campana'). The beginning of her vocal line, stuck on the pitch B, seems indeed to echo the B repeated by the orchestra immediately before she starts singing. The sound of a bell tolling finds immediate resonance and amplification in Wally's innermost self, of which her music is the direct manifestation – perhaps it is precisely the aural landscape around her that ignites Wally's emotions, which then betray their origin in their vocal manifestation (Ex. 5.6).

Wally spends most of Act 3 listening for noises coming from outside, and realises that Hagenbach is still alive when she hears his laments from the bottom of the ravine. Most noticeably, in the last act her sonic awareness is constantly alert, whether to fragments of the edelweiss song sung by Walter or to the wind. The final exchange with Hagenbach is in the first instance an exchange of voices, in turn heard, misheard, not heard, or heard all too well by Wally, who reacts most strongly not to the meaning of her beloved's words, but to their sound: 'The harmony of his words kills me!'

Ex. 5.6. Catalani, *La Wally*, Act 1: Wally, 'Ebben. . . Ne andrò lontana'.

('L'armonia delle sue parole m'uccide!'). When Hagenbach disappears to search for a path by which they can descend, they keep contact through their voices – 'He is calling me!. . . I hear you!' ('Mi chiama!. . . T'odo!'). Finally, she realises that Hagenbach has been killed by the avalanche – which produces a 'terrible roar' ('schianto terribile') – because he no longer responds. Silence is death – 'Dismal silence!. . . Death is down there!' ('Cupo silenzio!. . . La morte è laggiù!') – and she must now die. She leaps into the abyss, into the landscape, just as she leapt onto the stage out of the landscape at her first appearance. What matters most is not that she comes from landscape and to landscape she finally returns, but that, while on stage, she constantly listens to landscape and its sounds. The most striking novelty of Wally is not her strange mixture of violence and vulnerability, or her 'high' textual language and chromatic musical one. It is how she hears, and how she makes us hear in turn.

This aural investment in landscape not only constitutes the most important sign of *La Wally*'s new representational strategies and of the modernity of its heroine; it also participates in a larger socio-cultural discourse on the Alps that emerged in fin-de-siècle Italy, a discourse to which *La Wally* provided the most original operatic contribution.

IN SEARCH OF PURITY

The intimate interaction between landscape and character staged in *La Wally* contrasts in revealing ways with another successful opera from the 1890s, Umberto Giordano's *Fedora*, to a libretto by Arturo Colautti (Milan, Teatro Lirico, 1898). Act 3 takes place at Fedora's villa in the Swiss Oberland. The protagonist, a Russian princess from St Petersburg responsible for the death of her lover Loris's brother and mother, has moved to the Alps in search of peace for her tormented soul. The final act of the opera's source, Victorien Sardou's play *Fédora* (1882), took place not in Switzerland, however, but in Fédora's Paris apartment. Why did Colautti and Giordano decide on such a radical change of setting? Perhaps the history of opera played a significant part in their decision. Fedora longs for her lost innocence (if not, strictly speaking, her virginity) and, like the educated opera-goer she is, believes she can find it in the Swiss landscape. But Alpine nature fails to resolve Fedora's problems of conscience: she commits suicide by drinking poison, although Loris pardons her immediately before her death.

The dramatisation of Fedora's quest for purity rests on an initial accumulation of the usual markers of Alpine local colour. The act opens with French horns in the wings playing a *ranz des vaches* complete with echo effects; then an off-stage chorus of peasant girls sings a rustic song – rustic in its simple textual syntax as well as in its stubborn refusal to leave the tonic – about spring and birds and a hurdy-gurdy; immediately following this song the orchestra plays a *ländler*-like dance, although there is no dancing on stage; finally, Fedora enters to orchestral repetitions of fragments of the *ranz des vaches* and the song, underpinned by a continuous tremolo. After Loris has welcomed her with an ecstatic 'how beautiful you are!' ('quanto sei bella!'), she 'looks admiringly to the various bunches of flowers; then runs from one to the other, picking them and dropping them in her upturned skirt' ('guarda ammirata d'intorno i cespi fioriti; corre poi dall'uno all'altro, e si riempie la gonna rimboccata di fiori'):

FEDORA
Oh, che bei fiori! Oh, quanti!. . .
(*a Loris*)
Non ami, dunque, i fior?

LORIS (*teneramente le si avvicina*)
Te sola io guardo, o umano fior,
O fior perfetto, o fior di giovinezza,
O fior di passione, o fior dei fiori,
O fior d'amor!
(*la bacia lungamente*)[49]

FEDORA: What beautiful flowers! So many! (*to Loris*) You don't like flowers, then?
LORIS: (*moving tenderly towards her*) I have eyes only for you, human flower, perfect flower, flower of youth, flower of passion, flower of flowers, flower of love!
(*he gives her a long kiss*)

The scene is brought to a close by one final round of *ranz des vaches* and tremolos building up to a concluding fortissimo.[50] *C'est trop.* Fedora seems to be trying to become one with the landscape, with nature surrounding her, but the sheer accumulation of local colour, and above all the orchestral passage accompanying her entrance, lend her quest a tinge of desperation, a slightly hysterical edge, as if deep down she were aware that the landscape will not save her, that she is doomed.[51]

This redemptive failure of landscape is dramatised later in the act as a stark juxtaposition between ambience music and Fedora's music. After she has learned that she is the unwilling cause of the death of

Loris's brother and mother, and that Loris will soon find this out, she is left alone on stage, devastated. At this point bells are heard calling the evening prayer, their sound echoing in the valley, and a young Savoyard boy walking off-stage accompanies himself on a concertina for what sounds like the refrain of a missing *couplet*. On the last chord of the song Fedora launches into the first of her two solos of the act, 'Dio di giustizia', a prayer to God to save her love; but no attempt is made to connect her musical idiom, a broad cantabile sustained by arpeggiated chords in the orchestra, with the sounds of landscape. Giordano opts instead for stark juxtaposition, emphasised by yet another repetition of a *ranz des vaches* fragment and its echo as soon as the aria ends. The sounds of landscape and the sounds of the character's interiority are brought into contact but kept apart. Fedora cannot communicate with the landscape because she does not seem capable of hearing its voice: here lies her tragedy. At the very end the Savoyard boy is heard again, following with a fragment of his song Fedora's second solo, 'Tutto tramonta', and then concluding the opera with another fragment, after the heroine's death. His is the last voice we hear, the voice of an ultimately indifferent landscape from which Fedora has been excluded.[52]

Mercedes Viale Ferrero has suggested another reason why Colautti and Giordano moved *Fedora*'s third act from Paris to the Bernese Oberland: the recent vogue among the European higher classes of tourism, especially sport tourism.[53] Loris's costume for this act is in fact that of 'a mountaineer' ('da alpinista').[54] Italy's most famous mountaineer of the 1890s was perhaps Queen Margherita of Savoy, whose passion for climbing trips in the Alps was well known. But the impact of tourism on the operatic representation of the Alps in late-nineteenth-century Italy went well beyond Loris's mountaineering costume and even Colautti and Giordano's choice of ambience for Act 3 of *Fedora*. Significant aspects of the works mentioned thus far in this chapter, in fact, acquire meaning only when considered within the context of the increasing impact of tourism on the cultural construction of the Alps in the second half of the century.

As mentioned in chapter 2, Italy did not contribute significantly to European Alpine iconography in the first part of the century, nor did the Alps feature as a prominent theme in Italian poetry.[55] It was left to *I promessi sposi* and above all to opera to present the Alpine landscape to educated Italians; but, as we have seen, these works offered a view of the Alps from their foot. Alpine tourism had been popular in northern European countries, especially France and Great Britain, for several decades, but it did not take hold in Italy until well after unification. The first and most prominent organisation devoted to its promotion, the 'Club Alpino Italiano', was founded in Turin in 1863, but its membership initially remained confined to a relatively small number of eager mountaineers. It was only towards the end of the century that tourism in general and Alpine tourism in particular became a frequent experience for the Italian upper classes, at least in the northern regions.[56] No longer restricted to English gentlemen on their *grand tour* or French painters in search of picturesque views – the *buffo* of Pedrotti's *Fiorina* is a 'pittore francese', 'one of those who do the tour of Switzerland on foot' ('uno di coloro che fanno il viaggio della Svizzera a piedi') – the Alps were 'invaded' by the bourgeois, including Italians, brought there by railways, which start 'penetrating' the Alpine region from the 1860s.[57]

The rhetoric of invasion and penetration, of defloration of a virgin landscape, dominated the discourse on the Alps towards the end of the nineteenth century. Many angry voices could be cited, for example that of Jules Michelet in his *La Montagne* of 1868. But perhaps the most resonant outcry was by John Ruskin, in the following apostrophe to his contemporaries in *Sesame and Lilies*:

> You have despised Nature. . .You have put a railroad-bridge over the falls of Schaffhausen. You have tunnelled the cliffs of Lucerne by Tell's chapel. . . The Alps themselves, which your own poets used to love so reverently, you look upon as soaped poles in a bear-garden, which you set yourselves to climb and slide down again, with 'shrieks of delight'. When you are past shrieking, having no human articulate voice to say you are glad with, you fill the quietude of their valleys with gunpowder

blasts, and rush home, red with cutaneous eruptions of conceit, and voluble with convulsive hiccoughs of self-satisfaction.[58]

How could the popularity of the Alps as a tourist destination be reconciled with their ongoing cultural idealisation as sublime or idyllic? This was the contradiction that enraged Ruskin. While there is no Italian equivalent to Ruskin in his fury, a similar problem presented itself to a culture that, on the one hand, was absorbing the idealisation of this landscape from northern countries but, on the other, was also looking at this same landscape from an ever closer perspective. In 'Idillio', one of the 'human portraits' included in *La desinenza in A*, Carlo Dossi, the subtlest observer of Italy's contradictory relationship with modernity in the closing decades of the nineteenth century, went for parody. A young man writes a long letter to a friend celebrating life in the mountains (where he has recently moved from a city), the love of a peasant girl and his intention to 'educate' her: all the commonplaces surrounding the Alps and its inhabitants are displayed in an increasingly emphatic accumulation, eventually bordering on the grotesque. The second and final letter is much shorter: all it contains is a request for stavesacre, a pomade used to get rid of headlice.[59] Dossi's heavy irony and virtuosic rhetoric are not, however, representative of Italian attitudes at this time. Two other examples better illustrate Italy's uncomfortable combination of remoteness and closeness, idealisation and realism: those of Giovanni Segantini and Giosuè Carducci.

Segantini was one of the most successful painters of the Italian fin de siècle and a prominent exponent of divisionism. Originally from the province of Trento, after a period in Milan in 1880 he moved to the Brianza region, north of the city, to paint *en plein air*. In 1886 he settled in Savognin, a village in the Grisons canton, Switzerland, but six years later he decided to move even higher up, to an isolated *chalet* near the Maloja, in the Engadine valley. His quest for the luminous atmospheric clarity of high mountains went hand in hand with a progressively more exclusive focus on episodes of rural life set in the empty, dramatic spaces of the Engadine Alps. In the last decade of his life these episodes acquired ever more resonant symbolic meanings, eventually leaving behind any suggestion of the quotidian to focus on allegory (for example in *Punishment of the Lustful Women*, 1891, and the famous *Wicked Mothers*, 1894). In the words of art historian Aurora Scotti Tosini, 'the vast spaces of the Alpine landscape around Maloja were chosen by Segantini as the only setting able to give adequate resonance to the moral values he wished to express'.[60] Shortly before his death he tried to promote a multi-media installation for the Paris Exposition Universelle of 1900, a panorama of the Engadine in which gigantic paintings as well as water and sound machines would recreate the experience of the high mountains as realistically as possible, with a view to promoting tourism in the region.[61] One famous reaction to Segantini's art was that of the futurist Umberto Boccioni, who polemically proclaimed that he could not understand paintings that looked as if they had been commissioned by a tourist board – the 'Touring Club Italiano', the first Italian national organisation for the promotion of tourism, had been founded in Milan in 1894.[62]

Carducci's *œuvre* is perhaps the most significant example of the prominence of the Alps in Italian poetry at the fin de siècle. The themes of Carducci's extensive exploration are already evident in one of the earliest poems dedicated to the Alps, 'Mattino alpestre' (from *Rime nuove*, 1887), which opens with the image of the first rays of the sun progressively illuminating an Alpine landscape 'like the eyes of a virgin who answers to a new love' ('come occhi d'una vergine che a nuovo amor risponde').[63] This exploration reaches its climax in Carducci's last collection, *Rime e ritmi* (1899), where the Alps are evoked in poem after poem as the site of untouched, virginal nature, of pure snow, blinding sun, clear skies, profound silence; a site of 'serenity, intensity and infinity', to adapt a line from the famous 'Mezzogiorno alpino' ('Alpine midday'): 'Regna sereno intenso ed infinito / nel suo grande silenzio il mezzodì' ('Midday reigns serene, intense and infinite in its great silence').[64] Paradoxically, this poetic representation of the Alps is directly linked to Carducci's experience of them as a tourist, as the names of locations placed at the end of many poems or directly cited in them indicate, from Piano d'Arta (Carnia, Eastern Alps) to Pieve di Cadore (Dolomites), from Madesimo to Spluga (both in the Lombard Alps), from Courmayeur and Gressoney-la-Trinité (Val d'Aosta) to Ceresole Reale (Piedmont).

I would suggest that both Segantini and Carducci undertook a reconsecration of the Alps for Italian culture. They tried both to bring the landscape close to viewers/readers and to distance it from them, to make it at once familiar and remote, domestic and fantastic. They wanted to preserve the landscape's exclusive moral qualities while making it available, visually and textually if not experientially, to an inclusive, potentially amoral public. Segantini's ever more allegorical subjects are nonetheless always set in a landscape whose capacity to give 'adequate resonance to the moral values he wished to express' (to recall Scotti Tosini's words) depends on what he considered its fiercely realistic representation. He employed his divisionist technique to render with accurate realism the exceptional qualities of light and atmosphere in the upper Engadine. Similarly, Carducci's descriptions of Alpine landscapes insist on their untouched purity, their total remoteness, their existence apart from any form of human habitation. When humans make a rare appearance, they tend to do so as part of the landscape, almost indistinguishable from glaciers and trees, rivers and birds.[65] And yet both Segantini and Carducci were deeply implicated in the machine of tourism, the first as a promoter, the second as a consumer.

This dialectical relationship to the Alps is central to *La Wally*'s representational aesthetics. I have already mentioned that Catalani and Hohenstein travelled to the Oetz valley 'in order to copy the costumes and landscapes from reality'. The resulting four scenes, however, are anything but realistic, at least judging from Hohenstein's colour sketches. It is difficult to pinpoint what contributes most to the poetic effect of the scenes. The restricted choice of colour, its predominance of pastel tones, seems to suggest that this is a world in which colours – and therefore people and life – are simple and 'natural', in obvious opposition to the complexities, chromatic and otherwise, of the modern, 'artificial' urban existence of the audience. Similar considerations might be suggested by the proximity of human dwellings and vegetation, which goes significantly further than in any previous stage designs I have examined, and may recall both Segantini's rustic scenes and Carducci's representation of human beings as part of the landscape. The final effect is fairy-tale-like, and betrays an intention to place the action in an 'other' location on purely geographical terms, without any recourse to the historicising signs normally employed by nineteenth-century Italian stage designers (Figs. 5.1–5.4).

Why go to the Oetz valley to copy landscape and costumes, then, if the result was to place the action in an 'other', fairy-tale location? Perhaps the journey to the Oetztal served this aesthetics precisely, if at first sight paradoxically. If the landscape had to be that of an 'other' location, it could be so only if it attempted to reproduce realistically not just any Alpine landscape, but a very specifically located Alpine landscape: not Chamonix, or Courmayeur, or Cortina d'Ampezzo, or Thun, but Sölden in the Oetztal, then not yet reached by mass tourism, at least by Italians. A new kind of Alpine virgin could be portrayed in new ways only as part of a landscape that was both familiar and remote, not only in its location but also in the way it was represented. Illica and Catalani's use of all the topoi familiar from the Alpine virgin operas to portray a new kind of interaction between landscape and characters seems therefore comparable to Hohenstein's fairy-tale realism in its combination of the familiar with the remote, in its interpenetration of old and new. In other words, the landscape of *La Wally* is both presented for theatrical consumption to a public who could, and in many cases would, consume it in reality, and depicted as ultimately not for consumption, since this public could never aspire to enter its representational aesthetics, which 'morally' belonged only in this real and fantastic place called 'Oetztal'.

That entering this representation of the Alps in fin-de-siècle Italian culture was merely an illusion is made clear by *Fedora*, whose protagonist I have pointedly called earlier an avid opera-goer. What

Fig. 5.1. Adolf Hohenstein, stage design for Act I of Catalani's *La Wally* (Milan, Teatro alla Scala, 1892).

Fig. 5.2. Adolf Hohenstein, stage design for Act 2 of Catalani's *La Wally* (Milan, Teatro alla Scala, 1892).

Fig. 5.3. Adolf Hohenstein, stage design for Act 3 of Catalani's *La Wally* (Milan, Teatro alla Scala, 1892).

Fig. 5.4. Adolf Hohenstein, stage design for Act 4 of Catalani's *La Wally* (Milan, Teatro alla Scala, 1892).

is most significant is that *Fedora* stages the failure to break into this world in both its narrative and its representational techniques, in both content and form. Besides being an opera-goer, Fedora is a tourist, and therefore cannot hear the landscape as Wally does: she simply does not belong to it, despite her best efforts to the contrary. She can travel to the Alps, walk on them, pick their flowers; but she cannot become part of their 'morality'. She is prevented from doing so also by another fatal condition: besides being an opera-goer and a tourist, she is not a virgin.

The classics of the Alpine virgin tradition, *La sonnambula* and *Linda di Chamounix*, reached their lowest point in popularity in the early twentieth century. The compromised morality of the Alpine landscape in fin-de-siècle Italy certainly did not help their fortunes: the growing vogue of the Alps as a tourist destination was constructed as a process of defloration, threatening their idealisation as a prime site for moral and bodily purity. The third act of *Fedora* staged, in both narrative and representational terms, the failure of Segantini, Carducci and Illica/Catalani to make this landscape both consumable and unattainable. In Pietro Mascagni's *Amica*,[1] set in Savoy, no attention is paid to the Alpine landscape after the introductory chorus, despite Amica's suicide by jumping into a gorge – an obvious reference to *La Wally* but one without any meaningful intertextual connection. In any case, *Amica*'s Alpine setting was by now a rarity. More generally, as Luigi Baldacci has observed, while *La sonnambula* belonged to a culture within which the pastoral idyll had a well-defined place, in Italy this theme seemed to have exhausted its signifying potential by 1900.[2]

The Alpine virgin convention did not disappear without trace, however: its shadow looms large in at least one Italian opera of the new century, Puccini's *La fanciulla del West* (libretto by Carlo Zangarini and Guelfo Civinini, premièred at the Metropolitan Opera in New York on 10 December 1910). Viewing *Fanciulla* via its connections with this tradition can provide an entry into the dramaturgy and significance of a work that, after nearly a century, has not found a position within the history of Italian opera, or even within Puccini's *œuvre*. This point of view may also help connect the opera with trends that shaped Italian culture and society of the time, but have rarely played a part in Puccini criticism. Taking them into account may even suggest new ways in which we can discuss Puccini's attempts to come to terms with the aesthetics of modernism – attempts that left a profound mark on Puccini's operas starting precisely with *La fanciulla del West*, but have seldom been discussed in other than musical-stylistic terms.

THE VIRGIN OF THE SIERRA NEVADA

The connections between *La fanciulla del West* and the Alpine virgin tradition are self-evident: Puccini's opera is set in a miners' camp on the Californian Sierra Nevada and its protagonist, Minnie, is a virgin. Both the setting and the heroine's purity are explicitly and extensively thematised. Closely following the opera's source, David Belasco's play *The Girl of the Golden West*, the action takes place 'at the foot of the Cloudy Mountains in California' ('ai piedi delle Montagne delle Nubi [*Cloudy Mountains*] in California').[3] The mountains dominate the action of each act from afar. In Act 1 they are seen through the large door and window at the back of the main room of the 'Polka' saloon: 'The valley can be glimpsed, with its wild vegetation of elders, oaks and short conifers, baked in the flaming light of sunset. In the distance, the snowy mountains fade into golden and purple tones' ('Si scorge la valle, con la sua vegetazione selvaggia di sambuchi, quercie, conifere basse, tutta avvolta nel fiammeggiare del tramonto. Lontano, le montagne nevose si sfumano di toni d'oro e di viola'). Act 3 takes place in a forest clearing on a mountain slope, with 'very high, snow-capped mountain peaks' ('picchi nevosi altissimi di montagne') in the background among the trees and shining brightly when the sunlight hits them half-way through the act.[4] No mountains are mentioned in the setting of Act 2, Minnie's cabin, as described in the libretto (and in Belasco), but a staging manual probably connected to the first production asks for a backdrop of 'snow-capped mountains' to be glimpsed through the two windows in the back wall of the cabin.[5]

In Act 1 Minnie tells Johnson that she lives in a cabin 'half-way up the mountain' ('a mezzo il monte'), but it is in Act 2 that she reveals

to him the full meaning of her closeness to the mountains. To his
reflection 'how strange your life must be high up on this mountain,
alone and so far from the world!' ('che cosa strana la vostra vita, su
questa montagna solitaria, lontana dal mondo!'), she answers 'with
gaiety':

> Oh, se sapeste
> Come il vivere è allegro!
> Ho un piccolo polledro
> Che mi porta a galoppo
> Laggiù per la campagna;
> Per prati di giunchiglie,
> Di garofani ardenti,
> Per riviere profonde
> Cui profuman le sponde
> Gelsomini e vainiglie!
> Poi ritorno ai miei pini,
> Ai monti della Sierra,
> Così al cielo vicini
> Che Iddio passando pare
> La sua mano v'inclini,
> Lontani dalla terra
> Così, che vien la voglia
> Di battere alla soglia
> Del cielo, per entrare!. . .

> Oh, if only you knew what a happy life it is! I've got a little colt and
> I gallop all over the countryside, through fields of jonquils and fiery
> carnations, by deep rivers, with scented banks of jasmine and vanilla!
> Then I return to my pines, the mountains of the Sierra, so close to
> Heaven that God in passing seems to stretch down his hand, so far
> from earth that you suddenly feel like knocking on the gate of heaven
> to be let in![6]

Never in the century-long tradition of Alpine operas had the symbolic meaning of mountains as a site of spiritual elevation, of re-
moval from wordly concerns, been so explicitly invoked. Nor had the
bond between the mountains and the protagonist been so obvious:

this landscape literally belongs to Minnie, who at the end of the opera will say farewell to California, the Sierra and the snow emphasising that they are hers: 'Farewell, my sweet country; farewell, my California! Lovely Sierra mountains, snows, farewell!. . .' ('Addio, mia dolce terra; / addio, mia California! Bei monti della Sierra, o nevi, addio!. . .'). In 'Oh, se sapeste' Minnie's vocal line promotes her investment in the landscape by way of its overtly mimetic quality, first imitating the galloping colt with semiquaver turns on a descending scale at 'un piccolo polledro che mi porta a galoppo', and then describing the ascent to the mountains and the sky with a progressively ascending tessitura, up to a sustained high A on 'cielo' followed by a B on 'entrar'. Minnie keeps a faithful image of the landscape in her soul, and therefore knows how to represent this landscape in song.

'Oh, my mountains – I'm leaving you – Oh, my California, I'm leaving you – Oh, my lovely West – my Sierras! – I'm leaving you!' are the final words of Minnie and Johnson in Belasco's play, whose second act also contains Minnie's monologue on the landscape – where she declares, rather more explicitly than in the opera, that 'God's in the air here, sure'.[7] But while in the play the two lovers say goodbye to an invisible landscape, in the opera the snow-capped peaks bask in sunlight. The libretto closely follows Belasco's play for the first two acts, but Puccini himself devised the last act of the opera as a fusion of Belasco's Acts 3 and 4, which take place in 'the dance hall of the "Polka"' and then on 'the boundless prairies of the West', with no mountains to be seen in the background.[8] In fact, Belasco's Minnie explicitly comments on the disappearance of the mountains from her horizon: '(*Looking towards the unseen hills in the distance.*) Another day. . . Look back. . . the foothills are growing fainter – every dawn – farther away. Some nights when I am going to sleep, I'll turn – and they won't be there – red and shining. That was the promised land'.[9] It was Puccini who invented the setting of Act 3 in the forest clearing with the mountains in the background. As Mercedes Viale Ferrero has suggested, this forest is reminiscent of the one at the beginning of *Pelléas et Mélisande* (at least in the way they are devised in the two operas' staging manuals) and perhaps even of the one in *Parsifal* (especially as conceived by Adolphe Appia), all subscribing to the topical symbolism of the forest as the site where people get lost and find each other again in fatal encounters – Parsifal with Gurnemanz and Kundry, Golaud with Mélisande, Minnie with Johnson and his lynch-mob.[10] But the presence of the mountains in the background emphasises the connection between this ambience and previous Alpine operas, giving visual impact to the heroine's final farewell to 'her' landscape.

Minnie's virginity is explicitly declared in her description at the start of the libretto: she is 'fiercely virginal' ('fieramente verginale'). As she confesses to Johnson in Act 1, she has never danced in her life, despite running a saloon where dancing regularly takes place; what is more, she has never been kissed. According to Johnson, her innocence is guaranteed by her lack of self-consciousness and self-awareness: 'You don't know yourself. You are a good, pure-hearted creature. . . and you have the face of an angel' ('Voi non vi conoscete. Siete una creatura d'anima buona e pura. . . e avete un viso d'angelo'). It will come as no surprise, then, that she knows little about dressing up to make herself look good for Johnson, whose direct approaches she resists at first, with embarrassed confusion.

But Minnie is not simply virginal, she is *fiercely* so. Her full description paints a more complex portrait compared to Amina, Linda, Luisa and their younger sisters: 'A strange type, sweet and energetic, a mixture of the wild and the civilised, fiercely virginal, strong of both muscle and spirit' ('Tipo strano, dolce ed energico, un misto di selvaggio e di civilizzato, fieramente verginale, forte di muscoli e di spirito'). A comparison with *The Girl of the Golden West* proves that the libretto's description is not simply a condensation of the one in the play: 'The character of the girl is rather complex. Her utter frankness takes away all suggestion of vice – showing her to be unsmirched, happy, careless, untouched by the life about her. Yet she has a thorough knowledge of what the men of her world generally want. She is used to flattery – knows exactly how to deal with men –

is very shrewd – but quite capable of being a good friend to the camp boys'.[11] Her 'fierce virginity' is thus an addition of the libretto. While directly drawing attention to Minnie's bodily purity, and therefore connecting her to previous Italian opera virgins, this reference also distances her from her sisters. She is thus a virgin, but a new kind of virgin: not only 'sweet', but also 'energetic', 'strong of both muscle and spirit', a description hardly fitting Amina or Linda.[12]

On the one hand, then, La fanciulla del West exhibits important connections to the Alpine virgin tradition of Italian opera; on the other, it introduces significant innovations into this conventional coupling of a mountain setting and a virginal heroine. For these reasons, Puccini's opera can function as a privileged point of view from which to consider the ambiguous relationship between the works of the so-called 'giovane scuola' of Italian opera, of which Puccini was the most important member, and their Bellinian, Donizettian and Verdian predecessors. This relationship has been investigated mostly in two directions: musicologists have concentrated on musical innovations, especially formal and tonal, while literary critics have scrutinised changes in libretto style, especially from a linguistic point of view. Only rarely have themes and genres played a prominent role in this discussion; sustained attention to larger socio-cultural trends has been even rarer, especially if the music is kept in sight. In this chapter I first investigate the opera's portrayal of its protagonist from a gender-sensitive point of view, placing this portrayal in the context of contemporary Italian discourse on gender. Following this discourse in connecting gender to place, I then address the Italian reception of the American West at the turn of the twentieth century, returning to Fanciulla for an exploration of its representation of landscape and space.

ON LEARNING FEMININE RHETORICS

If Minnie's virginal, innocent side is depicted in a few, boldly drawn moments, her wild, 'muscular' side is perhaps even more boldly drawn, beginning with her entrance. At the moment when an

argument between Sonora, one of the miners, and the sheriff Jack
Rance is about to turn into a brawl, she suddenly appears and puts an
end to the commotion with a mixture of moral authority and bodily
strength:

> [*Sonora e Rance*] *si azzuffano; gli altri cercano di dividerli, ma non fanno a
> tempo: una donna è entrata d'un balzo, li ha, con fermo polso, divisi
> violentemente, strappando dalle mani di Sonora la pistola. È Minnie. Bello
> la segue, fermandosi al banco a guardare, ammirato. Un grido scoppia da
> tutte le parti: l'ira cade subitamente: solo Rance si apparta, tutto cupo,
> nella sua sedia di sinistra.*
>
> TUTTI (*con entusiasmo, agitando i cappelli*)
> Hello, Minnie! Hello, Minnie!
>
> MINNIE (*avanzandosi, con autorità*)
> Che cos'è stato?. . .
> (*severa, a Sonora*)
>   Sempre tu, Sonora?
>
> TRIN
> Nulla, Minnie; sciocchezze. . . Si scherzava!
>
> MINNIE (*adirata*)
> Voi manderete tutto alla malora!
> Vergogna!

*Sonora and Rance fight; the others try to separate them, but they are too late:
a woman leaps in and violently divides them with a firm hand, taking
the pistol away from Sonora. It is Minnie. Bello follows her, stopping
at the bar to watch in admiration. A shout explodes from all sides and
tempers calm down immediately; only Rance, very sombre, sits apart on
the left.*

ALL: (*enthusiastically, waving their hats*) Hello, Minnie! Hello,
Minnie!

MINNIE: (*advancing, with authority*) What's happened?
(*severely, to Sonora*) You again, Sonora?

TRIN: It's nothing, Minnie; just nonsense. . . we were only joking!

MINNIE: (*angry*) You'll ruin everything! Shame on you!

Minnie's entrance recalls Wally's leap onto the stage in Act 1 of Catalani's opera, both women putting an end to a fight by using violence themselves. These two characters, both explicitly designated as 'strange' ('strana creatura' Wally, 'strano tipo' Minnie), are set apart from the communities to which they nominally belong: Wally through her behaviour and her language; Minnie not only through her behaviour, but also simply through her gender, since she is the only woman, or at least the only Western woman, living amidst a community of men (Wowkle, the 'Indian squaw' and Minnie's servant, is defined almost exclusively in terms of her race; she and her man Billy are clearly not considered members of this community). In this sense, Minnie advances a more radical novelty than Wally, her 'strangeness' more emphatically and exclusively linked to her gender.

Puccini sets Minnie's entrance to a theme that has been interpreted in rather different ways, to say the least. To take three prominent critics, Mosco Carner considers the 'expansive, lyrical theme' a representation of 'the young girl, dreaming of the bliss of pure, innocent love'.[13] For Michele Girardi, the theme fixes 'the image of an authoritative and passionate woman. [. . .] The sonority of the orchestra (più che fortissimo), with horns at every octave, reflects the unusual situation of a woman disarming two men. This moment of emphasis is necessary to the action, but at the same time, more subtly, the two augmented chords reveal Minnie's sentimental side'.[14] Most recently, Julian Budden indicates in this theme 'one of the main pillars of the score, being associated exclusively with the heroine, whose authority over the men is considerably greater than that of Rance. It is very much the "new" Puccini: short phrases with wide intervals, each concluding with a dissonance that remains unresolved until its successor brings a change of harmony'.[15]

One way to interpret this disagreement would be to point to the problematic methodological grounds on which such precise identifications rest – in this sense Budden's restraint seems a virtue. Another way, perhaps more fruitful to my argument, is to suggest that this theme seems to strive towards a multiplicity of meanings, a complexity of characterisation that will reduce Minnie neither to a young

Ex. 6.1. Puccini, *La fanciulla del West*, Act 1: Minnie's entrance.

girl dreaming of the bliss of pure, innocent love – a Western version of Mimì – nor to an authoritative and passionate woman – a wild-West Tosca. In this sense it is precisely a 'new' Puccini we meet here, a Puccini trying to embody in one musical idea the multiple and often contradictory sides of a different kind of heroine. Besides the jagged melodic profile, the major seventh, ninth and augmented chords, the unresolved dissonances and sudden tonal shifts, and the lack of proper resolution, it should not go unmentioned that, immediately before Minnie's entrance, the orchestra had seemed to prepare a move to G, so that the theme's disruption of tonal expectations emphasises the unusual woman whose appearance it accompanies (Ex. 6.1).[16]

In the next scene the miners offer Minnie not only a bunch of wild flowers – entirely in keeping with her virginal, 'natural' state – but also a ribbon 'deep red like your mouth' ('color porpora come la vostra bocca') and a silk handkerchief 'light blue like your eyes' ('azzurro, come il vostro sguardo'), both the objects and their colours suggesting a 'frivolous' side to Minnie. At the same time

Minnie herself dismisses the 'adventuress' Nina Micheltorena, the only other woman of the camp, as 'a siren who uses lampblack to give herself a languid eye' ('una sirena che fa molto consumo di nerofumo per farsi l'occhio languido') – who, in other words, performs femininity in a way Minnie deems improper.[17]

What constitutes a proper performance of femininity and masculinity emerges as one of the central themes of the opera. When in Act I Rance tries to convince Minnie to marry him by telling her that 'you can't stay here alone' ('tu non puoi star qui sola'), she answers 'with pride' ('con fierezza'):

> Rance, basta! M'offendete!
> Vivo sola così, voi lo sapete,
> Perché così mi piace. . .
> (*frugandosi in petto e facendo luccicare in faccia a Rance una pistola*)
> (*basso, sommesso, ma con forza*)
> Con questa compagnia sicura e buona,
> Che mai non m'abbandona. . .
> Rance, lasciatemi in pace.

> Enough, Rance! You insult me! I live alone like this because I like it, as you know. . . (*pulling a pistol from her breast and waving it in Rance's face*) (*in a low, quiet voice, but forcefully*). . . with this good, faithful companion that never deserts me. . . Rance, just leave me in peace.

What Minnie proposes here is a new conception of femininity, one that emphasises independence and self-reliance. But this new femininity seems too fragile to command respect on its own (at least in a Californian mining camp): it needs a pistol to help it along. What is more, Minnie draws the pistol out of her cleavage, a gesture underlining the hybrid nature of this femininity, defended by a male-connotated object emerging out of a crucial part of the female body. By contrast, Johnson's masculinity is called into question, both before and after this moment: when Minnie hears that he has ordered whisky and water, she exclaims in disbelief 'what kind of joke is this?' ('che son questi pasticci?'), adding 'we'll make his hair curl' ('gli aggiusteremo i ricci') – later Rance will call him 'that fine-haired dog

from Sacramento' ('quel can di pelo fino giunto da Sacramento').
But this interpretation of masculinity, decidedly unusual among
the miners, emerges as the winning one, the one that eventually
conquers Minnie.

The initial description of Johnson's character emphasises the
positive aspects of his gender performance: 'Handsome man of
about thirty, with a soft, healthy and delicate face, the aspect of a
gentleman, and a civil, easy, simple and proud bearing. He wears
riding boots, a leather jacket and corduroy trousers: a travelling
outfit, with details suggesting a habit of elegance' ('Bell'uomo: circa
trent'anni: viso morbido, sano e delicato: aria di gentiluomo, porta-
mento civile, disinvolto, semplice, fiero. Stivali da cavallo, giacca di
cuoio, pantaloni di velluto: vestito da viaggio, con particolari di
abituale eleganza'). His face is soft and delicate, but at the same time
healthy; he wears regular male clothes, but showing his habitual
attention to detail. This is a man dressed to show how secure he is in
his masculinity precisely because of his 'feminine' attention to detail.

By contrast, Jack Rance's version of masculinity is riddled with
unresolved contradictions: 'He has a pale, nasty face: black hair;
black, drooping moustache; slightly feminine hands; a big diamond
on his finger. A white, richly embroidered shirtfront, with diamonds
for buttons there and at the wrists; a long, expensive chain hangs on
his neck, supporting his watch; a perfectly-cut redingote, with tight-
fitting trousers, according to the fashion of the time; a beaver top
hat. Cynical and sensual' ('Ha una faccia pallida e cattiva: capelli
neri; baffi neri, spioventi; le mani un poco femminee; al dito un
grosso diamante. Sparato candido, riccamente lavorato; diamanti
alla camicia e ai polsi; una lunga preziosa catena gli scende dal collo,
reggendogli l'orologio; *redingote* di taglio perfetto, calzoni attillati,
secondo il costume del tempo; cappello di castoro a cilindro. Cinico
e sensuale'). Rance's masculinity is problematic not simply because
of its negatively 'feminine' features (he is too fond of jewels and
fancy clothes, for example), but more so because he seems keenly
aware of its performative nature. While Johnson wears clothes,
Rance wears a costume, committing that capital sin for a man: he

is a fashion victim. Both cynical and sensual, he seems a modern, more sinister version of the old libertine (more *Luisa*'s Wurm than *Linda*'s Marchese, but smarter than both).[18]

In Acts 1 and 3 Minnie, like Johnson, wears clothes: 'She wears the very common dress of a bar owner, with bright colours among which red prevails' ('Veste l'abito assai comune di una tenitrice di bar a colori vivaci, con prevalenza di rosso'). In Act 2, however, we witness her putting on a costume, that of 'proper', 'traditional' femininity. The description of her cabin is that of a rustically simple space with some feminine touches to it – the flower-decorated bed canopy, the 'objects for female *toilette*' ('oggetti destinati alla toilette femminile') on the bedside table. She enters in her Act 1 costume, but immediately starts to change: she removes the pistol from her breast and exchanges it for red roses in her hair; after much effort, she manages to put on a pair of very tight white shoes that she had worn in Monterey, when she first met Johnson; her gloves are also tight, and too short: she has not worn them for a year. The transformation completed, she has doubts; 'awkward and happy' ('impacciata e contenta') she asks Wowkle: 'Won't the effect on him be of too much elegance?' ('Non gli farò l'effetto d'essere poi troppo elegante?'). Puccini set a shorter line, however: 'Won't I be too elegant?' ('Non sarò poi troppo elegante?'). She is unsure of her ability to perform traditional femininity, something in which she obviously has little practice – perhaps her hands and feet have grown larger since that first meeting in Monterey, coarsened by labour and difficult living; perhaps spending all her time with men has made her forget how to be a 'proper' woman. Puccini emphasises her naïveté by simplifying her last sentence, which in the original libretto was rather sophisticated grammatically and syntactically in the context of Minnie's portrayal thus far, showing a perhaps too knowing awareness that she is preparing a show for Johnson, that what counts is the effect the show will have.

Minnie's conflicted femininity is explored in several other moments of the opera, perhaps most famously in the card scene at the end of Act 2, when she cheats with 'manly' cold-bloodedness and determination by hiding the winning cards in a feminine garment, her stockings. As suggested above, however, at stake in *La fanciulla del West* is not only Minnie's femininity – or, less prominently, Johnson's and Rance's masculinity – but also the performative nature of this femininity, and of gender in general. Beside the scenes already mentioned, this debate comes to the fore when Minnie convinces the miners to spare Johnson's life in Act 3.

As they prepare to hang him, she bursts on stage on horseback like a warrior – 'gangster's moll, Fury and Valkyrie rolled into one' (Carner)[19] – and takes control with manly forcefulness. Rance desperately tries to call the miners' attention to the fact that she is 'just' a woman, that hers is an act, shouting 'mind your tongue, woman!' ('bada, donna, alle tue parole!') and 'has none of you got blood in your veins? Are you scared of a skirt?' ('nessun di voi ha sangue nelle vene? Una gonna vi fa sbiancare il viso?') – also implying that her behaviour calls into question their masculinity. It is only when Minnie's femininity is positively evoked by Sonora, when he cries that Johnson's biggest crime is to have stolen her heart from them, that, 'suddenly becoming affectionate' ('fatta d'un subito affettuosa'), she reverts to performing this femininity. In the long monologue that follows, she reminds the miners of all the 'feminine' acts she performed for them: she kept watch over sick Harry, who in his delirium mistook her for his sister Maud; she accepted flowers from Joe; she guided Trin's hand as he wrote his first letters back home. She continues reminding Bello that his eyes are those of a child (thus implying her role as his mother), and that they are all her brothers. Finally, in a highly symbolic gesture, she throws away her pistol, and, just in case they have missed the point, tells them how to read the action:

Ecco, getto quest'arma!
Torno quella che fui per voi,
L'amica, la sorella
Che un giorno v'insegnò
Una suprema verità d'amore:
Fratelli, non v'è al mondo

Peccatore cui non s'apra
Una via di redenzione!

Look, I throw away this gun! I'm again what I used to be for you,
your friend, your sister, who once taught you the supreme truth of
love: my brothers, there is not a sinner in the whole world to whom
a way to salvation is not open!

At this point Johnson, acting on everybody's behalf, 'moved, kneels
and kisses the hem of Minnie's dress, while she puts her hand on his
head as if blessing him' ('s'inginocchia commosso, bacia il lembo
della veste di Minnie mentre essa pone la mano sulla testa di lui quasi
benedicendolo').[20] Not only has Minnie returned to being a purely
feminine woman, a mother to all the men on stage: Johnson's
gesture promotes her to an incarnation of the mother of all mothers,
the Virgin Mary, who protectively blesses her sons while they dare
kiss only the hem of her garment.

Puccini set Minnie's speech and the miners' interjections as a kind
of *largo concertato* for soprano, *comprimari* (Sonora the most prominent) and chorus, 'E anche tu lo vorrai, Joe'. This piece has received a
certain amount of critical attention, commentators focusing especially on the rich fabric of themes and motives from earlier in the
score. Since these motives had earlier been assigned a more or less
precise semantic association, had been made to mean something,
their reappearance at this crucial point is taken by critics to contribute to the overall meaning of the piece.[21] I would rather suggest that
what counts most is not which specific themes are brought back, but
simply that so many different themes are reprised, and from very
different and distant moments in the opera. One conclusion is surely
that Minnie has reached a point in her evolution as a character where
she can be a mother, a sister, a friend and a lover at the same time,
where the different aspects of her femininity are reconciled in one
final complex picture.

But another, perhaps more radical conclusion is that Minnie has
learned that this complex femininity is a performance, that she can
draw on all these different materials in order to construct a new kind

of gender identity for herself, which she can somehow control. This claim is, of course, radical mainly because it ignores the composer's authority, granting Minnie a significant degree of control on the musical material and assigning her a compositional agency independent from that of Puccini. If we are willing to grant her this compositional agency, then the newly found control of her musical destiny emerges as the subject of the *largo concertato*, what this *sui generis* piece is all about: Minnie, firmly at the helm, enjoying full access to so many themes and motives and playing freely with them. She can throw away the gun because she wields a far more powerful weapon, that of rhetoric, musical as well as textual. Johnson's kneeling gesture interprets the sentiments of all the men on stage (except Rance) in worshipping a supremely skilled musical dramatist who is also a supremely skilled woman.

In light of this interpretation of the concluding *largo concertato*, the conflicting decodings of Minnie's entrance theme discussed above (docile and demure versus forceful and authoritative) may be read as responses to music ushering in a character who is still unaware of the rhetorical manipulations to which music can be submitted. As I have suggested above, this theme tries to embody the multiple and contradictory sides of a new kind of character; now I would add that this character has not yet learnt how to reconcile these widely different sides into a coherent and integrated performance – a situation which opens up space for widely different interpretations. By the end of the opera Minnie is not only both docile and forceful, demure and authoritative, but knows it. Crucially, she also knows that knowing how to be all these things at once is fundamental to her success as a woman and a character – as a female character.

In a sense, *La fanciulla del West* seems to say that the superior way to be an operatic character is to be a female one. Shortly before the *largo concertato* Johnson sings the only 'true' aria of the opera, 'Ch'ella mi creda libero e lontano', the only melody that generations of critics have recognised as in the old Puccinian mould, and which has become by far the most famous bit of *Fanciulla*. By forging an entirely new melody and the only self-contained piece in the opera, however, he reveals that he is a less advanced musical dramatist than Minnie, that he is still wedded to an old rhetoric and ultimately an old aesthetic of characterisation in opera, one that relies on self-contained solos and memorable melodies rather than on the combination and manipulation of multiple themes. I will explore the larger aesthetic implications of this interpretation below. For the moment I want to emphasise not simply the fundamental role of gender in *Fanciulla*'s textual and musical dramaturgy, but rather how a questioning of gender roles is central to this dramaturgy. (No surprise, then, that the conventional tools of feminist musicology play a larger part in this chapter than in any of the previous ones.) This questioning acquires wider resonances once we place the opera in the context of debates about femininity and gender that characterised the European fin de siècle.

'A FOOLISH VIRGIN WHOSE MISTAKES ARE WISE'

This is not the place for a discussion of the profound changes that affected conceptions and practices of femininity and gender between the 1880s and the outbreak of the First World War, about which an immense literature exists. Suffice it to say that in Italy these changes took place only slightly after those in northern Europe, and were significantly inflected by the immense influence of Catholicism and the Catholic Church on Italian society and culture – one need not read beyond Sibilla Aleramo's hugely successful *Una donna* of 1906 to obtain a good perspective on the Italian climate of the time.[22]

Minnie, however, is not simply another stereotypical 'new woman'. Hers could be the portrait of a dangerously masculine woman: she lives alone 'because she likes it', has a man's job, cheats at cards, rides horses and knows how to use a pistol; moreover, she has never danced with or kissed a man and she is not comfortable in overtly feminine attire. But she could also be a paragon of traditional femininity: she acts as the miners' mother and sister, taking care of their education as if they were her children; her dream is to reproduce the happy family that she remembers from her childhood, and especially the happy marriage between her parents; and she is ready to do anything to save her man's life. In this sense she is different from Wally, a more straightforwardly 'modern' woman, whose unbridled sexuality is never channelled into dreams of marriage and family, and who in fact abandons her father's house in open rebellion against his attempt to impose a husband on her. Minnie seems to embody the contradictions of 'modern' womanhood as envisaged by Puccini and his librettists, who, like Belasco before them, were embedded in a culture that fiercely debated womanhood, femininity and gender.[23] That equally fierce debates raged about masculinity, and especially about the feminising effects that new kinds of womanhood could have on men, may go some way towards understanding the different models of masculinity contrasted in the opera, especially Johnson's versus Rance's.

What is more, Minnie is not just a woman: she is also a virgin. Hers is not just a new kind of womanhood: it is also a new kind of virginity. Many different representations of 'new virginity' in Italian culture of the time could be brought to bear on Minnie's portrayal: the protagonists of some of Gabriele D'Annunzio's short stories ('Terra vergine', 'La vergine Orsola', 'La vergine Anna') come immediately to mind. One text seems especially apt, however, for reasons that will soon become clear, Guido Gozzano's poem 'Ketty', left unpublished at the author's death in 1916 and inspired by a journey to South Asia, of which significant excerpts follow:

> Bel fiore del carbone e dell'acciaio
> Miss Ketty fuma e zufola giuliva
> Altoriversa sulla sedia a sdraio.

> Sputa. Nell'arco della sua saliva
> M'irroro di freschezza: ha puri i denti,
> Pura la bocca, pura la genciva.

> Cerulo-bionda, le mammelle assenti,
> Ma forte come un giovinetto forte,
> Vergine folle da gli error prudenti,

Ma signora di sé della sua sorte
Sola giunse a Ceylon da Baltimora
Dove un cugino le sarà consorte.

Ma prima delle nozze, in tempo ancora
Esplora il mondo ignoto che le avanza
E qualche amico esplora che l'esplora.

Error prudenti e senza rimembranza:
Ketty zufola e fuma. La virile
Franchezza, l'inurbana tracotanza

Attira il mio latin sangue gentile.
[. . .]

L'attiro a me (l'audacia superando
Per cui va celebrato un cantarino
Napolitano, dagli Stati in bando. . .).

Imperterrita indulge al resupino,
Al temerario – o Numi! – che l'esplora
Tesse gli elogi di quel suo cugino,

Ma sui confini ben contesi ancora
Ben si difende con le mani tozze,
Al pugilato esperte. . . In Baltimora

Il cugino l'attende a giuste nozze.[24]

Beautiful flower of coal and steel, Miss Ketty smokes and whistles happily,
relaxing on a lounge chair. She spits. Under the arch of her saliva I bathe
in freshness: she has pure teeth, a pure mouth, pure gums. Light blonde,
with no breasts, but strong like a strong boy, a foolish virgin whose
mistakes are wise, but mistress of herself, of her destiny, she came alone
to Ceylon from Baltimore, where a cousin will be her consort. But, before
the wedding, she still has time to explore parts of the world still unknown
to her, and explores a few friends who explore her in turn. Wise mistakes,
ones not remembered: Ketty whistles and smokes. Her virile frankness,
her unkind arrogance attract my gentle Latin blood. [. . .] I pull her
towards me (outdoing the boldness for which a Neapolitan singer,
banned from the States, is celebrated. . .). She indulges the lying one

unperturbed; to the reckless one who explores her – o Gods! – she sings the praises of that cousin of hers, but on the well-fought boundaries she defends herself well with her squat hands, expert in boxing. . . In Baltimore the cousin expects her for their rightful marriage.

While some of Ketty's traits are obviously not Minnie's, whose California is far removed from industrial Baltimore, Gozzano's portrayal of a new virgin resonates with Puccini's – even if Gozzano's ambiguously repelled (and perhaps repulsive) eroticism is far removed from *Fanciulla*. Equally pure and independent, Ketty can allow physical contact and at the same time keep it on her own terms, thanks to strength of both mind and body. On the road to marriage, she can make 'wise mistakes' which will leave no memory because they have no real meaning. While her masculine traits (no breasts) and behaviour (smoking, whistling and spitting) may suggest an un-virginal knowingness, she remains pure, her frankness, however virile, 'taking away all suggestion of vice', to say it with Belasco's words about Minnie. Most significantly, both Minnie and Ketty are American.

For Italian culture of the time, steeped in Catholicism, these new models of femininity were located especially in protestant countries such as Britain; but the breeding ground for the most extreme types of behaviour was the United States. Italian discourses on femininity and America overlap revealingly. On the one hand, for example, Scipio Sighele's essay *La donna nova* (1898) concludes with a chapter on American women, their supposed lack of inclination towards marriage and family, and the high rate of divorce in the country, for which the author considers them solely responsible.[25] On the other, Federico Garlanda's two books on America, *La nuova democrazia americana* (1891) and *La terza Italia. Lettere di un yankee* (1903), contain lengthy descriptions of the supposed supremacy and independence enjoyed by women in America, praising them in the first volume but deprecating them twelve years later, with arguments remarkably similar to Sighele's.[26] In short, if Minnie presented a new, modern kind of femininity, then there was no better place for her to be than America. But what did 'America' mean for turn-of-the-century Italy?

LOOKING WEST FROM ITALY: BUFFALO BILL AND BRET HARTE

For Puccini's Italian contemporaries, as for many Europeans, America was a land of nature and freedom, of opportunity and democracy; unspoilt natural landscapes and imposing urban ones represented the violent opposites characterising this imagined space.[27] In the last years of the nineteenth century, however, a new factor began to alter this generalised, distant perception: a massive wave of emigration brought to America millions of Italians, especially from the South. Italian discourse on America acquired new layers: a mixure of shame at the fact that Italy was not able to support all her 'children' and of imagined nostalgia on the part of the emigrants, whose poor living conditions and social marginalisation were evoked in novels and especially travelogues.[28] In the chapter devoted to 'Italians in the United States' of *Impressioni d'America*, the account of a journey to the United States by none other than Puccini's librettist Giuseppe Giacosa, the author had to admit with profound humiliation that in American public opinion 'Italians are, if not at the second last, at the third last place. Below them there are only the Chinese and the Negroes'.[29] But the shadow of emigration darkened the Italian perception of those parts of the United States where the Italian presence was concentrated, that is to say, mostly the big industrial cities of the East Coast and the Midwest. The one part of the United States that had a separate identity in Italian culture and whose identity was not implicated in the discourse on emigration was the West.

Although it is difficult to separate a specific view of the West from the larger Italian discourse on the United States, since so many tropes belong to both, the turn-of-the-century West still seemed to embody some of the characteristics that Giacomo Leopardi had attributed to California in his *Inno ai patriarchi* of 1822: the last frontier of the Rousseauvian myth of the noble savage, the most remote place, yet to be violated by the cares of civilisation. The Gold Rush during which *Fanciulla* is set had been described by Antonio Caccia, one of the very few Italians who took part in it, as early as 1850, while a few others had cast the West in a utopian light, as the place where the 'spirito americano' could be found unadulterated.[30] But it seems that the main contributors to the Italian image, at least judging from Puccini's experience, were two Americans, Buffalo Bill (William Cody) and Bret Harte. Apart from Belasco (who was from San Francisco), these are the only two 'western' names mentioned by the composer. Buffalo Bill appears in a letter to his brother Michele of 1890 in which Puccini says that he has attended his 'Wild West Show'.[31] This show – a stagecoach robbery, gunfights, riding contests, buffaloes, and so on – took Europe by storm starting from 1887. In 1890 it reached Italy, where it was greeted by huge crowds in Naples, Rome, Florence, Bologna, Turin, Milan, Verona (they performed in the Roman amphitheatre, since 1913 home of the summer opera festival), Padua and Venice.[32] Perhaps Puccini remembered some of its more spectacular scenes when he had the idea for the horse-back man-hunt in Act 3 of *Fanciulla*.

More important for the opera, however, were the works of Bret Harte. Puccini mentioned them in an interview to the American press in New York in January 1907, during his first visit to the United States, in which the possibility of a Western opera was first mentioned: 'If I could get a good Western American libretto [. . .] I would undoubtedly write the music. [. . .] Something stunning could be made of the '49 period. I only know the West through Bret Harte's novels, but I admire them very much, as I have read them in translation'.[33] Bret Harte and his 'unforgettable Californian short stories' are also mentioned by Giacosa as epitomising American literature, together with some of Poe's works, in *Impressioni d'America*.[34] His Western stories had been hugely popular in the United States in the late 1860s and 1870s, but by the turn of the century had disappeared from the public eye. If Puccini's and Giacosa's voices are at all representative, however, they still constituted the most powerful incarnation of the West for turn-of-the-century Italy.[35] At least one American reviewer of the première of *Fanciulla* thought so: 'The West it depicts is, of course, the West as an Italian who has never seen the West imagines it, as a composer who has based his ideas not only on the Belasco play, but on a steady diet of Bret Harte and other pioneer American writers feels its whiskey-stimulated passions, emotions, and its life of vigor and rigors should be pictured in music'.[36]

According to Lee Clark Mitchell, Harte invented many of the recurring figures of the popular Western, from 'the whore with a heart of gold' to the 'prim but passionate eastern schoolmarm', from the 'blusteringly drunk, astonishingly competent stage driver' to the 'poised, tight-lipped southern gambler'. 'The road agents and outlaws, recluses and lonely eccentrics, Chinese immigrants and hard-knuckled miners all emerged from his brief sketches to become stock characters of the genre. Nearly single-handed, as it were, Harte concocted the dramatis personae for the Western'.[37] Several of these dramatis personae, especially from Harte's numerous stories set in miners' camps – 'The Luck of Roaring Camp', 'The Outcasts of Poker Flat' and 'Miggles' (mistress of a 'Polka' saloon) are among the most famous – would reappear in Belasco's play and Puccini's opera.

What neither Buffalo Bill's show nor Harte's stories provided, however, was a recognisable Western landscape in which the cowboys and miners could act. Mitchell reads Harte's descriptive vagueness as an erasure of 'the dialectical tension that exists in [James Fenimore] Cooper's novels between narrative and description, action and landscape', and ultimately a flattening of moral distinctions.[38] But in turn-of-the-century Italy this descriptive vagueness meant that the Western landscape could be 'virgin', available to be imbued with new meanings when placed in new contexts. *Fanciulla* is just one such context, in which the Californian Sierra becomes the new mountain landscape in which a new kind of femininity can be represented. Both the landscape and the character are first found in *The Girl of the Golden West*, of course, but there they belong to a different context, that of *American* discourse on the American West, incomparably richer and more complex, especially in a visual sense, than its Italian equivalent.[39] While invoking the real, historic women of the American frontier as Minnie's prototypes makes sense from an American point of view, and therefore either for Belasco's play or for the American reception of *Fanciulla*, the same cannot be said of the Italian context to which the opera belongs, where these women had little or no presence.[40] A similar claim can be made for the Western landscape: the paintings of Albert Bierstadt, for example, so compellingly analysed by Mitchell, have no relevance for a discussion of landscape in *Fanciulla*. It is rather to Segantini and Carducci that we must turn in search of a meaningful context. Even more relevant, however, are the landscapes of *La Wally*, *Fedora* and the other operatic predecessors of *Fanciulla* in the coupling of virginity and mountains. It is in this context that *Fanciulla*'s new representational strategies emerge in sharpest profile.

EXPLORING SONIC SPACE

The mountains of the Sierra dominate the action of *Fanciulla*. They link the opera with the Alpine virgin tradition of Italian opera, but they are not the Alps. A new virgin such as Minnie demanded a new landscape. This demand could be best fulfilled by the mountains of the American West, thanks not only to the meanings they had acquired in turn-of-the-century Italian culture, but also to the relative limitation of these meanings, one that left them open to new, additional layers. Although the Sierra Nevada is not the Alps, it could then fulfil a function similar to theirs in Italian opera and culture for most of the nineteenth century – that of a virgin land. The landscape of *Fanciulla* was thus both old and new, both generic (mountains) and specific (the mountains of California), both close (just like the Alps) and distant (not at all like the Alps).

Perhaps because of this double set of overlapping meanings, of this constituent ambivalence, in *Fanciulla* landscape receives an attention unprecedented in Puccini. As mentioned above, the mountains are glimpsed in the background of all three acts, deepening the stage space and constantly reminding the viewer of dimensions beyond that immediately visible in the foreground. Their uninterrupted presence keeps the natural landscape at the centre of attention as the larger location of the action, even when this action takes place indoors. The natural setting was already emphasised in *The Girl of the Golden West*, for which Belasco devised an opening sequence of two panorama-like views painted on foreground drops: the first 'a wild range of the Sierra peaks' in the distance and an external view of Minnie's cabin in the foreground; the second 'the exterior of the "Polka" saloon l[eft], at the foot of the mountain, showing the dark mountainside in the background'.[41] After a moment of complete darkness, Act 1 begins in the interior of the 'Polka'. Although dispensing with Belasco's initial panoramas, *Fanciulla* keeps the double outdoor/indoor perspective by showing the mountains and Minnie's cabin through the wide door and the window in the back wall of the 'Polka''s interior – a double perspective that will be repeated in Act 2 and also, in a sense, in Act 3, if we consider the clearing in the thick forest as an enclosed space comparable to the interior. Before this double perspective is revealed to the audience, however, an orchestral prelude is heard.

This prelude has been interpreted along broadly similar lines in the literature on *Fanciulla*, most commentators emphasising the descriptive function of its main theme as 'outdoor' music, evoking gusts of wind and swaying branches of giant trees.[42] If we follow this interpretation, we can enlist the prelude as the first manifestation of landscape music, and perhaps even as Puccini's attempt to convey musically what Belasco's panoramas had conveyed visually.[43] There is another way to interpret this prelude, however, one that relies less on attaching precise meanings to themes and motives. A self-contained prelude played by the orchestra before the curtain is raised, not heard in Puccini since *Le Villi* and quite rare in turn-of-the-century Italian opera, has the effect of establishing the orchestra itself as a separate and independent source of sound, and therefore of calling attention to an enlarged sonic space in the theatre, one that goes beyond the stage. I am less interested in elevating the orchestra to a Wagnerian omniscient voice than in establishing it as a sound source located elsewhere than the stage. And I would argue that this enlargement of sonic space continues after the curtain is raised to reveal the interior of the 'Polka'.

Visually, as the stage direction specifies, 'the violent light outside, which diminishes rapidly, makes the interior of the "Polka" even darker. In the darkness one can barely make out the contours of things' ('La luce violenta dell'esterno, che va calando rapidamente, rende anche più oscuro l'interno della "Polka"'). The light outside illuminates the valley with its wild vegetation and the snow-capped mountains, and it is as if this light locates where the first sounds come from. In this sense, what the orchestra plays can indeed be called 'outdoor' music. A barcarolle-like accompaniment on a tonic pedal supports echoing oboe and flute calls, the combination sounding like a reminiscence of the openings of previous Alpine virgin operas, or, more generally, of pastoral scenes from the nineteenth-century tradition. What is more, the first voices heard in the opera come from afar, from that space illuminated by the 'violent light'. Both the libretto and the score emphasise that these voices come from 'outside' ('fuori') and 'afar' ('lontano'), the score even distinguishing between 'molto lontano' and simply 'lontano'. As Allan Atlas has noted, 'là lontano' are also the first sung words (as opposed to shouted) in the opera, by a baritone anticipating the first few bars of the ballad 'Che faranno i vecchi miei', heard later in the act.[44] Moreover, according to the score, the word 'lontano' is sung by a 'distant voice' ('voce lontana') – the libretto calls it 'a refrain from very far away' ('un ritornello lontanissimo') (Ex. 6.2).

Atlas has discussed the centrality of 'lontano' in *Fanciulla*, a word he considers a 'verbal leitmotiv' (together with 'tornare' and 'redenzione'). These leitmotives, whose first important occurrences correspond musically to what he calls the 'redemption *tinta*', find their most explicit musical expression in Jake Wallace's song. In Atlas's interpretation, the leitmotives 'spell out the opera's underlying theme: to redeem Johnson, Minnie must leave behind the often

Ex. 6.2. Puccini, *La fanciulla del West*, Act 1: Beginning.

seamy life of the mining camp [. . .] and return to a distant state of moral and emotional innocence, which, from a musical point of view, is expressed most explicitly by the simplicity of Jake's minstrel song'.[45] Leaving redemption aside, I would like to focus on 'lontano' and 'tornare' – which, as Atlas suggests, are linked in both libretto and score – and their spatial implications. As we have seen, the beginning of the opera establishes 'lontano' as a source of sound – a place where voices come from – and, what is more, verbally and musically thematises this distance. The combination of the orchestral prelude and the opening scene creates a uniquely articulate sense of sonic space, one characterised by a perspective comparable to the deep visual spaces of the stage picture. If mimesis can be invoked for the opening music of *Fanciulla*, it is more as an effort to reproduce musically the spatial articulation of the visual field than to imitate objects or movements in themes and motives.

Fanciulla both opens and closes with music that articulates space through sound: at the end of the opera Minnie and Johnson, already out of sight, are heard repeating their farewell to California, 'moving further away' ('allontanadosi'). That the opera begins and ends with musical explorations of sonic space should alert us to this crucial aspect of the opera. Voices and sounds coming from afar, from the 'natural' outdoor space, are heard with remarkable frequency: whistles, gunshots, gusts of wind – Act 2 is punctuated by the sound of gusting wind, the voice of raging nature, heard each time the door of Minnie's cabin is open – shouts, shrieks, galloping horses, and so on.

The scene where this articulation of space through sound takes centre stage is undoubtedly the first part of Act 3, the man-hunt for Johnson, entirely of Puccini's devising – in fact it is among his first ideas about the opera, coming as early as August 1907, well before even the libretto had been drafted.[46] What makes this scene so remarkable is the music's attempt to stage an action that happens mostly out of sight, in the thick forest, by means of a careful placement of choir members and soloists at different and changing locations in the wings, so as to reproduce sonically the effect of people moving swiftly.[47] Revelatory in this sense are not only the specific indications in the score about the location of the voices heard from the wings and behind the scenery – 'lontano', 'più vicino', 'vicinissimo'; 'interno vicino', 'più vicino', 'vicinissimi', and so on – but also the need on the part of characters on stage to make sure that others have heard the sounds coming from beyond the visible field – 'sheriff, have you heard?' ('sceriffo, avete udito?'), 'did you hear? ('udiste?'), and so on. The speed of the action in this scene has led critics to suggest an anticipation of film techniques.[48] But film is characterised by a movable point of view and of hearing, the eye/ear of the camera that can follow fast-moving action. What Puccini attempts in *Fanciulla*, and specifically in the man-hunt scene, is an expansion and internal articulation of the fixed space of the theatre by means of a multiplication and strategic placement of the sound sources. In the impossibility of moving the ear to follow the sources of sound as a way of substituting for a movable eye, Puccini tries to create a particularly powerful ear, a giant one, capable of hearing the action beyond the fixed field of visibility – an ear capable of 'seeing' the action that the eye cannot see. This innovative construction of sonic space and of the means to hear it acquires richer meaning once it is brought to bear on critical interpretations of *Fanciulla*, especially the question of its 'Americanness'.[49]

AN OPERATIC EMIGRATION

Literary critics and historians of the Italian language have repeatedly called attention to the radical linguistic innovations present in the libretto of *Fanciulla*. Whereas those archaic, literary expressions and constructions common to nineteenth-century librettos were still present in earlier works by Puccini and other Italian composers at the turn of the century, in *Fanciulla* they have almost completely disappeared. The language of the libretto is thoroughly modern, characterised by the tones of spoken Italian of the time.[50] Even more innovative are its plurilingualism and interlingualism: never had an Italian opera libretto contained so many words in foreign languages, or featured characters whose condition as non-native speakers had been so prominently displayed (Billy and Wowkle at the beginning of Act 2).[51] One of the most frequently used words in present-day Italian, 'bar', commonly employed from the 1920s, makes one of its very first appearances in *Fanciulla*.[52] Puccini himself intervened directly on this aspect of the text, setting 'Mister Johnson' every time the libretto presented him with 'Signor Johnson'.

Fanciulla shares these linguistic features with a poem by Giovanni Pascoli, 'Italy' (1904), about a family of Italian emigrants to the United States that has temporarily returned to the Tuscan village of their origin. In both *Fanciulla* and 'Italy' plurilingualism symbolises the lack of geographical, psychological and emotional roots among the characters who speak this mixed, impure language. Everybody in *Fanciulla* is from somewhere else, a place for which most of them feel acute nostalgia: 'Nostalgia, homesickness' ('Nostalgia, mal di terra natia') is the miners' 'usual illness' ('solito male'), according to the bartender Nick in Act I. This place, whose memory is so painful, is 'lontano'; and Luigi Baldacci has quipped that the miners in *Fanciulla* are all 'lucchesi', from the province of Lucca, like Puccini, and therefore Tuscan, like Pascoli's emigrants to 'La Merica' of 'Italy'.[53]

Does Puccini's music present a similar case of plurilingualism? The degree to which the music of *Fanciulla* can be considered 'American' was hotly debated in the US press even before the opera's première. Linda B. Fairtile has thoroughly documented this debate, which included reports on Puccini's supposed study of 'Indian music', and in which the composer's own voice played a significant if ambiguous part. On the one hand, in an interview he claimed that he had made 'a special study of American music', which made him succeed in 'obtaining the required local color. As a matter of fact, there are some tunes that could be taken as purely American, although, of course, the score is Puccinian in character'.[54] But on another occasion he denied that the music could be called 'American'. In the same interview, leaving aside all claims to 'authenticity', he asserted that he had composed music that 'reflects the spirit of the American people and particularly the strong, vigorous nature of the West. [. . .] With very few exceptions I have borrowed no themes. All practically are of my own invention. It is American music, though Puccini at the same time'.[55]

Amidst salvos of nationalistic rhetoric, perhaps the most perceptive remarks came from the composer and ethnographer Arthur

Farwell, who, in a long article in *Musical America*, suggested that the composer had altered the few original American melodies incorporated into the score to such an extent as to strip them of their national character – if they had one in the first place.[56] Not only in Farwell's article, but throughout the debate, in fact, what was at stake was the very existence of a distinctly American music. What would this music sound like, anyway? Farwell makes the point that the Native American melodies used by Puccini are 'not yet familiar to Americans', and therefore 'such of his music as is based upon them is foredoomed to fall upon deaf ears, so far as American sympathies are concerned'.[57] If even Americans could not recognise these melodies as American, Europeans could certainly not be expected to do so. And the same applies to other supposedly 'American' themes in the opera, whether based on original material or newly composed by Puccini.

The difference with *Madama Butterfly*, for example (to take the work immediately preceding *Fanciulla*), lies in the lack of sufficiently distinctive markers of musical 'Americanness' available to composers at the beginning of the twentieth century – especially composers adopting a 'modern' sound world such as Debussy or Puccini.[58] Even what could arguably be the only immediately recognisable 'American' theme, the fanfare in cakewalk rhythm heard first at the end of the prelude and then again at Johnson's entrance, is open to different interpretations: for Girardi, for example, it is a touch of local colour, while for Budden it carries 'a Latin American flavour appropriate for one who is believed, however falsely, to be Mexican' (that is, Johnson as the bandit Ramerrez).[59] The truth is that, from this point of view, America was still a musically virgin land for Europe – not for long: 'jazz' would take the continent by storm in the 1920s. The answer to the question of whether Puccini's music presents a case of plurilingualism similar to that of the libretto must therefore be negative. The miners in *Fanciulla* may speak like emigrants to the United States, but they almost always sound as if they had never left the mountains near Lucca, at least if one listens to their melodies, harmonies and rhythms.

But the characters of *Fanciulla* are not on the mountains near Lucca, or the Alps. They are somewhere else. The opera is set in an 'other' place, but this sense of otherness is not achieved through the use of 'exotic' melodies, harmonies or rhythms. This is a new place because its space is articulated by sound in ways literally unheard. In *Fanciulla* the American West becomes the destination of an operatic emigration in search of new representational strategies: there one hears differently, with a giant ear – perhaps the sonic equivalent of what is known as the 'big sky' of the West. Minnie's new femininity, the new landscape of the Sierra Nevada, and the opera's new modes of operatic representation, crucially articulated as new modes of hearing space, make the American West of *La fanciulla del West* a radical experiment not only for Puccini, but also in the history of Italian opera. *Fanciulla* is a thoroughly modern work not only because of the new conceptions of gender and landscape that it portrays, but also because of its search for a new representational aesthetic.

The opera's modernity, then, lies not so much, or not only, in its much-discussed 'advanced' compositional vocabulary – its highly chromatic harmonies, disjunct and 'unmemorable' melodies, and Debussian orchestral colours – but in its attempt to explore new sonic spaces and to construct new ways of hearing them. The Puccini of *Fanciulla* is not the slow follower of compositional modernism, guardedly incorporated into an essentially conservative musical fabric, familiar from past and present literature.[60] The journey to California may have been initially intended as a search for a new musical ambience, for a source of an unheard kind of *couleur locale*, but Puccini must have soon realised that there was little scope there for the kind of musical exoticism that he had perfected in *Madama Butterfly*. What became possible instead in virgin California was a different way of representing sound and hearing, and ultimately reality.

Perhaps this is what Engelbert Humperdinck sensed when, leaving the theatre after *Fanciulla*'s première, he told journalists that 'the opera of the future will be the opera of Realism'.[61] Puccini's well-known preoccupation with stagings which reproduced reality as accurately as possible reached unprecedented levels with *Fanciulla*. More important, this preoccupation became a recurring theme in public pronouncements not only by Puccini, but also, for example, by Belasco, who took an active part in the first production of the opera.[62] These reiterated invocations of realism should not be read, however, as belated manifestations of a naturalist, *verismo* aesthetic, at least on Puccini's part. What the composer tried to protect with his repeated calls for constant attention to the most minute details of staging was the opera's spatial dramaturgy – perhaps realising its fragility. That this dramaturgy was subsumed early on under the banner of realism and has remained there ever since simply testifies to the wide gap between aesthetic practice and critical discourse that is a characteristic trait of the reception of Puccini's operas. *Fanciulla's* conception of sonic space goes beyond reality since it attempts to construct an unrealistically powerful way of hearing this space. The capabilities of the giant ear that the opera offers its audience go beyond anything of which any human ear is capable: they allow us to hear beyond reality.

In the light of these considerations, 'Ch'ella mi creda' sounds not only like a symptom of Johnson's masculine dramaturgical back-wardness, but also like a remnant of Puccini's own former operatic aesthetic, a piece of *La Bohème*, *Tosca* or *Madama Butterfly* thrown into *Fanciulla* in order to highlight by contrast the very different musico-theatrical context in the midst of which it is placed. In this sense, its effect is in some ways comparable to that of 'Di rigori armato il seno', the aria sung by the Italian tenor in Act 1 of *Der Rosenkavalier* (premièred less than two months after *Fanciulla*) – even if parody seems out of the question in Puccini's opera. It is as if Johnson's lyricism were in scare quotes by virtue of its very melodiousness, its overt *cantabilità*, whose distance from what surrounds it has the effect of pointing to the novelty of these surroundings.[63] If, as Gary Tomlinson has suggested, these Puccinian moments of 'culminating melodic distillation [. . .] harken back to an era when the noumenal cry seemed plausible', and are therefore the means through which Puccini enlists the audience's 'willfully nostalgic engagement', then

Fanciulla can be seen as questioning precisely this kind of lyric nostalgia.[64] *Perhaps paradoxically, nostalgia is at the emotional centre of the opera, but this Western nostalgia moves through space, not time – Jack Wallace wonders 'Che faranno i vecchi miei, là lontano?' ('What will my old folks be doing way back home?'), but now, in the present. And at the end of the opera nostalgia does not prevent Minnie and Johnson from moving on. The future is another place.*

But this future was never reached. Puccini's exploration of modern operatic aesthetics certainly continued with *Il trittico* (1918) and *Turandot* (1926), but in directions different from the one he attempted in *Fanciulla*. Although in many ways more modern, and perhaps even modernist, than *Fanciulla*, *Il trittico* and *Turandot* are not primarily concerned with space and modes of hearing, nor do they eschew the self-contained lyrical moments so subtly questioned there – in this sense not even *Il tabarro*, the work closest to *Fanciulla* in purely musical terms, shares its predecessor's aesthetics. Perhaps Puccini thought that his emigration to California had failed – and the opera's lukewarm success and relatively slow circulation certainly did nothing to dissuade him. In any case, as a result *Fanciulla* has been critically assessed as either a 'no longer' (*Bohème*, *Tosca* and *Butterfly*) or a 'not yet' (*Il trittico* and *Turandot*), and ultimately censured – nor has its popularity ever remotely reached the levels of Puccini's earlier and later works. If considered in the context of Puccini's *œuvre*, it seems almost unavoidable that this should be its fate. Locating this opera in a differently conceived context, however, allows its dramaturgy and aesthetics to make better sense than they have done thus far, and to emerge in all their startling novelty. Only by placing *Fanciulla* at the end of a venerable genealogy that counts among its ancestors *La sonnambula*, *Linda di Chamounix*, *Luisa Miller* and *La Wally* can we see its modernity.

THE POWER OF LANDSCAPE

Fanciulla suggests one final observation about landscape. In this book I have insisted on the constructedness of mountainous landscape as a cultural object, viewing it as a malleable receptacle of meanings. A significant part of my efforts has gone into charting these meanings and the changes they underwent over the course of the nineteenth century and into the twentieth – as I have done for female virginity. But the example of *Fanciulla* brings to the fore the active role that landscape, real or imagined, can have, its power to make certain kinds of representation and of rhetoric possible, but not others. As Franco Moretti recently put it, 'geography is not an inert container, is not a box where cultural history "happens", but an active force, that pervades the literary [or operatic] field and shapes it in depth'.[65] Paradoxically, only the Californian Sierra Nevada makes it possible for the mountains to find their own voice and sound world in Italian opera – paradoxically, of course, because 'mountains' had almost always meant 'Alps' in nineteenth-century Italy, on and off the stage.

At the same time, as W. J. T. Mitchell honestly reminds us in a book that investigates precisely how landscape works as an instrument of cultural force, the power of landscape 'is a relatively weak power compared to that of armies, police forces, governments, and corporations'.[66] Nowhere is this more evident than in the case of the Alps for twentieth-century Italian culture; and never has this been described with more touching simplicity than in Mario Rigoni Stern's novel *Storia di Tönle*, set on the Asiago Alps, in the Veneto:

> La mattina di buon'ora del giorno ventiquattro Tönle aveva guidato le pecore verso i soliti pascoli; poi si sedette ad accendere la pipa e a godersi il giorno. Sentì dapprima come un brontolio per il cielo, poi uno scoppio lontano. Si alzò in piedi e guardò attorno; non vide niente ma ancora sentì quel brontolio e lo scoppio ripetersi, e susseguirsene altri più numerosi. Allora capì: era incominciata la guerra e i forti del Campolongo e del Verena sparavano a quelli di Luserna e di Vezzena.[67]

> On the early morning of the twenty-fourth Tönle had taken the sheep to the usual pastures; then he sat down to light his pipe and enjoy the day. First he heard a sort of rumbling in the sky, then an explosion far away. He stood up and looked around; he saw nothing but heard that rumbling again and another explosion, and several others following it.

And then he understood: the war had begun and the Campolongo and Verena forts were shooting at the Luserna and Vezzena ones.

On 24 May 1915 Italy declared war on the Austro-Hungarian Empire, thus entering the First World War. For three and a half years hundreds of thousands of men died on what was then the Austrian front: on the Adamello, the Dolomites, the Monte Grappa, the Carso. The Alps would never be the same for Italians, on and off the operatic stage: the war brutally brought to an end the process of their defloration and turned them into places of death. When, as a teenager, I used to go on hiking trips to the Dolomites with family and friends, we always looked out for empty bomb shells, bullets, mess tins and other signs of that war from so many years ago, and found them, often emerging from snow and ice. Perhaps this book was begun then.

1 VIRGINS, MOUNTAINS, OPERA

1 'Da lontano si scorgono assai pittoresche montagne, che fanno bellissima e solenne veduta, mentre il sole, che nasce, va gradatamente illuminandole, siccome poi rischiara tutta la scena'; Carlo Pepoli, *I Puritani e i Cavalieri, opera-seria in due parti, parole del Signor C. Pepoli, musica del Sr. Maestro Bellini* (Paris: Delaforest, 1835), p. 1.

2 *Carmen, opéra-comique en quatre actes* (Paris: Michel Lévy Frères, 1875), p. 8. The description of Micaëla's costume comes almost *verbatim* from a reference in the source of the opera, Prosper Mérimée's novella of the same title, to the young José's naïve belief that there could not be 'beautiful young women without blue skirts and braids falling on their shoulders' ('je ne croyais pas qu'il y eût de jolies filles sans jupes bleues et sans nattes tombant sur les épaules'); Mérimée himself explains in a footnote that this was the traditional costume of young peasant girls from Navarre; Prosper Mérimée, *Carmen* (1846), ed. Maxime Revon (Paris: Garnier, 1960), pp. 32 and 273.

3 H. Marshall Leicester, Jr., 'Discourse and the Film Text: Four Readings of *Carmen*', *Cambridge Opera Journal* 6 (1994), pp. 245–82: 275–6.

4 Judg. 11: 37–8, 40; the translation is from *The New American Bible for Catholics* (Washington, DC: The Confraternity of Christian Doctrine, 1970), variously reprinted.

5 *The Biblical Antiquities of Philo*, trans. M. R. James (New York: Ktav, 1971), p. 194. The Latin reads: 'Audite montes trenum meum, et intendite colles lacrimas oculorum meorum. [. . .] Inclinate arbores ramos vestros et plangite iuventutem meam. Venite fere silve et conculcate supra virgines meas'; Pseudo-Philo, *Liber antiquitatum biblicarum*, ed. Guido Kisch (Notre Dame, Indiana: University of Notre Dame, 1949), pp. 221–2.

6 Giacomo Carissimi, *Jephte*, ed. Adelchi Amisano (Milan: Ricordi, n.d. [1977]), p. xxiii.

7 Elisja Schulte van Kessel, 'Virgins and Mothers between Heaven and Earth', *A History of Women in the West*, ed. Georges Duby and Michelle Perrot, vol. III, *Renaissance and Enlightenment Paradoxes*, ed. Natalie Zemon Davis and Arlette Farge, trans. Arthur Goldhammer (Cambridge, Mass.: Harvard University Press, 1993), pp. 132–66: 142.

8 For a Protestant (and wonderfully comic) view on virginity's decidedly mixed blessings, see the dialogue between Helen and Parolles in Act I, scene I of Shakespeare's *All's Well That Ends Well*.

9 Eric A. Nicholson, 'The Theater', *Renaissance and Enlightenment Paradoxes*, pp. 295–314: 314. In the Italian context, Luigi Baldacci has pointed to Vittorio Alfieri's plays and Ugo Foscolo's poetry as evident examples of this late-eighteenth- and early-nineteenth-century de-eroticisation of literature; see Baldacci, *Ottocento come noi. Saggi e pretesti italiani* (Milan: Garzanti, 2003), pp. 401–2.

10 Anne Ubersfeld, 'Les Bons et le méchant', *Revue des sciences humaines* 41 (1976), 193–203: 197.

11 'Cruel! que t'avait fait cette jeune et innocente fille, pour lui percer le cœur, lorsque tu sais qu'elle ne peut aimer sans être malheureuse? Pourquoi dirigeais-tu vers les barreaux de sa fenêtre ce beau jeune homme, que tu lui montres de bien de loin, sans doute; mais où ne voit pas l'oeil d'une vierge de quinze ans?'; A! A! A! [Abel Hugo, Armand Malitourne and Jean-Joseph Ader], *Traité du mélodrame* (Paris: Delaunay–Pélicier–Plancher, 1817), p. 21.

12 For a discussion of the tensions inherent in representing virginity in nineteenth-century literature in English, see *Virginal Sexuality and Textuality in Victorian Literature*, ed. Lloyd Davis (Albany: SUNY Press, 1993), especially the editor's 'The Virgin Body as Victorian Text: An Introduction', pp. 3–24.

13 For the progressive emergence of mountains in early modern European imagination, see Simon Schama, *Landscape and Memory* (London: Fontana Press, 1995), pp. 474–8.

14 For a classic wide-ranging account of the opposition between city and country in Western imagination, see Raymond Williams, *The Country and the City* (1973) (London: The Hogarth Press, 1985).

15 John Ruskin, *Modern Painters*, vol. IV (1856), *The Works of John Ruskin*, ed. E. T. Cook and Alexander Wedderburn, 39 vols. (London: George Allen, 1903–12), vol. VI, p. 420.

16 John Tyndall, *Hours of Exercise in the Alps* (London: Longman, 1871), quoted in Jim Ring, *How the English Made the Alps* (London: Murray, 2000), p. 98.

17 'Der Dichter, sagte ich, ist entweder Natur, oder er wird sie suchen. Jenes macht den naiven, dieses den sentimentalischen Dichter'; Friedrich Schiller, *Über naïve und sentimentalische Dichtung*, ed. William F. Mainland (Oxford: Blackwell, 1957), p. 22. It should be noted that Schiller's idiosyncratic use of the adjective 'sentimental' ('sentimentalisch') is different from its common meaning in English (better rendered in German with 'empfindsam').

18 Denis E. Cosgrove, *Social Formation and Symbolic Landscape*, 2nd edn (Madison: The University of Wisconsin Press, 1998), pp. 1, 15.

19 Ruskin, *Modern Painters*, p. 418.

20 See, among other studies, Gillian Rose, *Feminism and Geography: The Limits of Geographical Knowledge* (Cambridge: Polity Press, 1993), and Catherine Nash, 'Reclaiming Vision: Looking at Landscape and the Body', *Gender, Place and Culture: A Journal of Feminist Geography* 3 (1996), pp. 149–69.

21 The only sexualisation of mountains as male that I have come across was by the French climber Henriette d'Angeville, who, in a published account of her ascent of Mont Blanc in 1838, referred to it as a 'wedding' with her 'frozen lover', feeling pangs of frustrated desire when prevented from attempting the climb by bad weather: 'I was late for my wedding, for my marriage with the face of Israel . . . for the delicious hour when I could lie on his summit'; quoted in Schama, *Landscape and Memory*, p. 497. 'Mont' is masculine in French, as 'monte' is in Italian, and therefore 'Mont Blanc/Monte Bianco' is gendered masculine in both languages (on the other hand, 'montagne' is feminine, as 'montagna' is in Italian).

22 See Nicolas Giudici, *La Philosophie du Mont Blanc. De l'alpinisme à l'économie immatérielle* (Paris: Grasset, 2000), p. 358.

23 'O virgin! [. . .] I adore the whiteness of your forehead surrounded by stars. In you everything is splendid and pure, even your name. Only the sky drinks your breath from your sacred lips; your blue-veined breast, blushing at dawn, allows only God to pick on its reddened snow the Eastern roses planted by the sun' ('O vierge! [. . .] J'adore en sa blancheur ton front chargé d'étoiles. / En toi, jusqu'à ton nom, tout est splendide et pur! / Le ciel seul boit ton souffle à ta lèvre sacrée; / Ton sein veiné d'azur, rougissant au

réveil, / Laisse à Dieu seul cueillir, sur sa neige empourprée, / Les roses d'Orient qu'y sème le soleil'); Victor de Laprade, 'L'Alpe vierge', *La Revue des deux mondes* 19 (1849), pp. 539–41: 539.

24 *Ibid.*, pp. 540–1.

25 To Gérard de Nerval's ears the voice of the 'jeunes filles' of Saint-Germain-en-Laye sounded 'pure and with a good timbre, as in the mountains' ('pure et bien timbrée, comme dans les pays de montagne'); Nerval, *Promenades et souvenirs* (1855), in *Œuvres complètes*, ed. Jean Guillaume and Claude Pichois, 3 vols. (Paris: Gallimard, 1984–93), vol. III, p. 675.

26 For a recent survey of the relationship between music and nature (from which, predictably, Italian opera is virtually absent), see Helga de la Motte-Haber, *Musik und Natur: Naturanschauung und musikalische Poetik* (Laaber: Laaber Verlag, 2000), especially pp. 51–78 (on echo), to be read together with Alexander Rehding's probing discussion of this and other recent publications in German on music and nature in his 'Ecomusicology', *Journal of the Royal Musical Association* 127 (2002), pp. 305–20.

27 It is therefore not surprising that Italian opera is conspicuously absent from a survey of mountainous *couleur locale* in nineteenth-century opera from the point of view of musical style; see Hubert Unverricht, 'Das Berg- und Gebirgsmilieu und seine musikalische Stilmittel in der Oper des 19. Jahrhunderts', *Die 'Couleur locale' in der Oper des 19. Jahrhunderts*, ed. Heinz Becker (Regensburg: Bosse, 1976), pp. 99–119. Markus Engelhardt has noticed the relatively little attention paid by Donizetti to Swiss local colour in his *dramma giocoso Betly, ossia La capanna svizzera* (1836) vis-à-vis its significant presence in Adolphe Adam's *opéra comique Le Chalet* (1834), whose libretto, by Scribe and Duveyrier, is the direct source of Donizetti's opera, translated by the composer himself; see Engelhardt, 'Goethe, Scribe, Donizetti: *Betly, ossia La capanna svizzera*', *Donizetti, Napoli, l'Europa*, ed. Franco Carmelo Greco and Renato Di Benedetto (Naples: Edizioni Scientifiche Italiane, 2000), pp. 21–32.

2 'AT THE FOOT OF THE ALPS': THE LANDSCAPE OF LA SONNAMBULA

1 The only earlier Italian works that have constantly been performed since their premières are *Don Giovanni* and *Il barbiere di Siviglia*, but in the former's case this is true only in the German-speaking countries and, to a lesser extent, in Great Britain.

2 'La Scène se passe en Provence, dans l'île de la Camargue, auprès d'Arles'; *La Somnambule, ou l'Arrivée d'un nouveau seigneur, ballet-pantomime en trois actes, par MM. Scribe et Aumer* (Paris: Barba, 1828), p. 1.

3 All quotations are from *La sonnambula. Melodramma di Felice Romani da rappresentarsi nel Teatro Carcano la Quaresima del 1831* (Milan: Fontana, 1831); reprinted with critical notes by Eduardo Rescigno as Vincenzo Bellini, *La sonnambula. Melodramma in due atti di Felice Romani* (Milan: Ricordi, 1990).

4 See Marjorie Hope Nicolson, *Mountain Gloom and Mountain Glory: The Development of the Aesthetics of the Infinite* (Ithaca: Cornell University Press, 1959; rpt Seattle: University of Washington Press, 1997), chapter 1, 'The Literary Heritage', pp. 34–71.

5 Note in particular the reference to the Savoy Alps in Immanuel Kant, *Critique of Aesthetic Judgement*, trans. and ed. James Creed Meredith (Oxford: Clarendon Press, 1911), p. 130; see also Kant, *Observations on the Feeling of the Beautiful and Sublime* (1764).

6 For classic accounts of eighteenth-century sublime, see Samuel H. Monk, *The Sublime: A Study of Critical Theories in Eighteenth-Century England* (Ann Arbor: University of Michigan Press, 1960; 1st edn, New York: Modern Language Association of America, 1935), and Thomas Weiskel, *The Romantic Sublime: Studies in the Structure and Psychology of Transcendence* (Baltimore: Johns Hopkins University Press, 1976). For the relationship between sublime and mountains, see Hope Nicolson, *Mountain Gloom and Mountain Glory*, and Simon Schama, *Landscape and Memory* (London: Fontana, 1995), pp. 447–78.

7 See Jean-Jacques Rousseau, *Emile*, ed. Charles Wirz and Pierre Burgelin, in Rousseau, *Œuvres complètes* (Paris: Gallimard, 1959–), vol. IV, pp. 594–600.

8 On Rousseau's Alps, see Paul Guichonnet, 'L'homme devant les Alpes', *Histoire et civilisation des Alpes*, ed. Paul Guichonnet, 2 vols. (Toulouse and Lausanne: Privat–Payot, 1980), vol. II, pp. 169–248; on the philosophical aspects of Rousseau's Arcadian ideal, see Richard Noble, *Language, Subjectivity, and Freedom in Rousseau's Moral Philosophy* (New York: Garland, 1991), pp. 90–132.

9 'J'aurois passé tout le tems de mon voyage dans le seul enchantement du paysage, si je n'en eusse éprouvé un plus doux encore dans le

commerce des habitans. Vous trouverez dans ma description un léger crayon des leurs mœurs, de leur simplicité, de leur égalité d'âme, et de cette paisible tranquillité qui les rend heureux par l'exemption des peines plutôt que par le goût des plaisirs'; Jean-Jacques Rousseau, *Julie, ou La Nouvelle Héloïse*, ed. Henri Coulet and Bernard Guyon, in Rousseau, *Œuvres complètes*, vol. II, p. 79; *Eloisa, or A Series of Original Letters Collected and Published by Mr. J. J. Rousseau*, trans. William Kenrick, 4 vols. (London: Vernor and Hood, 1803; facsimile reprint in 2 vols., Oxford: Woodstock Books, 1989), vol. I, p. 121.

10 'Les touchans attraits de la nature, et l'inaltérable pureté de l'air, et les mœurs simples des habitans, et leur sagesse égale et sûre, et l'aimable pudeur du sexe, et ses innocentes graces'; *La Nouvelle Héloïse*, p. 83; *Eloisa*, p. 128.

11 'Il semble qu'en s'élevant au dessus du séjour des hommes on y lasse tous les sentimens bas et terrestres, et qu'a mesure que l'on s'approche des régions éthérées, l'âme contracte quelque chose de leur inaltérable pureté. [. . .] Le spectacle a je ne sais quoi de magique, de surnaturel qui ravit l'esprit et les sens; on oublie tout, on s'oublie soi-même, on ne sait plus où l'on est'; *La Nouvelle Héloïse*, pp. 78–9; *Eloisa*, pp. 119–21.

12 Jean Starobinski, *Jean-Jacques Rousseau: Transparency and Obstruction*, trans. Arthur Goldhammer (Chicago: The University of Chicago Press, 1988), p. 83.

13 Mary Shelley and Percy Bysshe Shelley, *History of a Six Weeks' Tour Through Parts of France, Switzerland, Germany, and Holland, With Letters Descriptive of a Sail round the Lake of Geneva, and of the Glaciers of Chamouni* (London: Hookam–Ollier, 1817; facsimile reprint, Oxford: Woodstock Books, 1989), pp. 162–3 (P. B. Shelley to Thomas Love Peacock, 22 July 1816). However, the previous letter, dated 12 July, is full of references to the 'sacred name of Rousseau' and the novel: 'I read Julie all day; an overflowing, as it now seems, surrounded by the scenes which it has so wonderfully peopled, of sublimest genius, and more than human sensibility' (pp. 127–8, 138).

14 Byron in a note to *Childe Harold's Pilgrimage*, book 3, stanza 99, which begins 'Clarens! sweet Clarens, birth-place of deep Love!'; *The Complete Poetical Works of Lord Byron*, ed. Jerome J. McGann, 7 vols. (Oxford: Clarendon Press, 1980–1993), vol. II, p. 312.

15 John Murray, *A Handbook for Travellers in Switzerland* (London, 1838; facsimile reprint, Leicester: Leicester University Press, 1970), p. 146, quoted in David Hill, *Turner in the Alps: The Journey Through France and Switzerland in 1802* (London: George Philip, 1992), pp. 94–5.

16 *History of a Six Weeks' Journey*, p. 128.

17 See *Passages romantiques des Alpes*, ed. Daniel Sangsue (Lausanne: Favre, 1990), especially the editor's introduction, pp. 3–19.

18 'La surabondance d'un esprit qui se plaît au tableau de la nature'; cited in Jean Roussel, *Jean-Jacques Rousseau en France après la révolution, 1795–1830* (Paris: Colin, 1972), p. 169.

19 'Les personnes habituées à la vie des montagnes [. . .] trouvent le paysage des hautes vallées autrement sévère, sobre et précis que notre poète ne l'a créé dans sa magnifique idylle luxuriante'; 'outré vraiment et comme irrité de cette douceur blonde et bleue et de cet optimisme indéfini'; Saint-Beuve in the *Revue des deux mondes*, 1 March 1839, quoted in Roger Lefèvre, 'Le Printemps alpestre de *Jocelyn*, ou l'imagination lamartinienne du bonheur', *Lamartine. Le Livre du centenaire*, ed. Paul Viallaneix (Paris: Flammarion, 1971), pp. 97–106: 104–5; for the larger context in which both Chateaubriand's and Lamartine's Alpine descriptions are situated, see Pauline Lacoste-Veysseyre, *Les Alpes romantiques. Le Thème des Alpes dans la littérature française de 1800 à 1850*, 2 vols. (Geneva: Slatkine, 1981), vol. I, pp. 163–87 (the vogue of the Alps after 1820), 335–54 (Chateaubriand), 504–73 (Lamartine).

20 *Oh! Che originali, farsa; Nina o La pazza per amore, dramma semiserio* (Milan: Fontana, 1829). Pasta sang *Nina* also in London in 1824, 1826 and 1828, and Verona and Mantua in 1830, repeating the role in Paris in 1824, 1825 and 1826. In Naples in 1827 and in Vienna in 1830 she was partnered by the tenor Giovanni Battista Rubini, who would also be at her side at the première of *La sonnambula*. See Giorgio Appolonia, *Giuditta Pasta, gloria del belcanto* (Turin: EDA, 2000), pp. 279–305.

21 See Stefano Castelvecchi, 'From *Nina* to *Nina*: Psychodrama, Absorption and Sentiment in the 1780s', *Cambridge Opera Journal* 8 (1996), pp. 91–112.

22 See Lucio Tufano, '*La Nina o sia La pazza per amore* di Giovanni Paisiello: testi e contesti', doctoral dissertation, University of Pavia (2000), pp. 22–8.

23 'Il desiderio de' piaceri semplici dell'innocente natura'; cited in *ibid.*, pp. 57–8, from Andrea Della Corte, *Settecento italiano* (Milan: Bocca, 1922), pp. 178–9.

24 See Pietro G. Beltrami, *La metrica italiana* (Bologna: Il Mulino, 1991), pp. 286–9; Alberto Mario Cirese, *Ragioni metriche* (Palermo: Sellerio, 1988), pp. 35–153.

25 A hundred years after Paisiello, Mascagni used a song of the *strambotto* family to locate his opera musically as well as poetically: Turiddu's 'O Lola, ch'hai di latti la cammisa' at the beginning of *Cavalleria rusticana* (1890).

26 The most explicit critic was Michele Scherillo in his once-influential *Vincenzo Bellini. Note aneddotiche e critiche* (Ancona: Morelli, 1882), p. 131. One can cite, among others, P[aul] Scudo, *Critique et littérature musicales* (Paris: Amyot, 1850), p. 96; Arthur Pougin, *Bellini. Sa vie, ses œuvres* (Paris: Hachette, 1868), p. 211; Francesco Florimo, *Bellini. Memorie e lettere* (Florence: Barbera, 1882), p. 45; Francesco Degrada, 'Prolegomeni a una lettura della *Sonnambula*', *Il melodramma italiano dell'Ottocento. Studi e ricerche per Massimo Mila*, ed. Giorgio Pestelli (Turin: Einaudi, 1977), pp. 319–50: 326–7; Friedrich Lippmann, 'Vincenzo Bellini e l'opera seria del suo tempo. Studi sul libretto, la forma delle arie e la melodia', in Maria Rosaria Adamo and Friedrich Lippmann, *Vincenzo Bellini* (Turin: ERI, 1981), pp. 313–555: 318–19, 339–40.

27 'Ti giuro che se il libretto non sarà capace di profonde sensazioni, è pieno però d'effetti teatrali pel colorito, e posso dire essere il fondo del genere come la Sonnambula o la Nina di Paisiello, aggiunto a del militare robusto ed a qualche cosa di severo Puritano'; Vincenzo Bellini, *Epistolario*, ed. Luisa Cambi (Milan: Mondadori, 1943), p. 442; see Pierluigi Petrobelli, *Music in the Theater: Essays on Verdi and Other Composers*, trans. Roger Parker (Princeton: Princeton University Press, 1994), pp. 162–92.

28 Petrobelli sums up the similarities between *Nina* and *I Puritani* with the word *tinta*, 'that most useful of Verdian terms'; Petrobelli, *Music in the Theater*, p. 188.

29 Stendhal, *Life of Rossini*, trans. Richard N. Coe, 2nd edn (London and New York: Calder–Riverrun, 1985), p. 271.

30 The stage direction ('dietro alla collina') does not appear in Rossini's autograph, although the composer almost never included stage

directions in his scores; the passage constitutes the first section of what in the autograph is called 'Coro e cavatina Giannetto'; see *La gazza ladra, melodramma in due atti di Giovanni Gherardini, musica di Gioachino Rossini*, ed. Alberto Zedda, Edizione critica delle opere di Gioachino Rossini, Sezione I, vol. XXI, 2 vols. (Pesaro: Fondazione Rossini, 1979).

31 Stendhal, *Life of Rossini*, p. 267.

32 For standard historical accounts of this change in the Italian context, see, for example, Stuart Woolf, *A History of Italy, 1700–1860 : The Social Constraints of Political Change* (London: Methuen, 1979; rpt London and New York: Routledge, 1991), pp. 283–92; Marco Meriggi, 'Società, istituzioni e ceti dirigenti', *Storia d'Italia*, ed. Giovanni Sabbatucci and Vittorio Vidotto, 6 vols., vol. I, *Le premesse dell'unità: dalla fine del Settecento al 1861* (Rome and Bari: Laterza, 1994), pp. 119–228, especially 119–30.

33 Alessandro Manzoni, *I promessi sposi*, ed. Vittorio Spinazzola (Milan: Garzanti, 1966), pp. 6–7; *The Betrothed*, trans. Bruce Penman (London: Penguin, 1972), pp. 25, 27.

34 *I promessi sposi*, p. 116; *The Betrothed*, p. 164.

35 Letter to Perucchini, dated 3 January 1831, in Bellini, *Epistolario*, 265.

36 See Michael Fend, 'Literary Motifs, Musical Form and the Quest for the "Sublime": Cherubini's *Eliza ou Le Voyage aux glaciers du Mont St Bernard*', *Cambridge Opera Journal* 5 (1993), pp. 17–38.

37 Fend goes so far as to say that 'the Alps [. . .] provoke his decision to commit suicide'; *ibid.*, p. 27.

38 See *ibid.*, pp. 29–38. More generally on the sublime and the Alps in music, see Michael Fend, 'Die ästhetische Kategorie des Erhabenen und die Entdeckung der Alpen in der Musik', *Schweizer Töne: Die Schweiz im Spiegel der Musik*, ed. Anselm Gerhard and Annette Landau (Zurich: Chronos, 2000), pp. 29–43.

39 Although *Guillaume Tell* had not been performed in Italy when Bellini was composing *La sonnambula*, Bellini and Rossini met in Milan in late August 1829, shortly after the triumphant première of *Tell* at the Paris Opéra. In a letter to Vincenzo Ferlito dated 28 August, Bellini describes the encounter and mentions the opera; see Francesco Pastura, *Bellini secondo la storia* (Parma: Guanda, 1959), pp. 218–23. Between August 1829 and January 1831 Bellini could easily have acquired or seen a vocal score of *Tell*, most probably the one published by the Neapolitan firm

of Girard in 1830; see *Guillaume Tell, opéra en quatre actes di Victor Joseph Etienne de Jouy e Hippolyte Louis Florent Bis, musica di Gioachino Rossini*, ed. M. Elizabeth C. Bartlet, Edizione critica delle opere di Gioachino Rossini, Sezione 1, vol. XXXIX, commento critico, 2 vols. (Pesaro: Fondazione Rossini, 1992), vol. 1, p. 45.

40 Benjamin Walton, 'Looking for the Revolution in Rossini's *Guillaume Tell*', *Cambridge Opera Journal* 15 (2003), pp. 127–51; see also Anselm Gerhard, '"Schweizer Töne" als Mittel der motivischen Integration: Gioachino Rossinis *Guillaume Tell*', *Schweizer Töne*, pp. 99–106.

41 *Elisa* was never published: I have consulted the manuscript copy in the Biblioteca Marciana, Venice (It. Cl. IV 844 [=10250]), which lacks the frontispiece (on the last page, fol. 213, a note reads 'Dalla Cop:ria di Giov.i Carcano in Venezia').

42 'La Musica esprime il comparire del sole'; *Elisa, dramma sentimentale in un atto per musica, da rappresentarsi nel Teatro Nobilissimo Venier in S. Benedetto la Primavera* 1804 (Venice: Casali, 1804), p. 5.

43 'Intanto da lontano si sente allegra Musica, accompagnata da Lire, Triangoli, e Cimbaletti, e voci diverse, che accostandosi in Coro di dentro [cantano]'; *ibid.*, pp. 8–9.

44 See Victor Ducange, *Thérèse, ou l'Orpheline de Genève, mélodrame en trois actes* (Paris: Barba, 1821).

45 *L'orfanella della Svizzera, dramma in tre atti, traduzione dal francese di Luigi Marchionni* (Leghorn: Vignozzi, 1824; rpt Rome: Ajani, 1827; and Milan: Visaj, 1830). *L'orfana ginevrina, ossia L'ombra di un vivo, ballo in tre atti espressamente composto per la prima volta da Antonio Monticini* (Vicenza: Parise, 1826); this *ballo* was performed in Milan, at the Teatro Carcano, in 1828, and again in 1830 at the Teatro della Canobbiana. Another *ballo* on the same subject was choreographed by Giuseppe Turchi: unfortunately, the copy of the scenario at the Biblioteca Braidense, Milan (*L'orfannella di Ginevra, ossia L'ombra di un vivo, azione mimica in 4 atti di Giuseppe Turchi*) has been detached from the opera libretto it was published with, and therefore it is impossible to establish the date and place of the performances of this *ballo*.

46 [Felice Romani], *Amina ovvero L'innocenza perseguitata, melodramma semiserio* (Milan: Pirola, 1824); [Romani], *Amina ovvero L'innocenza perseguitata, melodramma semiserio* (Trieste: n.e., 1825); [Romani and Andrea Leone Tottola], *Amina ovvero L'orfanella da Ginevra, melodramma*

comico-sentimentale (Naples: Flautina, 1825); [Romani and Jacopo Ferretti], *L'orfanella di Ginevra, melodramma* (Milan: Truffi, 1832). For the attribution to Romani of this anonymous text and of the alterations to Tottola and Ferretti, see Alessandro Roccatagliati, *Felice Romani librettista* (Milan and Lucca: Ricordi–LIM, 1996), pp. 88, 298.

47 In the copy of the libretto of Ricci's opera printed for the 1832 performances at the Canobbiana now at the Archivio Storico Ricordi, Milan (without shelf number), several leaves with manuscript alterations have been glued over the original printed text. The first stage direction, 'the park of the castle' ('parco nel Castello'), has been replaced with 'the scene represents a range of beautiful hills, with the Alps in the background' ('la scena rappresenta una catena di amene colline, in lontananza le Alpi').

48 See the chorus that precedes Amina's *cavatina*, 'La bella innamorata', and the waltz-like 'Allegria!' that concludes the *introduzione*. Since all the *pezzi staccati* published by Ricordi and reprinted in Luigi Ricci, *'Chiara di Rosembergh' and Excerpts from 'Colombo' and 'L'orfanella di Ginevra'*, ed. Philip Gossett (New York and London: Garland, 1990), are arias or duets, I have consulted Ricci's autograph score in the Archivio Storico Ricordi (without shelf number), a collection of unbound fascicles and single sheets (mostly misplaced).

49 This had by no means always been the case: in Gaetano Rossi's successful *melodramma sentimentale* in one act *Adelina* (music by Pietro Generali, Venice, 1810), the story of the tribulations of a woman who has had a child out of wedlock (a rather daring subject for an opera at the time) is set in a village near Zurich with a beautiful vista of the Alps.

50 See Lacoste-Veysseyre, *Les Alpes romantiques*, vol. 1, pp. 298–9. Lacoste-Veysseyre's observation refers mainly to the Romantic *Alpes épouvantes*, with their forests, storms and glaciers, a popular version of the more literary, sublime Alps (the name of the mountain looming large on the action of the 1822 *mélodrame Le Solitaire ou l'Exilé du Mont Sauvage* is 'Le Pic Terrible').

51 'Si richiede [. . .] di non parlar della bellezza, e gioventù dell'orfana [e] render l'Orfana meno giovane. E se si potesse anche cambiare senza nuocere all'essenziale il titolo d'Orfana, in un altro ciò renderà più accettabile l'Opera'; letter by Giuseppe Maria Franchetti, the Austrian

Government's representative to La Scala administrative board, to Felice
Romani, dated 24 November 1823, transcribed in Roccatagliati, *Felice
Romani*, p. 323.

52 See, however, the manuscript stage direction in the libretto of Ricci's
opera in the Archivio Storico Ricordi mentioned above.

53 Apparently only the costumes for Teresa, Elvino and Alessio were
published at the time of the première. The simplicity and atemporality
of Pasta's costume for Amina can be observed in a coloured engraving
on the back cover of *Galleria Teatrale d'Italia. Almanacco per l'anno 1833*
(Milan: Canadelli, 1833), which also reproduces part of the stage design
for the last scene of *La sonnambula* identical with Figure 2.3.

54 See *'Guillaume Tell' di Gioachino Rossini: fonti iconografiche*, ed. M.
Elizabeth C. Bartlet with Mauro Bucarelli (Pesaro: Fondazione Rossini,
1996); Mercedes Viale Ferrero, *'Guglielmo Tell* a Torino (1839–40) ovvero
una "procella" scenografica', *Rivista italiana di musicologia* 14 (1979),
pp. 378–94.

55 For the iconographical repertoire of early-nineteenth-century Italian
painting, especially in Lombardy, see Enrico Piceni and Mario
Monteverdi, *Pittura lombarda dell'Ottocento* (Milan: Cassa di Risparmio
delle Province Lombarde, 1969). See also the large iconographical
repertoire collected in *Les Alpes à travers la gravure du XIXe siècle*, ed. Aldo
Audisio, Bruno Guglielmotto-Ravet and Annie Bertholet (Paris: Berger–
Levrault, 1982).

56 'Quella [la scena] del primo atto che figura una stanza d'osteria, da
quanto dice il libretto, ci parve da prima poco adatta, a cagione di que'
quadri che la costituiscono una galleria di antico castello anzicché una
camera d'alloggio di povero villaggio; ma meglio informati abbiamo
saputo che tutta quella scena di ritratti costituiva gli antenati dell'oste,
il quale in origine sarà stato forse il feudatario del paese, o qualche cosa
di simile'; *Gazzetta privilegiata di Milano*, 8 March 1831, cited in Pastura,
Bellini secondo la storia, pp. 281–2.

57 See, for example, Degrada, 'Prolegomeni a una lettura della
Sonnambula', pp. 334–6, which cites Giulio Confalonieri, *Storia della
musica*, 2nd edn, ed. Alfredo Mandelli (Milan: Sansoni, 1968), p. 505.

58 For a more extensive treatment of the scenographic tradition of *La
sonnambula* in the nineteenth century, see Emanuele Senici, 'Amina e il
C.A.I.: vedute alpine ottocentesche', *Vincenzo Bellini nel secondo*

centenario della nascita, ed. Graziella Seminara and Anna Tedesco (Florence: Olschki, 2004), pp. 569–79, which contains an earlier version of the few preceding paragraphs.

59 These sketches, now in the library of the Accademia Chigiana, Siena, were discovered and described by Franco Schlitzer, *Mondo teatrale dell'Ottocento* (Naples: Fiorentino, 1954), p. 18.

60 The first to point out this similarity has been Degrada, 'Prolegomeni a una lettura della *Sonnambula*', p. 336.

61 A few quotes from across the century: 'Colour of pastoral melody' ('Tinta di pastorale melodia'); review published in the *Gazzetta privilegiata di Milano* on 15 March 1831 (in Pastura, *Bellini secondo la storia*, pp. 282–3). 'A bright, welcoming, pleasant [opera], like a delightful village illuminated by the sun and surrounded by flowers' ('Lucida, agevole, amena come un paese ridente, irraggiato dal sole e seminato di fiori'); review by Felice Romani published in the *Gazzetta piemontese* on 3 January 1856, quoted in Emilia Branca, *Felice Romani e i più riputati maestri di musica del suo tempo* (Milan: Sonzogno, 1882), pp. 191–2. 'A bucolic composition from Virgil's and Theocritus' country' ('Une vrai bucolique du pays de Virgile et de Théocrite'); P[aul] Scudo, *L'Année musicale*, 3 vols. (Paris: Hachette, 1860–2), vol. I, p. 69. 'An idyll, a delightful dream under the spell of the perfume of an orange tree grove, with the far-away echo of Theocritus' and Meli's melancholic tunes' ('Un idillio, un sogno delizioso al rezzo d'un boschetto d'aranci, che ne porta di lontano le malinconiche note di Teocrito e del Meli'); Florimo, *Bellini*, p. 43. 'The idyllic taste that, so to speak, the composer tasted in his mother's milk in Theocritus' and Meli's homeland' ('Quel sapore idillico, già da lui succhiato quasi col latte nella terra di Teocrito e del Meli'); Scherillo, *Vincenzo Bellini*, pp. 63, 70.

62 Giovanni Meli was a Sicilian poet of the late eighteenth century who wrote pastoral poems in Sicilan dialect; references to him, therefore, recall Bellini's Sicilian birth and connect it with his supposedly 'Sicilian' art.

63 'Bellini colla *Sonnambula* diveniva il Teocrito, il Gessner della musica'; Florimo, *Bellini*, p. 44, who cites as his source Felix Clément's *Les Musiciens célèbres*, 2nd edn (Paris: Hachette, 1868), where I have not

been able to find this sentence. 'Si direbbe che il Bellini sia ito ad ispirarsi in Elvezia ai soavi canti della musa Gessner per isposarli ai bei numeri della greca melodia'; Romani in the *Gazzetta piemontese* of 7 September 1836, cited in Mario Rinaldi, *Felice Romani dal melodramma classico al melodramma romantico* (Rome: De Santis, 1965), p. 250.

64 The popularity of Gessner's *Idyllen* in late-eighteenth- and early-nineteenth-century Europe (Italy included) is discussed in John Hibberd, *Salomon Gessner: His Creative Achievement and Influence* (Cambridge: Cambridge University Press, 1976), pp. 127–41; see also Lacoste-Veysseyre, *Les Alpes romantiques*, pp. 19, 22; especially relevant for the Italian context is Aurelio De' Giorgi Bertola, *Elogio di Gessner* [1789], ed. Michèle and Antonio Stäuble (Florence: Olschki, 1982).

65 See Branca, *Felice Romani*, pp. 161–2; Scherillo, *Vincenzo Bellini*, pp. 69–70; see also Pastura, *Bellini secondo la storia*, pp. 250–3.

66 See Degrada, 'Prolegomeni a una lettura della *Sonnambula*', p. 332.

67 See Quirino Principe, '*La sonnambula*' di Vincenzo Bellini (Milan: Mursia, 1991), pp. 81–2.

68 See Luigi Baldacci, *La musica in italiano. Libretti d'opera dell'Ottocento* (Milan: Rizzoli, 1997), pp. 33–5; Guido Paduano, 'La verità del sogno: *La sonnambula*', in his *Il giro di vite* (Florence: La Nuova Italia, 1992), pp. 67–83.

69 See Degrada, 'Prolegomeni a una lettura della *Sonnambula*', pp. 326–30.

70 Romani's autograph text of this scene, now housed in the Archivio Storico Civico, Milan, has been published by Marco Mauceri, 'Inediti di Felice Romani. La carriera del librettista attraverso nuovi documenti dagli archivi milanesi', *Nuova rivista musicale italiana* 25 (1992), pp. 391–432: 426–9, but its existence had been known since its mention in Branca, *Felice Romani*, pp. 162–3. Changes in the libretto caused by the rejection of this scene are documented in the autograph material at the Accademia Chigiana, Siena, mentioned above; see Schlitzer, *Mondo teatrale dell'Ottocento*, pp. 15–22.

71 See Mauceri, 'Inediti di Felice Romani', p. 429.

72 For a discussion of the links between dramaturgy and morality in *mélodrame*, see chapter 4 below.

73 See Paduano, 'La verità del sogno', pp. 82–3.

74 See *ibid.*, p. 82.

75 See Fabrizio Della Seta, 'Affetto e azione. Sulla teoria del melodramma italiano dell'Ottocento', *Atti del XIV Congresso della Società Internazionale di Musicologia. Trasmissione e recezione delle forme di cultura musicale*, ed. Lorenzo Bianconi, F. Alberto Gallo, Angelo Pompilio, Donatella Restani, 3 vols. (Bologna: Il Mulino, 1990), vol. III, pp. 395–9: 396.

76 Although the last phrase repeats the final couplet of text, I label it a''' rather than coda because in a'' the voice cadences on the mediant of E flat rather than on the tonic: another, more stable repetition is needed, one that is integral to the form (the lyric form model is notoriously unsatisfactory in dealing with the final section of a movement).

77 This affective potential will be weakened once the lyric form becomes the default mode for slow movements as well as for cabalettas – which, according to Mary Ann Smart, in Bellini's operas happens only from *Norma*; see Smart, 'Bellini, Vincenzo', *The New Grove Dictionary of Music and Musicians*, 2nd edn, ed. Stanley Sadie and John Tyrrell (London: Macmillan, 2001), vol. III, pp. 194–212: 204–5.

78 Except for the aborted feint towards F minor at 'a lei vola, è in lei rapita di dolcezza e di piacer', the rest, solidly rooted in A flat, is almost entirely diatonic.

79 In the fourth line Bellini substitutes 'vezzo' for 'riso'.

80 See Mary Ann Smart, 'Bellini's Fall from Grace', *Opera* 53/3 (March 2002), pp. 278–84: 282.

81 In Romani's text Elvino's first line ended with 'amante', like Amina's; 'errante' is Bellini's.

82 This point is made by Luca Zoppelli in 'L'idillio borghese', programme notes for a production of *La sonnambula* at the Teatro La Fenice, Venice, in June 1996 (Venice: Edizioni del Teatro La Fenice, 1996), pp. 49–62.

83 'Oh dì funesto' appears in the printed libretto, but was not set by Bellini.

84 Verdi's letter to Camille Bellaigue of 2 May 1898, in *I copialettere di Giuseppe Verdi*, ed. Gaetano Cesari and Alessandro Luzio (Milan: Commissione esecutiva per le onoranze a Giuseppe Verdi nel primo centenario della nascita, 1913), p. 415.

85 See Smart, 'Bellini's Fall from Grace', p. 283.

86 Bellini substitutes 'recarti' for 'donarti'.

87 Carl Dahlhaus, *Nineteenth-Century Music*, trans. J. Bradford Robinson (Berkeley and Los Angeles: University of California Press, 1989), pp. 117–19.

88 See Smart, 'Bellini's Fall from Grace', p. 283.

89 The only exception could be Imogene's *cavatina* in *Il pirata*, but there Bellini seems to operate outside the frame of reference of the lyric form, rather than subvert it from within as in 'Ah! non credea mirarti'.

90 See Lippmann, 'Vincenzo Bellini', p. 411; Paduano, 'La verità del sogno', pp. 77–8; Zoppelli, 'L'idillio borghese', p. 62.

91 See Lippmann, 'Vincenzo Bellini', p. 411.

92 The cadenza in Bellini's autograph score, shorter than the one in the current Ricordi vocal score, contains both the A and the A flat; see Vincenzo Bellini, *'La sonnambula' [. . .] partitura d'orchestra in fac-simile dell'autografo* (Milan: Ricordi, 1934), p. 371.

93 See Smart, 'Bellini's Fall from Grace', pp. 282–3.

94 The time of the action is not specified in the libretto. The entry in the *New Grove Opera* locates *La sonnambula* in the early nineteenth century, without further comment; see Julian Budden, Elizabeth Forbes and Simon Maguire, *'La sonnambula'*, *The New Grove Dictionary of Opera*, ed. Stanley Sadie, 4 vols. (London: Macmillan, 1992), vol. IV, pp. 452–4. In his edition of the libretto, Quirino Principe comments at length on the fact that the time of the action is not defined, and, on the basis of a few clues in the text, opts for the late eighteenth or, better, the early nineteenth century; see Principe, *'La sonnambula'*, p. 107.

95 See the engraving entitled 'Madame Malibran de Beriot, in her celebrated character of *La sonnambula*', published in Pierre Brunel, *Vincenzo Bellini* (Paris: Fayard, 1978), unnumbered pages following p. 224; a lithograph from a sheet music cover dating from 1847, the year Lind sang *La sonnambula* at Her Majesty's Theatre in London, published in Elizabeth Forbes, 'Lind, Jenny', *The New Grove Dictionary of Opera*, vol. III, p. 128; a photograph of Adelina Patti as Amina dating from the 1860s published in John Frederick Cone, *Adelina Patti: Queen of Hearts* (Portland: Amadeus Press, 1993), unnumbered pages following p. 40; and another photograph presumably taken in 1890, the year of Patti's *La sonnambula* at the Metropolitan in New York, published in F. Hernandez Girbal, *Adelina Patti, la reina del canto* (Madrid: Lira, 1979), unnumbered pages following p. 69. In an engraving of the last

scene of the opera by P. Oggioni, dating from 1835, the Conte is the only character whose costume proves to be chronologically specific, and it points unambiguously to the nineteenth century; see *La sonnambula*, programme book for a production of the opera at La Scala, Milan, in March 1986 (Milan: Edizioni del Teatro alla Scala, 1986), p. 60.

96 'Agnesi, toujours parfait, en bon maître qu'il est, a bien rendu le rôle du comte. Mais pourquoi cette redingote noire, ce képi des nos jours, ce ruban rouge, toutes choses qui jurent avec la contexture de la pièce et le costume des autres personnages? Pourquoi ne pas endosser un habit militaire Louis XV, puisqu'il est le *seigneur* du château? Le chant est une langue fictive qui sied mal au costume de tous les jours. Il lui faut une décoration, sinon fictive, au moins assez ancienne pour que l'imagination du spectateur puisse se prêter à l'illusion musicale'; Review by J. De Filippi in the Parisian *Menager des théâtres*, 15 November 1868.

97 For more on the costumes for *La sonnambula* in the nineteenth century, see Senici, 'Amina e il C.A.I.'.

98 Alessandro Roccatagliati and Luca Zoppelli, 'Testo, messinscena, tradizione: le testimonianze dei libretti', *Vincenzo Bellini: verso l'edizione critica. Atti del convegno internazionale, Siena, 1–3 giugno 2000*, ed. Fabrizio Della Seta and Simonetta Ricciardi (Florence: Olschki, 2004), pp. 271–90: 288.

99 The following paragraphs are based on portions of my essay 'Per una biografia musicale di Amina', *Vincenzo Bellini: verso l'edizione critica*, pp. 297–314.

100 Letter not dated to Francesco Florimo and letter dated 16 May 1833 to Alessandro Lamperi, in *Bellini. Epistolario*, pp. 363–70. On the authenticity of the letter to Florimo, see John Rosselli, *The Life of Bellini* (Cambridge: Cambridge University Press, 1996), pp. 9–10.

101 See *The celebrated opera La Sonnambula, composed by Bellini, adapted to the English stage by Henry R. Bishop* (London: Boosey, n.d., no plate number).

102 'Scritta a Milano / Rappresentata al Real Teatro del Fondo L'anno 1833'; Naples, Biblioteca del Conservatorio 'S. Pietro a Maiella', Ms. 24.3.7/8. The only significant difference from the autograph consists in the relocation of Lisa's 'De' lieti auguri' immediately after the chorus at the beginning of Act 2. This was clearly done at a later stage, after the manuscript had been copied.

103 See 'Come per me sereno / Sovra il sen' (London: Duff & Hodgson, n.d., plate number D&H 1833) (C–F instead of E flat–A flat); 'Ah non credea / Ah non giunge' (London: Leader & Cock, n.d., plate number L&C 2103) (G–G instead of A–B flat); *La sonnambula, Die Nacht-wandlerinn, Oper von V. Bellini, Kleiner Clavierauszug mit deutschem und italienischem Texte für den Umfang jeder Stimme eingerichtet von Ant. Diabelli* (Vienna: Diabelli, n.d., plate number 4492) (*cavatina* in D with cabaletta in E flat; final aria ['Romanze'] in G with cabaletta ['Schluss-Cavatine'] in A).

104 'Rubini fu trovato sublime e pel suo canto (che t'assicuro, mio caro, che ogni nota toccava la più profonda fibra del cuore) e per l'anima ed azione che mise in tutta l'opera. Ma, per renderlo padrone della sua parte, ho abbassato la sua cavatina da Si bemolle a La ed il largo e la stretta del finale ancora di mezzo tono, poiché ora la voce di Rubini possiede l'effetto un mezzo tono più basso della tessitura che sei anni sono richiedeva; perciò non potea dire con più enfasi e ricavare tanti effetti come nell'esecuzione di iersera'; Bellini to Florimo, 24 October 1834, in Cambi, *Epistolario*, p. 462.

105 'Spostasi una voce sotto', i.e., in A rather than B flat; *La sonnambula, fac-simile dell'autografo*, fol. 32r.

106 See *La sonnambula, melodramma di Felice Romani posto in musica dal M° Bellini* (Milan: Ricordi, n.d., plate numbers 5271–88 [1831]); *La sonnambula, opera seria in due atti del signor Maestro Vincenzo Bellini* (Paris: Launer, n.d., plate numbers 2978–81, 2734–43 [1834]).

107 See *La sonnambula, fac-simile dell'autografo*, fols. 63, 95.

108 See *La sonnambula, melodramma di Felice Romani posto in musica dal M° Bellini [. . .] nuova edizione* (Milan: Ricordi, n.d., plate numbers 30481–501 [1858]).

109 Biblioteca del Conservatorio, Rome, G.Ms. 716/717.

110 Biblioteca del Conservatorio, Rome, G.Ms. 714/715; Bibliothèque Nationale, Paris, Ms. D.850/851. For information on the two Roman manuscripts I am indebted to Philip Gossett, 'Trasporre Bellini', *Vincenzo Bellini: verso l'edizione critica*, pp. 163–85.

111 British Library, London, Hirsch II.46, 2 vols. of unnumbered sheets.

112 Gossett, 'Trasporre Bellini', p. 180.

113 *La sonnambula (The Somnambulist), a lyric drama, written by Felice Romani and rendered into English from the Italian by J. Wrey Mould, the music [. . .]*

by Vincenzo Bellini, revised from the orchestral score by W. S. Rockstro, pupil of Dr. Felix Mendelssohn Bartholdy (London: Boosey, n.d. [1849]), p. v.

114 *La Sonnambula, opéra complet pour piano et chant, paroles italiennes, musique de Bellini* (Paris: Vve Launer, n.d., plate number 3221 [1841]); *La sonnambula (La Somnambule), opéra en deux actes, paroles françaises de Mr Maurice Bourges, musique de Bellini* (Paris: Schlesinger, n.d., plate number 4262 [1845]); *La Somnambule, drame lyrique en 3 actes, paroles françaises de Crevel de Charlemagne, musique de V. Bellini* (Paris: Leduc, n.d., no plate number [*c.* 1872]).

115 *La sonnambula (La Somnambule)*, pp. 68–70.

116 'uniss. col tenore'; *ibid.*, pp. 92, 95.

117 British Library, London, H.799.b.; the first page of the score reads: *La sonnambula, atto primo [. . .] stampato in luogo di manoscritto* (Milan: Ricordi, n.d., plate number 96343 [*c.* 1895]); for the cuts, see p. 252.

118 See Georges Voisin, 'Discographie: airs séparés', in *La Somnambule, L'Avant-Scène Opéra*, n. 178 (July–August 1997), pp. 75–7; for the period of acoustic recording (up to *c.* 1925), Voisin lists fourteen recordings of 'Ah! non credea mirarti', eight of 'Ah, non giunge' and eleven of the two movements together, while 'Prendi, l'anel ti dono' with tenor *and soprano* was recorded seven times and 'Son geloso' four.

119 'Son geloso del zefiro errante', Amelita Galli-Curci and Tito Schipa, conductor Rosario Bourdon, Victor 8067-B (1923), in *Amelita Galli-Curci, 'Prima voce'*, CD Nimbus, NI 7806 (1990); 'D'un pensiero, d'un accento', Maria Gentile and Dino Borgioli, Orchestra of La Scala, Milan, conductor not indicated, Columbia GQX 10154 (1927), in *The Record of Singing, vol. III, 1926–1939*, LP EMI, EX 29 0169 3 (1984); 'Prendi, l'anel ti dono', Toti Dal Monte and Tito Schipa, Orchestra of La Scala, Milan, conductor Franco Ghione, Grammofono DA1351 (1933), in *Toti Dal Monte in Opera and Song*, CD Pearl, Gemm CD9195 (1996); *La sonnambula*, Lina Pagliughi and Ferruccio Tagliavini, RAI Orchestra of Turin, conductor Franco Capuana, LP Cetra, LPC 1240 (1952); *La sonnambula*, Joan Sutherland and Nicola Monti, Chorus and Orchestra of the Maggio Musicale Fiorentino, conductor Richard Bonynge, LP Decca, 239/41 (1963).

120 This recording has constantly been in the EMI catalogue, recently in CD format (CDS 747378/9).

121 CD Legato Classics, SRO-841-2 (n.d.).

122 The most recent recording of the opera keeps to the interpretative and textual choices of Callas's one: see *La sonnambula*, Luba Orgonasova and Raúl Giménez, Dutch Radio Chamber Orchestra, conductor Alberto Zedda, CD Naxos, 8.660042/3 (1997).

3 LINDA DI CHAMOUNIX AND THE IDEOLOGY OF CHASTITY

1 Sigmund Freud, 'The Taboo of Virginity', *The Standard Edition of the Complete Psychological Works of Sigmund Freud*, trans. James Strachey with Anna Freud, Alix Strachey and Alan Tyson, 24 vols. (London: The Hogarth Press–The Institute of Psychoanalysis, 1953–1974), vol. XI, pp. 193–208: 193.

2 Luigi Baldacci, *Ottocento come noi. Saggi e pretesti italiani* (Milan: Rizzoli, 2003), p. 402. There should be no need to stress the distance between ideology and everyday practices, especially as pertains to the lower strata of society. For a recent discussion of these practices in an Italian context, see Paolo Sorcinelli, *Storia e sessualità. Casi di vita, regole e trasgressioni tra Ottocento e Novecento* (Milan: Bruno Mondadori, 2001).

3 For a recent reflection on these issues, see Peter Brooks, 'Introduction', *Whose Freud? The Place of Psychoanalysis in Contemporary Culture*, ed. Peter Brooks and Alex Woloch (New Haven: Yale University Press, 2000), pp. 1–12.

4 I paraphrase a sentence from Eve Kosofsky Sedgwick, 'Paranoid Reading and Reparative Reading; Or, You're So Paranoid, You Probably Think This Introduction is About You', *Novel Gazing: Queer Readings in Fiction*, ed. Eve Kosofsky Sedgwick (Durham: Duke University Press, 1997), pp. 1–37: 30.

5 'Linda, vous le savez, c'est la *Grâce de Dieu*, ce drame célèbre applaudi pendant si long-temps au théâtre de la Gaîté; la *Grâce de Dieu*, c'est *Fanchon la vielleuse*, cette comédie si long-temps applaudie au théâtre du Vaudeville, et arrangée avec variations sur le thème d'une romance de mademoiselle Loïsa Puget, si long-temps applaudie dans les salons et dans mille autres lieux. Quelle origine glorieuse! quelle généalogie retentissante! quels succès de drame, de vaudeville, de romance, avant-coureurs d'un succès d'opéra!'; review by 'A.Z.' in the *Revue et Gazette Musicale de Paris* 9 (1842), pp. 455–6 (20 November 1842), in Annalisa

Bini and Jeremy Commons, *Le prime rappresentazioni delle opere di Donizetti nella stampa coeva* (Rome–Milan: Accademia Nazionale di Santa Cecilia–Skira, 1997), p. 1073.

6 *La Grâce de Dieu, ou la Nouvelle Fanchon, drame en cinq actes (mêlé de chant)* (Paris: Tresse, 1841). Donizetti mentions that he saw the play in Paris in a letter to Antonio Vasselli dated 24 December 1841; see Guido Zavadini, *Donizetti. Vita, musiche, epistolario* (Bergamo: Istituto italiano d'arti grafiche, 1948), p. 570. For the literary and theatrical tradition of the two Savoyards, or the 'vielleuse' (hurdy-gurdy player) and the Savoyard, to which *Linda* clearly belongs, see Emilio Sala, 'La "vielleuse" e il savoiardo: tradizione e drammaturgia', *Donizetti, Parigi e Vienna. Atti del convegno internazionale, Roma, 19–20 marzo*, Atti dei convegni Lincei 156 (Rome: Accademia Nazionale dei Lincei, 2000), pp. 47–77.

7 *Fanchon la vielleuse, comédie en trois actes, mêlée de vaudevilles [. . .] par MM. J. N. Bouilly et Joseph Pain* (Paris: Barba, 1803); for a list of later editions, see John Ralyea, 'The Savoyard Plays, Including the Plays Based on the Fanchon Legend', in his *Shepherd's Delight*, 2nd edn (Chicago: The Hurdy-Gurdy Press, 1981), pp. 125–92: 129. This play was translated into Italian as *Cecchina suonatrice di ghironda*, on which Gaetano Rossi himself based his *melodramma comico* of the same title set to music by Pietro Generali in 1810; see Sala, 'La "vielleuse" e il savoiardo', pp. 74–5.

8 Puget's songs often circulated in manuscript form well before their publication; see Austin B. Caswell, 'Loïsa Puget and the French *Romance*', *Music in Paris in the Eighteen-Thirties*, ed. Peter Bloom (Stuyvesant: Pendragon Press, 1987), pp. 97–115, which contains an edition of 'A la grâce de Dieu' based on a manuscript copy once owned by the soprano Laure Cinti-Damoreau and practically identical to the text reproduced here, transcribed from a late impression (*c.* 1880), published by 'Ancienne Maison Meissonier–E. Gérard et C.ie.', of plates originally prepared by the publishing firm 'Compagnie Musicale' around 1858 (plate no. 'C.M. 6701'); see Sala, 'La "vielleuse" e il savoiardo', for a reproduction of these plates with a different frontispiece. For a sympathetic, if at times ironic, assessment of Puget's output, see P[aul] Scudo, 'Esquisse d'une histoire de la romance depuis son origine jusqu'à nos jours', in his *Critique et littérature musicales* (Paris: Amyot, 1850), pp. 342–78: 372–4; see also Caswell, 'Loïsa Puget'.

9 'Marie, machinalement, chante le refrain de *la Grâce de Dieu*'; *La Grâce de Dieu*, p. 33.

10 See John McCormick, *Popular Theatres of Nineteenth-Century France* (London and New York: Routledge, 1993), pp. 187–8. Reviewing the Parisian première of *Linda*, 'H.W.' of the *Revue des deux mondes* was categorical: 'What brought extraordinary success to this *mélodrame* was the popularity of the song. This song encapsulated the whole story, the whole affect, the whole colour of the play; it was its soul' ('Ce qui valut au mélodrame ce succès inoui [. . .] ce fut la popularité de la romance. [. . .] Cette romance était toute l'intrigue, toute l'émotion, toute la couleur de la pièce; elle en était l'âme'); 'Revue musicale', *Revue des deux mondes* 32 (1842), pp. 853–66: 854.

11 In the letter to Vasselli mentioned above, Donizetti, after summarising the plot, adds: 'Don't tell me you don't like it, because I have seen the play in Paris. It is short and serves my purpose' ('Non dirmene male, perché ho vista la *pièce* a Parigi. È corta e mi serve a proposito').

12 In a letter in French to Michele Accursi dated 13 January 1842, published in *Studi donizettiani* 1 (1962), pp. 76–8: 77. See also the opinion of the reviewer of the Parisian première of *Linda* in *Le Ménestrel* of 20 November 1842: 'There are very few stories as interesting as that of *La Grâce de Dieu*, and that lend themselves so well to the needs of musical drama' ('Il est peu de sujets aussi intéressans que celui de la *Grâce de Dieu* et qui se prêtent aussi bien aux exigences du drame musical') (in Bini and Commons, *Le prime rappresentazioni*, p. 1076). Perhaps Donizetti got hold of a copy of Puget's song (beside of course having heard it in the play): in a letter to Antonio Dolci dated 18 December 1841, immediately before starting to compose *Linda*, Donizetti asks the addressee: 'Thank Bonesi on my behalf, who remembered to send me the Savoyard song' ('Dirai mille cose per me a Bonesi che ebbe la buona memoria d'inviarmi la canzone Savojarda'); Zavadini, *Donizetti*, p. 569. In any case, Pierotto's *ballata* in the opera bears no musical resemblance to Puget's song apart from the 6/8 metre.

13 In the letter to Accursi mentioned in the preceding note, Donizetti refers to this character as 'prêtre'.

14 This plot summary is adapted from the one compiled by Francesca Rescigno for the booklet accompanying the recording of the opera conducted by Gabriele Bellini with Mariella Devia in the title role (CD ARTS 447151–2, released by Pilk UK Ltd in 1994).

15 All quotations from *Linda*'s libretto follow the preliminary version of the opera's critical edition by Gabriele Dotto (Milan: Ricordi, 1994, for rent only), but have been checked against the librettos of both the first, Viennese version (*Linda di Chamounix, melodramma in tre atti, parole di Gaetano Rossi, musica del Maestro Cav. Gaetano Donizetti* [Vienna: Ullrich, 1842]) and the second, Parisian one (*Linda de Chamouni [sic], opéra en trois actes, musique de M. Gaétan Donizetti, paroles de M. Gaetano Rossi* [Paris: Lange Lévy, 1842]). In the case of Pierotto's *ballata* they present only two minor differences: 'ricercar' for 'rintracciar' in the first stanza, and 'tapina' for 'fanciulla' in the second.

16 See, for example, the three descriptions of Paris found at the beginning of the three novels constituting *L'Histoire des Treize*: *Ferragus*, *La Duchesse de Langeais* and *La Fille aux yeux d'or*. It is worth noting that at this time the provinces seemed to have become susceptible to corruption because their gaze was constantly fixed upon Paris (as in Balzac's *Scènes de la vie de province* and Stendhal's *Mémoires d'un touriste*).

17 'L'histoire éternelle qui faisait les délices de nos pères et dont on a bercé encore notre pâle génération: 'Aux montagnes de la Savoie, / Je naquis de pauvres parens; / Voilà qu'à Paris l'on m'envoie, / Car nous étions beaucoup d'enfans' etc. O montagnes! Que vous ont fait les plaines pour les accabler de vos vertus! O campagnes, que vous ont faits les villes! O Savoie, que t'a fait la France, où tu n'apportes que des marmottes en vie, et d'où tu remportes tant de petits sous! Est-il besoin que les Savoyards viennent à Paris pour se corrompre?'; Théophile Gautier, review of *Linda di Chamounix* in *La Presse*, 23 November 1842, reprinted in his *Histoire de l'art dramatique en France depuis vingt-cinq ans*, 6 vols. (Paris: Hetzel, 1856–8), vol. II, pp. 297–301: 298, partially reproduced in Bini and Commons, *Le prime rappresentazioni*, pp. 1078–80: 1079. The works cited by Gautier as precedents for *La Grâce de Dieu* are successful plays and novels identified by Bini and Commons (*La Paysanne pervertie* is misidentified as *Le Paysan perverti*, an *histoire* also by Rétif as well as a play by Théaulon: Gautier is obviously referring to Rétif's *Paysanne*).

18 See Sala, 'La "vielleuse" e il savoiardo', pp. 58–61, for a reproduction of this song and an analysis of its music.

19 Jacques Joly, '"Romance" popolare e melodramma colto. Da *Fanchon la vielleuse* a *Linda di Chamounix*', in his *Dagli Elisi all'inferno. Il melodramma*

tra Italia e Francia dal 1730 al 1850 (Florence: La Nuova Italia, 1990), pp. 229–43: 241.

20 See Mary Ann Smart, '"Dalla tomba uscita": Representations of Madness in Nineteenth-Century Italian Opera', Ph.D. dissertation, Cornell University (1994), for a multifaceted exploration of madness in nineteenth-century Italian opera, drawing on ideas from feminist literary and film theory and addressing questions of style, convention and drama.

21 'Oh! monsieur, cela se dit et ne se raconte pas. . . Je suis déshonorée, perdue. [. . .] Il n'y a plus de repos pour moi! Je ne veux pas d'autre repos que celui de la tombe'; Honoré de Balzac, *Splendeurs et misères des courtisanes*, ed. Pierre Barbéris (Paris: Gallimard, 1973), p. 330.

22 'Elle chanta des ritournelles d'airs gracieux, et tour à tour vociféra certaines phrases horribles qu'elle avait entendues! Sa belle figure était marbrée de teintes violettes. Elle mêlait les souvenirs de sa vie si pure à ceux de ces dix jours d'infamie'; *ibid.*, p. 331.

23 'Placez cette fille-là dans une maison de santé, si elle ne recouvre pas la raison en accouchant, si toutefois elle devient grosse, elle finira ses jours folle-mélancolique'; *ibid.*, p. 335.

24 The opening scene of *Linda* is discussed more in detail in chapter 4 below.

25 Donizetti made this utterance the climax of the duet between Antonio and the Prefetto, and the Viennese public was deeply impressed; see, for example, the review by Carl Kunt in the *Wiener Zeitschrift für Kunst, Literatur, Theater und Mode* no. 104 (25 May 1842), pp. 827–32 (in Bini and Commons, *Le prime rappresentazioni*, pp. 1059–64), translated into Italian in Rudolph Angermüller, 'Il periodo viennese di Donizetti', *Atti del primo convegno internazionale di studi donizettiani*, 2 vols. (Bergamo: Azienda Autonoma di Turismo, 1983), vol. II, pp. 619–95: 663; and the anonymous review in the *Wiener Zeitung* no. 175 (27 June 1842), pp. 1312–13 (in Bini and Commons, *Le prime rappresentazioni*, pp. 1071–2), translated in Angermüller, 'Il periodo viennese', pp. 670–2.

26 See the reviews by Heinrich Adami in the Viennese *Allgemeine Theaterzeitung* no. 121 (21 May 1842), pp. 535–6 (in Bini and Commons, *Le prime rappresentazioni*, pp. 1049–53; translated in Angermüller, 'Il periodo viennese', pp. 647–51); 'A.Z.' in the *Revue et Gazette Musicale de Paris*, p. 456 (Bini and Commons, *Le prime rappresentazioni*, pp. 1073–4);

and 'G. Romani' in the Milanese *Figaro* 12, no. 19 (6 March 1844), pp. 73–4. French reviewers were possibly influenced by a plot summary printed on a single sheet and probably distributed to the audience of the Parisian première, which reads: 'Pierotto comes to inform Linda of Sirval's wedding, which is about to take place nearby. Upon hearing this news, Linda loses her mind' ('Pierrot vient prévenir Linda qu'il a appris le mariage du vicomte de Sirval, qui va se célébrer dans le voisinage. Linda, à cette nouvelle, devient folle'). A copy of this plot summary is found in the *dossier d'œuvre* for *Linda* in the Bibliothèque de l'Opéra, Paris.

27 A few attentive reviewers realised the true cause of Linda's madness, among them Théophile Gautier: 'Her father Antoine finds her in Paris wearing a rich dress, and, believing her dishonoured, curses her; Linda faints, and wakes up mad' ('Son père, Antoine, en la retrouvant à Paris sous un riche costume, la croit désonorée et lui donne sa malediction; Linda tombe évanouie, et ne se reveille que folle'); Gautier's review in *La Presse* cited above, in *Histoire de l'art dramatique en France depuis vingt-cinq ans*, p. 299 (unfortunately Gautier's plot summary is omitted in Bini and Commons, *Le prime rappresentazioni*, p. 1079).

28 Michel Foucault, *The History of Sexuality*, vol. I, *An Introduction*, trans. Robert Hurley (New York: Random House, 1978), p. 110.

29 This prohibition is first discussed by Thomas Aquinas in his *Summa Theologiae*; see L. G. Miller, 'Incest', *The New Catholic Encyclopedia*, ed. the Editorial Staff at the Catholic University of America, 15 vols. (New York: McGraw–Hill, 1967), vol. VII, p. 419.

30 Foucault, *The History of Sexuality*, p. 109.

31 For a summary of nineteenth-century attitudes towards female virginity in the context of the family, see Michelle Perrot, 'The Family Triumphant', *A History of Private Life*, ed. Philippe Ariès and Georges Duby, vol. IV, *From the Fires of Revolution to the Great War*, ed. Michelle Perrot, trans. Arthur Goldhammer (Cambridge, Mass.: Harvard University Press, 1990), pp. 99–165: 150.

32 Yvonne Knibiehler, 'Bodies and Hearts', *A History of Women in the West*, ed. Georges Duby and Michelle Perrot, vol. IV, *Emerging Feminism from Revolution to World War*, ed. Geneviève Fraisse and Michelle Perrot, trans. Arthur Goldhammer (Cambridge, Mass.: Harvard University Press, 1993), pp. 325–69: 340.

33 See Michela De Giorgio, 'The Catholic Model', *Emerging Feminism from Revolution to World War*, pp. 166–97: 188.

34 See *ibid.*, pp. 169–72. Purity was especially relevant in the cult of Saint Philomena, the patron saint of virgins, which reached a peak in the 1830s and 1840s: see Alain Corbin, 'The Secret of the Individual', *From the Fires of Revolution to the Great War*, ed. Perrot, pp. 457–547: 492.

35 See Isabelle Bricard, *Saintes ou pouliches. L'Education des jeunes filles au XIXe siècle* (Paris: Michel, 1985), pp. 264–74; and *L'educazione delle donne. Scuole e modelli di vita femminile nell'Italia dell'Ottocento*, ed. Simonetta Soldani (Milan: Angeli, 1991). *When she was in her teens, my mother, born in Italy in 1935, was customarily sent to play outside when my grandmother wanted to talk with friends about 'sexuality'. This command might seem unremarkable; but for my grandmother the sphere of 'sexuality' could include even the simple mention of an acquaintance's pregnancy.*

36 'Une petite fontaine en pierre, où, dans une niche, se trouve une petite statue de la Vierge'; *Mise en scène de 'Linda de Chamouny', Opéra en trois actes, Paroles de M. Hyppolyte Lucas, Musique de M. Gaëtan Donizetti, Mise en scène de M. L. Palianti* (Paris: Chez l'Auteur, n.d. [1844]). Marian Smith tentatively links Palianti's staging with the first performance of *Linda* in the French translation by Lucas, which took place in Brussels on 1 February 1844; see her 'The *Livrets de Mise en Scène* of Donizetti's Parisian Operas', *L'opera teatrale di Gaetano Donizetti. Atti del convegno internazionale di studio, Bergamo, 17–20 settembre*, ed. Francesco Bellotto (Bergamo: Comune di Bergamo, 1993), pp. 371–89: 388.

37 See De Giorgio, 'The Catholic Model', pp. 184, 188–9.

38 Pasquale Contini, *Nuova raccolta di poesie morali e civili ad uso delle scuole e delle famiglie italiane* (Milan: Agnelli, 1866), p. 70.

39 Freud, 'Charcot', *The Standard Edition*, vol. III, pp. 9–23, especially 20–3.

40 See Evelyne Ender, *Sexing the Mind: Nineteenth-Century Fictions of Hysteria* (Ithaca: Cornell University Press, 1995), pp. 25–65.

41 See Jan Goldstein, *Console and Classify: The French Psychiatric Profession in the Nineteenth Century* (Cambridge: Cambridge University Press, 1987), pp. 322, 331–2.

42 See Foucault, *History of Sexuality*, pp. 30–1, 104.

43 *Ibid.*, p. 113; see also pp. 129–31.

44 See William J. McGrath, *Freud's Discovery of Psychoanalysis: The Politics of Hysteria* (Ithaca: Cornell University Press, 1986), especially chapter 4, 'The Architecture of Hysteria', pp. 152–96.

45 Paul Robinson has recently argued along similar lines for a coupling of Verdi and Freud as 'the artistic memorialist and the psychological analyst of the new romance between parent and child'; Paul Robinson, 'Verdi's Fathers and Daughters', in his *Opera, Sex, and Other Vital Matters* (Chicago: The University of Chicago Press, 2002), pp. 112–22: 122.

46 Freud and Josef Breuer, *Studies on Hysteria, The Standard Edition*, vol. II, pp. 125–34. The case of Katharina, surely the least studied of the five presented, is discussed by Patrick J. Mahoney, *On Defining Freud's Discourse* (New Haven: Yale University Press, 1989), chapter 2, 'The Dawn of Psychoanalysis: Katharina's Case History', pp. 25–58.

47 *Studies on Hysteria*, p. 125.

48 *Ibid.*, p. 127.

49 *Ibid.*, p. 134.

50 *Ibid.*, p. 132.

51 See Luigi Baldacci, *La musica in italiano. Libretti d'opera dell'Ottocento* (Milan: Rizzoli, 1997), p. 40.

52 'Vendre cette chaumière, où nous nous sommes mariés!. . . où ma mère est morte! où notre fille Marie est née! Est-ce-t-y Dieu possible? Qu'allons-nous devenir, Antoine, qu'allons-nous devenir?'; *La Grâce de Dieu*, p. 3.

53 'MADELEINE: Oh! je ne crains pas la fatigue et les veilles, moi!. . . je suis forte! PIERROT: Ce n'est pas comme mamzelle Marie!. . . on ne dirait jamais qu'elle est de vous, celle-là!. . . elle a plutôt l'air d'une demoiselle de la ville, que d'une Savoyarde!. . . ous qu'all'est donc, à c' matin? MADELEINE: Elle dort!. . . C'est jeune. . . ça a besoin de sommeil!. . . mais, moi, je travaille!. . . ça fait qu'comme ça, elle dort plus long-temps et que l'ouvrage n'en souffre pas'; *La Grâce de Dieu*, pp. 1–2.

54 *Ibid.*, p. 9.

55 'Marie pousse un cri terrible et se retire de la fenêtre avec horreur; à partir de ce moment, elle regarde le public d'un œil fixe et hagard'; *Ibid.*, p. 32.

56 According to Freud, this is not anomalous: 'In the absence of fear of castration the chief motive is lacking which leads boys to surmount the Oedipus complex. Girls remain in it for an indeterminate length of time:

they demolish it late and, even so, incompletely'; 'Femininity', *The Standard Edition*, vol. XXII, pp. 112–35: 129.

57 Freud, 'Female Sexuality', *The Standard Edition*, vol. XXI, pp. 223–43: 238–9.

58 *Ibid.*, p. 227.

59 Another operatic character born the same year as Linda, Senta in Wagner's *Der fliegende Holländer*, has been portrayed as a hysteric, most famously in Harry Kupfer's 1978 Bayreuth production; and *Der fliegende Holländer* is another 'ballad opera' with many points of contact with *Linda*.

60 Peter Brooks, *Psychoanalysis and Storytelling* (Oxford: Blackwell, 1994), pp. 25, 35–6.

61 See Tim Dean, 'What's the Point of Psychoanalytic Criticism?', *Beyond Redemption: The Work of Leo Bersani*, ed. Timothy Clark and Nicholas Royle, special issue of *The Oxford Literary Review* 20 (1998), pp. 143–62.

62 'Non andar cercando nella storia il soggetto di Vienna. Son ragazzi che partono dalla Savoia per Parigi onde guadagnar pane. V'è chi è buono e chi è cattivo. Una ragazza sta più volte per lasciarsi sedurre, ma, ogni volta, sente la canzone del paese, e pensa al padre, alla madre e resiste. . . Poi non resiste più. . . il seduttore vuole sposare un'altra. Poi essa diviene pazza (auff); poi torna al paese con un povero ragazzo che la fa camminare a forza di suonarle la canzone: se no, s'arresta. . . Muoion quasi di fame tutti e due; il seduttore arriva. . . non ha sposato. La ragazza rinviene, chè a sentire. . . la donna rinviene subito'; Zavadini, *Donizetti*, p. 570.

63 Gabriele Dotto's edition, based on the autograph score, offers the exact repetition of 'A consolarmi affrettisi / Tal giorno desiato' (Donizetti, *Linda di Chamounix*, ed. Dotto, pp. 246–7, 824), as does the current Ricordi vocal score (Gaetano Donizetti, *Linda di Chamounix, melodramma in tre atti di Gaetano Rossi* [Milan: Ricordi, plate no. 42056], pp. 71, 229). The printed libretto for the first performance has 'A consolarmi affrettisi, / O giorno sospirato' in Act 1 and 'A consolarmi affrettati, / Momento fortunato' in Act 3 (*Linda di Chamounix, melodramma in tre atti*, pp. 14, 43), while the printed libretto for the revised Parisian version gives 'A consolarmi affrettisi, / O giorno sospirato' in Act 1 and 'A consolarmi affrettisi, / Momento fortunato' in Act 3 (*Linda de Chamouni, opéra en trois actes*, pp. 20, 70).

64 Gabriele Dotto has suggested that, on repeated hearings, Donizetti would eventually have realised his mistake and cut the first Larghetto; see his '*Linda di Chamounix*: percorsi di una struttura drammaturgica e scelte esecutive', forthcoming in the proceedings of the conference *Donizetti e il teatro musicale europeo* (Venice, Teatro La Fenice, 1997) (Bergamo: Fondazione Donizetti).

65 See *Linda di Chamounix*, ed. Dotto, p. 263; this pianissimo reprise of the melody made a great impression on the first audiences, as numerous reviews testify: see, for example, the already-cited review by Heinrich Adami in the *Allgemeine Theaterzeitung* (Bini and Commons, *Le prime rappresentazioni*, p. 1052; Angermüller, 'Il periodo viennese', p. 651).

66 'Quasi piangente. . . a mezza voce' is present in Dotto's edition (*Linda di Chamounix*, ed. Dotto, p. 578), but not in the Ricordi vocal score.

67 The first, Viennese version of the opera featured a slow movement, 'Nel silenzio della sera', positioned between the reprise of 'A consolarmi affrettisi' and the cabaletta and cut by Donizetti in the summer of 1842, well before the other alterations made for the Parisian première; see Dotto, '*Linda di Chamounix*', for the text of this movement and a discussion (Dotto calls it a 'cavatina'). It is worth noting that Linda's hallucinatory description of her wedding to Carlo establishes a strong intertextual link with previous mad scenes, most famously Lucia's in *Lucia di Lammermoor*, but also Anna's in *Anna Bolena* and Amina's sleepwalking in Act 2 of *La sonnambula*. I would suggest that one of the reasons why Donizetti decided to cut this movement may have been a desire to distance this scene from its too-famous predecessors. The formal result is an aria without the slow movement.

68 In bars 3–4 of 'No, non è ver' Donizetti gives the singer the choice of singing C–B flat–A–B flat–G or A flat–G–F sharp–G–E flat, accompanied by the two clarinets playing both lines; the clarinets also provide the doubling at the unison and a third below to the melody of 'A consolarmi affrettisi'.

69 Compare Freud's and Breuer's conclusion that 'hysterics suffer mainly from reminiscences'; *Studies on Hysteria*, p. 7.

70 In the Viennese and Parisian librettos Linda sings 'Egual voce, eguale accento / Così un dì mi lusingò'.

71 In the Viennese and Parisian librettos Carlo sings 'Oh! sì, Linda, lo rammento!' Translating 'accento' as 'words' empties the word of the

musical resonances the term has in Italian: it could perhaps be rendered better with 'tune'.

72 'Questa cabaletta può esser cantata da Linda la 2a volta'; *Donizetti a Casa Ricordi. Gli autografi teatrali*, ed. Alessandra Campana, Emanuele Senici and Mary Ann Smart (Bergamo: Fondazione Donizetti, 1998), p. 70.

73 The autograph score does not name this number. Printed vocal scores customarily divide long numbers like this into smaller units, and *Linda's* are no exception: see the 'Preludio, Scena ed Aria / Preghiera–Quintetto a voci sole / Scena e Duetto Finale' of the current Ricordi vocal score. In his edition Dotto calls it 'Finale ultimo'.

74 See Michel Poizat, *La Voix du diable. La Jouissance lyrique sacrée* (Paris: Métailié, 1991); Mladen Dolar, 'The Object Voice', *Gaze and Voice as Love Objects*, ed. Renata Salecl and Slavoj Žižek (Durham: Duke University Press, 1996), pp. 7–31; Corrado Bologna, *Flatus vocis. Metafisica e antropologia della voce*, 2nd edn. (Bologna: Il Mulino, 2000).

75 'Il est inouï toute la puissance que l'oreille a sur notre âme'; Denis Diderot, *Correspondance*, ed. Georges Roth with Jean Varloot, 16 vols. (Paris: Minuit, 1955–70), vol. XVI, p. 60.

76 'Il est reçu, parmi les véritables libertins, que les sensations communiquées par l'organe de l'ouïe sont celles qui flattent davantage et dont les impressions sont les plus vives. En conséquence, nos quatre scélérats, qui voulaient que la volupté s'imprégnât dans leur cœur aussi avant et aussi profondément qu'elle y pouvait pénétrer, avaient à ce dessein imaginé une chose assez singulière. Il s'agissait, après s'être entouré de tout ce qui pouvait le mieux satisfaire les autres sens par la lubricité, de se faire en cette situation raconter avec les plus grands détails, et par ordre, tous les différents écarts de cette débauche, toutes ses branches, toutes ses attenances, ce qu'on appelle en un mot, en langue de libertinage, toutes les passions'; Marquis de Sade, *Le Cent vingt journées de Sodome, ou L'école du libertinage* (1789), ed. Michel Delon, in *Œuvres*, vol. I (Paris: Gallimard, 1990), p. 39.

77 Until recently, however, Lacanian critics themselves neglected this aspect of his work, as can be inferred, for example, from the absence of entries for 'voice' or 'ear' in Dylan Evans, *An Introductory Dictionary of Lacanian Psychoanalysis* (London and New York: Routledge, 1996). Even more significant is the almost total absence of voice from a book-length reflection on opera by two of the most prominent present-day

Lacanians, Slavoj Žižek and Mladen Dolar, despite the fact that one of them, Dolar, is the author of a fundamental essay on voice in general, the already-cited 'The Object Voice'; see their *Opera's Second Death* (New York and London: Routledge, 2002).

78 The first quote comes from 'The Line and Light' and the second from 'From Love to the Libido', both in Jacques Lacan, *The Four Fundamental Concepts of Psychoanalysis*, ed. Jacques-Alain Miller, trans. Alan Sheridan (New York: Norton, 1978), pp. 104 and 195 respectively.

79 Jacques Lacan, 'The Subversion of the Subject and the Dialectic of Desire in the Freudian Unconscious', *Ecrits: A Selection*, trans. Alan Sheridan (New York: Norton, 1977), p. 319.

80 'The Line and Light', p. 103.

81 Bruce Fink, *The Lacanian Subject: Between Language and Jouissance* (Princeton: Princeton University Press, 1995), p. 59.

82 Julia Kristeva, 'Stabat Mater', in her *Tales of Love*, trans. Leon S. Roudiez (New York: Columbia University Press, 1987), pp. 243–63: 248, 257.

83 Kaja Silverman, *The Acoustic Mirror: The Female Voice in Psychoanalysis and Cinema* (Bloomington: Indiana University Press, 1988), p. 112. Other prominent feminist critiques of Kristeva's conception of the maternal voice are Domna C. Stanton, 'Difference on Trial: A Critique of the Maternal Metaphor in Cixous, Irigaray and Kristeva', *The Poetics of Gender*, ed. Nancy K. Miller (New York: Columbia University Press, 1986), pp. 157–82; and Claire Kahane, 'Questioning the Maternal Voice', *Genders* 3 (November 1988), pp. 82–91.

84 The orchestral music of the pantomime presents first the motive on which Linda had sung the words 'non è ver' in the Act 2 finale, then fragments of the *ballata*, and eventually works these two ideas together in the seven-bar codetta of this short yet impressive contrapuntal and harmonic *tour de force*.

85 See Carolyn Abbate, *Unsung Voices: Opera and Musical Narrative in the Nineteenth Century* (Princeton: Princeton University Press, 1991), p. 120.

86 Marco Beghelli, 'Il ruolo del musico', *Donizetti, Napoli, l'Europa*, ed. Franco Carmelo Greco and Renato Di Benedetto (Naples: Edizioni Scientifiche Italiane, 2000), pp. 323–35: 334.

87 Donizetti seems to have conceived the first few scenes of Act 2, up to and including Carlo's *romanza* 'Se tanto in ira agli uomini', as one long single number, subsequently divided for publishing reasons into three

numbers: duet Linda–Pierotto, duet Linda–Marchese and *romanza* Carlo; see *Donizetti a casa Ricordi*, p. 69.

88 Heather Hadlock, '*Tancredi* and *Semiramide*', *The Cambridge Companion to Rossini*, ed. Emanuele Senici (Cambridge: Cambridge University Press, 2004), pp. 139–58: 156.

89 Donizetti has Pierotto sing these lines in the bridge between the two statements of the cabaletta rather than in its second statement (to which the libretto seems to assign them), so that Pierotto must repeat the first stanza of the text in the second statement.

90 Carolyn Abbate, *In Search of Opera* (Princeton: Princeton University Press, 2001), pp. 24–6. For other memorable variations on the voice and its echoes which have influenced my reading of *Linda*, see pp. 70–3, 131–4, 153–60.

91 For a discussion of dramaturgical differences between Donizetti and Verdi, illuminating despite its neglect of musical and vocal aspects, see Baldacci, *La musica in italiano*, pp. 49–61.

92 'Come on, always the same' ('E via, sempre lo stesso') is Pierotto's comment when Linda sings the fragment of the cabaletta theme in Act 3.

93 Compare Peter Brooks's recent pronouncement that 'the operatic aria [. . .] speaks the name of desire directly. It may be the most unrepressed speech of desire that art allows'; Peter Brooks, 'Body and Voice in Melodrama and Opera', *Siren Songs: Representations of Gender and Sexuality in Opera*, ed. Mary Ann Smart (Princeton: Princeton University Press, 2000), pp. 118–34: 122.

94 'They [the gaze and the voice] belong to the register of what Lacan calls the real, and resist imaginarisation and symbolisation. They are nevertheless closely related to the subject's most crucial experiences of pleasure and pain, excitement and disappointment, thrill and horror [i.e., *jouissance*]. They resist analytic action – which involves speech, putting things into words, trying to say what the problem is, to speak it – and are related to a *jouissance* that defines the subject's very being'; Fink, *The Lacanian Subject*, p. 92. For a Lacanian interpretation of opera not unlike the one I propose here, see Michel Poizat, *The Angel's Cry: Beyond the Pleasure Principle in Opera*, trans. Arthur Denner (Ithaca: Cornell University Press, 1992), especially pp. 99–106; Poizat, *La Voix du diable*, especially pp. 183–216. For a historicisation of this interpretation in

the context of Western philosophical constructions of subjectivity, see Gary Tomlinson, *Metaphysical Song: An Essay on Opera* (Princeton: Princeton University Press, 1999), pp. 83–7.

4 THE POLITICS OF GENRE IN LUISA MILLER

1 David Kimbell, *Verdi in the Age of Italian Romanticism* (Cambridge: Cambridge University Press, 1981), pp. 597–8.
2 Piero Weiss, 'Verdi and the Fusion of Genres', *Journal of the American Musicological Society* 35 (1982), pp. 138–56: 146–7.
3 Alessandro Roccatagliati, *Drammaturgia romantica verdiana: 'Luisa Miller' e 'Rigoletto'* (Bari: Il Coretto, 1989), p. 42. Peter Ross advances similar considerations in his 'Luisa Miller–ein "kantiger Schiller-Verschnitt"? Sozialkontext und ästhetische Autonomie der Opernkomposition im Ottocento', *Zwischen Opera buffa und Melodramma: Italienische Oper im 18. und 19. Jahrhundert*, ed. Jürgen Maehder and Jürg Stenzl (Frankfurt: Peter Lang, 1994), pp. 159–78, especially 164–5.
4 In the prose draft no specific mention of the Tyrol or the Alps is actually found: the action takes place in a village located amidst mountains; see *Carteggio Verdi–Cammarano (1843–1852)*, ed. Carlo Matteo Mossa (Parma: Istituto Nazionale di Studi Verdiani, 2001), pp. 105–9. The Tyrol first appears in the printed libretto and in Cammarano's notes for the staging of the opera, published in *ibid.*, pp. 363–5, and translated in Giuseppe Verdi, *Luisa Miller*, ed. Jeffrey Kallberg (Chicago and Milan: The University of Chicago Press–Ricordi, 1991), p. xxiii.
5 'Ha giovato molto in un subietto nel quale a prima giunta l'intervento dei Cori pareva piuttosto impossibile che difficile'; *Carteggio Verdi– Cammarano*, p. 129, trans. in *Luisa Miller*, ed. Kallberg, p. xix. Note that Cammarano does not say that he did so solely in order to provide room for the chorus, as Weiss and Markus Engelhardt claim. See Weiss, 'Verdi and the Fusion of Genres', p. 147; Markus Engelhardt, '"Something's Been Done to Make Room for Choruses": Choral Conception and Choral Construction in *Luisa Miller*', *Verdi's Middle Period, 1849–1859: Source Studies, Analysis, and Performance Practice*, ed. Martin Chusid (Chicago: The University of Chicago Press, 1997), pp. 197–205. The quotation in the title of Engelhardt's essay comes from Cammarano's letter to Verdi dated 15 May 1849, in which, however, no reference to the change of locale is found.

6 *La sonnambula, melodramma di Felice Romani, da rappresentarsi nel Teatro Carcano la Quaresima del 1831* (Milan: Fontana, 1831), pp. 9–10; reprinted with critical notes by Eduardo Rescigno as Vincenzo Bellini, *La sonnambula. Melodramma in due atti di Felice Romani* (Milan: Ricordi, 1990).

7 Gaetano Donizetti, *Linda di Chamounix*, preliminary version of the critical edition by Gabriele Dotto (Milan: Ricordi, 1994, for rent only), p. 74. The libretto for the première presents a slightly different text: 'E i perigli del viaggio degna il Cielo rischiarar' instead of 'Già dal Ciel fausto viaggio cominciamo ad implorar'; *Linda di Chamounix, melodramma in tre atti, parole di Gaetano Rossi, musica del Maestro Cav. Gaetano Donizetti* (Vienna: Ullrich, 1842), pp. 6–7.

8 The rustic connotations of 6/8 were a given of nineteenth-century musical culture. To cite only two Italian references related to an operatic context, Luigi Casamorata, reviewing the Florence première of Verdi's *Macbeth* (1847) for the *Gazzetta musicale di Milano*, complained that the music accompanying Duncan's arrival on stage in Act I, though lovely, is called 'rustic' ('villereccia') in the libretto, but, in fact, has nothing rustic about it except the metre; see *Verdi's 'Macbeth': A Sourcebook*, ed. Andrew Porter and David Rosen (New York: Norton, 1984), p. 388. Writing in the 1850s, Abramo Basevi claimed that the 6/8 metre 'has a special character that makes it apt for pastoral and hunting ambiences' ('ha un carattere speciale, che lo rende proprio ad esprimere ciò che ha attinenza col pastorale e colla caccia'); Abramo Basevi, *Studio sulle opere di Giuseppe Verdi* (Florence: Tofani, 1859; reprint Bologna: Forni, n.d. [1978]), p. 67.

9 See John Black, *Donizetti's Operas in Naples* (London: The Donizetti Society, 1982), p. 69.

10 See *Il teatro di San Carlo, 1737–1987*, vol. II, *La cronologia*, ed. Carlo Marinelli Roscioni (Naples: Guida, 1988). The correspondence between Verdi and Cammarano concerning *Luisa Miller* shows an ongoing concern for the cast that was eventually to sing at the première; even though they never mention that Salandri, Malvezzi and Selva were singing in *Linda*, it is difficult to think that it had no influence on the conception of *Luisa*.

11 For a discussion of Cammarano's production duties, see John Black, *The Italian Romantic Libretto: A Study of Salvadore Cammarano* (Edinburgh:

Edinburgh University Press, 1984), pp. 272–90. Cammarano's notes for the production of *Luisa Miller*, already mentioned, read almost exactly like the stage directions in the libretto.

12 All quotations are from *Luisa Miller, melodramma tragico, in tre atti [. . .] da rappresentarsi nel Real Teatro S. Carlo* (Naples: Flautina, 1849), p. 5.

13 'Alba' in Latin means 'white', gendered feminine; semantic connections granted by word derivation are hardly casual in the heavily literary language of Italian opera librettos, and 'literary language' in Italian is practically synonymous with 'classicising' and 'Latinising'; see, for example, 'sorgente', a Latin present participle used to form a relative clause (normally it would be 'che sorge'), or, later, 'ne (=Latin *nos*) invita' instead of 'ci invita'.

14 See Julian Budden, *The Operas of Verdi*, vol. I, *From 'Oberto' to 'Rigoletto'*, 2nd edn (Oxford: Oxford University Press, 1992), p. 425.

15 See William Ashbrook, *Donizetti and His Operas* (Cambridge: Cambridge University Press, 1982), p. 468. The *tyrolienne* was a triple-metre, waltz-like dance similar to the *ländler*, characterised by pastoral texts, simple, often triadic melodies, and echo and yodel effects. By 1842 its most famous operatic instance was the *Pas de trois et chœur tyrolien* 'Toi que l'oiseau ne suivrait pas' in Act 3 of *Guillaume Tell*, in which the voices adopt a prominent staccato articulation. This piece was called simply 'tyrolienne' in early printed librettos and reviews of the opera; see Gioachino Rossini, *Guillaume Tell, opéra en quatre actes di Victor Joseph Etienne de Jouy e Hippolyte Louis Florent Bis*, ed. M. Elizabeth C. Bartlet, commento critico (Pesaro: Fondazione Rossini, 1992), p. 206. Linda's piece, originally in D flat major, was inserted by Donizetti for the first performance of the opera at the Théâtre-Italien on 17 November 1842 at the request of Fanny Tacchinardi-Persiani. Eugenia Tadolini, Linda in the 1849 revival at the San Carlo, had included the aria since the first Viennese revival of *Linda* (1 April 1843), mounted under Donizetti's supervision, and she very probably sang it in Naples. Both versions of the opera, Viennese and Parisian, were published in vocal score in 1842 (the first in Milan by Ricordi, the second in Paris by Schoenenberger), and therefore Verdi was almost certainly acquainted with the piece. Lisa's *cavatina* within the *introduzione* of *La sonnambula*, an Allegro moderato cabaletta, might have provided a model for embedding a one-movement cabaletta within an *introduzione*.

16 In both cases the first line of each quatrain is a *verso sdrucciolo* (a line with the final accent on the antepenultimate syllable).

17 'Canto staccato' is Basevi's term. The critic was puzzled by the form and the position of this piece – he calls it 'a *romanza* for the soprano, which could be better called a *cabaletta*' ('una *romanza* del soprano, la quale meglio può dirsi *cabaletta*'); *Studio sulle opere di Giuseppe Verdi*, p. 162. It was Cammarano who suggested to Verdi the form of Luisa's *sortita* and of the following trio; see Cammarano's letter to Verdi on 23 May 1849 (*Carteggio Verdi–Cammarano*, p. 117; trans. in *Luisa Miller*, ed. Kallberg, p. xviii).

18 This connection is mentioned in Gilles de Van, *Verdi's Theater: Creating Drama Through Music*, trans. Gilda Roberts (Chicago: The University of Chicago Press, 1998), p. 191.

19 Perhaps Donizetti also tried to evoke the wide leaps typical of yodel and *tyrolienne*.

20 The remote predecent to these pieces might be Ninetta's *cavatina* in *La gazza ladra*, 'Di piacer mi balza il cor', in which the heroine sings of her heart throbbing at the happy thought of the imminent return of both her father and her lover. And of course Ninetta is a virgin, and *La gazza ladra* has much in common with *La sonnambula*, as discussed in chapter 2. But she does not sing in a prominently staccato style: the throbbing of her heart is evoked instead by the alternation of double-dotted quavers and demisemiquavers on 'mi balza il cor'. Elvira's 'Son vergin vezzosa' in *I Puritani* could also be meaningfully connected to this network of arias, and I wonder whether Gilda's 'Caro nome, che il mio cor festi primo palpitar', with its prominent quaver rests and its virginal evocation of 'le delizie dell'amor', might not owe something to Luisa's, Linda's and Amina's *sortite*.

21 I have examined reviews from the first half of the century, especially (but not exclusively) of performances of *La sonnambula* and *Linda di Chamounix* that appeared in newspapers and periodicals published in Milan, Paris and London, as well as the reviews of the Viennese première of *Linda*.

22 'Soltanto mi è d'uopo dirvi che io vorrei un soggetto, non a spettacolo, ma di sentimento, una specie di *Sonnambula*, o di *Linda*, staccandosi però da quel genere, perché è già conosciuto'; Giuseppe Verdi, *'Re Lear' e 'Ballo in maschera'. Lettere di Giuseppe Verdi ad Antonio Somma*, ed.

Alessandro Pascolato (Città di Castello: Lapi, 1902), p. 77 (letter not dated, but postmarked 5 April 1855).

23 'Vi dissi come io avrei desiderato di applicarmi a fare un dramma quieto, semplice, tenero: una specie di *Sonnambula* senz'essere un'imitazione della *Sonnambula*'; letter from Busseto dated 7 April 1856 (*ibid.*, p. 78). It seems that this project did not even reach the stage at which possible titles would have been mentioned.

24 References to previous examples of 'family-based' operas substantiate and clarify this discourse, as in the following excerpt from an 1847 review of Federico Ricci's *Rolla*: 'Ricci, who likes broad melodies so much (perhaps too much), has problems restricting himself to the modest proportions of the family-based drama – these proportions are, it seems, a middle road very hard to find. I mean that middle road so beautifully found (leaving aside Rossini, master of every genre) by Bellini in *La sonnambula*, Mercadante in *Elisa e Claudio*, Donizetti in *Linda*, Paer in *Agnese*, Paisiello and Coppola in their *Ninas*, and others too numerous to mention here' ('Il Ricci, che tanto si piace, anzi forse troppo, de' canti larghi, a stento si riduce nelle proporzioni modeste del dramma *famigliare* [*sic*], e che per verità sono, ne sembra, un giusto-mezzo assai arduo da raggiungere. Gli è quel giusto-mezzo nel quale seppero così bene starsi (lasciato Rossini da un lato, in ogni genere sommo), Bellini nella *Sonnambula*, Mercadante nell'*Elisa e Claudio*, Donizetti nella *Linda*, Paër nell'*Agnese*, Paesiello [*sic*] e Coppola nelle loro *Nine*, ed altri che troppo lungo sarebbe il numerare'); anonymous review of Federico Ricci's *Rolla* in the *Gazzetta musicale di Milano*, 12 May 1847.

25 See, for example, the review by one Lambertini of the first production of *La sonnambula* at La Scala in the *Gazzetta privilegiata di Milano*, 2 October 1834.

26 See Guilbert de Pixérécourt, 'Le Mélodrame', *Paris, ou Le Livre des cent-et-un*, vol. VI (Paris: Ladvocat, 1832), pp. 319–52: 332–3; see also the reference to Sedaine on p. 325.

27 *Mélodrame* and *semiseria* are esplicitly connected in Arnold Jacobshagen, 'Pixérécourt–Romanelli–Romani: *Margherita d'Anjou* und das Melodramma semiserio', *Meyerbeer und das europäische Musiktheater*, ed. Sieghart Döhring and Arnold Jacobshagen (Laaber: Laaber Verlag, 1998), pp. 41–63; and François Lévy, 'Bellini et l' "école frénétique": de *Bertram* (1822) à *Il pirata* (1827)', *L'Opéra en France et en Italie (1791–1925). Une scène*

privilégiée d'échanges littéraires et musicaux, ed. Hervé Lacombe (Paris: Société Française de Musicologie, 2000), pp. 37–60; for a more general connection between *semiseria* and French theatre, see Sieghart Döhring and Sabine Henze-Döhring, *Oper und Musikdrama im 19. Jahrhundert* (Laaber: Laaber Verlag, 1997), pp. 48–56; Jacobshagen, 'Opera semiseria', *Die Musik in Geschichte und Gegenwart*, 2nd edn, ed. Ludwig Finscher (Kassel–Stuttgart: Bärenreiter–Metzler, 1994–), *Sachteil*, vol. VII (1997), cols. 699–706.

28 'Ce qu'il y a de certain, c'est que dans les circonstances où il apparut, le mélodrame était une nécessité. Le peuple tout entier venait de jouer dans les rues et sur les places publiques le plus grand drame de l'histoire. Tout le monde avait été acteur dans cette pièce sanglante, tout le monde avait été ou soldat, ou révolutionnaire, ou proscrit. A ce spectateurs solennels qui sentaient la poudre et le sang, il fallait des émotions analogues à celles dont le retour de l'ordre les avait sevrés. [. . .] Il fallait leur rappeler dans un thème toujours nouveau de contexture, toujours uniforme de résultats, cette grande leçon dans laquelle se résument toutes les philosophies, appuyées sur toutes les religions: que même ici-bas, la vertu n'est jamais sans récompense, le crime n'est jamais sans châtiment. Et qu'on n'aille pas s'y tromper! ce n'était pas peu de chose que le mélodrame! C'était la moralité de la révolution'; Charles Nodier, 'Introduction', in Guilbert de Pixérécourt, *Théâtre choisi*, 4 vols. (Paris and Nancy: Tresse–L'Auteur, 1841–3), vol. I, pp. i–xvi: vii–viii; on Nodier as critic of *mélodrame*, see Pierre Reboul, 'Peuple Enfant, Peuple Roi, ou Nodier, mélodrame et révolution', *Revue des sciences humaines* 41 (1976), pp. 247–56.

29 Among the many discussions of the dramaturgy of *mélodrame*, I have found particularly useful Anne Ubersfeld, 'Les Bons et le méchant', *Revue des sciences humaines* 41 (1976), pp. 193–203. For a more detailed description of characters, see Jean-Marie Thomasseau, *Le Mélodrame sur les scènes parisiennes de 'Coelina' (1800) à 'L'Auberge des Adrets' (1823)* (Lille: Service de Réproduction des Thèses, 1974), pp. 173–321, summarised in his more easily available *Le Mélodrame* (Paris: Presses Universitaires de France, 1984), pp. 31–40.

30 Ubersfeld, 'Les Bons et le méchant', p. 200.

31 'Une disposition des personnages sur la scène, si naturelle et si vraie, que rendue fidèlement par un peintre, elle me plairait sur la toile, est un

tableau'; quoted in Pierre Frantz, *L'Esthétique du tableau dans le théâtre du XVIIIᵉ siècle* (Paris: Presses Universitaires de France, 1998), p. 7.

32 'A la fin de chaque acte, il faut avoir soin de réunir en groupe tous les personnages, et de les mettre chacun dans l'attitude qui convient à la situation de son âme. Par exemple: la douleur placera une main sur son front; le désespoir s'arrachera les cheveux, et la joie aura une jambe à l'air. Cet aspect général est désigné sous le nom de Tableau. On sent combien il est agréable au spectateur de ressaisir d'un coup d'œil l'état moral de chaque personnage'; A! A! A! [Abel Hugo, Armand Malitourne and Jean-Joseph Ader], *Traité du mélodrame* (Paris: Delaunay–Pélicier–Plancher, 1817), p. 47.

33 See Frantz, *L'Esthétique du tableau*, p. 168.

34 Roland Barthes, 'Diderot, Brecht, Eisenstein', in his *The Responsibility of Forms: Critical Essays on Music, Art, and Representation*, trans. Richard Howard (New York: Hill and Wang, 1985), pp. 89–97: 90–1.

35 For the performance of *mélodrame* as ritual, see Julia Przybos, *L'Entreprise mélodramatique* (Paris: Corti, 1987), pp. 187–90.

36 See Stefano Castelvecchi, 'Sentimental Opera: The Emergence of a Genre, 1760–1790', Ph.D. dissertation, The University of Chicago (1996), pp. 81–95.

37 See *ibid.*, p. 139.

38 On a performative level, a powerful source of interest was the presence on stage of one or more of the many famous actors specialising in *mélodrame*, true *divi* whose appeal to the audience was very similar to that exercised, then and now, by opera singers.

39 The audience's interest was kept alive not only by the immersion of the characters in new and unusual ambiences, but also by changes of locale within each *pièce*. While *mélodrame* usually respects the unities of action and time, it seldom features unity of space.

40 See Frantz, *L'Esthétique du tableau*, pp. 87–114.

41 See Marie-Antoinette Allevy, *La Mise en scène en France dans la première moitié du dix-neuvième siècle* (Paris: Droz, 1938), pp. 31–40 (treatises on *mise en scène*), 62–73 (*mise en scène* on the Boulevard stage).

42 See the testimony of Aléxandre Piccinni, a frequent musical collaborator of Pixérécourt, quoted in Thomasseau, *Le Mélodrame*, p. 48; in his 'Dernières réflexions' (p. 495) Pixérécourt is categorical: 'The dramatic author must be able to direct his texts' ('ll faut que l'auteur dramatique sache mettre lui-même sa pièce en scène').

43 See Peter Brooks, *The Melodramatic Imagination: Balzac, Henry James, Melodrama, and the Mode of Excess*, 2nd edn (New Haven: Yale University Press, 1995), pp. 62–8.

44 See Frantz, *L'Esthétique du tableau*, pp. 115–20.

45 See Annalisa Bini, '*Otto mesi in due ore, ossia Gli esiliati in Siberia*. Vicende di un'opera donizettiana', *Rivista italiana di musicologia* 22 (1987), pp. 183–260: 200.

46 Brooks, *The Melodramatic Imagination*, p. 66.

47 'Le crime lui [le public] apparissait toujours odieux, et toujours puni; la bonne foi triomphait, l'innocence était protégée par une invincible main: enfin, on ne lui montrait pas le monde comme il est, mais bien comme il devrait être'; J.-B.-A. de Pongerville, 'Notice sur *L'Homme à trois visages*', in Pixérécourt, *Théâtre choisi*, vol. i, p. 164, translated in Gabrielle Hyslop, 'Pixérécourt and the French Melodrama Debate: Instructing Boulevard Theatre Audiences', *Themes in Drama 14: Melodrama*, ed. James Redmond (Cambridge: Cambridge University Press, 1992), pp. 61–85: 65.

48 The costumes for Act 2 of *Linda*, which takes place in Paris, might have defined the time as eighteenth century, but the impression of contemporaneity given by Act 1 probably diminished their impact on the audience.

49 'Fu però il Verdi unico in Italia nell'esprimere seriamente gli affetti di personaggi della nostra moderna e *prosaica* società come nella *Traviata*. *La Sonnambula*, la *Linda* ec., sono soggetti simili, ma non prosaici'; Basevi, *Studio sulle opere di Giuseppe Verdi*, p. 300.

50 Not everybody was convinced by the 'poetic' qualities of *Linda*; one Parisian reviewer found that 'if anything goes against musical inspiration, it is surely the down-to-earth, prosaic and bourgeois character which dominates in works of this kind' ('si quelque chose répugne à l'inspiration musicale, c'est à coup sûr le terre-à-terre et l'élément prosaïque et bourgeois qui domine dans les pièces de ce genre'); 'H.W.', 'Revue musicale', *Revue des deux mondes* 32 (1842), pp. 853–66: 855.

51 *Intrigue et amour, drame en cinq actes et neuf tableaux, traduit de Schiller, par Alexandre Dumas, représenté pour la première fois, à Paris, sur le Théâtre Historique, le 11 Juin 1847* (Paris: Michel Lévy Frères, 1847); on this adaptation, see Emilio Sala, 'Verdi and the Parisian Boulevard Theatre,

1847–9', *Cambridge Opera Journal* 7 (1995), pp. 185–205; Weiss, 'Verdi and the Fusion of Genres', p. 147; *Luisa Miller*, ed. Kallberg, p. xvi.

52 When performed at the Théâtre Français in 1826 it was, according to Weiss, converted into a 'regular' tragedy and proved unsuccessful; see Weiss, 'Verdi and the Fusion of Genres', p. 147. It was occasionally presented in Italy – as *Amore e raggiro* – but the reviewer of a performance at the Milanese Teatro Re in 1834 stated that it was seldom seen on stage; see *Il barbiere di Siviglia*, 30 April 1834.

53 'Il est peut-être plus facile de faire admettre chez nous la réalité shakspearienne [*sic*], qui porte sur des sujets historiques et convention-nels, que le procédé analogue employé par Schiller pour des sujets modernes. Les détails de la vie bourgeoise mêlés aux situations où éclatent les passions les plus tragiques, risquent souvent de provoquer le sourire. [. . .] Le public français [. . .] n'a jamais admis complètement le mélange du plaisant et du sérieux; il accepte bien le niais du mélodrame, ou la scène familière succédant à la scène tragique; mais le rire strident, qui tout à coup se mêle au choc des passions exaltées, a quelque chose qui l'étonne encore'; *La Presse*, 14 June 1847, reprinted in Gautier, *Histoire de l'art dramatique en France depuis vingt-cinq ans*, 6 vols. (Paris: Hetzel, 1856–8), vol. v, pp. 112–13, translated in Weiss, 'Verdi and the Fusion of Genres', pp. 147–8.

54 'Ouvrages monstrueux [. . .] d'où est bannie précisément toute conscience, qui outragent à chaque scène le bon sens, la morale et la pudeur, ouvrages essentiellement licencieux qui ne peuvent inspirer que l'horreur de la société en nous la monstrant constamment sous un aspect hideux'; Pixérécourt, 'Le Mélodrame', p. 323.

55 See Lévy, 'Bellini et l'"école frénétique"'.

56 That this 'prosaicness' implies a moral judgement and does not refer to the everyday life quality of the opera is made clear by Basevi in the chapter on *La traviata*: 'In *Norma* Bellini portrayed a guilty woman, but he presented her blinded by such a strong passion that she cannot see the enormity of her sin. Furthermore, Norma's sin offends us much less [than Violetta's] because, thanks to the remote times and the difference of customs, it is much more difficult for us to identify ourselves with the character. But this is not the case with *La traviata*, in which we find characters not only close to us in time and customs, but also of common [i.e. not aristocratic] condition' ('Se il Bellini dipinse nella *Norma* la

donna colpevole, ce la presentò ad un' ora accecata siffattamente dalla passione, che non potesse vedere l'enormità del suo peccato. Senza che, la colpa di Norma tanto meno ci offende, quanto, per la lontananza de' tempi, e per la differenza de' costumi, più malagevole a noi riesce d'immedesimare la nostra coscienza con quella del detto personaggio. Il che non accade nella *Traviata*, ove troviamo non solo i personaggi a noi vicini e per tempo e per costumi, ma eziandio comuni per condizione'); Basevi, *Studio sulle opere di Giuseppe Verdi*, pp. 231–2.

57 'Formerly people chose only that which was good; but in these modern dramas we find nothing but monstrous crimes that revolt our sense of morality and modesty. Always and everywhere there is adultery, rape, incest, parricide, prostitution, each vice more shameless, filthy and disgusting than the last' ('Jadis on choisissait seulement ce qui était bon; mais dans les drames modernes, on ne trouve que des crimes monstrueux qui révoltent la morale et la pudeur. Toujours et partout l'adultère, le viol, l'inceste, le parricide, la prostitution, les vices les plus éhontés, plus sales, plus dégoûtants l'un que l'autre'); Pixérécourt, 'Dernières réflexions', pp. 497–8; translated in Hyslop, 'Pixérécourt and the French Melodrama Debate', p. 82.

58 See Anne Ubersfeld, *Le Roi et le bouffon. Etude sur le théâtre de Hugo de 1830 à 1839* (Paris: Corti, 1974), pp. 77–89.

59 'Quella scuola satanica, che adesso pare sia appena da pochi giorni nata e cresciuta in Francia, mercé l'opera di Hugo, Balzac, e compagni'; *Il barbiere di Siviglia*, 30 April 1834. This 'satanic school' had recently arrived on the Italian operatic stage in the form of Romani and Donizetti's *Lucrezia Borgia*, premièred at La Scala in December 1833, of which several critics pointed out the 'immorality'; see the reviews reprinted in *Le prime rappresentazioni delle opere di Donizetti nella stampa coeva*, ed. Annalisa Bini and Jeremy Commons (Rome–Milan: Accademia Nazionale di Santa Cecilia–Skira, 1998), pp. 366–89.

60 'La localité exacte est un des premiers éléments de la réalité. Les personnages parlants ou agissants ne sont pas les seuls qui gravent dans l'esprit du spectateur la fidèle empreinte des faits. Le lieu où telle catastrophe s'est passée en devient un témoin terrible et inséparable; et l'absence de cette sorte de personnage muet décompléterait dans le drame les plus grandes scènes de l'histoire. [. . .] On conçoit que, pour une œuvre de ce genre, si le poète doit choisir dans les choses (et il

le doit), ce n'est pas le beau, mais le caractéristique. Non qu'il convienne de faire, comme on dit aujourd'hui, de la couleur locale, c'est à dire d'ajouter après coup quelques touches criardes ça et là sur un ensemble du reste parfaitement faux et conventionnel. Ce n'est point à la surface du drame que doit être la couleur locale, mais au fond, dans le cœur même de l'œuvre, d'où elle se répand au dehors, d'elle-même, naturellement, également, et, pour ainsi parler, dans tous les coins du drame, comme la sève qui monte de la racine à la dernière feuille de l'arbre'; Victor Hugo, 'Préface' to *Cromwell*, in his *Théâtre complet*, ed. J.-J. Thierry and Josette Mélèze, 2 vols. (Paris: Gallimard, 1963–4), vol. I, pp. 409–54: 429, 437; translation modified from Hugo, *Dramas*, trans. I. G. Burnham, 10 vols. (Philadelphia: Barrie, 1895–96), vol. IX, pp. 7–117: 55, 75–6. Similar sentiments were voiced by Benjamin Constant, who had translated into French Schiller's *Wallenstein* trilogy in 1809, in his *Réflections sur la tragédie* of 1829 (see especially pp. 956–7 of the edition of this text in Constant's *Œuvres*, ed. Alfred Roulin (Paris: Gallimard, 1957)).

61 Pixérécourt praised *mélodrame* against *tragédie* precisely in terms of 'naturalness': 'I prefer melodrama to tragedy; I find it more truthful, more appealing, more theatrically skilful, and above all more natural. It touches me, stirs me, moves me; what it enacts for me becomes part of my behaviour in everyday life, whereas the great misfortunes true or otherwise of those heroes up on their stilts and speaking a bombastic language leave me at best indifferent' ('Je préfère le mélodrame à la tragédie: j'y trouve plus de vérité, plus d'intérêt, plus d'entente de la scène, et surtout plus de naturel. Il me touche, m'émeut, m'attendrit; ce qu'il me retrace rentre dans les habitudes de la vie ordinaire, tandis que les grandes infortunes vraies ou supposées de ces héros montés sur des échasses et parlant un langage emphatique me laissent au moins indifférent'); Pixérécourt, 'Le Mélodrame', pp. 345–6; translated in Hyslop, 'Pixérécourt and the French Melodrama Debate', p. 76.

62 'Conservare in tutta la parte di quest'ultimo quel certo non so che di comico che servirà a dare maggior risalto alle sue finezze e alle sue scelleraggini'; letter of 17 May 1849, in *Carteggio Verdi–Cammarano*, p. 113, trans. in *Luisa Miller*, ed. Kallberg, p. xvii; see also Weiss, 'Verdi and the Fusion of Genres', p. 149.

63 Wurm shares at least one aspect with many previous comic characters: he is a coward (he takes to flight when Rodolfo challenges him to a duel

in Act 2). But it seems difficult to hear any hint at a comic treatment of this situation in Verdi's music.

64 The unison triplets followed by trills played forte by the orchestra in the low register at the moment when 'a diabolic smile appears on Wurm's face', immediately before Luisa's cabaletta in Act 2, scene 2, could perhaps be interpreted as a depiction of the sinister comic – the smiling, mocking villain who twists his waxed moustache as he ties the girl to the railroad tracks. Budden hears this passage as an anticipation of Jago's 'Credo' (*The Operas of Verdi*, vol. I, p. 436). Closer to *Luisa*, Verdi makes use of the same musical devices when Rigoletto 'advances with mock gravity' and insults Monterone with equally mocking words in the *introduzione* of *Rigoletto*; see Péter Pál Várnai, 'Contributi per uno studio della tipizzazione negativa nelle opere verdiane: personaggi e situazioni', *Atti del Primo Congresso Internazionale di Studi Verdiani* (Parma: Istituto di Studi Verdiani, 1969), pp. 268–75: 269.

65 Basevi comments that in this movement Verdi did not follow convention, but composed a melody almost entirely independent from the initial theme; *Studio sulle opere di Giuseppe Verdi*, p. 168.

66 For an overview of Verdi's use of the lyric form, see Emanuele Senici, 'Words and Music', *The Cambridge Companion to Verdi*, ed. Scott L. Balthazar (Cambridge: Cambridge University Press, 2004), pp. 88–110, where an earlier version of the discussion of Luisa's Act 2 aria appears.

67 'Il Maestro, dopo di essere stato oltremonti, dopo avere studiate le leggerezze francesi, le combinazioni tedesche, la prosa diremmo armonica dei melodrammi parlati, e gli accompagnamenti a rilievo o picchettati, ha voluto tentare il genere campestre a fronte dell'eroico, l'innocenza dei villici di riscontro alla superbia baronale, un amor contrastato in fine, cui la morte mette compimento, toccando la corda quasi mai fallace della pietà e del terrore! [. . .] V'era d'uopo ricordare musiche francesi e tedesche? [. . .] Chi lasciava l'Italia, o moriva o s'infreddava: così Rossini, così Bellini, così Donizetti'; ample excerpts from this review are quoted in Marcello Conati, 'Verdi per Napoli', in *Il Teatro di San Carlo, 1737–1987*, vol. II, *L'opera, il ballo*, ed. Bruno Cagli and Agostino Ziino (Naples: Electa, 1987), pp. 225–66: 236–7. 'German combinations' probably means harmonic and contrapuntal density; 'harmonic prose of spoken melodramas' might refer to those passages of orchestral music of pantomimic quality usually found in French

mélodrames; '*picchettati* accompaniments' tries to explain some musical devices of this 'harmonic prose' – 'picchettati' implies some kind of staccato. The precise meaning of the musical references in this passage, however, remains rather obscure.

68 'Il canto [. . .] procede più tranquillo. Le cantilene sono meno *larghe*, o più leggiere; i ritmi più mobili, e più scoperti'; Basevi, *Studio sulle opere di Giuseppe Verdi*, pp. 158–9. Other critics speak of *Luisa* as the beginning of a new direction in Verdi's output: see, for example, the review by Giovanni Veroli of the first Milanese production (Teatro Carcano, September 1850) for the local *Gazzetta dei teatri* (10 September 1850); the review of a production that opened in Bologna a month later, originally published in the Bolognese newspaper *L'osservatorio* (10 October 1850) and reprinted in the *Gazzetta dei teatri* (15 October); and the review of the first production of the opera at La Scala that appeared in the Milanese *La fama* on 29 December 1851.

69 On *Lucrezia* and *Rigoletto*, see Gary Tomlinson, 'Opera and *Drame*: Hugo, Donizetti, and Verdi', *Studies in Music History 2: Music and Drama* (New York: Broude Brothers, 1988), pp. 171–92; see also Winton Dean, 'Some Echoes of Donizetti in Verdi's Operas', in *Atti del Terzo Convegno Internazionale di Studi Verdiani* (Parma: Istituto di Studi Verdiani, 1974), pp. 122–47, who hears local echoes of *Belisario* and *Lucia di Lammermoor* in *Luisa Miller*, but does not claim any substantial intertextual link between these operas and *Luisa*.

70 'Al Verdi giovarono quelle forti passioni su cui posa l'intreccio del dramma. E perché gli animi non erano più capaci di assaporare l'entusiasmo, non disdissero que' personaggi, i quali a prima giunta non si rendono importanti per quel prestigio, che ricevono dall'antichità del fatto, o che tolgono dal loro grado, o acquistano dagli effetti che per essi vengono operati: onde la tragedia prende il nome di borghese, e che noi diremmo domestica'; Basevi, *Studio sulle opere di Giuseppe Verdi*, pp. 159–60.

71 In fact, 'Süd-Tirol', in Italian 'Alto Adige', is now a largely German-speaking part of the Italian Republic, assigned to Italy in 1919 by the treaty of Saint Germain because it is located south of the Alpine watershed.

72 See Cristina Trivulzio di Belgioioso, 'La Guerre dans le Tyrol italien', *Revue des deux mondes* 19 (1849), pp. 201–30.

73 See Mary Jane Phillips-Matz, *Verdi: A Biography* (Oxford: Oxford University Press, 1993), p. 50.

74 'L'Autriche possède à un degré supérieur l'art de déraciner les peuples du sol où ils ont pris naissance, d'égarer les nationalités par la création de nationalités factices, n'ayant de base ni de cause que le caprice, ou, ce qui est encore pis, la politique du souverain'; 'La Guerre dans le Tyrol italien', p. 209.

75 'Les Autrichiens, redevenus les maîtres, déclarèrent Trente en état de siège; les arrestations, les confiscations, les exécutions se succédèrent. Les bourgs, les villages, les chaumières, furent livrés au pillage'; *ibid.*, p. 222.

76 'Les vallées du Tyrol italien sont retombées sous la domination autrichienne. La police impériale y sévit avec un rigueur impitoyable. Le Tyrol, jusque dans ses vallons les plus reculés, est tranformé en un vaste camp soumis à la loi militaire, et sur plusieurs points on a vu des soldats autrichiens commettre des violences qui rappellent les plus tristes scènes de la Gallicie [*sic*]'; *ibid.*, p. 230.

77 'Cotesto disegno di sinfonia è insolito per l'Italia; ma se ne trovano esempj nelle sinfonie dei musicisti oltremontani'; Basevi, *Studio sulle opere di Giuseppe Verdi*, p. 160.

78 In his review of the first performance of *Luisa Miller* in Milan mentioned above, Giuseppe Veroli wrote that 'the overture is very beautiful, and the intelligent ones admire its remarkable learning' ('la sinfonia è molto bella, e gli intelligenti ne ammirano la molta scienza'). In the aesthetic climate of mid-century Italy, saying that 'gli intelligenti' admired a work's 'scienza' suggested that the majority could be left cold by it.

79 See Tomlinson, 'Opera and *Drame*', and Tomlinson, 'Italian Romanticism and Italian Opera: An Essay in Their Affinities', *19th-Century Music* 10 (1986), pp. 43–60; Weiss, 'Verdi and the Fusion of Genres'. In a letter to Cammarano about the operatic project that Verdi toyed with immediately before *Luisa*, *L'assedio di Firenze*, the composer mentions 'this mixture of comic and terrible (à la Shakespeare')' ('questo misto di comico e di terribile (a uso Shaespeare [*sic*]'); letter to Cammarano from Paris dated 24 March 1849, *Carteggio Verdi–Cammarano*, p. 100, trans. in Weiss, 'Verdi and the Fusion of Genres', p. 144.

80 'Verdi and the Fusion of Genres', p. 155.

81 Roger Parker, 'Luisa Miller', *The New Grove Dictionary of Opera*, ed. Stanley Sadie, 4 vols. (London: Macmillan, 1992), vol. III, p. 82.

82 Tomlinson is the critic who most explicitly links musical and dramaturgical experimentation, in his discussion of *Rigoletto* in 'Opera and *Drame*', pp. 187–90, but many do so implicitly. On *Macbeth* see, for example, Martin Chusid, 'Evil, Guilt, and the Supernatural in Verdi's Macbeth: Toward an Understanding of the Tonal Structure and Key Symbolism', *Verdi's 'Macbeth': A Sourcebook*, pp. 249–60; and Pierluigi Petrobelli, 'Verdi's Musical Thought: An Example from *Macbeth*', in his *Music in the Theater: Essays on Verdi and Other Composers*, trans. Roger Parker (Princeton: Princeton University Press, 1994), pp. 141–52. On *Stiffelio*, see Harold S. Powers, '"Aria sfasciata", "duetto senza l'insieme": le scene di confronto tenore–soprano nello Stiffelio/Aroldo di Giuseppe Verdi', *Tornando a Stiffelio: popolarità, rifacimenti, messinscena, effettismo e altre 'cure' nella drammaturgia del Verdi romantico. Atti del convegno internazionale di studi (Venezia, 17–20 dicembre 1985)*, ed. Giovanni Morelli (Florence: Olschki, 1986), pp. 141–88.

83 A welcome corrective to this tendency are James Hepokoski's analyses of *La traviata* and *Il trovatore* from the point of view of their mixture of formal types: see James A. Hepokoski, 'Genre and Content in Mid-Century Verdi: "Addio, del passato" (*La traviata*, Act III)', *Cambridge Opera Journal* 1 (1989), pp. 249–76; Hepokoski, 'Ottocento Opera as Cultural Drama: Generic Mixtures in *Il trovatore*', *Verdi's Middle Period*, pp. 147–96.

84 'La *Traviata* è tale composizione, che per la qualità de' personaggi, per gli affetti domestici, e per la mancanza dello spettacolo s'accosta alla commedia. Il Verdi iniziò una terza maniera, che in più parti s'avvicina al genere francese dell'Opera comica'; Basevi, *Studio sulle opere di Giuseppe Verdi*, p. 230.

5 DEFLOWERING THE ALPS: FROM I PROMESSI SPOSI TO LA WALLY AND FEDORA

1 *I promessi sposi, melo-dramma in tre atti tratto dal romanzo del signor Manzoni di simil titolo da Giuseppe Checcherini pel Teatro Nuovo nell'inverno dell'anno 1830* (Naples: Severino, 1830), p. 25.

2 *I promessi sposi, melo-dramma semi-serio in due atti da rappresentarsi nel Teatro Valle [. . .] nel Carnevale dell'Anno 1834* (Rome: Puccinelli, 1834). See, for example, Lucia's entrance aria 'Sì: quel canto al cor mi dice', or her *rondò* 'Ch'io respiri almen lasciate'.

3 *I promessi sposi, melodramma in quattro atti posto in musica dal Maestro Amilcare Ponchielli, da rappresentarsi per la prima volta nel Teatro della Concordia in Cremona l'Autunno 1856* (Cremona: Manini, 1856), p. 5.

4 *I promessi sposi, melodramma in quattro parti, musica di Amilcare Ponchielli* (Milan: Ricordi, n.d. [1872?]), p. 7. On the authorship of the libretto and Praga's revision, see Stefania Franceschini, 'Tanti librettisti per un'opera di Ponchielli a lungo rimaneggiata (1856–1874)', *Nuova rivista musicale italiana* 30 (1996), pp. 365–82.

5 *I promessi sposi, melodramma di Pietro Micheletti e di Emanuele Bardare, posto in Musica dal Maestro Andrea Traventi, da rappresentarsi nel Teatro Argentina nella stagione di Autunno 1858* (Rome: Stabilimento Tipografico, 1858), p. 5.

6 The only operatic version of *I promessi sposi* that stages it is Ponchielli's, although in Ghislanzoni's libretto for Petrella Lucia mentions the vow in the last act, only for Padre Cristoforo to release her from it, as in the source.

7 'The novel by the famous Manzoni suggested the idea of this libretto, but the vast canvas of that story is not developed here, owing to the restrictions of the theatre. What is more, the number of characters has been reduced, and the unities of time and place have been respected, sometimes emphasising things which are barely mentioned in the novel' ('Il Romanzo del celebre Manzoni suggerì il concetto di questo libretto; ma poiché le esigenze del teatro non lo permettevano, non vi si vede sviluppata tutta la vasta tela ond'è ordito quel racconto. Anzi si limitò il numero dei personaggi, si unirono le circostanze di tempo e di luogo dando talvolta maggior risalto a cose di cui nel Romanzo è appena fatto cenno'); *I promessi sposi [. . .] di Amilcare Ponchielli*, p. 5.

8 'Tutti quanti gli spettatori recheranno in teatro la piena conoscenza del romanzo. [. . .] Qualche volta ho copiato quasi testualmente; e sempre, poi, mi sono studiato di imitare, fin dove i versi lo consentono, quella naturalezza e semplicità di linguaggio, di che il Manzoni è maestro insuperabile'; *I promessi sposi, melodramma in quattro atti di Antonio Ghislanzoni, musica del M.° Cav.ᵉ Errico Petrella* (Milan: Lucca, n.d. [1873?]), p. 3.

9 *Ibid.*, p. 31.

10 'Addio, monti sorgenti dall'acque, ed elevati al cielo; cime inuguali, note a chi è cresciuto tra voi; [. . .] torrenti [. . .] ville sparse e biancheggianti sul pendìo, come branchi di pecore pascenti; addio!' Alessandro

Manzoni, *I promessi sposi*, ed. Vittorio Spinazzola (Milan: Garzanti, 1966), p. 116; *The Betrothed*, trans. Bruce Penman (London: Penguin, 1972), p. 164. For an analysis of further passages directly invoking the novel, see Bianca Barattelli, 'I *Promessi sposi* di Antonio Ghislanzoni', *Esperienze letterarie* 11/4 (October–December 1986), pp. 41–79.

11 'Renzo e Lucia sono due contadini *reali*, riprodotti scrupolosamente dal vero, due contadini quali voi ne vedrete ancora a centinaia *su quel di Lecco*. [. . .] Per poco che vi diate la pena di consultare il romanzo, voi rimarrete convinto che il loro frasario è perfettamente identico a quello che essi parlano nel mio libretto. Poteva, doveva io idealizzare, laddove Manzoni si è mostrato così grande, così inimitabile nel *vero*? [. . .] Mio primo e assoluto proposito fu quello di conservarmi, il meglio che potessi, fedele al testo. In molti luoghi ho copiato quasi letteralmente, sacrificando la forma del verso e le facili ostentazioni della poetica fraseologia, al compito di essere vero'; Antonio Ghislanzoni in a letter to the newspaper *La Lombardia*, 27 May 1871, replying to a review by the critic E. Torelli Viollier in the *Corriere di Milano*, cited in Barattelli, 'I *Promessi sposi* di Antonio Ghislanzoni', p. 63. 'Su quel di Lecco' is a Lombardism clearly derived from dialect, meaning 'in the area around Lecco'.

12 'L'autore ha seguito il metro e la bizzarra struttura di due canzoni popolari lombarde, di data antichissima, menzionate anche dall'illustre storico Cesare Cantù ne' suoi *Documenti alla Storia Universale*. Il maestro Petrella, per dare al quadro una tinta affatto locale, volle espressamente riprodurre quelle tradizionali melodie'; *I promessi sposi [. . .] di Antonio Ghislanzoni*, p. 7. The reference is to Cesare Cantù, 'Della poesia popolare e specialmente delle romanze spagnuole', originally in *Rivista europea* 2 (1839); reprinted in Cantù, *Della letteratura* (part 5 of his *Documenti alla Storia Universale*), first published in 1841, but which circulated widely in Italy in its three-volume 8th edition (Turin: Unione Tipografico-Editrice, 1857–8), vol. II, pp. 422–6.

13 *I promessi sposi [. . .] di Antonio Ghislanzoni*, pp. 7–8.

14 I have traced the text of the women's song, usually entitled 'L'uccellin del bosco', to Oreste Marcoaldi, *Canti popolari inediti umbri liguri piceni piemontesi* (Genoa: Sordo-Muti, 1855), pp. 157–8: although located in the section of songs from Piedmont, the text was transcribed in Oleggio, a town in the province of Novara close to the border between Piedmont

and Lombardy, and its language is clearly a Lombard rather than a Piedmontese dialect; Georg Widter and Adolf Wolf, *Volkslieder aus Venetien* (Vienna: Hof- und Staatsdruckerei, 1864), p. 35; J[oseph] Caselli, *Chants populaires de l'Italie* (Paris: Librairie Internationale, 1865), pp. 201–2; Giuseppe Ferraro, *Canti popolari monferrini* (Turin and Florence: Loescher, 1870), p. 111; Domenico Giuseppe Bernoni, *Canti popolari veneziani* (Venice: Fontana–Ottolini, 1872), pp. 15–16. Costantino Nigra, *Canti popolari del Piemonte* (Turin: Loescher, 1888), pp. 445–7, gives several different versions of the song, and compares it with the numerous appearances of the same theme in French folk songs, citing many sources. For a more recent treatment, see Vittorio Santoli, *I canti popolari italiani. Ricerche e questioni*, 2nd edn (Florence: Sansoni, 1968), pp. 253–61. The men's song has proved more difficult to track down precisely, probably given its generic theme and brevity; Bianca Barattelli points to the frequent operatic appearances of this theme, for example in the chorus 'Giovinette che fate all'amore' in Da Ponte and Mozart's *Don Giovanni*; see Barrattelli, 'I *Promessi sposi* di Antonio Ghislanzoni', p. 65. Neither song appears in two important collections of popular songs from the province of Como, which could include Lecco (it did from the 1920s to the 1990s, for example): *Canti comaschi*, vol. II of *Canti popolari lombardi*, piano accompaniment by Giulio Ricordi and Italian text by Leopoldo Pullé (Milan: Ricordi, 1858), and *Canzoni popolari comasche*, ed. Giovanni Battista Bolza (Vienna: I. R. Tipografia di Corte e di Stato, 1867).

15 See the sources listed in the previous footnote for various northern Italian regions; for Tuscany, see Michele Barbi, *Poesia popolare pistoiese* (Florence: Carnesecchi, 1895), pp. 26–7.

16 According to a contemporary witness who accompanied Petrella on walks around Lecco during the composition of the opera, the first time the composer heard the songs sung by labourers and peasants walking home from work in the evening, he was so struck that he went back day after day to hear them again; see Giacomo De Santis, *Antonio Ghislanzoni e il teatro di Lecco* (Lecco: Bartolozzi, 1977), p. 47, cited in Sebastian Werr, *Die Opern von Errico Petrella: Rezeptionsgeschichte, Interpretationen und Dokumente* (Vienna: Praesens, 1999), p. 159.

17 Compare Verdi's requests for samples of 'authentic', 'real' Sicilian folk music during the composition of *Les Vêpres siciliennes* and his complaints about the 'lack of character' of the songs sent to him; see Marcello

Conati, 'Ballabili nei *Vespri* con alcune osservazioni su Verdi e la musica popolare', *Studi verdiani* I (1982), pp. 21–46, especially 22–3 and 39–41.

18 *Il trovatore*, 16, no. 40 (7 October 1869), p. 2.

19 Originally published in Correnti's *Rivista europea*; reprinted in *I periodici popolari del Risorgimento*, ed. Dina Bertoni Jovine, 3 vols. (Milan: Feltrinelli, 1958–60), vol. II, pp. 82–9.

20 See Piero de Tomaso, *Il racconto campagnolo nell'Ottocento italiano* (Ravenna: Longo, n.d. [1973]).

21 'Les mœurs pures, les sentiments tendres et l'équité primitive sont ou peuvent être encore de ce monde'; George Sand, second preface (written in 1851) to *La Petite Fadette* (1849), ed. Geneviève van den Bogaert (Paris: Garnier–Flammarion, 1967), p. 40.

22 'Une scène réelle que j'eus sous les yeux [. . .] l'art n'est pas une étude de la réalité positive; c'est une recherche de la vérité idéale'; George Sand, *La Mare au diable* (1846), ed. Pierre Reboul (Paris: Garnier–Flammarion, 1964), pp. 23, 30.

23 'Le chant des paysans est le plus pur et le meilleur, parce qu'il s'inspire davantage de la nature, qu'il est en contact plus direct avec elle'; George Sand, preface to *François le Champi* (1848) (Paris: Gallimard, 1973), p. 47.

24 *Fiorina, o La fanciulla di Glaris, melodramma semiserio in due atti, musica di Carlo Pedrotti* (Milan: Ricordi, n.d. [post 1865]).

25 See *Fiorina, o La fanciulla di Glaris, melodramma semiseria [sic] in due atti posto in musica [. . .] da Carlo Pedrotti* (Paris: Léon Escudier, n.d., pl. no. L.E. 1535 [*c*. 1855]), pp. 44–5.

26 *La savojarda, dramma lirico in 3 atti di Francesco Guidi posto in musica da Amilcare Ponchielli, da rappresentarsi nel Teatro della Concordia in Cremona pel Carnevale 1860–61* (Cremona: Manini, 1861); *Lina, dramma lirico in tre atti di F. Guidi e C. D'Ormeville, musica di Amilcare Ponchielli, Teatro Dal Verme, Autunno 1877* (Milan: Ricordi, n.d. [1877]).

27 No vocal score of *La savojarda* was published.

28 See *Lina, dramma lirico in tre atti di F. Guidi e C. D'Ormeville, musica di Amilcare Ponchielli* (Milan: Ricordi, n.d., pl. no. 45228).

29 'Il colore idillico, campestre, affettuoso vi domina, e il Ponchielli musicando i casti affetti di Lina ha trovato delle frasi soavemente melodiche, degli accenti belliniani [. . .] Questa *Lina*, con tutta la buona volontà di cavarne una *Sonnambula* o una *Linda*, non è riuscita che un pasticcio'; Filippo Filippi in *La perseveranza*, 19 November 1877, quoted in

Angelo Pompilio, 'La carriera e le opere di Ponchielli nei giudizi della critica italiana (1856–1887)', in Nino Albarosa *et al.*, *Amilcare Ponchielli 1834–1886. Saggi e ricerche nel 150° anniversario della nascita* (Casalmorano: Cassa Rurale ed Artigiana, 1984), pp. 7–92: 46.

30 'Uda' in *La Lombardia*, 19 November 1877, quoted in Pompilio, 'La carriera e le opere di Ponchielli', pp. 46–7.

31 *Le Villi, opera-ballo in due atti di Ferdinando Fontana, musica di Giacomo Puccini, Teatro alla Scala, Carnevale–Quaresima 1884–85* (Milan: Ricordi, 1885), p. 11.

32 *Le Villi, opera-ballo*, pp. 6–7. The aria was added for the second version of the opera, first performed at Turin's Teatro Regio on 26 December 1884; for a discussion of the various versions of *Le Villi*, see Michele Girardi, *Puccini: His International Art*, trans. Laura Basini (Chicago: The University of Chicago Press, 2000), pp. 26–7.

33 *Edgar, dramma lirico in quattro atti di Ferdinando Fontana, musica di Giacomo Puccini, Teatro alla Scala, Carnevale–Quaresima 1888–89* (Milan: Ricordi, 1889), p. 7.

34 See Virgilio Bernardoni, 'La drammaturgia dell'aria nel primo Puccini. Da "Se come voi piccina" a "Sola, perduta, abbandonata"', *Studi pucciniani* 1 (1998), pp. 43–56.

35 See Alfred de Musset, *La Coupe et les lèvres*, in *Premières poésies, 1829–1835*, vol. 1 of *Œuvres complètes*, ed. Edmond Biré, 9 vols. (Paris: Garnier, n.d. [1908]), pp. 195–262: 204–6.

36 *Ibid.*, p. 213.

37 On the cover of the first edition of the libretto, cited above, Fidelia is depicted picking the almond blossom: she looks like any peasant girl in her Sunday best, with no hint of Flanders, let alone of 1302.

38 See Julian Budden, *Puccini: His Life and Works* (New York: Oxford University Press, 2002), pp. 69–70. Budden also points to the similarity between the orchestration of *Edgar*'s opening music and that of the introduction to Anna's aria in *Le Villi*.

39 *L'amico Fritz, commedia lirica in tre atti di P. Suardon (Nicola Daspuro) dal romanzo di Erckmann–Chatrian, musica di Pietro Mascagni* (Milan: Sonzogno, 1986), p. 20.

40 See *Fior d'Alpe, opera in tre atti, parole di Leo Di Castelnovo, musica di Alberto Franchetti* (Milan: Sonzogno, 1894).

41 *Ibid.*, p. xix.

42 See Verdi's letter to Boito dated 14 March 1894 and Boito's response on 16 March in Hans Busch, *Verdi's 'Falstaff' in Letters and Contemporary Reviews* (Bloomington: Indiana University Press, 1997), pp. 470–2.

43 *La Wally di W. De Hillern, riduzione drammatica in quattro atti di Luigi Illica, musica di Alfredo Catalani, Teatro alla Scala, 1891–92* (Milan: Ricordi, 1892), p. 14; translation modified from the one by Peggie Cochrane printed in the booklet accompanying the 1990 Eurodisc recording of the opera conducted by Pinchas Steinberg (Eurodisc 69073-2-RC).

44 *'La Wally* è [. . .] l'alta montagna portata nel teatro in musica. [. . .] Nella *Wally* il colore locale si mette sollecitamente e spontaneamente in prima linea'; Giuseppe Depanis, *Alfredo Catalani. Appunti e ricordi* (Turin: Roux, 1893), quoted (without page number) by Michelangelo Zurletti, *Catalani* (Turin: EDT, 1982), p. 179.

45 Letter to Giuseppe Depanis dated 16 July 1891, in Richard M. Berrong, *The Politics of Opera in Turn-of-the-Century Italy as Seen Through the Letters of Alfredo Catalani* (Lewiston: Edwin Mellen Press, 1992), p. 88.

46 See *ibid.*, p. 89 (letter to Depanis dated 31 July 1891).

47 See Alfredo Catalani, *La Wally, dramma lirico in quattro atti [. . .] riduzione per canto e pianoforte di Carlo Carignani* (Milan: Ricordi, n.d., pl. no. 95257), pp. 116ff. For an overview of the musical language of *La Wally*, see Jay Nicolaisen, *Italian Opera in Transition, 1871–1893* (Ann Arbor: UMI Research Press, 1980), pp. 176–85.

48 Catalani, *La Wally*, p. 125.

49 *Fedora, dramma di Victorien Sardou, ridotto in tre atti per la scena lirica da Arturo Colautti, musica di Umberto Giordano* (Milan: Sonzogno, 1997), p. 55. This libretto reflects the vocal score published by Edoardo Sonzogno in 1898 (pl. no. E984S); this in turn includes a complete libretto, which, however, differs, sometimes significantly, from the text in the score. In general Giordano's interventions amount to cuts, as in this scene, which in the libretto includes an initial exchange between Fedora and Loris before the chorus, and a slightly longer text for the passage quoted here.

50 See Umberto Giordano, *Fedora*, vocal score (Milan: Edoardo Sonzogno, 1898), pp. 167–77.

51 Fedora's friend Olga, a comic character, gives voice to these doubts about the power of landscape in the following scene: 'Always the same green, the same blue, the same white lambs, the same dirty children!

The symphony of crickets, the kingdom of flies!' ('Sempre lo stesso verde! Sempre l'azzurro istesso, gli stessi agnelli candidi, gli stessi bimbi sudici! La sinfonia dei grilli, il regno delle mosche!'); *Fedora, dramma*, p. 56.

52 For a more general discussion of the music's indifference to characters in *Fedora*, see Virgilio Bernardoni, 'Il linguaggio musicale della *Fedora* di Umberto Giordano', in *Ultimi splendori. Cilea, Giordano, Alfano*, ed. Johannes Streicher (Rome: Ismez, n.d. [1999]), pp. 347–61.

53 See Mercedes Viale Ferrero, 'Da *Fédora* a *Fedora*: smontaggio e rimontaggio di uno scenario (melo)drammatico', *Il saggiatore musicale* 2 (1995), pp. 93–104: 101–2; and Viale Ferrero, '"Come su ali invisibili". Viaggiatori immaginari tra provincie e capitali', *Nazionalismo e cosmopolitismo nell'opera fra Ottocento e Novecento. Atti del 3o convegno internazionale 'Ruggero Leoncavallo nel suo tempo'*, ed. Lorenza Guiot and Jürgen Maehder (Milan: Sonzogno, 1998), pp. 229–38.

54 This is specified only in the original libretto, not in the text reproducing the vocal score.

55 The most famous appearance of the Alps in Italian poetry before the unification is probably Martino's description of his journey through them in Act 2 of Manzoni's tragedy *Adelchi* (1822), where they are described as 'steep, naked, awesome, uninhabited' ('erti, nudi, tremendi, inabitati').

56 See Alessandro Pastore, *Alpinismo e storia d'Italia dall'Unità alla Resistenza* (Bologna: Il Mulino, 2003), pp. 15–53.

57 See Paul Guichonnet, 'L'homme devant les Alpes', *Histoire et civilisation des Alpes*, ed. Paul Guichonnet, 2 vols. (Toulouse and Lausanne: Privat–Payot, 1980), vol. ii, pp. 169–248, especially 216–21; Nicolas Giudici, *La Philosophie du Mont Blanc* (Paris: Grasset, 2000), pp. 355–437; Pastore, *Alpinismo e storia d'Italia*, pp. 33–53.

58 John Ruskin, *Sesame and Lilies* (1865), in *The Works of John Ruskin*, ed. E. T. Cook and Alexander Wedderburn, 39 vols. (London: George Allen, 1903–1912), vol. xviii, pp. 89–90.

59 Carlo Dossi, *La desinenza in A (Ritratti umani)* (1878; rev. edn. 1884), in *Opere*, ed. Dante Isella (Milan: Adelphi, 1995), pp. 776–83.

60 Aurora Scotti Tosini, 'Segantini, Giovanni', *The Dictionary of Art*, ed. Jane Turner, 34 vols. (London: Macmillan, 1996), vol. xxviii, pp. 354–7: 357. Gabriele D'Annunzio's ode 'Per la morte di Giovanni Segantini' is

a powerful document of Segantini's early reception in terms of the morality of his landscapes: its final stanza begins with an apostrophe to mountains, 'purity of untouched things' ('purità delle cose intatte'); D'Annunzio, *Elettra* (1904), in *Laudi del cielo, del mare, della terra e degli eroi* (Milan: Mondadori, 1939), p. 434.

61 See Dora Lardelli, 'Panorama dell'Engadina', in *Segantini*, ed. Gabriella Belli (Milan: Electa, 1987), pp. 52–8.

62 See Umberto Boccioni, 'Carlo Fornara' (1916), quoted in *Giovanni Segantini (1858–1899)* (Zurich: Kunsthaus, 1990), p. 256.

63 Giosuè Carducci, 'Mattino alpestre', in *Rime nuove* (1887), *Edizione nazionale delle opere di Giosuè Carducci*, 30 vols. (Bologna: Zanichelli, 1935–1940), vol. III, p. 201.

64 Carducci, 'Mezzogiorno alpino', in *Rime e ritmi* (1899), *Edizione nazionale*, vol. IV, p. 230.

65 See, for an eloquent example, 'L'ostessa di Gaby', in *Rime e ritmi*, p. 231. It seems significant that D'Annunzio, a poet far removed from Carducci in aesthetic and ideological terms, comes very close to sounding Carduccian in his poem 'Alle montagne' (1896), in which peaks are 'virginal', springs 'uncorrupted', silence 'sacred', and so on; D'Annunzio, *Laudi*, pp. 345–7.

6 LA FANCIULLA DEL WEST: A NEW LANDSCAPE FOR A NEW VIRGIN

1 French libretto by Paul Bérel, pseudonym of the publisher Paul de Choudens, translated into Italian by Giovanni Targioni-Tozzetti (Monte Carlo, 1905).

2 See Luigi Baldacci, 'Mascagni senza teatro' (1985), in his *La musica in italiano. Libretti d'opera dell'Ottocento* (Milan: Rizzoli, 1997), pp. 159–81: 175–6.

3 All quotations are from Giacomo Puccini, *La fanciulla del West, opera in tre atti di Guelfo Civinini e Carlo Zangarini*, ed. Eduardo Rescigno (Rome: Ricordi, 2002), p. 22. This edition reproduces the first edition of the libretto (1910), but also refers to Puccini's revision of the opera (1922) and the current edition of the score (ed. Mario Parenti, Ricordi, pl. no. 113300, [1960?]). The most richly documented account of the various versions of the opera is Dieter Schickling, *Giacomo Puccini: Catalogue of the Works* (Kassel: Bärenreiter, 2003), pp. 294–314.

4 The peaks are clearly visible in a well-known photograph of the moment when Minnie saves Johnson taken during the first run of performances at the Metropolitan Opera, as well as in the stage design by Angelo Parravicini for the first Italian production of *Fanciulla* (Rome, Teatro Costanzi, 1911); both images are reproduced in *La scena di Puccini*, ed. Vittorio Fagone and Vittoria Crespi Morbio (Lucca: Fondazione Ragghianti, 2003), pp. 270–1.

5 'Grand fond montagnes couvertes de neige'; *La Fille du West [. . .] Mise en Scène de Monsieur Jules Speck, Régisseur de la scène du Métropolitan Opéra, New-York* (Paris: Ricordi, n.d. [1911?]), p. 41. Jules Speck was stage manager at the Metropolitan Opera between 1908 and 1917 and is identified as such in the playbill of the first performance of *Fanciulla* (reproduced in *Tutti i libretti di Puccini*, ed. Enrico Maria Ferrando, 2nd edn. [Milan: Garzanti, 1995], p. 291). The relationship between this staging manual (compiled in French so that it could be rented throughout the world) and the first *mise en scène* of the opera is not proven beyond doubt, given some discrepancies between this document and a few photographs taken from the first production; for an assessment of the evidence, see Ilaria Castellazzi, '*La fanciulla del West*, tra musica e messa in scena', *tesi di laurea*, University of Pavia (2001), chapter 3; see also Mercedes Viale Ferrero, 'Riflessioni sulle scenografie pucciniane', *Studi pucciniani* 1 (1998), pp. 19–42: 37.

6 Translations of the libretto are taken, often with alterations, from the translation by Gwyn Morris printed in the booklet accompanying the 1978 Deutsche Grammophon recording of *Fanciulla* conducted by Zubin Mehta (DG 419 640–2).

7 David Belasco, *The Girl of the Golden West* (1905), in *American Melodrama*, ed. Daniel C. Gerould (New York: Performing Arts Journal Publications, 1983), 183–247: 247, 215.

8 Belasco's stage direction asks for foothills in the far background 'with here and there a suggestion of a winding trail leading to the West' (*ibid.*, 246).

9 *Ibid.*

10 See Viale Ferrero, 'Riflessioni sulle scenografie pucciniane', pp. 37–8.

11 Belasco, *The Girl of the Golden West*, p. 194.

12 This description fits well the only other Minnie of the Italian twentieth century, the protagonist of Massimo Bontempelli's comedy *Minnie la*

candida (1928), whose first name may indeed owe something to a memory of Puccini's Minnie.

13 Mosco Carner, *Puccini: A Critical Biography*, 3rd edn (London: Duckworth, 1992), pp. 461–2.

14 Michele Girardi, *Puccini: His International Art*, trans. Laura Basini (Chicago: The University of Chicago Press, 2000), p. 297. The reference is to the two chords on the third beat of the second and third bars of the theme.

15 Julian Budden, *Puccini: His Life and Works* (New York: Oxford University Press, 2002), p. 310.

16 For an interpretation of Minnie's entrance not dissimilar to mine, see Allan W. Atlas, '*Lontano-tornare-redenzione*: Verbal Leitmotives and Their Musical Resonance in Puccini's *La fanciulla del West*', *Studi musicali* 21 (1992), pp. 359–98: 370. Helen M. Greenwald calls attention to the change in metre (from 4/4 to 12/8), which introduces a 'new "compound" sonority'; 'Character Distinction and Rhythmic Differentiation in Puccini's Operas', *Giacomo Puccini. L'uomo, il musicista, il panorama europeo*, ed. Gabriella Biagi Ravenni and Carolyn Gianturco (Lucca: LIM, 1997), pp. 495–515: 500.

17 Minnie's description of Nina as 'una finta spagnuola nativa di Cachuca' (in Belasco 'one of them Cachuca girls, with droopy Spanish eyes') points to her probable Mexican identity. This negative opinion of Nina's femininity is part of a complex discourse on race that the libretto derives from its source, albeit in a toned-down version. Minnie's is the only viable version of femininity also (and perhaps first) because she is the only 'white' woman around (Nina is Mexican and Wowkle is Native American).

18 In Belasco's play Johnson's masculinity is also inflected by his elevated manner of speaking, which contrasts with the rough speech of Rance and the miners (and Minnie), undoubtedly contributing to his characterisation as 'the one man in the place who has the air of a gentleman' (*The Girl of the Golden West*, p. 199). This differentiation is not preserved in the libretto, in which everybody remains on roughly the same linguistic level.

19 Carner, *Puccini*, p. 466.

20 The staging manual simply repeats word for word the libretto's stage direction.

21 See, for example, Atlas, '*Lontano–tornare–redenzione*', pp. 377–80, and Girardi, *Puccini*, pp. 322–4, for the details of thematic and motivic recall.

22 For a summary of Italian attitudes towards gender and femininity at the turn of the century, see Michela De Giorgio, *Le italiane dall'unità a oggi. Modelli culturali e comportamenti sociali* (Rome and Bari: Laterza, 1992), especially pp. 20–8 (on the 'new woman' in Italy) and 74–89 (on virginity); for an interpretation of the reception of Puccini's works and image in the light of these attitudes, see Alexandra Wilson, 'Torrefranca vs. Puccini: Embodying a Decadent Italy', *Cambridge Opera Journal* 13 (2001), pp. 29–53.

23 Catherine Clément's celebration of Minnie as an antiheroine 'made for tomorrow' originates in a somewhat comparable cultural climate, that of 1970s France; *Opera, or the Undoing of Women* (1979), trans. Betsy Wing (Minneapolis: University of Minnesota Press, 1988), p. 95.

24 Guido Gozzano, 'Ketty', *Tutte le poesie*, ed. Andrea Rocca (Milan: Mondadori, 1980), pp. 314–17.

25 Scipio Sighele, *La donna nova* (Rome: Voghera, 1898), pp. 185–200.

26 See Federico Garlanda, *La nuova democrazia americana. Studi e applicazioni* (Rome: Società Editrice Laziale, 1891), p. 26; and Garlanda, *La terza Italia. Lettere di un yankee* (Rome: Società Editrice Laziale, 1903), p. 379. Both volumes are discussed in Andrew J. Torrielli, *Italian Opinion on America as Revealed by Italian Travelers, 1850–1900* (Cambridge, Mass.: Harvard University Press, 1941), pp. 196–9. The independence of North American women was already a theme in a number of late-eighteenth-century *buffa* librettos, such as Nunziato Porta's *L'americana in Olanda* (1777) and Giuseppe Palomba's *La quakera spiritosa* (1783); see Pierpaolo Polzonetti, '*Opera buffa* and the American Revolution', Ph.D. dissertation, Cornell University (2003), chapter 3.

27 See Torrielli, *Italian Opinion on America*, pp. 253–97.

28 See Giuseppe Massara, *Viaggiatori italiani in America (1860–1970)* (Rome: Edizioni di Storia e Letteratura, 1976), chapter 2; Massara, *Americani. L'immagine letteraria degli Stati Uniti in Italia* (Palermo: Sellerio, 1984), pp. 153–216.

29 'Gli italiani tengono, nella pubblica stima, se non il penultimo, il terz'ultimo posto. Al disotto di essi, non ci sono che i cinesi ed i negri'; Giuseppe Giacosa, *Impressioni d'America*, 2nd edn (Milan: Cogliati, 1902), pp. 170–1.

30 Antonio Caccia's *Europa ed America. Scene della vita dal 1848 al 1850*, published in Monaco in 1850, is discussed in Massara, *Americani* (p. 41), where utopian texts such as Ermolao Rubieri's *D'Italia in California* (1878) and Francesco Domenico Guerrazzi's *Il secolo che muore* (1885) are also introduced (pp. 42–3).

31 'Buffalo Bill has been here, and I liked it. Buffalo Bill is a company of North Americans, with a number of Redskins and buffaloes, who do splendid shooting tricks and reproduce for real scenes that went on at the frontier' ('C'è stato qui Buffalo Bill che mi piacque. Buffalo Bill è una compagnia di americani del Nord, con una quantità di indiani pellirosse e di bufali, che fanno dei giuochi di tiro splendidi e riproducono al vero delle scene successe alla frontiera'); Puccini to Michele Puccini, 24 April 1890, in *Carteggi pucciniani*, ed. Eugenio Gara (Milan: Ricordi, 1958), p. 38, trans. in Girardi, *Puccini*, p. 326.

32 Robert A. Carter, *Buffalo Bill Cody: The Man behind the Legend* (New York: John Wiley, 2000), pp. 333–6, 411. The show returned to Italy in 1905 for a shorter tour (Carter does not specify which cities were visited). Lively accounts of the show's visit to Verona, originally published in a local newspaper, can be read in Emilio Salgari, *Una tigre in redazione. Le pagine sconosciute di un cronista sempre in viaggio con la fantasia*, ed. Silvino Gonzato (Venice: Marsilio, 1994), pp. 53–75. Salgari was Italy's most famous and prolific writer of adventure novels and short stories for children, still read in Italy to this day. Between the 1890s and the 1910s he published several works set in the American West, some with a Gold Rush theme. In *La sovrana del Campo d'Oro* (1904) Buffalo Bill himself rescues the father of the protagonist from a mine where he was kept captive by rebel miners, after she had put herself up for auction in order to raise the money to pay the ransom asked for his freedom. See Ann Lawson Lucas, *La ricerca dell'ignoto. I romanzi d'avventura di Emilio Salgari* (Florence: Olschki, 2000), p. 19. At the very least, Salgari's books must have had an impact on the image of the American West of Italian opera audience members of the 1910s who had been children or teenagers in the 1890s and 1900s (provided that the parents did not also read books ostensibly intended for their children).

33 'Puccini Suggests an American Opera', *Musical America*, 26 January 1907, p. 3.

34 'Indimenticabili *Racconti californiesi* [*sic*]'; Giacosa, *Impressioni d'America*, p. III. For a general discussion of European images of the American West in the nineteenth century (in which Italy is hardly mentioned, however), see Ray Allen Billington, *Land of Savagery, Land of Promise: The European Image of the American Frontier in the Nineteenth Century* (New York and London: W. W. Norton, 1981).

35 Several stories had been published in two collections: *Racconti californiani* (Milan: Treves, 1877), with an important introduction by E. Torelli Viollier, and *Nuovi racconti californiani* (Milan: Brigola, 1880). Pietro Floridia's opera *La colonia libera* (Rome, 1899; rev. ed. Turin, 1900), on a libretto by Luigi Illica, is based on Harte's short story *M'liss: An Idyll of the Red Mountain*, first published in 1863 and in Italian, as *Mliss*, in *Racconti californiani*, pp. 39–63. A reading of Illica's libretto shows a few similarities with *Fanciulla* that may be due to more than just the operas' chronological and geographical contiguity: among others, the forest setting of the third act, to which the two lovers Juanita and Salvador have escaped after he has committed a crime, only to be tracked down by the inhabitants of the colony; and the final tableau of the two lovers leaving the colony, to which they bid repeated farewells, amidst the other characters' pleadings to stay at least one day longer. Puccini, who had the idea of setting *Fanciulla*'s third act in a forest clearing, may have been acquainted with the libretto or the score of *La colonia libera*, or at least heard about it.

36 Unnamed critic writing for a Philadelphia newspaper, cited in Eric Myers, 'Opera at Land's Edge', *Opera* 55/4 (April 2004), pp. 396–400: 396–7.

37 Lee Clark Mitchell, *Westerns: Making the Man in Fiction and Film* (Chicago: The University of Chicago Press, 1996), pp. 77–8.

38 *Ibid.*, p. 75.

39 The literature on this American discourse is immense but hardly relevant here. This situation is exactly the reverse of the Italian discourse on the West at the turn of the twentieth century, of which no readily available discussion exists, at least as far as I have been able to ascertain. Opera's adventurousness in the Italian cultural landscape is a decidedly mixed blessing for the context-conscious musicologist, forcing him or her, as it often does, to temp as pioneering literary critic and cultural historian.

40 For the claim that 'what is fascinating about Puccini's representation of American frontier life in *La fanciulla* is its likeness to historical reality', see Mary Jane Phillips-Matz, 'Puccini's America', in *The Puccini Companion*, ed. William Weaver and Simonetta Puccini (New York and London: W. W. Norton, 1994), pp. 202–27: 211.

41 David Belasco, *The Girl of the Golden West* (New York: Samuel French, 1933; first published 1915), pp. 11, 13. The text published in *American Melodrama*, ed. Gerould, does not include the lengthy description of the opening pictures. This panorama-like device, used extensively by Belasco and central to his aesthetics of realism, is discussed in Helen M. Greenwald, 'Realism on the Opera Stage: Belasco, Puccini, and the California Sunset', in *Opera in Context: Essays on Historical Staging from the Late Renaissance to the Time of Puccini*, ed. Mark A. Radice (Portland: Amadeus Press, 1998), pp. 279–96: 288–9.

42 See, for example, William Ashbrook, *The Operas of Puccini* (Ithaca: Cornell University Press, 1985; first published 1968), pp. 145–6; Greenwald, 'Realism on the Opera Stage', p. 290; Budden, *Puccini*, p. 305. Girardi, on the other hand, hears the thematic sequence of the prelude as symbolising 'love as a redemptive force'; Girardi, *Puccini*, p. 286.

43 This is the position of Greenwald, 'Realism on the Opera Stage', and Budden, *Puccini*.

44 See Atlas, '*Lontano–tornare–redenzione*', pp. 363–4.

45 See *ibid.*, p. 369. Atlas interprets the role of Minnie as a gradual appropriation of the style characteristics of this *tinta* through a 'long musical-metaphoric path' that will eventually lead her to quote Jake Wallace's song in the final concertato.

46 'I have the idea of a grandiose scene, a clearing in the vast Californian forest with colossal trees, but it needs eight or ten "horse-supers" ' ('Ho l'idea di uno scenario grandioso, una spianata nella grande foresta californiana cogli alberi colossali, ma occorrono 8 o 10 cavalli-comparse'); letter to Giulio Ricordi, 26 August 1907, in *Carteggi pucciniani*, p. 353.

47 For a detailed analysis of the scene, see Girardi, *Puccini*, pp. 317–19.

48 For example *ibid.*, p. 319.

49 This detailed articulation of space in both libretto and music, which makes the use of a staging manual superfluous in a sense, may go some way towards explaining the apparently poor circulation of the stage manual prepared by Speck, at least judging from the small number of its

surviving copies (no major library holds one, a fact also due to *Fanciulla*'s relative lack of success, of course). The amount of literal repetition from the libretto contained in this document is certainly much greater than in any of the staging manuals published by Ricordi in the final decades of the nineteenth century.

50 See Baldacci, *La musica in italiano*, p. 258; Luca Serianni, *Viaggiatori musicisti poeti. Saggi di storia della lingua italiana* (Milan: Garzanti, 2002), pp. 133, 153.

51 See Serianni, *Viaggiatori musicisti poeti*, pp. 143, 155. The German soldier proudly displaying his foreign accent and speaking in the infinitives of such eighteenth-century comic operas as Goldoni's *La buona figliola* was by now a very distant memory if at all present in the collective linguistic conscience of Italian opera. Perhaps some very old spectators could remember the German tenor Guglielmo of Donizetti's *Le convenienze ed inconvenienze teatrali* (1827–31), probably the last descendant of this by then thoroughly conventional type.

52 See Paolo D'Achille, 'Prime apparizioni di ideofoni ed esotismi in libretti d'opera', *Lingua nostra* 62/1 (March 1996), pp. 1–6.

53 Baldacci, *La musica in italiano*, p. 256.

54 'Puccini Studies American Music in Writing *Girl of the Golden West*', *Musical America* 12, no. 6 (18 June 1910), p. 3, quoted in Linda B. Fairtile, '"No Such Thing as American Music": Nationalist Sentiments and the Early Reception of *La fanciulla del West*', *Studi pucciniani* (forthcoming).

55 'Setting Poker to Music', *Musical America* 13, no. 1 (12 November 1910), p. 19, quoted in Fairtile, '"No Such Thing as American Music"'.

56 Arthur Farwell, 'The Music of Puccini's Opera', *Musical America* 13, no. 6 (17 December 1910), pp. 4–5, extensively quoted and discussed in Fairtile, '"No Such Thing as American Music"'. On original American melodies in *Fanciulla* and Puccini's compositional interventions, examined through their evolution in sketches and drafts, see Allan W. Atlas, 'Belasco and Puccini: "Old Dog Tray" and the Zuni Indians', *The Musical Quarterly* 75 (1991), pp. 362–98.

57 Farwell, 'The Music of Puccini's Opera', p. 5.

58 Michael Saffle concludes his attempt to analyse 'exotic' harmony in *Fanciulla* and *Turandot* with the following: 'From one point of view these examples demonstrate clearly that Puccini's harmonic idiom is filled with quasi-exotic harmonic devices. From another point of view,

however, these examples also demonstrate how elusive Puccini's harmonic idiom can be. At some points in *La fanciulla del West* it is difficult to determine whether Puccini's music is – or is intended to be – "American"'; Michael Saffle, '"Exotic" Harmony in *La fanciulla del West* and *Turandot*', *Esotismo e colore locale nell'opera di Puccini. Atti del I convegno internazionale sull'opera di Giacomo Puccini. Torre del Lago, Festival Pucciniano 1983*, ed. Jürgen Maehder (Pisa: Giardini, 1985), pp. 119–29: 129.

59 Girardi, *Puccini*, p. 289; Budden, *Puccini*, p. 306.

60 A work that shares with *Fanciulla* not only its exploration of new sonic spaces and hearing, but also its mixed critical fortunes, is Schreker's near-contemporary *Der ferne Klang* (1912), which is also crucially concerned with gender and femininity; see Peter Franklin, 'Distant Sound–Fallen Music: *Der ferne Klang* as "Woman's Opera"?', *Cambridge Opera Journal* 3 (1991), pp. 159–72.

61 As reported in *Musical America* 13, no. 6 (17 December 1910), p. 4. Humperdinck was in New York for the first performance of *Königskinder* (which took place on 28 December), an opera which can hardly be called 'realist' – and it seems therefore difficult to read Humperdinck's remark as unqualified praise of *Fanciulla*.

62 See, for example, Puccini's interview in the *Gazzetta di Torino* of 11 November 1911, the day of the Turinese première of the opera (published in *La fanciulla del West*, programme book [Milan: Edizioni del Teatro alla Scala, 1995], pp. 77–81); and a letter to Alfredo Colombo about the German première (Berlin, March 1913) in which Puccini insists on a German translation of the staging manual and regrets that the theatre was not supplied with a detailed guide to 'effetti scenici' (published in *Quaderni pucciniani* 5 [1996], p. 207). For Belasco, see his article in *Musical America* 13, no. 7 (24 December 1910), p. 28. For Belasco's collaboration on the first production, see Shelby J. Davis, 'David Belasco and Giacomo Puccini: Their Collaborations', *Opera and the Golden West: The Past, Present, and Future of Opera in the U.S.A.*, ed. John L. DiGaetani and Josef P. Sirefman (Rutherford – London and Toronto: Farleigh Dickinson University Press – Associated University Presses, 1994), pp. 129–39; Greenwald, 'Realism on the Opera Stage'.

63 Conceding to Johnson's request to give a speech about 'the woman I love', Rance warns him: 'One minute. . . be brief' ('Un minuto. . . sii breve'). This remark highlights the performative nature of 'Ch'ella mi

creda', almost turning it into a stage song. In this sense, Rance here is the voice of the 'new' Puccini warning his 'old' dramaturgical self to be brief with his set piece (which lasts only about 1 minute and 40 seconds, making it perhaps Puccini's shortest aria).

64 Gary Tomlinson, *Metaphysical Song: An Essay on Opera* (Princeton: Princeton University Press, 1998), pp. 148–9. It is interesting that Tomlinson, who is suspicious of what he calls Puccini's 'pushy salesman' aesthetic, finds Act 1 of *Fanciulla* 'the best single act Puccini ever wrote' ('Puccini Turns Respectable', *The New York Times*, 15 December 2002, Section 7, p. 14).

65 Franco Moretti, *Atlas of the European Novel, 1800–1900* (London and New York: Verso, 1998), p. 3.

66 W. J. T. Mitchell, 'Preface to the Second Edition of *Landscape and Power*: Space, Place, and Landscape', *Landscape and Power*, ed. Mitchell, 2nd edn (Chicago: The University of Chicago Press, 2002), p. vii.

67 Mario Rigoni Stern, *Storia di Tönle* (1978) (Turin: Einaudi, 1993), pp. 52–3.

BIBLIOGRAPHY

PRIMARY SOURCES

Librettos, plays, staging manuals

Belasco, David. *The Girl of the Golden West.* New York: Samuel French, 1933
  The Girl of the Golden West. In Daniel C. Gerould, ed. *American Melodrama.*
  New York: Performing Arts Journal Publications, 1983, 183–247
Bouilly, Jean-Nicolas and Joseph Pain. *Fanchon la vielleuse, comédie en trois
  actes, mêlée de vaudevilles.* Paris: Barba, 1803
Cammarano, Salvadore. *Luisa Miller. Melodramma tragico, in tre atti [. . .] da
  rappresentarsi nel Real Teatro S. Carlo.* Naples: Flautina, 1849
Checcherini, Giuseppe. *I promessi sposi, melo-dramma in tre atti tratto dal
  romanzo del signor Manzoni di simil titolo da Giuseppe Checcherini pel
  Teatro Nuovo nell'inverno dell'anno 1830.* Naples: Severino, 1830
Civinini, Guelfo and Carlo Zangarini. *Giacomo Puccini, La fanciulla del West,
  opera in tre atti di Guelfo Civinini e Carlo Zangarini.* Ed. Eduardo
  Rescigno. Rome: Ricordi, 2002
Colautti, Arturo. *Fedora, dramma di Victorien Sardou, ridotto in tre atti per la
  scena lirica da Arturo Colautti, musica di Umberto Giordano.* Milan:
  Sonzogno, 1997
Daspuro, Nicola. *L'amico Fritz, commedia lirica in tre atti di P. Suardon (Nicola
  Daspuro) dal romanzo di Erckmann-Chatrian, musica di Pietro Mascagni.*
  Milan: Sonzogno, 1986
D'Ennery, Adolphe and Gustave Lemoine. *La Grâce de Dieu, ou la Nouvelle
  Fanchon, drame en cinq actes (mêlé de chant).* Paris: Tresse, 1841
Ducange, Victor. *Thérèse, ou l'Orpheline de Genève, mélodrame en trois actes.*
  Paris: Barba, 1821
  *L'orfanella della Svizzera, dramma in tre atti, traduzione dal francese di Luigi
  Marchionni.* Leghorn: Vignozzi, 1824
Ferrando, Enrico Maria, ed. *Tutti i libretti di Puccini.* 2nd edn. Milan:
  Garzanti, 1995

Fontana, Ferdinando. *Le Villi, opera-ballo in due atti di Ferdinando Fontana, musica di Giacomo Puccini, Teatro alla Scala, Carnevale–Quaresima 1884–85.* Milan: Ricordi, 1885

   Edgar, dramma lirico in quattro atti di Ferdinando Fontana, musica di Giacomo Puccini, Teatro alla Scala, Carnevale–Quaresima 1888–89. Milan: Ricordi, 1889

Franchetti, Alberto. *Fior d'Alpe, opera in tre atti, parole di Leo Di Castelnuovo, musica di Alberto Franchetti.* Milan: Sonzogno, 1894

Ghislanzoni, Antonio. *I promessi sposi, melodramma in quattro atti di Antonio Ghislanzoni, musica del M.° Cav.ᵉ Errico Petrella.* Milan: Lucca, n.d. [1873?]

Guidi, Francesco. *La savojarda, dramma lirico in 3 atti di Francesco Guidi posto in musica da Amilcare Ponchielli, da rappresentarsi nel Teatro della Concordia in Cremona pel Carnevale 1860–61.* Cremona: Manini, 1861

   Lina, dramma lirico in tre atti di F. Guidi e C. D'Ormeville, musica di Amilcare Ponchielli, Teatro Dal Verme, Autunno 1877. Milan: Ricordi, n.d. [1877]

Illica, Luigi. *La Wally di W. De Hillern, riduzione drammatica in quattro atti di Luigi Illica, musica di Alfredo Catalani, Teatro alla Scala, 1891–92.* Milan: Ricordi, 1892

Meilhac, Henri and Ludovic Halévy. *Carmen, opéra-comique en quatre actes.* Paris: Michel Lévy Frères, 1875

Mérimée, Prosper. *Carmen.* Ed. Maxime Revon. Paris: Garnier, 1960

Micheletti, Pietro and Emanuele Bardare. *I promessi sposi, melodramma di Pietro Micheletti e di Emanuele Bardare, posto in musica dal Maestro Andrea Traventi, da rappresentarsi nel Teatro Argentina nella stagione di Autunno 1858.* Rome: Stabilimento Tipografico, 1858

Monticini, Antonio. *L'orfana ginevrina, ossia L'ombra di un vivo, ballo in tre atti espressamente composto per la prima volta da Antonio Monticini.* Vicenza: Parise, 1826

Musset, Alfred de. *Œuvres complètes.* Ed. Edmond Biré. 9 vols. Paris: Garnier, n.d. [1908]

Oh! Che originali, farsa; Nina o La pazza per amore, dramma semiserio. Milan: Fontana, 1829

Palianti, Louis. *Mise en scène de 'Linda de Chamouny', Opéra en trois actes, Paroles de M. Hyppolyte Lucas, Musique de M. Gaëtan Donizetti, Mise en scène de M. L. Palianti.* Paris: Chez l'Auteur, n.d. [1844]

Pepoli, Carlo. *I Puritani e i Cavalieri, opera-seria in due parti, parole del Signor C. Pepoli, musica del Sr. Maestro Bellini.* Paris: Delaforest, 1835

I promessi sposi, melo-dramma semi-serio in due atti da rappresentarsi nel Teatro Valle [. . .] nel Carnevale dell'Anno 1834. Rome: Puccinelli, 1834

I promessi sposi, melodramma in quattro atti posto in musica dal Maestro Amilcare Ponchielli, da rappresentarsi per la prima volta nel Teatro della Concordia in Cremona l'Autunno 1856. Cremona: Manini, 1856

Romani, Felice. *Amina ovvero L'innocenza perseguitata, melodramma semiserio.* Milan: Pirola, 1824

Amina ovvero L'innocenza perseguitata, melodramma semiserio. Trieste: n.p., 1825

La sonnambula, melodramma di Felice Romani, da rappresentarsi nel Teatro Carcano la Quaresima del 1831. Milan: Fontana, 1831

Vincenzo Bellini. La sonnambula. Melodramma in due atti di Felice Romani. Ed. Eduardo Rescigno. Milan: Ricordi, 1990

Romani, Felice and Andrea Leone Tottola. *Amina ovvero L'orfanella da Ginevra, melodramma comico-sentimentale.* Naples: Flautina, 1825

Romani, Felice and Jacopo Ferretti. *L'orfanella di Ginevra, melodramma.* Milan: Truffi, 1832

Rossi, Gaetano. *Elisa, dramma sentimentale in un atto per musica, da rappresentarsi nel Teatro Nobilissimo Venier in S. Benedetto la Primavera 1804.* Venice: Casali, 1804

Linda di Chamounix, melodramma in tre atti, parole di Gaetano Rossi, musica del Maestro Cav. Gaetano Donizetti, da rappresentarsi nell'I.R. Teatro di Corte alla Porta Carinzia in Vienna. Vienna: Ullrich, 1842

Linda de Chamouni [sic], opéra en trois actes, musique de M. Gaétan Donizetti, paroles de M. Gaetano Rossi. Paris: Lange Lévy, 1842

Schiller, Friedrich. *Intrigue et amour, drame en cinq actes et neuf tableaux, traduit de Schiller, par Alexandre Dumas, représenté pour la première fois, à Paris, sur le Théâtre Historique, le 11 Juin 1847.* Paris: Michel Lévy Frères, 1847

Scribe, Eugène. *La Somnambule, ou l'Arrivée d'un nouveau seigneur, ballet-pantomime en trois actes, par MM. Scribe et Aumer.* Paris: Barba, 1828

Serenelli Honorati, Luigi. *Fiorina, o La fanciulla di Glaris, melodramma semiserio in due atti, musica di Carlo Pedrotti.* Milan: Ricordi, n.d. [post 1865]

Speck, Jules. *La Fille du West [. . .] Mise en Scène de Monsieur Jules Speck, Régisseur de la scène du Métropolitan Opéra, New-York*. Paris: Ricordi, n.d. [1911?]

Turchi, Giuseppe. *L'orfanella di Ginevra, ossia L'ombra di un vivo, azione mimica in 4 atti di Giuseppe Turchi*. N.p.: n.e., n.d.

Scores

Bellini, Vincenzo. *La sonnambula, melodramma di Felice Romani posto in musica dal M° Bellini*. Milan: Ricordi, n.d. [1831], pl. nos. 5271–88

The celebrated opera La Sonnambula, composed by Bellini, adapted to the English stage by Henry R. Bishop. London: Boosey, n.d. [1833?], no plate number

La sonnambula, opera seria in due atti del signor Maestro Vincenzo Bellini. Paris: Launer, n.d. [1834], pl. nos. 2978–81, 2734–43

La sonnambula, Die Nachtwandlerinn, Oper von V. Bellini, Kleiner Clavierauszug mit deutschem und italienischem Texte für den Umfang jeder Stimme eingerichtet von Ant. Diabelli. Vienna: Diabelli, n.d. [1830s], pl. no. 4492

La Sonnambula, opéra complet pour piano et chant, paroles italiennes, musique de Bellini. Paris: Vve Launer, n.d. [1841], pl. no. 3221

La sonnambula (La Somnambule), opéra en deux actes, paroles françaises de Mr Maurice Bourges, musique de Bellini. Paris: Schlesinger, n.d. [1845], pl. no. 4262

La sonnambula (The Somnambulist), a lyric drama, written by Felice Romani and rendered into English from the Italian by J. Wrey Mould, the music [. . .] by Vincenzo Bellini, revised from the orchestral score by W. S. Rockstro, pupil of Dr. Felix Mendelssohn Bartholdy. London: Boosey, n.d. [1849], no plate number

La sonnambula, melodramma di Felice Romani posto in musica dal M° Bellini [. . .] nuova edizione. Milan: Ricordi, n.d. [1858], pl. nos. 30481–501

La Somnambule, drame lyrique en 3 actes, paroles françaises de Crevel de Charlemagne, musique de V. Bellini. Paris: Leduc, n.d. [c. 1872], no plate number

La sonnambula. Milan: Ricordi, n.d. [c. 1875], pl. no. 41686

La sonnambula, atto primo [. . .] stampato in luogo di manoscritto. Milan: Ricordi, n.d. [c. 1895], pl. no. 96343

La sonnambula, melodramma in due atti di Felice Romani, musica di Vincenzo Bellini, partitura d'orchestra in fac-simile dell'autografo. Milan: Ricordi, 1934

Canti comaschi. Piano accompaniment by Giulio Ricordi and Italian text by Leopoldo Pullé. Milan: Ricordi, 1858

Canzoni popolari comasche. Ed. Giovanni Battista Bolza. Vienna: I. R. Tipografia di Corte e di Stato, 1867

Carissimi, Giacomo. *Jephte.* Ed. Adelchi Amisano. Milan: Ricordi, n.d. [1977], pl. no. 131729

Catalani, Alfredo. *La Wally, dramma lirico in quattro atti [. . .] riduzione per canto e pianoforte di Carlo Carignani.* Milan: Ricordi, n.d. [1892], pl. no. 95257

Donizetti, Gaetano. *Linda di Chamounix, melodramma in tre atti di Gaetano Rossi.* Milan: Ricordi, n.d. [1870s], pl. no. 42056

Linda di Chamounix. Preliminary version of the critical edition. Ed. Gabriele Dotto. Edizione critica delle opere di Gaetano Donizetti. For rent only. Milan: Ricordi, 1994, pl. no. 136661

Giordano, Umberto. *Fedora.* Milan: Edoardo Sonzogno, 1898, pl. no. E984S

Paisiello, Giovanni. *Nina o sia La pazza per amore.* Ed. Fausto Broussard. Milan: Ricordi, 1981, pl. no. 132843

Pedrotti, Carlo. *Fiorina, o La fanciulla di Glaris, melodramma semiseria [sic] in due atti posto in musica [. . .] da Carlo Pedrotti.* Paris: Léon Escudier, n.d. [c. 1859], pl. no. L.E.1535

Ponchielli, Amilcare. *Lina, dramma lirico in tre atti di F. Guidi e C. D'Ormeville, musica di Amilcare Ponchielli.* Milan: Ricordi, n.d. [1877?], pl. no. 45228

I promessi sposi, melodramma in quattro parti, musica di Amilcare Ponchielli. Milan: Ricordi, n.d. [1872?], pl. no. 43444

Puccini, Giacomo, *La fanciulla del West.* Ed. Mario Parenti. Milan: Ricordi, n.d. [1940?], pl. no. 113300

Ricci, Luigi. *'Chiara di Rosembergh' and Excerpts from 'Colombo' and 'L'orfanella di Ginevra'.* Ed. Philip Gossett. New York and London: Garland, 1990

Rossini, Gioachino. *La gazza ladra, melodramma in due atti di Giovanni Gherardini, musica di Gioachino Rossini.* Ed. Alberto Zedda. 2 vols. Pesaro: Fondazione Rossini, 1979

*Guillaume Tell, opéra en quatre actes di Victor Joseph Etienne de Jouy e
Hippolyte Louis Florent Bis, musica di Gioachino Rossini*. Ed. M. Elizabeth
C. Bartlet. 4 vols. Pesaro: Fondazione Rossini, 1992
Verdi, Giuseppe. *Luisa Miller*, ed. Jeffrey Kallberg. The Works of Giuseppe
Verdi. Chicago and Milan: The University of Chicago Press–Ricordi,
1991

SECONDARY LITERATURE

A! A! A! [Hugo, Abel, Armand Malitourne and Jean-Joseph Ader]. *Traité du
mélodrame*. Paris: Delaunay–Pélicier–Plancher, 1817
Abbate, Carolyn. *Unsung Voices: Opera and Musical Narrative in the Nineteenth
Century*. Princeton: Princeton University Press, 1991
    In Search of Opera. Princeton: Princeton University Press, 2001
Allevy, Marie-Antoinette. *La Mise en scène en France dans la première moitié du
dix-neuvième siècle*. Paris: Droz, 1938
Angermüller, Rudolph. 'Il periodo viennese di Donizetti'. *Atti del primo
convegno internazionale di studi donizettiani*. 2 vols. Bergamo: Azienda
Autonoma di Turismo, 1983, vol. II, 619–95
Appolonia, Giorgio. *Giuditta Pasta, gloria del belcanto*. Turin: EDA, 2000
Ashbrook, William. *Donizetti and His Operas*. Cambridge: Cambridge
University Press, 1982
    The Operas of Puccini. Ithaca: Cornell University Press, 1985
Atlas, Allan W. 'Belasco and Puccini: "Old Dog Tray" and the Zuni Indians'.
The Musical Quarterly 75 (1991), 362–98
    'Lontano–tornare–redenzione: Verbal Leitmotives and Their Musical
Resonance in Puccini's *La fanciulla del West*'. *Studi musicali* 21 (1992),
359–98
Audisio, Aldo, Bruno Guglielmotto-Ravet and Annie Bertholet, eds. *Les
Alpes à travers la gravure du XIXe siècle*. Paris: Berger–Levrault, 1982
Baldacci, Luigi. *La musica in italiano. Libretti d'opera dell'Ottocento*. Milan:
Rizzoli, 1997
    Ottocento come noi. Saggi e pretesti italiani. Milan: Garzanti, 2003
Balzac, Honoré de. *Splendeurs et misères des courtisanes*. Ed. Pierre Barbéris.
Paris: Gallimard, 1973
Barattelli, Bianca. 'I *Promessi sposi* di Antonio Ghislanzoni'. *Esperienze
letterarie* 11/4 (October–December 1986), 41–79

Barbi, Michele. *Poesia popolare pistoiese*. Florence: Carnesecchi, 1895

Barthes, Roland. *The Responsibility of Forms: Critical Essays on Music, Art, and Representation*. Trans. Richard Howard. New York: Hill and Wang, 1985

Bartlet, M. Elizabeth C. with Mauro Bucarelli, eds. *'Guillaume Tell' di Gioachino Rossini: fonti iconografiche*. Pesaro: Fondazione Rossini, 1996

Basevi, Abramo. *Studio sulle opere di Giuseppe Verdi*. Florence: Tofani, 1859 Reprint, Bologna: Forni, n.d. [1978]

Beghelli, Marco. 'Il ruolo del musico'. In Franco Carmelo Greco and Renato Di Benedetto, eds. *Donizetti, Napoli, l'Europa*. Naples: Edizioni Scientifiche Italiane, 2000, 323–35

Bellini, Vincenzo. *Epistolario*. Ed. Luisa Cambi. Milan: Mondadori, 1943

Beltrami, Pietro G. *La metrica italiana*. Bologna: Il Mulino, 1991

Bernardoni, Virgilio. 'La drammaturgia dell'aria nel primo Puccini. Da "Se come voi piccina" a "Sola, perduta, abbandonata"'. *Studi pucciniani* 1 (1998), 43–56

'Il linguaggio musicale della *Fedora* di Umberto Giordano'. In Johannes Streicher, ed. *Ultimi splendori. Cilea, Giordano, Alfano*. Rome: Ismez, n.d. [1999], 347–61

Bernoni, Domenico Giuseppe. *Canti popolari veneziani*. Venice: Fontana–Ottolini, 1872

Berrong, Richard M. *The Politics of Opera in Turn-of-the-Century Italy as Seen Through the Letters of Alfredo Catalani*. Lewiston: Edwin Mellen Press, 1992

Bertoni Jovine, Dina, ed. *I periodici popolari del Risorgimento*. 3 vols. Milan: Feltrinelli, 1958–60

Billington, Ray Allen. *Land of Savagery, Land of Promise: The European Image of the American Frontier in the Nineteenth Century*. New York and London: W. W. Norton, 1981

Bini, Annalisa. '*Otto mesi in due ore, ossia Gli esiliati in Siberia*. Vicende di un'opera donizettiana'. *Rivista italiana di musicologia* 22 (1987), 183–260

Bini, Annalisa and Jeremy Commons, eds. *Le prime rappresentazioni delle opere di Donizetti nella stampa coeva*. Rome–Milan: Accademia Nazionale di Santa Cecilia–Skira, 1998

Black, John. *Donizetti's Operas in Naples*. London: The Donizetti Society, 1982

The Italian Romantic Libretto: A Study of Salvadore Cammarano. Edinburgh: Edinburgh University Press, 1984

Bologna, Corrado. *Flatus vocis. Metafisica e antropologia della voce.* 2nd edn. Bologna: Il Mulino, 2000

Brooks, Peter. *Psychoanalysis and Storytelling.* Oxford: Blackwell, 1994
   The Melodramatic Imagination: Balzac, Henry James, Melodrama, and the Mode of Excess. 2nd edn. New Haven: Yale University Press, 1995
   'Body and Voice in Melodrama and Opera'. In Mary Ann Smart, ed. *Siren Songs: Representations of Gender and Sexuality in Opera.* Princeton: Princeton University Press, 2000, 118–34

Brooks, Peter and Alex Woloch, eds. *Whose Freud? The Place of Psychoanalysis in Contemporary Culture.* New Haven: Yale University Press, 2000

Brunel, Pierre. *Vincenzo Bellini.* Paris: Fayard, 1978

Budden, Julian. *The Operas of Verdi.* 2nd edn. 3 vols. Oxford: Oxford University Press, 1992
   Puccini: His Life and Works. New York: Oxford University Press, 2002

Burke, Edmund. *Philosophical Inquiry into the Origin of Our Ideas of the Sublime and Beautiful.* Ed. James T. Boulton. London: Routledge–Kegan, 1958

Busch, Hans. *Verdi's 'Falstaff' in Letters and Contemporary Reviews.* Bloomington: Indiana University Press, 1997

Byron, George. *The Complete Poetical Works of Lord Byron.* Ed. Jerome J. McGann. 7 vols. Oxford: Clarendon Press, 1980–93

Campana, Alessandra, Emanuele Senici and Mary Ann Smart, eds. *Donizetti a Casa Ricordi. Gli autografi teatrali.* Bergamo: Fondazione Donizetti, 1998

Cantù, Cesare. *Della letteratura.* 8th edn. 3 vols. Turin: Unione Tipografico-Editrice, 1857–58

Carducci, Giosuè. *Edizione nazionale delle opere di Giosuè Carducci.* 30 vols. Bologna: Zanichelli, 1935–40

Carner, Mosco. *Puccini: A Critical Biography.* 3rd edn. London: Duckworth, 1992

Carter, Robert A. *Buffalo Bill Cody: The Man behind the Legend.* New York: John Wiley, 2000

Caselli, J[oseph]. *Chants populaires de l'Italie.* Paris: Librairie Internationale, 1865

Castellazzi, Ilaria. '*La fanciulla del West*, tra musica e messa in scena'. *Tesi di laurea.* University of Pavia, 2001

Castelvecchi, Stefano. 'Sentimental Opera: The Emergence of a Genre, 1760–1790'. Ph.D. disssertation. The University of Chicago, 1996

'From *Nina* to *Nina*: Psychodrama, Absorption and Sentiment in the 1780s'. *Cambridge Opera Journal* 8 (1996), 91–112

Caswell, Austin B. 'Loïsa Puget and the French *Romance*'. In Peter Bloom, ed. *Music in Paris in the Eighteen-Thirties*. Stuyvesant: Pendragon Press, 1987, 97–115

Chusid, Martin. 'Evil, Guilt, and the Supernatural in Verdi's *Macbeth*: Toward an Understanding of the Tonal Structure and Key Symbolism'. In Andrew Porter and David Rosen, eds. *Verdi's 'Macbeth': A Sourcebook*. New York: Norton, 1984, 249–60

Cirese, Alberto Mario. *Ragioni metriche*. Palermo: Sellerio, 1988

Clément, Catherine. *Opera, or the Undoing of Women*. Trans. Betsy Wing. Minneapolis: University of Minnesota Press, 1988

Conati, Marcello. 'Ballabili nei *Vespri* con alcune osservazioni su Verdi e la musica popolare'. *Studi verdiani* 1 (1982), 21–46

'Verdi per Napoli'. In Bruno Cagli and Agostino Ziino, eds. *Il Teatro di San Carlo, 1737–1987*. Vol. II. *L'opera, il ballo*. Naples: Electa, 1987, 225–66

Cone, John Frederick. *Adelina Patti: Queen of Hearts*. Portland: Amadeus Press, 1993

Confalonieri, Giulio. *Storia della musica*. Ed. Alfredo Mandelli. Milan: Sansoni, 1968

Constant, Benjamin. *Réflections sur la tragédie*. Ed. A. Roulin. Paris: Gallimard, 1957

Contini, Pasquale. *Nuova raccolta di poesie morali e civili ad uso delle scuole e delle famiglie italiane*. Milan: Agnelli, 1866

Cosgrove, Denis E. *Social Formation and Symbolic Landscape*. 2nd edn. Madison: The University of Wisconsin Press, 1998

D'Achille, Paolo. 'Prime apparizioni di ideofoni ed esotismi in libretti d'opera'. *Lingua nostra* 62/1 (March 1996), 1–6

Dahlhaus, Carl. *Nineteenth-Century Music*. Trans J. Bradford Robinson. Berkeley and Los Angeles: University of California Press, 1989

D'Annunzio, Gabriele. *Laudi del cielo, del mare, della terra e degli eroi*. Milan: Mondadori, 1939

Davis, Lloyd, ed. *Virginal Sexuality and Textuality in Victorian Literature*. Albany: SUNY Press, 1993

Davis, Shelby J. 'David Belasco and Giacomo Puccini: Their Collaborations'. In John L. DiGaetani and Josef P. Sirefman, eds. *Opera and the Golden West: The Past, Present, and Future of Opera in the U.S.A.* Rutherford–London and Toronto: Farleigh Dickinson University Press–Associated University Presses, 1994, 129–39

Dean, Tim. 'What's the Point of Psychoanalytic Criticism?'. In Timothy Clark and Nicholas Royle, eds. *Beyond Redemption: The Work of Leo Bersani*. Special issue of *The Oxford Literary Review* 20 (1998), 143–62

Dean, Winton. 'Some Echoes of Donizetti in Verdi's Operas'. In *Atti del Terzo Convegno Internazionale di Studi Verdiani*. Parma: Istituto di Studi Verdiani, 1974, 122–47

De' Giorgi Bertola, Aurelio. *Elogio di Gessner*. Ed. Michèle and Antonio Stäuble. Florence: Olschki, 1982

De Giorgio, Michela. *Le italiane dall'unità a oggi. Modelli culturali e comportamenti sociali*. Rome and Bari: Laterza, 1992

Degrada, Francesco. 'Prolegomeni a una lettura della *Sonnambula*'. In Giorgio Pestelli, ed. *Il melodramma italiano dell'Ottocento. Studi e ricerche per Massimo Mila*. Turin: Einaudi, 1977, 319–50

Della Corte, Andrea. *Settecento italiano*. Milan: Bocca, 1922

Della Seta, Fabrizio. 'Affetto e azione. Sulla teoria del melodramma italiano dell'Ottocento'. In Lorenzo Bianconi, F. Alberto Gallo, Angelo Pompilio and Donatella Restani, eds. *Atti del XIV Congresso della Società Internazionale di Musicologia. Trasmissione e recezione delle forme di cultura musicale*. 3 vols. Bologna: Il Mulino, 1990, vol III, 395–9

Depanis, Giuseppe. *Alfredo Catalani. Appunti e ricordi*. Turin: Roux, 1893

De Tomaso, Piero. *Il racconto campagnolo nell'Ottocento italiano*. Ravenna: Longo, n.d. [1973]

De Van, Gilles. *Verdi's Theater: Creating Drama Through Music*. Trans. Gilda Roberts. Chicago: The University of Chicago Press, 1998

Diderot, Denis. *Correspondance*. Ed. Georges Roth with Jean Varloot. 16 vols. Paris: Minuit, 1955–70

Döhring, Sieghart and Sabine Henze-Döhring. *Oper und Musikdrama im 19. Jahrhundert*. Laaber: Laaber Verlag, 1997

Dolar, Mladen. 'The Object Voice'. In Renata Salecl and Slavoj Žižek, eds. *Gaze and Voice as Love Objects*. Durham: Duke University Press, 1996, 7–31

Dossi, Carlo. *Opere*. Ed. Dante Isella. Milan: Adelphi, 1995

Dotto, Gabriele. '*Linda di Chamounix*: percorsi di una struttura dramma-turgica e scelte esecutive'. Proceedings of the conference *Donizetti e il teatro musicale europeo* (Venice, Teatro La Fenice, May 1997). Bergamo, Fondazione Donizetti, forthcoming

Ender, Evelyne. *Sexing the Mind: Nineteenth-Century Fictions of Hysteria*. Ithaca: Cornell University Press, 1995

Engelhardt, Markus. '"Something's Been Done to Make Room for Choruses": Choral Conception and Choral Construction in *Luisa Miller*'. In Martin Chusid, ed. *Verdi's Middle Period, 1849–1859: Source Studies, Analysis, and Performance Practice*. Chicago: The University of Chicago Press, 1997, 197–205

'Goethe, Scribe, Donizetti: *Betly, ossia La capanna svizzera*'. In Franco Carmelo Greco and Renato Di Benedetto, eds. *Donizetti, Napoli, l'Europa*. Naples: Edizioni Scientifiche Italiane, 2000, 21–32

Evans, Dylan. *An Introductory Dictionary of Lacanian Psychoanalysis*. London and New York: Routledge, 1996

Fagone, Vittorio and Vittoria Crespi Morbio, eds. *La scena di Puccini*. Lucca: Fondazione Ragghianti, 2003

Fairtile, Linda B. '"No Such Thing as American Music": Nationalist Sentiments and the Early Reception of *La fanciulla del West*'. *Studi pucciniani* (forthcoming)

La fanciulla del West. Programme book. Milan: Edizioni del Teatro alla Scala, 1995

Fend, Michael. 'Literary Motifs, Musical Form and the Quest for the "Sublime": Cherubini's *Eliza ou le Voyage aux glaciers du Mont St Bernard*'. *Cambridge Opera Journal* 5 (1993), 17–38

'Die ästhetische Kategorie des Erhabenen und die Entdeckung der Alpen in der Musik'. In Anselm Gerhard and Annette Landau, eds. *Schweizer Töne: Die Schweiz im Spiegel der Musik*. Zurich: Chronos, 2000, 29–43

Ferraro, Giuseppe. *Canti popolari monferrini*. Turin and Florence: Loescher, 1870

Fink, Bruce. *The Lacanian Subject: Between Language and Jouissance*. Princeton: Princeton University Press, 1995

Florimo, Francesco. *Bellini. Memorie e lettere*. Florence: Barbera, 1882

Foucault, Michel. *The History of Sexuality*. Vol. I. *An Introduction*. Trans. Robert Hurley. New York: Random House, 1978

Fraisse, Geneviève and Michelle Perrot, eds. *Emerging Feminism from Revolution to World War*. Trans. Arthur Goldhammer. Vol. IV of Georges Duby and Michelle Perrot, eds. *A History of Women in the West*. Cambridge, Mass.: Harvard University Press, 1993

Franceschini, Stefania. 'Tanti librettisti per un'opera di Ponchielli a lungo rimaneggiata (1856–1874)'. *Nuova rivista musicale italiana* 30 (1996), 365–82

Franklin, Peter. 'Distant Sound – Fallen Music: *Der ferne Klang* as "Woman's Opera"?'. *Cambridge Opera Journal* 3 (1991), 159–72

Frantz, Pierre. *L'Esthétique du tableau dans le théâtre du XVIIIe siècle*. Paris: Presses Universitaires de France, 1998

Freud, Sigmund. *The Standard Edition of the Complete Psychological Works of Sigmund Freud*. Trans. James Strachey with Anna Freud, Alix Strachey and Alan Tyson. 24 vols. London: The Hogarth Press – The Institute of Psychoanalysis, 1953–74

Gara, Eugenio, ed. *Carteggi pucciniani*. Milan: Ricordi, 1958

Garlanda, Federico. *La nuova democrazia americana. Studi e applicazioni*. Rome: Società Editrice Laziale, 1891

La terza Italia. Lettere di un yankee. Rome: Società Editrice Laziale, 1903

Gautier, Théophile. *Histoire de l'art dramatique en France depuis vingt-cinq ans*. 6 vols. Paris: Hetzel, 1856–8

Gerhard, Anselm. '"Schweizer Töne" als Mittel der motivischen Integration: Gioachino Rossinis *Guillaume Tell*'. In Anselm Gerhard and Annette Landau, eds. *Schweizer Töne: Die Schweiz im Spiegel der Musik*. Zurich: Chronos, 2000, 99–106

Giacosa, Giuseppe. *Impressioni d'America*. 2nd edn. Milan: Cogliati, 1902

Giovanni Segantini (1858–1899). Zurich: Kunsthaus, 1990

Girardi, Michele. *Puccini: His International Art*. Trans. Laura Basini. Chicago: The University of Chicago Press, 2000

Giudici, Nicolas. *La Philosophie du Mont Blanc. De l'alpinisme à l'économie immatérielle*. Paris: Grasset, 2000

Goldstein, Jan. *Console and Classify: The French Psychiatric Profession in the Nineteenth Century*. Cambridge: Cambridge University Press, 1987

Gossett, Philip. 'Trasporre Bellini'. In Fabrizio Della Seta and Simonetta Ricciardi, eds. *Vincenzo Bellini: verso l'edizione critica. Atti del convegno internazionale, Siena, 1–3 giugno 2000*. Florence: Olschki, 2004, 163–85

Gozzano, Guido. *Tutte le poesie*. Ed. Andrea Rocca. Milan: Mondadori, 1980

Greenwald, Helen M. 'Character Distinction and Rhythmic Differentiation in Puccini's Operas'. In Gabriella Biagi Ravenni and Carolyn Gianturco, eds. *Giacomo Puccini. L'uomo, il musicista, il panorama europeo*. Lucca: LIM, 1997, 495–515

'Realism on the Opera Stage: Belasco, Puccini, and the California Sunset'. In Mark A. Radice, ed. *Opera in Context: Essays on Historical Staging from the Late Renaissance to the Time of Puccini*. Portland: Amadeus Press, 1998, 279–96

Guichonnet, Paul, ed. *Histoire et civilisation des Alpes*. 2 vols. Toulouse–Lausanne: Privat–Payot, 1980

Hadlock, Heather. '*Tancredi* and *Semiramide*'. In Emanuele Senici, ed. *The Cambridge Companion to Rossini*. Cambridge: Cambridge University Press, 2004, 139–58

Harte, Bret. *Racconti californiani*. Milan: Treves, 1877

Nuovi racconti californiani. Milan: Brigola, 1880

Hepokoski, James A. 'Genre and Content in Mid-Century Verdi: "Addio, del passato" (*La traviata*, Act III)'. *Cambridge Opera Journal* 1 (1989), 249–76

'*Ottocento* Opera as Cultural Drama: Generic Mixtures in *Il trovatore*'. In Martin Chusid, ed. *Verdi's Middle Period, 1849–1859: Source Studies, Analysis, and Performance Practice*. Chicago: The University of Chicago Press, 1997, 147–96

Hernandez Girbal, F. *Adelina Patti, la reina del canto*. Madrid: Lira, 1979

Hibberd, John. *Salomon Gessner: His Creative Achievement and Influence*. Cambridge: Cambridge University Press, 1976

Hill, David. *Turner in the Alps: The Journey Through France and Switzerland in 1802*. London: George Philip, 1992

Hope Nicolson, Marjorie. *Mountain Gloom and Mountain Glory: The Development of the Aesthetics of the Infinite*. Ithaca: Cornell University Press, 1959. Reprint, Seattle: University of Washington Press, 1997

Hugo, Victor. *Théâtre complet*. Ed. J.-J. Thierry and Josette Mélèze. 2 vols. Paris: Gallimard, 1963–4

Dramas. Trans. I. G. Burnham. 10 vols. Philadelphia: Barrie, 1895–6

Hyslop, Gabrielle. 'Pixérécourt and the French Melodrama Debate: Instructing Boulevard Theatre Audiences'. In James Redmond, ed. *Themes in Drama 14: Melodrama*. Cambridge: Cambridge University Press, 1992, 61–85

Jacobshagen, Arnold. 'Pixérécourt–Romanelli–Romani: *Margherita d'Anjou* und das Melodramma semiserio'. In Sieghart Döhring and Arnold Jacobshagen, eds. *Meyerbeer und das europäische Musiktheater*. Laaber: Laaber Verlag, 1998, 41–63

Joly, Jacques. *Dagli Elisi all'inferno. Il melodramma tra Italia e Francia dal 1730 al 1850*. Florence: La Nuova Italia, 1990

Kahane, Claire. 'Questioning the Maternal Voice'. *Genders* 3 (November 1988), 82–91

Kant, Immanuel. *Critique of Aesthetic Judgement*. Trans. and ed. James Creed Meredith. Oxford: Clarendon Press, 1911

    Observations on the Feeling of the Beautiful and Sublime. Trans. John T. Goldthwait. Berkeley and Los Angeles: University of California Press, 1960

Kimbell, David. *Verdi in the Age of Italian Romanticism*. Cambridge: Cambridge University Press, 1981

Kosofsky Sedgwick, Eve. 'Paranoid Reading and Reparative Reading; Or, You're So Paranoid, You Probably Think This Introduction is About You'. In Eve Kosofsky Sedgwick, ed. *Novel Gazing: Queer Readings in Fiction*. Durham: Duke University Press, 1997, 1–37

Kristeva, Julia. *Tales of Love*. Trans. Leon S. Roudiez. New York: Columbia University Press, 1987

Lacan, Jacques. *Ecrits: A Selection*, trans. Alan Sheridan. New York: Norton, 1977

    The Four Fundamental Concepts of Psychoanalysis. Ed. Jacques-Alain Miller. Trans. Alan Sheridan. New York: Norton, 1978

Lacoste-Veysseyre, Pauline. *Les Alpes romantiques. Le Thème des Alpes dans la littérature française de 1800 à 1850*. 2 vols. Geneva: Slatkine, 1981

Laprade, Victor de. 'L'Alpe vierge'. *La Revue des deux mondes* 19 (1849), 539–41

Lardelli, Dora. 'Panorama dell'Engadina'. In Gabriella Belli, ed. *Segantini*. Milan: Electa, 1987, 52–8

Lawson Lucas, Ann. *La ricerca dell'ignoto. I romanzi d'avventura di Emilio Salgari*. Florence: Olschki, 2000

Lefèvre, Roger. 'Le Printemps alpestre de *Jocelyn*, ou l'imagination lamartinienne du bonheur'. In Paul Viallaneix, ed. *Lamartine. Le Livre du centenaire*. Paris: Flammarion, 1971, 97–106

Leicester, H. Marshall Jr. 'Discourse and the Film Text: Four Readings of *Carmen*'. *Cambridge Opera Journal* 6 (1994), 245–82

Lévy, François. 'Bellini et l'"école frénétique": de *Bertram* (1822) à *Il pirata* (1827)'. In Hervé Lacombe, ed. *L'Opéra en France et en Italie (1791–1925). Une scène privilégiée d'échanges littéraires et musicaux.* Paris: Société Française de Musicologie, 2000, 37–60

Lippmann, Friedrich. 'Vincenzo Bellini e l'opera seria del suo tempo. Studi sul libretto, la forma delle arie e la melodia'. In Maria Rosaria Adamo and Friedrich Lippmann. *Vincenzo Bellini.* Rome: ERI, 1981, 313–555

Mahoney, Patrick J. *On Defining Freud's Discourse.* New Haven: Yale University Press, 1989

Manzoni, Alessandro. *I promessi sposi.* Ed. Vittorio Spinazzola. Milan: Garzanti, 1966

The Betrothed. Trans. Bruce Penman. London: Penguin, 1972

Marcoaldi, Oreste. *Canti popolari inediti umbri liguri piceni piemontesi.* Genoa: Sordo–Muti, 1855

Marinelli Roscioni, Carlo. *La cronologia.* Vol. II of *Il teatro di San Carlo, 1737–1987.* Naples: Guida, 1988

Massara, Giuseppe. *Viaggiatori italiani in America (1860–1970).* Rome: Edizioni di Storia e Letteratura, 1976

Americani. L'immagine letteraria degli Stati Uniti in Italia. Palermo: Sellerio, 1984

Mauceri, Marco. 'Inediti di Felice Romani. La carriera del librettista attraverso nuovi documenti dagli archivi milanesi'. *Nuova rivista musicale italiana* 25 (1992), 391–432

McCormick, John. *Popular Theatres of Nineteenth-Century France.* London and New York: Routledge, 1993

McGrath, William J. *Freud's Discovery of Psychoanalysis: The Politics of Hysteria.* Ithaca: Cornell University Press, 1986

Meriggi, Marco. 'Società, istituzioni e ceti dirigenti'. In Giovanni Sabbatucci and Vittorio Vidotto, eds. *Storia d'Italia*, 6 vols. Vol. I: *Le premesse dell'unità. Dalla fine del Settecento al 1861.* Rome and Bari: Laterza, 1994, 119–228

Mitchell, Lee Clark. *Westerns: Making the Man in Fiction and Film.* Chicago: The University of Chicago Press, 1996

Mitchell, W. J. T. 'Preface to the Second Edition of *Landscape and Power*: Space, Place, and Landscape'. In W. J. T. Mitchell, ed. *Landscape and Power*. 2nd edn. Chicago: The University of Chicago Press, 2002

Monk, Samuel H. *The Sublime: A Study of Critical Theories in Eighteenth-Century England*. Ann Arbor: University of Michigan Press, 1960

Moretti, Franco. *Atlas of the European Novel, 1800–1900*. London and New York: Verso, 1998

Mossa, Carlo Matteo, ed. *Carteggio Verdi–Cammarano (1843–1852)*. Parma: Istituto Nazionale di Studi Verdiani, 2001

Motte-Haber, Helga de la. *Musik und Natur: Naturanschauung und musikalische Poetik*. Laaber: Laaber Verlag, 2000

Murray, John. *A Handbook for Travellers in Switzerland*. London, 1838. Reprint, Leicester: Leicester University Press, 1970

Myers, Eric. 'Opera at Land's Edge'. *Opera* 55/4 (April 2004), 396–400

Nash, Catherine. 'Reclaiming Vision: Looking at Landscape and the Body'. *Gender, Place and Culture: A Journal of Feminist Geography* 3 (1996), 149–69

Nerval, Gérard de. *Œuvres complètes*. Ed. Jean Guillaume and Claude Pichois. 3 vols. Paris: Gallimard, 1984–93

Nicolaisen, Jay. *Italian Opera in Transition, 1871–1893*. Ann Arbor: UMI Research Press, 1980

Nigra, Costantino. *Canti popolari del Piemonte*. Turin: Loescher, 1888

Noble, Richard. *Language, Subjectivity, and Freedom in Rousseau's Moral Philosophy*. New York: Garland, 1991

Paduano, Guido. *Il giro di vite. Percorsi dell'opera lirica*. Florence: La Nuova Italia, 1992

Pastore, Alessandro. *Alpinismo e storia d'Italia dall'Unità alla Resistenza*. Bologna: Il Mulino, 2003

Pastura, Francesco. *Bellini secondo la storia*. Parma: Guanda, 1959

Perrot, Michelle, ed. *From the Fires of Revolution to the Great War*. Trans. Arthur Goldhammer. Vol. IV of Philippe Ariès and Georges Duby, eds. *A History of Private Life*. Cambridge, Mass.: Harvard University Press, 1990

Petrobelli, Pierluigi. *Music in the Theater: Essays on Verdi and Other Composers*. Trans. Roger Parker. Princeton: Princeton University Press, 1994

Phillips-Matz, Mary Jane. *Verdi: A Biography*. Oxford: Oxford University Press, 1993

'Puccini's America'. In William Weaver and Simonetta Puccini, eds. *The Puccini Companion*. New York and London: W. W. Norton, 1994, 202–24

Philo of Alexandria. *Liber antiquitatum biblicarum*. Ed. Guido Kisch. Notre Dame, Ind.: University of Notre Dame, 1949

The Biblical Antiquities. Trans. M. R. James. New York: Ktav, 1971

Piceni, Enrico and Mario Monteverdi. *Pittura lombarda dell'Ottocento*. Milan: Cassa di Risparmio delle Province Lombarde, 1969

Pixérécourt, René-Charles Guilbert de. 'Le Mélodrame'. *Paris, ou Le Livre des cent-et-un*. Vol. VI. Paris: Ladvocat, 1832, 319–52

Théâtre choisi. 4 vols. Paris and Nancy: Tresse–L'Auteur, 1841–43

Poizat, Michel. *La Voix du diable. La Jouissance lyrique sacrée*. Paris: Métailié, 1991

The Angel's Cry: Beyond the Pleasure Principle in Opera. Trans. Arthur Denner. Ithaca: Cornell University Press, 1992

Polzonetti, Pierpaolo. 'Opera buffa and the American Revolution'. Ph.D. dissertation. Cornell University, 2003

Pompilio, Angelo. 'La carriera e le opere di Ponchielli nei giudizi della critica italiana (1856–1887)'. In Nino Albarosa *et al. Amilcare Ponchielli 1834–1886. Saggi e ricerche nel 150° anniversario della nascita*. Casalmorano: Cassa Rurale ed Artigiana, 1984, 7–92

Porter, Andrew and David Rosen, eds. *Verdi's 'Macbeth': A Sourcebook*. New York: Norton, 1984

Pougin, Arthur. *Bellini. Sa vie, ses œuvres*. Paris: Hachette, 1868

Powers, Harold S. '"Aria sfasciata", "duetto senza l'insieme": le scene di confronto tenore–soprano nello *Stiffelio/Aroldo* di Giuseppe Verdi'. In Giovanni Morelli, ed. *Tornando a Stiffelio: popolarità, rifacimenti, messinscena, effettismo e altre 'cure' nella drammaturgia del Verdi romantico. Atti del convegno internazionale di studi (Venezia, 17–20 dicembre 1985)*. Florence: Olschki, 1986, 141–88

Principe, Quirino. 'La sonnambula' di Vincenzo Bellini. Milan: Mursia, 1991

Przybos, Julia. *L'Entreprise mélodramatique*. Paris: Corti, 1987

Ralyea, John. *Shepherd's Delight*. 2nd edn. Chicago: The Hurdy-Gurdy Press, 1981

Reboul, Pierre. 'Peuple Enfant, Peuple Roi, ou Nodier, mélodrame et révolution'. *Revue des sciences humaines* 41 (1976), 247–56

Rehding, Alexander. 'Ecomusicology'. *Journal of the Royal Musical Association* 127 (2002), 305–20

Rigoni Stern, Mario. *Storia di Tönle*. Turin: Einaudi, 1993

Rinaldi, Mario. *Felice Romani dal melodramma classico al melodramma romantico*. Rome: De Santis, 1965

Ring, Jim. *How the English Made the Alps*. London: Murray, 2000

Robinson, Paul. *Opera, Sex, and Other Vital Matters*. Chicago: The University of Chicago Press, 2002

Roccatagliati, Alessandro. *Drammaturgia romantica verdiana: 'Luisa Miller' e 'Rigoletto'*. Bari: Il Coretto, 1989

  Felice Romani librettista. Milan and Lucca: Ricordi–LIM, 1996

Roccatagliati, Alessandro and Luca Zoppelli. 'Testo, messinscena, tradizione: le testimonianze dei libretti'. In Fabrizio Della Seta and Simonetta Ricciardi, eds. *Vincenzo Bellini: verso l'edizione critica. Atti del convegno internazionale, Siena, 1–3 giugno 2000*. Florence: Olschki, 2004, 271–90

Rose, Gillian. *Feminism and Geography: The Limits of Geographical Knowledge*. Cambridge: Polity Press, 1993

Ross, Peter. '*Luisa Miller* – ein "kantiger Schiller-Verschnitt"? Sozialkontext und ästhetische Autonomie der Opernkomposition im Ottocento'. In Jürgen Maehder and Jürg Stenzl, eds. *Zwischen Opera buffa und Melodramma: Italienische Oper im 18. und 19. Jahrhundert*. Frankfurt: Peter Lang, 1994, 159–78

Rosselli, John. *The Life of Bellini*. Cambridge: Cambridge University Press, 1996

Rousseau, Jean-Jacques. *Emile, ou de l'Education*. Ed. Charles Wirz and Pierre Burgelin. Paris: Gallimard, 1969

  Julie, ou La Nouvelle Héloïse. Ed. Henri Coulet and Bernard Guyon. Paris: Gallimard, 1969

  Eloisa, or A Series of Original Letters Collected and Published by Mr. J.J. Rousseau. Trans. William Kenrick. 4 vols. London: Vernor and Hood, 1803. Reprint, 2 vols. Oxford: Woodstock Books, 1989

Roussel, Jean. *Jean-Jacques Rousseau en France après la révolution, 1795–1830*. Paris: Colin, 1972

Ruskin, John. *The Works of John Ruskin*. Ed. E. T. Cook and Alexander Wedderburn, 39 vols. London: George Allen, 1903–12

Sade, Marquis de. *Les Cent vingt journées de Sodome, ou L'école du libertinage*. Ed. Michel Delon. Paris: Gallimard, 1990

Saffle, Michael. '"Exotic" Harmony in *La fanciulla del West* and *Turandot*'. In Jürgen Maehder, ed. *Esotismo e colore locale nell'opera di Puccini. Atti del I convegno internazionale sull'opera di Giacomo Puccini. Torre del Lago, Festival Pucciniano 1983*. Pisa: Giardini, 1985, 119–29

Sala, Emilio. 'Verdi and the Parisian Boulevard Theatre, 1847–9'. *Cambridge Opera Journal* 7 (1995), 185–205

'La "vielleuse" e il savoiardo: tradizione e drammaturgia'. *Donizetti, Parigi e Vienna. Atti del convegno internazionale, Roma, 19–20 marzo 1998*. Atti dei convegni Lincei 156. Rome: Accademia Nazionale dei Lincei, 2000, 47–77

Salgari, Emilio. *Una tigre in redazione. Le pagine sconosciute di un cronista sempre in viaggio con la fantasia*. Ed. Silvino Gonzato. Venice: Marsilio, 1994

Sand, George, *La Mare au diable*. Ed. Pierre Reboul. Paris: Garnier–Flammarion, 1964

La Petite Fadette. Ed. Geneviève van den Bogaert. Paris: Garnier–Flammarion, 1967

François le Champi. Paris: Gallimard, 1973

Sangsue, Daniel. *Passages romantiques des Alpes*. Lausanne: Favre, 1990

Santoli, Vittorio. *I canti popolari italiani. Ricerche e questioni*. 2nd edn. Florence: Sansoni, 1968

Schama, Simon. *Landscape and Memory*. London: Fontana Press, 1995

Scherillo, Michele. *Vincenzo Bellini. Note aneddotiche e critiche*. Ancona: Morelli, 1882

Schickling, Dieter. *Giacomo Puccini: Catalogue of the Works*. Kassel: Bärenreiter, 2003

Schiller, Friedrich. *Über naïve und sentimentalische Dichtung*. Ed. William F. Mainland. Oxford: Blackwell, 1957

Schlitzer, Franco. *Mondo teatrale dell'Ottocento*. Naples: Fiorentino, 1954

Scudo, P[aul]. *Critique et littérature musicales*. Paris: Amyot, 1850

L'Année musicale. 3 vols. Paris: Hachette, 1860–2

Senici, Emanuele. 'Per una biografia musicale di Amina'. In Fabrizio Della Seta and Simonetta Ricciardi, eds. *Vincenzo Bellini: verso l'edizione critica. Atti del convegno internazionale, Siena, 1–3 giugno 2000*. Florence: Olschki, 2004, 297–314

'Amina e il C.A.I.: vedute alpine ottocentesche'. In Graziella Seminara and Anna Tedesco, eds. *Vincenzo Bellini nel secondo centenario della nascita*. Florence: Olschki, 2004, 569–79

'Words and Music'. In Scott L. Balthazar, ed. *The Cambridge Companion to Verdi*. Cambridge: Cambridge University Press, 2004, 88–110

Serianni, Luca. *Viaggiatori musicisti poeti. Saggi di storia della lingua italiana.* Milan: Garzanti, 2002

Shelley, Mary and Percy Bysshe Shelley. *History of a Six Weeks' Tour Through Parts of France, Switzerland, Germany, and Holland: With Letters Descriptive of a Sail round the Lake of Geneva, and of the Glaciers of Chamouni.* London: Hookam–Ollier, 1817. Reprint, Oxford: Woodstock Books, 1989

Sighele, Scipio. *La donna nova.* Rome: Voghera, 1898

Silverman, Kaja. *The Acoustic Mirror: The Female Voice in Psychoanalysis and Cinema.* Bloomington: Indiana University Press, 1988

Smart, Mary Ann. '"Dalla tomba uscita": Representations of Madness in Nineteenth-Century Italian Opera'. Ph.D. dissertation. Cornell University, 1994

'Bellini's Fall from Grace'. *Opera* 53/3 (March 2002), 278–84

Smith, Marian. 'The *Livrets de Mise en Scène* of Donizetti's Parisian Operas'. In Francesco Bellotto, ed. *L'opera teatrale di Gaetano Donizetti. Atti del convegno internazionale di studio 1992, Bergamo, 17–20 settembre 1992.* Bergamo: Comune di Bergamo, 1993, 371–89

Soldani, Simonetta, ed. *L'educazione delle donne. Scuole e modelli di vita femminile nell'Italia dell'Ottocento.* Milan: Angeli, 1991

Sorcinelli, Paolo. *Storia e sessualità. Casi di vita, regole e trasgressioni tra Ottocento e Novecento.* Milan: Bruno Mondadori, 2001

Stanton, Domna C. 'Difference on Trial: A Critique of the Maternal Metaphor in Cixous, Irigaray and Kristeva'. In Nancy K. Miller, ed. *The Poetics of Gender.* New York: Columbia University Press, 1986, 157–82

Starobinski, Jean. *Jean-Jacques Rousseau: Transparency and Obstruction.* Trans. Arthur Goldhammer. Chicago: The University of Chicago Press, 1988

Stendhal. *Life of Rossini.* Ed. and trans. Richard N. Coe. 2nd edn. London and New York: Calder–Riverrun, 1985

Thomasseau, Jean-Marie. *Le Mélodrame sur les scènes parisiennes de 'Coelina' (1800) à 'L'Auberge des Adrets' (1823).* Lille: Service de Réproduction des Thèses, 1974

Le Mélodrame. Paris: Presses Universitaires de France, 1984

Tomlinson, Gary. 'Italian Romanticism and Italian Opera: An Essay in Their Affinities'. *19th-Century Music* 10 (1986), 43–60

'Opera and *Drame*: Hugo, Donizetti, and Verdi'. In *Studies in Music History 2: Music and Drama.* New York: Broude Brothers, 1988, 171–92

Metaphysical Song: An Essay on Opera. Princeton: Princeton University Press, 1999

'Puccini Turns Respectable'. *The New York Times*, 15 December 2002, Section 7, 14

Torrielli, Andrew J. *Italian Opinion on America as Revealed by Italian Travelers, 1850–1900*. Cambridge, Mass.: Harvard University Press, 1941

Trivulzio di Belgioioso, Cristina. 'La Guerre dans le Tyrol italien'. *Revue des deux mondes* 19 (1849), 201–30

Tufano, Lucio. '*La Nina o sia La pazza per amore* di Giovanni Paisiello: testi e contesti'. Doctoral dissertation. University of Pavia, 2000

Tyndall, John. *Hours of Exercise in the Alps*. London: Longman, 1871

Ubersfeld, Anne. *Le Roi et le bouffon. Etude sur le théâtre de Hugo de 1830 à 1839*. Paris: Corti, 1974

'Les Bons et le méchant'. *Revue des sciences humaines* 41 (1976), 193–203

Unverricht, Hubert. 'Das Berg- und Gebirgsmilieu und seine musikalische Stilmittel in der Oper des 19. Jahrhunderts'. In Heinz Becker, ed. *Die 'Couleur locale' in der Oper des 19. Jahrhunderts*. Regensburg: Bosse, 1976, 99–119

Várnai, Péter Pál. 'Contributi per uno studio della tipizzazione negativa nelle opere verdiane: personaggi e situazioni'. In *Atti del Primo Congresso Internazionale di Studi Verdiani*. Parma: Istituto di Studi Verdiani, 1969, 268–75

Verdi, Giuseppe. '*Re Lear*' e '*Ballo in maschera*': lettere di Giuseppe Verdi ad Antonio Somma. Ed. Alessandro Pascolato. Città di Castello: Lapi, 1902

I copialettere di Giuseppe Verdi. Ed. Gaetano Cesari and Alessandro Luzio. Milan: Commissione esecutiva per le onoranze a Giuseppe Verdi nel primo centenario della nascita, 1913

Viale Ferrero, Mercedes. '*Guglielmo Tell* a Torino (1839–40) ovvero una "procella" scenografica'. *Rivista italiana di musicologia* 14 (1979), 378–94

'Da *Fédora* a *Fedora*: smontaggio e rimontaggio di uno scenario (melo) drammatico'. *Il saggiatore musicale* 2 (1995), 93–104

'"Come su ali invisibili". Viaggiatori immaginari tra provincie e capitali'. In Lorenza Guiot and Jürgen Maehder, eds. *Nazionalismo e cosmopolitismo nell'opera fra Ottocento e Novecento. Atti del 3o convegno internazionale 'Ruggero Leoncavallo nel suo tempo'*. Milan: Sonzogno, 1998, 229–38

'Riflessioni sulle scenografie pucciniane'. *Studi pucciniani* 1 (1998), 19–42

Voisin, Georges. 'Discographie: airs séparés'. *La Somnambule, L'Avant-Scène Opéra* 178 (July–August 1997), 75–7

Walton, Benjamin. 'Looking for the Revolution in Rossini's *Guillaume Tell*'. *Cambridge Opera Journal* 15 (2003), 127–51

Weiskel, Thomas. *The Romantic Sublime: Studies in the Structure and Psychology of Transcendence.* Baltimore: Johns Hopkins University Press, 1976

Weiss, Piero. 'Verdi and the Fusion of Genres'. *Journal of the American Musicological Society* 35 (1982), 138–56

Werr, Sebastian. *Die Opern von Errico Petrella: Rezeptionsgeschichte, Interpretationen und Dokumente.* Vienna: Praesens, 1999

Widter, Georg and Adolf Wolf. *Volkslieder aus Venetien.* Vienna: Hof- und Staatsdruckerei, 1864

Williams, Raymond. *The Country and the City.* London: The Hogarth Press, 1985

Wilson, Alexandra. 'Torrefranca vs. Puccini: Embodying a Decadent Italy'. *Cambridge Opera Journal* 13 (2001), 29–53

Woolf, Stuart. *A History of Italy, 1700–1860: The Social Constraints of Political Change.* London: Methuen, 1979. Reprint, London and New York: Routledge, 1991

Zavadini, Guido. *Donizetti. Vita, musiche, epistolario.* Bergamo: Istituto Italiano d'Arti Grafiche, 1948

Zemon Davis, Natalie and Arlette Farge, eds. *Renaissance and Enlightenment Paradoxes.* Trans. Arthur Goldhammer. Vol. III of Georges Duby and Michelle Perrot, eds. *A History of Women in the West.* Cambridge, Mass.: Harvard University Press, 1993

Žižek, Slavoj and Mladen Dolar. *Opera's Second Death.* New York and London: Routledge, 2002

Zoppelli, Luca. 'L'idillio borghese'. *La sonnambula.* Programme book. Venice: Edizioni del Teatro La Fenice, 1996, 49–62

Zurletti, Michelangelo. *Catalani.* Turin: EDT, 1982

INDEX

Abbate, Carolyn, 136, 139
Aleramo, Sibilla, 243
   Una donna, 243
Ambrose, St, 131
   On the Education of Virgins, 131
   On Virginity, 131
Antier, Benjamin, 163
   L'Auberge des Adrets, 163, 164
Appia, Adolphe, 232
Atlas, Allan, 252, 254
Auber, Daniel-François-Esprit, 1
   La Muette de Portici, 1
Aumer, Jean-Pierre, 23, 43, 89, 90
   *La Somnambule ou l'Arrivée d'un
   nouveau seigneur*, 23, 34, 55, 90

Baldacci, Luigi, 55, 93, 94, 112, 228, 256
Balzac, Honoré de, 102, 103, 106,
   164, 193
   Scènes de la vie parisienne, 102
   *Splendeurs et misères des
   courtisanes*, 103
Barbier, Jules, 1
Bardare, Emanuele, 183, 184
Barthes, Roland, 157
Bartlet, M. Elizabeth C., 46, 47
Basevi, Abramo, 161, 163, 175, 177, 180
   *Studio sulle opere di Giuseppe
   Verdi*, 161
Beaumarchais, Pierre Augustin Caron
   de, 157
Beethoven, Ludwig van, 2, 19
   Fidelio, 2

Pastoral Symphony, 19
Beghelli, Marco, 136
Belasco, David, 229, 231, 244, 246, 248,
   249, 250, 251, 259
   The Girl of the Golden West, 229, 232,
   249, 251
Bellini, Vincenzo, 1, 2, 3, 4, 21–92, 137,
   144, 149, 150, 153, 158, 166, 174,
   190, 192, 202, 205
   Adelson e Salvini, 158
   I Capuleti e i Montecchi, 58
   Norma, 137
   Il pirata, 58
   I Puritani, 1, 2, 33, 105, 140, 141
   La sonnambula, 3, 4, 5, 8, *21–92*, 93,
   140, 141, 144, 147, 149, 150, 151, 153,
   154, 161, 163, 175, 177, 180, 181, 183,
   184, 190, 192, 198, 199, 199, 200,
   203, 205, 228, 260
   La straniera, 58
Belloc, Teresa, 43
Berlioz, Hector, 19
   Fantastic Symphony, 19
Bernstein, Leonard, 89
Bierstadt, Albert, 250
Bishop, Henry R., 81, 83
Bizet, Georges, 2
   Carmen, 2, 3, 210
Boccioni, Umberto, 220
Boito, Arrigo, 204
Bologna, Corrado, 131
Bonynge, Richard, 89
Boosey, publishing firm, 83, 86, 87

Bordese, Luigi, 182
Borgioli, Dino, 88
Bouilly, Jean Nicolas, 95
  Fanchon la vielleuse, 95, 102, 103
Branca, Emilia 54
Bresciani, Pietro, 183
Bretonne, Rétif de la, 102
  *Les Nuits de Paris, ou Le spectateur
    nocturne*, 102
  *La Paysanne pervertie, ou Les dangers
    de la ville*, 102
Brooks, Peter, 116, 159
Budden, Julian, 150, 203, 235, 257
Buffalo Bill (William Cody), 7, 248, 249
Burke, Edmund, 24, 25
  *Philosophical Inquiry into the Origin of
    Our Ideas of the Sublime and
    Beautiful*, 24
Byron, George, 27

Caccia, Antonio, 248
Caigniez, Louis-Charles, 34, 158
  *La Pie voleuse ou la Servante de
    Palaiseau*, 34, 36, 158
Callas, Maria, 89, 90
Cammarano, Salvatore, 5, 143, 144, 148,
    149, 153, 162, 165, 166, 168, 169, 173,
    174, 175, 176, 179, 188
Cantù, Cesare, 188
  Documenti alla storia universale, 188
Carafa, Michele, 158
  Le nozze di Lammermoor, 158
Carcano, Giulio, 193
Carducci, Giosuè, 6, 219, 220, 221, 222,
    228, 250
  Rime e ritmi, 220
  Rime nuove, 220
Carissimi, Giacomo, 9, 12, 15, 18
  Jephte, 9, 12, 15, 18
Carner, Mosco, 235, 240

Carpani, Giuseppe, 52
Carré, Michel, 1
Castelvecchi, Stefano, 157
Catalani, Alfredo, 3, 5, 181, 205–22,
    228, 235
  La Wally, 3, 5, 6, 181, *205–22*, 228,
    250, 260
Cavalli, Francesco, 24
  Ormindo, 24
Chapponier, Alexis, 163
  L'Auberge des Adrets, see Antier,
    Benjamin
Charcot, Jean-Martin, 109, 110, 381
Chateaubriand, François-René de, 28
  Essai sur les révolutions, 28
Checcherini, Giuseppe, 182
Cherubini, Luigi, 4, 38, 39, 40, 42
  *Eliza ou Le Voyage aux glaciers du
    Mont St. Bernard*, 4, 38, 40, 44
Cicéri, Pierre-Luc-Charles, 40
Cioni, Renato, 89
Civinini, Guelfo, 228
Clairon, Mademoiselle, 159
Clément, Catherine, 103
Colautti, Arturo, 215, 217
Contini, Pasquale, 108
  'La traviata', 108
Cooper, James Fenimore, 249
Corneille, Pierre, 165
Correnti, Cesare, 193
  'Della letteratura popolare', 193
Cosgrove, Denis E., 16, 17
Cotrubas, Ileana, 22
Cozens, Alexander, 46
Cozens, John Robert, 88

Dahlhaus, Carl, 66
Dal Monte, Toti, 88
D'Annunzio, Gabriele, 244
  'La vergine Anna', 244

'La vergine Orsola', 244
'Terra vergine', 244
Dante Alighieri, 44
  Inferno, 44
D'Antoni, Antonio, 41
Da Ponte, Lorenzo, 14
D'Arienzo, Marco, 196
D'Aubigny, Jean-Marie-Théodore-
  Baudouin, 34
  *La Pie voleuse ou la Servante de
  Palaiseau*, see Caigniez,
  Louis-Charles
David, Jacques-Louis, 46, 47
Debussy, Claude, 257
  Pelléas et Mélisande, 231
Degrada, Francesco, 55
Delamarre, Prospère, 158
  Adelson et Salvini, 158
D'Ennery, Adolphe Philippe, 95,
  102, 111
  La Grâce de Dieu, 5, 95, 98, 100, 101,
  103, 109, 110, 111, 112, 114, 115, 117,
  120, 135
Depanis, Giuseppe, 210
Diabelli, Anton, 81
Di Castelnovo, Leo, 204
Diderot, Denis, 131, 156, 157, 159
  Entretiens sur 'Le Fils naturel', 156
Disney, Walt, 139
  Snow White, 139
Dolar, Mladen, 131
Donizetti, Gaetano, 3, 4, 93–142, 144,
  149, 150, 151, 153, 158, 159, 166, 174,
  175, 202, 205
  Anna Bolena, 136
  Chiara e Serafina, 158
  Il furioso all'isola di San Domingo, 158
  Linda di Chamounix, 3, 4, 5, 8, *93–142*,
  144, 147, 149, 150, 151, 153, 154, 161,
  163, 174, 175, 177, 180, 181, 183, 184,

198, 199, 200, 203, 204, 205, 211,
  228, 239, 260
  Lucia di Lammermoor, 105, 140, 141
  Lucrezia Borgia, 175
  Maria di Rohan, 136
  Maria Stuarda, 175
  Otto mesi in due ore, 158, 159
D'Ormeville, Carlo, 198
Dossi, Carlo, 219
  La desinenza in A, 219
Ducange, Victor, 41, 42, 43, 158
  La Fiancée de Lammermoor, 158
  Thérèse ou l'Orpheline de Genève,
  41, 42
Dumas, Alexandre, 162, 164
  Antony, 164
  Henri III et sa cour, 164
  Intrigue et amour, 162

Esquirol, Jean-Etienne-Dominique, 110

Fairtile, Linda B., 256
Farwell, Arthur, 256, 257
Faustini, Giovanni, 24
Fend, Michael, 38
Ferretti, Jacopo, 42, 43
Filippi, Filippo, 199
Filippi, J. de, 74
Fink, Bruce, 134, 142
Florimo, Francesco, 33, 53, 81, 82
Fontana, Ferdinando, 200, 202, 203
Foucault, Michel, 106, 110
Franchetti, Alberto, 204
  Fior d'Alpe, 204
Frantz, Pierre, 156, 159
Freud, Sigmund, 4, 18, 93, 110, 111,
  112, 115
  'Female Sexuality', 115
  'Femininity', 115
  Studies in Hysteria, 111, 115

Galli-Curci, Amelita, 88
Garlanda, Federico, 246
　La nuova democrazia americana, 246
　La terza Italia. Lettere di un
　　yankee, 246
Garrick, David, 159
Gautier, Théophile, 102, 103, 162
Gazzetta privilegiata di Milano, 48
Gentile, Maria, 88
Gervasi, Luigi, 183
Gessner, Salomon, 53
　Idyllen, 53
Gherardini, Giovanni, 34, 35
Ghislanzoni, Antonio, 183, 186, 187, 188,
　　190, 192, 193, 194
Giacosa, Giuseppe, 247, 248
　Impressioni d'America, 247, 248
Giordano, Umberto, 5, 181, 215–17
　Fedora, 6, 181, *215–27*, 228, 250
Girardi, Michele, 235, 257
Goldoni, Carlo, 29
Goldstein, Jan, 110
Gossett, Philip, 86
Gozzano, Guido, 244, 246
　'Ketty', 244
Grétry, André-Ernest-Modeste, 38
　Guillaume Tell, 38
Grisi, Giulia, 82
Guarini, Giovanni Battista, 154
　Il pastor fido, 154
Guidi, Francesco, 198

Hadlock, Heather, 137
Halévy, Ludovic, 2
Haller, Albrecht von, 24
　Die Alpen, 44
Harte, Bret, 7, 248, 249
　'The Luck of Roaring Camp', 249
　'The Outcasts of Poker Flat', 249
Hillern, Wilhelmine von, 205, 211

Die Geyer-Wally, 205
Hohenstein, Adolf, 6, 211, 221, 222
Horace, 15
Hugo, Victor, 19, 43, 164, 165, 166,
　　178, 179
　Cromwell, 19, 164
　Hernani, 43, 164
　Lucrèce Borgia, 164, 165
　Marion De Lorme, 164
　Le Roi s'amuse, 164
Humperdinck, Engelbert, 258

Illica, Luigi, 205, 222, 228

Joan of Arc, 176
Joly, Jacques, 103
Jouy, Etienne de, 165
Juvenal, 15

Kant, Immanuel, 24, 25
　Critique of Judgement, 24
Kimbell, David, 143
Knibiehler, Yvonne, 107
Kristeva, Julia, 4, 134, 135

Lacan, Jacques, 4, 116, 132, 133, 134, 135
Lacoste, Amand, 163
　L'Auberge des Adrets, see Antier,
　　Benjamin
Lacoste-Veysseyre, Pauline, 42
Lamartine, Alphonse de, 28, 36, 37
　Jocelyn, 28
Lamperi, Alessandro, 81
Laprade, Victor de, 18
　'L'Alpe vierge (à la Jungfrau)', 18
Launer, publishing firm, 82, 87, 88
Leduc, publishing firm, 87
Legge, Walter, 89
Leicester, H. Marshall, 3
Lemaître, Frédérick, 163

Robert Macaire, 163

Lemoine, Gustave, 95, 111

La Grâce de Dieu, see D'Ennery,
  Adolphe Philippe

Leopardi, Giacomo, 247

  Inno ai patriarchi, 247

Linck, Jean-Antoine, 46

Lind, Jenny, 74

Lippmann, Friedrich, 33

Lorenzi, Giambattista, 31, 52

Lory, Gabriel, 46

Louis XV, King of France, 80

Malibran, Maria, 43, 74, 81

Malvezzi, Settimio, 148

Mann, Thomas, 21

  The Magic Mountain, 21

Manzoni, Alessandro, 3, 5, 36, 37, 38, 52,
  92, 181–94

  I promessi sposi, 3, 5, 36, 37, 52,
    181–94, 218

Marelli, Marco Arturo, 21, 91

Margherita of Savoy, Queen of
  Italy, 217

Maria Adelaide of Savoy, 108

Mary, mother of Jesus Christ, 18, 105,
  107, 108, 185, 241

Mascagni, Pietro, 202, 228

  Amica, 228

  L'amico Fritz, 202, 204

Massenet, Jules, 2

  Werther, 2

Mayr, Giovanni Simone, 40, 41, 42, 86

  Elisa, ossia Il monte S. Bernardo, 40,
    41, 87

Meilhac, Henry, 2

Meli, Giovanni, 53

Mercadante, Saverio, 5, 181, 196

  Violetta, 196, 198

Mercier, Louis Sébastien, 102, 157

Le Nouveau Paris, 102

  Tableau de Paris, 102

Metastasio, Pietro, 14

Meyerbeer, Giacomo, 1, 2

  Le Pardon de Ploërmel, 1, 2

Michelet, Jules, 218

  La Montagne, 218

Micheletti, Pietro, 183, 184

Mitchell, Lee Clark, 249, 250

Mitchell, W. J. T., 261

Monteverdi, Claudio, 105

Monti, Nicola, 89

Moretti, Franco, 261

Mould, J. Wrey, 87

Mozart, Wolfgang Amadeus, 14, 29

  Così fan tutte, 14

  La finta giardiniera, 29

  Die Zauberflöte, 177

Musical America, 257

Musset, Alfred de, 202, 203

  La Coupe et les lèvres, 202

Napoleon Bonaparte, 35, 36

Nievo, Ippolito, 193

Nigra, Costantino, 190

  Canti popolari del Piemonte, 190

Nodier, Charles, 155, 163

Omnibus, L', 46

Paduano, Guido, 55

Pagliughi, Lina, 88, 89

Pain, Joseph-Marie, 95

  Fanchon la vielleuse, see Bouilly, Jean
    Nicolas

Paisiello, Giovanni, 4, 28, 29, 30, 31, 32,
  33, 34, 35, 38, 52, 154

  La Nina o sia La pazza per amore, 4, 8,
    18, 28, 29, 32, 33, 34, 35, 43,
    52, 154

Palianti, Louis, 108
Parker, Roger, 34, 179
Pascoli, Giovanni, 256
  'Italy', 256
Pasta, Giuditta, 29, 90
Patti, Adelina, 74
Pedrotti, Carlo, 5, 181, 194, 198, 218
  Fiorina o La fanciulla di Glaris, 194,
    198, 218
Pepoli, Carlo, 1
Percoto, Caterina, 193
Peroni, Filippo, 74
Petrella, Errico, 183, 186, 188, 190, 192,
  194, 211
  I promessi sposi, 192, 193, 194, 211
Petrobelli, Pierluigi, 33, 34
Philo of Alexandria, Pseudo-, 9
  Antiquitates biblicae, 9
Piccinni, Niccolò, 29
  La buona figliola, 29
Pius IX, Pope, 107, 108
Pixérécourt, Guilbert de, 155, 156, 158,
  163, 164, 165, 166
  La Citerne, 158
  La Fille de l'exilé ou Huit mois en deux
    heures, 158, 165
  'Le mélodrame', 163
  Robinson Crusoe, 158
  Théâtre choisi, 164
Poe, Edgar Allan, 248
Poizat, Michel, 4, 131
Ponchielli, Amilcare, 183, 184, 186, 198,
  199, 200
  Lina, 198, 199, 200, 203
  La savojarda, 198, 199, 200, 203
Praga, Enrico, 183
Puccini, Giacomo, 3, 5, 6, 7, 181, 200,
  201, 202, 203, 205, 228–60
  La Bohème, 259, 260
  Edgar, 5, 181, 200, 201, 202, 203

  La fanciulla del West, 3, 6, 7, 8,
    228–61
  Madama Butterfly, 257, 258, 259, 260
  Il tabarro, 260
  Tosca, 259, 260
  Il trittico, 260
  Turandot, 260
  Le Villi, 5, 181, 200, 202, 203, 251
Puccini, Michele, 248
Puget, Loïsa, 95, 99, 100, 101
  'A la Grâce de Dieu', 95, 98, 101,
    113, 117

Racine, Jean, 165
Rastrelli, Giuseppe, 41
  Amina ovvero L'innocenza
    perseguitata, 41
Rescigno, Nicola, 89
Revue des deux mondes, 28, 176
Ricci, Luigi, 42
  L'orfanella di Ginevra, 42
Ricordi, publishing firm, 82, 83, 88
Rigoni Stern, Mario, 261
  Storia di Tönle, 261
Roccatagliati, Alessandro, 80, 143
Rockstro, W. S., 87
Romani, Felice, 4, 21, 23, 34, 38, 41, 43,
  44, 46, 51, 52, 53, 55, 56, 57, 64, 66,
  72, 91, 92
  Amina ovvero L'innocenza perseguitata,
    41, 43, 44
Rosenkavalier, Der, 259
Rosi, Francesco, 3
Rossi, Gaetano, 40, 43, 93, 104, 111, 112,
  114, 115, 117, 133, 135, 141
Rossini, Gioachino, 1, 4, 19, 28, 34, 35,
  39, 40, 42, 137, 174, 175
  Il barbiere di Siviglia, 1, 35
  La gazza ladra, 28, 34, 35, 36, 137,
    154, 158

Guillaume Tell, 4, 19, 39, 40, 44, 46,
  47, 88, 174
L'italiana in Algeri, 14
Rodolfo di Sterlinga, 46, 47, 48
Semiramide, 137
Vallace, 46, 47, 48
Rousseau, Jean-Jacques, 3, 24, 25, 26,
  27, 28, 38, 55, 56, 159
  *Discourse on the Origins of
    Inequality*, 25
  Emile, 25
  La Nouvelle Héloïse, 3, 24, 25, 27, 28
  The Social Contract, 25
Rubini, Giovanni Battista, 82
Ruskin, John, 15, 17, 218, 219
  Sesame and Lilies, 218

Sade, Marquis de, 131, 132, 142
  Les Cent vingt journées de Sodome, 131
Saint-Beuve, Charles-Augustin, 28, 36
Saint-Cyr, Jacques Antoine de
  Révéroni, 38, 40
Salandri, Teresa, 148
Sand, George, 193, 194
  La Mare au diable, 193
Sanquirico, Alessandro, 4, 44, 45, 46,
  48, 51, 91, 92
Sardou, Victorien, 215
  Fédora, 215
Scherillo, Michele, 33, 54
Schiller, Friedrich, 5, 16, 24, 143, 162,
  164, 166, 175, 178, 179, 180
  Kabale und Liebe, 5, 143, 149, 162, 180
  On Naïve and Sentimental Poetry, 16
  On the Sublime, 24
Schipa, Tito, 88
Schlesinger, publishing firm, 87, 88
Schulte van Kessel, Elisja, 12
Scotti Tosini, Aurora, 220, 221
Scotto, Renata, 22

Scribe, Eugène, 23, 43, 55, 90
  *La Somnambule ou l'Arrivée d'un
    nouveau seigneur, see* Aumer, Jean-
    Pierre
Sedaine, Michel-Jean, 38
Segantini, Giovanni, 6, 219, 220, 221,
  222, 228, 250
  Punishment of the Lustful Women, 220
  Wicked Mothers, 220
Selva, Antonio, 148
Senancour, Etienne Pivert de, 28
  Oberman, 28
Serenelli Honorati, Luigi, 194
Serra, Luciana, 22
Shakespeare, William, 178
Shelley, Mary, 26, 27, 55
Sighele, Scipio, 246
  La donna nova, 246
Silverman, Kaja, 4, 135
Smart, Mary Ann, 63, 65, 66, 68
Somma, Antonio, 153
Soumet, Alexandre, 165
Starobinski, Jean, 26
Stendhal (Henri Beyle), 35
  Life of Rossini, 35
Strepponi, Giuseppina, 176
Sutherland, Joan, 22, 88, 89

Tacchinardi-Persiani, Fanny, 119, 183
Tadolini, Eugenia, 147
Tagliavini, Ferruccio, 88
Tasso, Torquato, 154
  Aminta, 154
Tetrazzini, Luisa, 22
Theocritus, 53
Tomlinson, Gary, 178, 259
Töpffer, Rodolphe, 18
Torelli, Vincenzo, 45, 177
Tottola, Andrea Leone, 42, 43
  Traité du mélodrame, 13, 14, 156

Traventi, Andrea, 183, 184
Trivulzio di Belgioioso, Cristina, 176
  'La Guerre dans le Tyrol italien', 176
Turner, William, 46
Tyndall, John, 16

Ubersfeld, Anne, 13, 156

Vaccaj, Nicola, 43
  Malvina, 43
Valentini, Carlo, 42
  Amina ovvero L'orfanella di Ginevra, 42
Varesi, Felice, 148
Vasselli, Antonio, 117
Verdi, Giuseppe, 1, 3, 5, 65, 140, 143–80,
    204, 205
  Aida, 210
  Amore e raggiro, 149, 164
  Un ballo in maschera, 140
  Luisa Miller, 3, 5, 8, *143–80*, 181, 184,
      188, 194, 198, 203, 239, 260
  Macbeth, 178, 179
  Nabucco, 175
  Re Lear, 153
  Rigoletto, 14, 19, 175, 178, 179, 180
  Simon Boccanegra, 1, 19

Stiffelio, 179
  La traviata, 14, 161, 163, 164, 180
  Il trovatore, 179, 180, 192
Viaggio pittorico nei monti di Brianza, 51
Viale Ferrero, Mercedes, 46, 47,
    217, 231
Virgil, 15, 53
Visconti, Luchino, 89
Voltaire (François-Marie Arouet), 165
Votto, Antonino, 89

Wagner, Richard, 2
  Die Meistersinger von Nürnberg, 2
  Parsifal, 232
  Der Ring des Nibelungen, 2
  Siegfried, 2
  Die Walküre, 2
Walton, Benjamin, 39
Weber, Carl Maria von, 19
  Der Freischütz, 19
Weiss, Piero, 143, 178, 179
Wise, Robert, 4
  The Sound of Music, 3, 204

Zangarini, Carlo, 228
Zoppelli, Luca, 80